LIFE IN THE ANCIENT NEAR EAST, 3100–332 B.C.E.

LIFE IN THE
ANCIENT NEAR EAST

3100–332 B.C.E.

DANIEL C. SNELL

YALE UNIVERSITY PRESS · NEW HAVEN AND LONDON

Designed by Sonia L. Scanlon
Set in Adobe Garamond type by The Marathon
Group, Inc., Durham, North Carolina.
Printed in the United States of America by Vail-Ballou
Press, Binghamton, New York.

Library of Congress Cataloging-in-Publication-Data
Life in the ancient Near East, 3100–332 B.C.E.
p.   cm.
ISBN 0-300-06615-5 (cloth: alk. paper)
0-300-07666-5 (pbk.: alk. paper)
1. Middle East—History—To 622—Bibliography.
2. Middle East—Social conditions—Bibliography.
3. Middle East—Economic conditions—Bibliography.
Z3014.H55L54   1997
[DS62.23]
016.956—dc20   96-32549
CIP

A catalogue record for this book is available from the
British Library.

The paper in this book meets the guidelines for per-
manence and durability of the Committee on Production Guidelines for Book Longevity of the Council on
Library Resources.

10 9 8 7 6 5 4 3 2

For Jim and Doris Barwick

CONTENTS

ILLUSTRATIONS

1. Drawing of Khafaje Temple and surrounding walls; Courtesy of the Oriental Institute of the University of Chicago.

2. Photograph of the Ziggurat of Ur-Nammu at Ur. Reproduced with permission of the Trustees of the British Museum.

3. Drawing by A. H. Layard of BM 124905, 124906 from Kuyunjik. Reproduced with permission of the Trustees of the British Museum.

4. Drawing by F. C. Cooper of a relief from the South-West Palace of Sennacherib at Nineveh. Reproduced with permission of the Trustees of the British Museum.

5. Ship from a wall painting in Thera, the Aegean. Reproduced with permission of the Greek National Archaeological Museum.

6. Drawing of a cylinder seal, reproduced with permission of the Ashmolean Museum.

7. Photograph of the front of a Puzriš-Dagan tablet, reproduced by permission of the Oklahoma Museum of Natural History, University of Oklahoma, and Prof. A. J. Heisserer.

8. Photograph of the water drawer from the Theban tomb of Ipuy. Reprinted with the permission of the Metropolitan Museum of Art.

9. Drawing from the tomb chapel of Nebamun at Thebes. Reproduced with permission of the Trustees of the British Museum.

10. Photograph of woman in a Syrian village, reproduced by permission of Dr. Katie Barwick-Snell.

PREFACE

This book is addressed first to the educated lay reader who has some interest in the ancient world but no detailed knowledge of it. I hope a junior or a senior in college would not find it overly mystifying, and anyone with an interest would find something of value.

I also seek to put matters well known to scholars in the field in a new perspective, and in doing so I will certainly have slighted important developments in all the fields covered. I believe it is inevitable in a work that tries both to synthesize and to advance the field.

By *Ancient Near East* I mean the areas of the modern countries of Iran, Iraq, Turkey, Syria, Lebanon, Israel, and Egypt. The terms *Near East* and the synonymous *Middle East* both are imprecise and focused on Europe, but the term *Western Asia* seems not to be widely used, and it is not understood by the public at large.

Few will doubt the need for a book such as this, for two reasons. First, the field of ancient economic and social history is becoming so vast that people who study one part of it have trouble keeping up with other parts of it. This book may make that slightly easier because it provides a background to current scholarly work. Second, as the field is becoming more specialized and more arcane, it has lost the voices that used to address a general audience. This is a deplorable development. The scholar's study must always be open to the public because it is the public ultimately who pays the scholar for her or his time and work. And the work in this field is so fascinating and so far-reaching in its implications for the understanding of human life now that it must be pressed forward on all fronts. And to be seriously pursued it must be widely understood.

Three recent books tend in the direction in which I am interested, and I have learned much from each. J. N. Postgate's *Early Mesopotamia* stops with the Old Babylonian period around 1600 B.C.E. M. Liverani's *Antico Oriente: Storia, società, economia* and *Kulturgeschichte des alten Vorderasien*, edited by H. Klengel and others, both slight Egypt and, to varying degrees, ancient Israel.

On the question of why one should be interested in social and economic history, one must in the end give a personal answer. Eckart Otto in a brief essay has suggested that the interest in the field among Christian biblicists derives from their sense that today faith and daily life are separated in people's lives, and to study ancient Israel's society may be a way for them to see how faith and daily life were once integrated and perhaps could be again. This is not my motivation. My interest derives from my having grown up in a family that for many years struggled economically; I have always wanted to know who pays and who benefits, and I have always cared little for what people said about their motives and more for what they did. I see my interests as part of Western culture's desire to question received opinion about the past and to get behind political propaganda to an economic and social reality.

ACKNOWLEDGMENTS

Charles Grench of Yale University Press suggested to me in 1986 that a book like this should be written and that I should write it. Although I did not take him too seriously at the time, I appreciate his suggestion, which was certainly correct.

A fellowship at the National Humanities Center in 1989–90 enabled me to embark on the project. The fellowship granted by the center was funded by the National Endowment for the Humanities. Earlier a summer fellowship from the Research Council of the University of Oklahoma allowed me to begin reading in the summer of 1989, and the Humanities Research Centre at the Australian National University at Canberra provided me with further time in the summer of 1990 to work on the manuscript.

For the encouragement of friends in Norman, Chapel Hill-Durham, and Canberra, I am deeply appreciative. Miguel Civil, W. W. Hallo, A. J. Heisserer, and Marvin Powell were especially helpful in advancing the project. The staff of the Interlibrary Loan Office of the Bizzell Memorial Library at the University of Oklahoma was extremely obliging, as were the librarians at the National Humanities Center. Philip Curtin of Johns Hopkins University and the other members of his National Endowment for the Humanities Summer Seminar in 1993 offered stimulating insights. My student J. Brett McClain read and commented on the manuscript at a late stage. David Snell reiterated a suggestion that I finally accepted.

I am thankful for the aid of these institutions and persons but refuse to share with them the blame for errors, which I have crafted by myself. My children, James and Abigail, and my wife, Dr. Katie Barwick-Snell, were instrumental in making the work possible. I dedicate the work to my wife's parents, who have given me warm parental support and encouragement now that I am fresh out of regular parents. Doris Barwick in particular gave me a laywoman's response to the manuscript, and her advice has proved invaluable.

ABBREVIATIONS

AfO	*Archiv für Orientforschung*
ANET	J. Pritchard, ed., *Ancient Near Eastern Texts*
ASJ	*Acta Sumerologica* (Japan)
A.V.	Anniversary Volume, or *Festschrift*
BiOr	*Bibliotheca Orientalis*
FS	*Festschrift*
JANES	*Journal of the Ancient Near Eastern Society*
JAOS	*Journal of the American Oriental Society*
JBL	*Journal of Biblical Literature*
JCS	*Journal of Cuneiform Studies*
JESHO	*Journal of the Economic and Social History of the Orient*
JNES	*Journal of Near Eastern Studies*
OrNS	*Orientalia Nova Series*
RA	*Revue d'Assyriologie*
RlA	*Reallexikon der Assyriologie*
VDI	*Vestnik Drevnei Istorii*
WZKM	*Wiener Zeitschrift für die Kunde des Morgenlandes*
ZA	*Zeitschrift für Assyriologie*

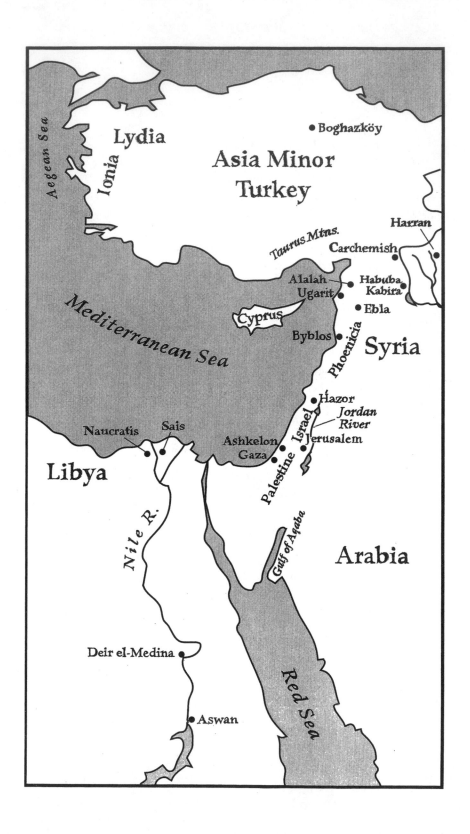

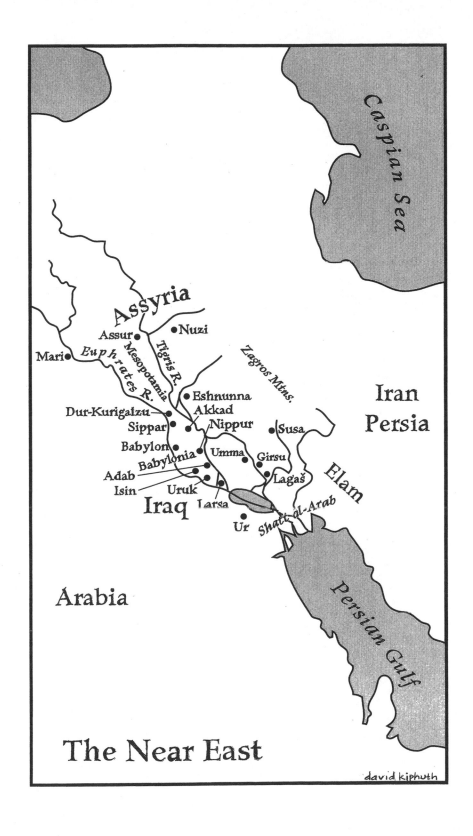

The Near East

david kiphuth

CHRONOLOGICAL TABLE OF PERIODS

	Mesopotamia	Egypt	Israel-Palestine	Anatolia
Time (all dates B.C.E. unless otherwise indicated)				
5500–5000	Halaf			
5000–3500	Ubaid			
3500–3100	Uruk			
3100–3000	Jemdet-Nasr	3100–2686	3150–2200	
3000–2800	Early Dynastic I	Early Dynastic	Early Bronze	
2800–2500	Early Dynastic II			
2500–2334	Early Dynastic III	2686–2200 Old Kingdom		
2334–2197	Sargonic = Old Akkadian			
2197–2112	Guti	2200–2040		
2112–2004	Ur III	1st Intermediate		
2004–1595	Old Babylonian	2040–1786 Middle Kingdom	2000–1200 Middle Bronze II	
				1700–1595 Hittite Old Kingdom
1595–1375	Dark Age	1786–1558 2nd Intermediate		
				1375–1200 Hittite New Kingdom = Empire
1375–1155	Kassite = Middle Babylonian = Middle Assyrian	1558–1085 New Kingdom	1100 "Conquest"	
			1050–925	
1155–626	Neo-Assyrian		United Kingdom	
625–539	Neo-Babylonian		586 Exile	
539–332	Persian		539 Return	
332–143	Alexander and successors			
143 B.C.E.–240 C.E.	Parthians			
240–636 C.E.	Sassanians			
637 C.E. – present	Arabs			

INTRODUCTION

This book surveys what is known about social and economic life in the Ancient Near East from the beginning of writing to the coming of Alexander the Great, a period of almost three thousand years. This enormous task is worth trying because we know a great deal about some of the periods, although never as much as we would like to know.

By the *Ancient Near East* I mean the areas of the modern countries of Iran, Iraq, Turkey, Syria, Lebanon, Israel, and Egypt. All the modern languages of the region with which I am familiar use *Middle East* for the area. Students of the ancient world tend to use *Near East* to refer to the region, and that is what I shall do here.

There seem to be no standards for a social and economic history; data have led authors in other periods to talk of all sorts of things, including political history, the one area that, one would think, would not loom large in social and economic history. Here I, too, will be led by what is known and by my own view of what is important in understanding society—the ways people in groups relate to each other—and in understanding economy—the ways people use the resources they have. As will be clear in the Appendix, there is no dominant theory of the ancient societies and economies studied here that might help organize the material.

The periods we shall be considering differ in what we know of them, but I shall try to cover similar topics in the social and economic history of each. Each chapter concerns a politically defined period of time and deals with the following topics:

> 1. *Real People.* Near the beginning of each chapter is an exploration of the social reality behind a significant text from the period. There is a tendency, one to which I myself sometimes unfortunately succumb, to lose sight of the fact that real people lived in the Ancient Near East, and an imaginative recreation may help us focus on what their lives were like.[1] I have not created imaginary situations; all are attested either in the archaeological or the textual record. I have, however, taken the liberty of imagining thoughts and speeches.
>
> 2. *Population Distribution.* Surface survey—an archaeological technique in which a researcher picks up pottery sherds from the surface of a tell, or ruin-hill, created by the destruction of human habitation—allows us to say quite a lot about

where people lived in different periods even if we cannot be
sure about their absolute numbers. The theory of surface
survey is that the sherds from any period in which the tell was
occupied by a large number of people are likely to be present
even on the surface. The prerequisite for a surface survey is
that one know the pottery chronology of the region, that is,
how exactly styles changed in pottery making. A pottery
chronology can be compiled only by study of excavations in
sites that have more than one period of occupation.[2] The
advantage of surface survey is that it is relatively easy and
cheap; one does not need a large team working for months on
end to get a general idea of what sites were occupied in what
periods. The disadvantages are that short periods of occupation may not show up in pottery on the surface, and some
periods may not have really distinctive pottery, so that it is
difficult for the researcher to attribute the site to a specific
period.

3. *Social Groups.* I discuss whether texts from the period
allow us to describe any particular social groups or classes that
played prominent roles in the period.[3] Ethnic divisions will be
reviewed, although one must always guard against the tendency, common in Western civilization, to make social generalizations on the basis of racial and ethnic differences.
Sometimes that is justified by ancient practice, but frequently
it is not.

4. *Family.* What we know about family structure is limited, but I try to formulate what texts tell us about the roles
and status of children and other family members in the
period, and whether nuclear or more extended families seem
to be important.

5. *Women.* It seems sensible to consider independently
what is known about the status of women because they sometimes were not totally defined by their roles within families. I
explore what texts tell us about women's legal and economic
power.

6. *Work.* How labor was managed and paid is a theme.
Hired labor was not usually an important factor in the
Ancient Near East, but forced labor, or corvée, frequently
was, as governments exacted taxes not only in money and
kind but also in labor.

7. *Land and Agriculture.* I examine how land was divided, sold (if it was sold), and redistributed.

8. *Animal Management.* The ways people exploited animals dominated the economic life of important parts of the population, and texts frequently reveal what the methods of control were and who was involved.

9. *Crafts.* The Ancient Near East was the premier locus for the production of the best tools and the most interesting fancy things, the New York and Paris of the age. Texts sometimes reveal how production was organized, who was involved, and how the goods were distributed.

10. *Trade.* Commerce in craft goods but in many other things as well is attested in all periods, and interregional or foreign commerce is particularly well documented in many periods. It also may be significant for the intercultural exchange of ideas.[4]

11. *Money and Prices.* We have information about how goods were used in some of the functions of modern money. And we have the prices for specific commodities. Sometimes we have series of prices, which are prices coming from one organization over time. Such series are the most reliable indication of a level of prices because they are not subject to the whims of individuals and they reveal the short-term fluctuations in prices. Prices usually come from economic texts in which the buyer and seller wanted it to be clear what was paid. Literary and legal texts too sometimes mention prices.

12. *The Government and the Economy.* We have texts that reveal something about government policies or at least about attitudes toward dealing with economic problems. Although much of the information about the matters discussed above comes from texts produced by governments, I examine separately what policies were and whether they were successfully imposed.[5]

13. *Egypt.* The detailed information I use in discussing the features outlined above usually is not available for Egypt. The reason is starkly simple but frequently overlooked. The areas around the valley of the Nile are very dry, and the climate preserves even delicate materials well, but the Nile is a swiftly running river that does not deviate from its banks, and only its floodplain is habitable by people. And so ancient people

usually lived exactly where modern people live. Archaeological excavation has consequently concentrated on the uninhabited regions in which people buried their dead. The picture we have of Egyptian civilization is skewed toward death, and although tombs occasionally reveal a great deal about some of the questions we will be considering, we usually cannot hope to discover anything like the complexity of texts that we find from the rest of the Ancient Near East.[6] But we will try to see what is known about society and economy in Egypt

14. *Israel.* In Israel there are fewer problems with people living exactly where the ancients lived, but we have a lot less information—especially in early periods—about the questions of interest here. Unlike that in the other areas considered, the major textual information from Israel is not contemporary to events, but rather is found in the Bible, which comes down to us through copies made every generation or two. The oldest complete text of the Hebrew Bible, or Old Testament, dates only from 900 of our era. Although there is every indication that the transmission of the text was usually faithful, we are at least a thousand years removed from the original form of the texts for most of the Hebrew Bible. Many though not all of the categories of information listed above can be guessed at through judicious use of the Bible. This is not a simple matter, though, and I do not want to be understood as implying that it is. Unlike most of the texts used in this book, the Bible was and is a document of faith revered by believing communities; but it is wrong to neglect it just because people revere it still.

15. *The Rest of the World.* Outside the Ancient Near East very little is known in most of the period we are considering, but it is a good idea to try to place the Near East in a larger context. Usually I shall be able to assert only that the rest of the world appeared to be a backwater compared to the Ancient Near East, but this contrast in apparent development may be due to the lack of preserved texts outside the Ancient Near East. Over time there are interesting developments recorded in archaeology and writing from far afield.

It is usually best in theory to strive for a history that deals with the whole hemisphere, in this case Europe, Asia, and Africa, because any interconnecting region may have influ-

enced another even if direct traces of contact are not preserved.[7] The paucity of evidence, especially of written evidence, impedes our making connections. We will not be able
to change that situation without becoming aware at least in a
general way of developments elsewhere in the same periods.

I propose a view of ancient economies and societies that is focused on
Mesopotamia.[8] This may be surprising to those weaned on the glories of Egypt,
but it is determined by the wealth of information, especially on economic and
social matters, that comes down to us in cuneiform, the Mesopotamian writing
system. We almost always know a lot more about matters social and economic
in Mesopotamia than anywhere else, and so one must begin there.

Mesopotamia is central not only because it has more data, but also because
it has no boundaries. The mountains on its north and east are permeable to
travelers, and in most periods the cultural interactions are clear across those
mountains as well as to the west of the river valleys. This situation contrasts
with that of Egypt, which is geographically isolated by deserts to the east and
west; there is Egyptian cultural interaction with the rest of the Ancient Near
East, too, but it appears in contrast to Mesopotamian interaction to be sporadic and limited.

We are not used to seeing Mesopotamia as central to ancient history because
we are more directly affected by later cultures, those of Israel and Greece and
Rome. It is arguable, however, that important aspects of the societies and
economies of those places shared much with Mesopotamia, and certainly tech-
nologically there was much in common. Openness to long-distance trade is an
important feature of both the Ancient Near East and the classical world of
Greece and Rome. And the dependence on unfree labor appears also to be a
shared aspect, although the nature of the unfree labor varied.

One ought not to assume, however, that in any given period conditions in
Mesopotamia were similar to those elsewhere. Geographically and culturally
Mesopotamia was unique in the ancient world, and it frequently may have
been economically and socially too. The record its people have left is immea-
surably rich, though, and it must be the basis for any such book as this.

THE GROUNDWORK

The groundwork for books like this one consists mainly in the reading and
publishing of ancient texts. By publishing I mean that we transliterate the text
into Roman letters, photograph it or copy it as faithfully as possible, translate
it, and annotate it, trying to solve its problems and make it understandable to

other students of the past. These publications appear in the form of books and journal articles, in a never-ending flow that is difficult to absorb. The texts themselves continue to be found both in archaeological excavations and in museums. The texts got to the museums mostly when it was legal to bring antiquities out of the Near East, in Iraq before 1933. The texts may have been sold by collectors as souvenirs and then given to museums or bought by them. Internal criteria, like the language in which the texts are written, the writing system used, the way they are inscribed, and even things like systems used for dating events mentioned in them, may help us to say from which site the text comes. But texts in museums usually do not come from modern excavations, and we never will know where exactly they were found.

We sometimes have a lot of information about texts that come from excavations, but that information varies with how careful the person recording the excavation was and what methods were used. Since Robert Koldewey (1855–1925) excavated Babylon just before World War I, a very high standard for accuracy and completeness has been set.[9] But not every excavator has managed to live up to it.

So even after we have published a text, much may remain unknown about it, and basic things may not be understood. To a large extent this ignorance results from the dearth of living traditions connecting us directly to the cultures of the Ancient Near East. We have no worthies to whom we can turn for answers to difficult language questions, and we have few modern groups who feel themselves connected to these times and places and would be willing to sponsor and encourage their study.

Knowledge of the ancient languages and their scripts faded after the beginning of the common era (here: B.C.E.), which is the same as the Christian era. Although knowledge of the Egyptian language's descendant, Coptic, did not totally die out, Coptic did cease to be the spoken language of Egyptian Christians long before the nineteenth century. The situation was even worse in the east, where first the Aramaic language had replaced most of the older tongues by 600 B.C.E., and later, after the Muslim conquest, Arabic became more and more the first language of most people, even of people who did not become Muslims.

The closest we come to a continuing tradition is that of the Jews. The Bible, the only significant written relic of Israel from early antiquity, has been consistently studied over the entire intervening period. But it has not always been studied with a historical purpose in mind. Rather, the goal has usually been a theological one aimed at the edification of contemporary congregations. Only after the Enlightenment in Europe did scholars begin to examine the Bible, which had become of course very much a part of Christian culture, too, from a historical perspective.[10] Persian traditions as well have been handed down in religion, but again it was only in the eighteenth and more vigorously in the nineteenth centuries that they began to be examined for what they could tell us about history.

The breakthroughs in understanding the ancient texts were made by several people at various times, and they constitute one of the most impressive achievements of nineteenth-century scientific thought. Jean-François Champollion (1790–1832) was the earliest to crack an important ancient script, the Egyptian.[11] He was able to do so because of his study of Coptic and because of the growing number of accurately copied texts with which he could work. The Rosetta Stone, found by Napoleon's troops in 1799 near the Rosetta Mouth of the Nile, offered Champollion a bilingual inscription from a late Egyptian ruler, and one of the languages was Greek, which Champollion knew well. Champollion made guesses about how personal names were to be read in Egyptian on the basis of the Greek and his knowledge of Coptic, and he tried his hypotheses on other texts.

The decipherment of cuneiform script, the wedge-shaped script used in ancient Iraq and Persia, was a more communal affair. A German schoolteacher, Georg Grotefend (1775–1853), in 1802 and 1803 used accurate copies of inscriptions brought back by travelers to guess that the script was syllabic, expressing not individual phonemes but pairs of them, *ta, ti, tu,* rather than *a, b, c.* And in 1847 the English adventurer Henry Rawlinson climbed the mighty rock at Besitun in Iran to get a papier-mâché squeeze of the inscription, which allowed him to decipher the Old Persian version of that text. Other scholars studying Rawlinson's material and using new inscriptions were able to decipher the Akkadian version of the same inscription, and within ten years the Royal Academy in London felt confident enough to declare that the script had been definitively deciphered.[12]

Scholars then began a period, which continues today in the study of both ancient Egypt and the rest of the Near East, of text publication. And there is no end in sight to this activity because there are thousands of documents still unread and unstudied.[13]

Although we are permanently compelled to publish texts, we are bound in a way to nineteenth-century ideology about the study of the past. Edward Said in 1978 argued that the approach of Europeans and Americans to the Middle East in general and even to the Ancient Near East was largely determined by the interest of their governments in imperial domination of the region. This assertion has been attacked by other students, and to me it seems facile.[14] There were many other motivations besides the desire to dominate that led people to the study of the Orient. And yet it must be admitted that these westerners brought with them their cultural baggage, and when they encountered the East they did not do so without preconceptions.

One nineteenth-century preconception that still dominates the field is that kings were important, and what kings did and said constitutes a central part of history. This preconception is supported by the fact that in all of the cultures we study in the ancient world access to literacy was much more limited than it is now, and a lot of what there is to read does come from kings or people paid by kings.

The fixation on monarchy derives from the sources and also from what was happening in nineteenth-century Europe, especially Germany, which was being unified under a dynasty of strong kings. And it did throw up extremely difficult problems, especially of chronology, that are certainly basic to any historical understanding. One has to know the order of dynasties and which of two kings came first just to put their subjects' actions in chronological order. And these chronological questions are not fully resolved even today, although there is a much wider consensus on them than there was even in 1900.[15]

Another nineteenth-century preconception that persists is that the ideal kind of scholarship is scholarship that tries to be objective, to present the past more or less as it actually happened. Increasingly in the twentieth century it has become clear that although an objective reality may once have existed, we have a great deal of work to do to sift through the viewpoints and prejudices of the ancients about events.[16] And we also have to contend with the fact that our own cultures endow us with ideas about how societies worked and should work that may keep us from seeing explanations for institutions and events.

Historians in general are not pessimistic about the possibility of keeping this torrent of viewpoints under control and presenting syntheses that might be of value into the next century. And yet such considerations do lead many students to stick with the safe, yet nonetheless valuable task of getting the texts out and hoping a later scholar will create a synthesis when more texts are available and more is known.[17] I would rather that scholars produce a series of tentative syntheses and attempt more frequently to address a broad public.

PERIODS

How might one best divide the periods to be studied? Traditionally, and functionally in this book too, we have divided ancient history into political periods, defined largely by what dynasties were in power. The problem with relying on political periods is that one cannot always be sure that they do not mask underlying social and economic continuities. We doubt that things are always as bad economically as they are depicted by apologists for regimes active in restoring former glories. It would be naive to accept, for example, what the scribes of the Old Babylonian ruler Ishme-Dagan, who reigned about 1953–1935 B.C.E., thought about the fall of the city of Ur around 2004 B.C.E. as if it were the whole truth.[18]

But we are at a loss as to what other periodization might make more sense because we have not usually managed to isolate features of social and economic life that last longer than a single political period. It is one of the functions of this book to try to suggest such continuities and discontinuities. But now there seems to be no reason to insist on a new overall periodization in ways that might seem odd to other students or to people generally familiar with the ancient world.

Nonetheless, I hypothesize that interregional trade may be a key to periodizations that makes more sense for social and economic developments than political periods do. I suggest that periods in which interregional trade is firmly attested, regardless of the persons and agencies involved, were less likely than other periods to be ones in which households turned in upon themselves and tried to become self-sufficient. By focusing on trade I do not want to advance the idea that trade was necessarily economically important. It was in fact not central to the economies with which we are concerned. But the fact that foreign trade goods were available indicates that channels were open to the broader world.

We cannot be sure that a period in which interregional trade is significantly attested really corresponded to a period of increased availability of goods and services to all households. We know little about nonofficial households in most periods. When there was little interregional trade, then households were obviously focusing on supplies of things nearer to home. But we cannot assume that the lack of evidence in texts for trade is a real indication of the end of trade. The trade in certain practical things like obsidian blades was probably not formal enough to be recorded or to be impeded by slowdowns in economic conditions unless they were acute. And it seems that other light and relatively valuable things kept circulating even in the most impacted periods of economic history. It must be kept in mind, however, that political fragmentation, which might affect trade or at least trade records, did not necessarily correlate with economic or cultural decline.[19]

Some trade goods, like obsidian, which any enterprising traveler might stuff in his pack as insurance against destitution in foreign lands, would leave traces in the archaeological record, but not necessarily in texts. Grain and wool, which Mesopotamia exported, decayed and would not be preserved archaeologically, but such bulky items might well occur in texts. We must keep an eye out for trade and for other elements that seem similar over long periods, and of course for discontinuities that occur within single politically defined periods. We cannot now solve the problem of a proper periodization, but we can be aware of it as we move through the framework that political history has bequeathed us.

THE ORIGINS OF CITIES

5500–2300 B.C.E.

There they are, a band of travelers on the horizon; you can see them distinctly though it is still quite early in the morning. They must have started long before dawn, for they probably come from several miles away. They are moving along slowly on foot, and the children among them impede their progress. But they apparently know that they cannot enter the city before the gates are open, and the gates are only just now opening. There are ten or twenty of them, as it seems from this distance, and they are carrying bundles, probably with a bit of food. They may comprise five or six families and be related to one another; maybe they all come from the same village.

Why are they coming to the city? We cannot be sure, but people like them have been abandoning the outlying villages for some time now, and they have the impression that life will be easier in the city. They must surely have heard about what a hard life most people lead here, and especially about the diseases. Cities like this are frequently devastated by diseases that physicians cannot treat, and only the rich can afford physicians.

And still they come. We could ask them, of course, but they would be uncommunicative. Peasants don't trust city people, so why should they discuss this most basic decision of their lives with the likes of us? Perhaps the attraction of the city is the stimulation it offers, of which they hear tales in the country-side. But really these peasants are not likely to learn the craftsmen's skills or how to build buildings or what the administrators are planning. They are coming simply because they think that they and their children, who are already afflicted with eye diseases, will have a chance to live a better life. The administrators would prefer that they stay out in the country, but who can blame them for trying something new? It is this willingness to take risks that makes us human.[1]

PRELUDE: THE EARLY PERIODS

That the peasants actually did come is very clear. In southern Iraq the period from 5500 to 2300 B.C.E. is one of great change, though it may not have been change that would have been perceived as occurring very fast. Already at the beginning of the period human beings living in the foothills of the Near East had experimented with agriculture and learned that after a few years grains increased in size when human beings planted, tended, and harvested them. Animals too changed some of their characteristics when they were domesticated, and both animals and plants were more convenient for people and more reliable than they had been before people were planting and managing them.

The geological shape of the region had been established long before people arrived. Scholars are unsure only whether the shore of the Persian Gulf reached nearer to the heartland of cities in southern Mesopotamia than it now does. Rivers lay down silt, and one might think that the mouth of the Shatt al-Arab, the waterway formed after the rivers join in marshes, would grow out over time into the gulf. Others argue that most of the silt is dropped in the beds of the slow-moving rivers, and the slight upthrust of the Zagros Mountains might be enough to keep the gulf in its present position. Climate seems, from the evidence of pollen core samples, not to have changed since 5000 B.C.E., though seasonable variation in rain can make a big difference in an arid region like the Near East. Over time, nonetheless, human beings have profoundly affected their environment, especially in the decimation of the forests.[2]

Humans had been at work altering their environment in the hill country that surrounds Mesopotamia, especially by domesticating plants and animals. Questions remain about why domestication occurred. The reason this is problematic is that a family can easily harvest enough grain from still-existing wild wheat stands in the region to last an entire year. One theory is that perceived population pressure led groups to move to less productive land and to bring along seeds and animals that they were used to back home. It was then discovered that plants grew more luxuriantly and animals could be conveniently managed.[3]

These discoveries eventually led to sedentarization, people's settling down and living in one place all of the time, and the techniques that made living in a village possible were apparently fairly quickly shared throughout the region. For example, goats, which are found wild in Iraq, appear fairly soon in Syria-Palestine, and emmer, which is wild there, found its way to Iraq. Before sedentarization there had been trade contacts throughout the region, which we can trace by looking for obsidian, a volcanic rock found in the region only in the mountains of central Turkey and used to make knives. It seems probable that at first the obsidian trade did not involve long-distance travel by the traders but just the passing along from group to group of the valuable stone, although in fact the volume of stone does not diminish the farther one gets from the sources, so perhaps it was not such an informal process of trade. Knowledge about domestication possibly spread in the ways that obsidian had.[4] However it spread, the entire hill region was settled with small agricultural villages by around 5500.

Pottery had been invented already, perhaps in imitation of wicker baskets, and pottery, of course, had been broken. This may seem a minor matter, but it looms large in the study of the past because humans quite reasonably did not take great pains to dispose of the pottery but just threw it out or swept it out of their way. And today archaeologists find pottery the single most useful artifact for dating sites because the pottery styles slowly changed, and if you have a stratified site, one with successive occupations one on top of another, you have a good chance of establishing a pottery chronology that can be used to date other sites too.[5]

By 5500 in the foothills there had been several identifiable cultures that produced different and sometimes quite carefully made pottery, sometimes on potter's wheels. We cannot be sure if these cultures differed in language, customs, and social organization because all we have is the archaeological remains, but possibly a great deal of social complexity had already developed. The Samarra period has been singled out by scholars as one in which the really fancy pots indicate that there probably was a marked difference between people who could afford the pots and others who settled for simpler wares. Some have argued that this period marks the beginning of chieftaincies, in which villages were ruled by headmen who were chosen because they had more goods than others. Ambitious headmen may have tried to get control of decision making in neighboring villages, too, forming bigger chieftaincies. It seems probable that these and other developments had happened before 5500 B.C.E. Perhaps in the Halaf period, before 5000 B.C.E., pottery variety was replaced by a single style; this may not argue directly for chieftaincies, but it does argue for better communication given that a single style could be known in so vast a region. So-called ranked societies tend to have recognized leaders but not permanent institutions to support them, and their settlements are likely to be in areas where they might strive to be self-sufficient instead of relying on exchange with other settlements.[6] This appears to be the case in Mesopotamia at least until the Ubaid period (5000–3500 B.C.E.)

People began to venture out of the parts of the foothills that got enough water for rainfall agriculture onto the Iraqi plain. On that plain there was never enough rainfall to grow things, and so people had to experiment with irrigation. This turned out to be easy because one of the great rivers that created the plain, the Euphrates, is a slow-moving, meandering stream that is easy to tap and divert to riverside fields.[7] And irrigation, even more than domestication, enhanced the size of the grain, so that even more food was produced from the same area of land. What was a necessity turned out to be a gift of abundance.

Large-scale irrigation was relatively late, and the scattered early sites do not suggest centralized control. Land in Mesopotamia has no value at all without water, and large amounts of land that might be irrigated were always available.[8]

The move onto the plain had likely begun tentatively even before 5000 B.C.E., and the motives for it may have been similar to those for domestication itself. People may have perceived that their villages were getting too crowded, even if they may not have been crowded at all by later standards. And so they moved out into the forbidding frontier area, which turned out to be extremely productive agriculturally.[9]

When they moved, they probably brought their village social structure and preconceptions to the new riverine environment. And they no doubt continued to be in communication with people back home because the rivers made travel easy. And the pottery culture that dominated after 5000 B.C.E., which we call the Ubaid after an archaeological site near the southern Iraqi city of Ur, stretched not only across the plain but also into the foothills and into what is now Syria. It was the most widespread pottery style of any we have yet identified. It is probable that the plain had been settled in some places slightly earlier by people using different pots, but they are attested so far only at a few southern sites.[10]

Surface survey of southern Iraq shows that Ubaid villages stretched along the Euphrates and along many smaller canals that emerged from it either naturally or owing to human intervention. The surface survey results are perhaps a little circular in asserting that there were such canals, because usually the only evidence of their existence is a string of tells with Ubaid remains.[11] But since we know that these villages could not have survived on the meager rainfall that the plain gets, and since it is not likely that the climate has changed much in the intervening millennia, it seems safe to assume that the villages perched along canals, which they tapped to water their fields.

In the villages, which consisted of small mud huts without specialized rooms, there were also public buildings. In the far southern site of Eridu is a building that seems to have been a temple, perhaps dedicated to the god of fresh water because excavators have found a great many fish bones in it.[12]

Very likely the Ubaid period saw an increasing specialization of labor, and a few people could count on the rest of the population to support them with their agricultural surpluses while they carried out agriculturally unproductive duties that the community thought were useful. There probably were priests and there were political leaders of some sort, and they may not have had to work, or at least to work full-time, as farmers.[13]

There is a controversy about who these Ubaid people were, whether they were direct ancestors of the groups we see when writing was invented. And because of the muteness of the archaeological record, it does not seem likely

that the controversy will ever be resolved. It is sometimes termed the Sumerian Problem because it involves the question of where the Sumerians, the first historically attested group in the region, came from. Were they Ubaidians? It seems likely that they were because there are no major archaeological breaks after the Ubaid—but in fact we may never know for sure.[14]

Around 3500 B.C.E. there was a change in pottery style and perhaps a quickening in the development of complexity. We call the new style, and the new period, the Uruk, after a large southern site. In this period we see the growth of several large villages into something like cities. We are not sure how many people lived in these settlements, but probably their numbers were fairly small, not more than ten thousand even in the biggest. The population growth was not uniform. Survey shows population decline in the Nippur-Adab area from the middle of the Uruk period, just when Uruk itself was increasing in population.[15]

Some villages grew because they were advantageously situated for trade on crossroads of canals; some were near the sea, the Persian Gulf, which was becoming important for trade too. Others may have grown because the people in charge increased the agricultural productivity of their region by organizing the digging of new canals. That there were people in charge seems clear from the growth of public buildings. The temple at Uruk got bigger in the period, and the precinct around it was built up to create a big platform, presumably for ceremonial and religious activities.[16] Someone had control of a tremendous agricultural surplus and was spending it on building magnificent things.

But it was not just in large things that the opulence of the period can be seen. Small statues, too, show that stone was being imported; the Iraqi plain lacks large stone because it is river-laid. And although the statues may not strike us as realistic or attractive, they obviously required a lot of someone's time and effort, which was being freed from agricultural work.

Also from this period we get for the first time a trinket that was to become the typical sign of what we call Mesopotamian civilization: the cylinder seal. This is a small, cylindrical bit of stone or other hard material that has been carved so that when you roll it out on soft clay, it makes a design. By analogy to later periods, we think that people used these as medieval European notables used signet rings, to sign documents and attest to their authenticity.[17]

One unusual aspect of the Uruk period is the sending forth of colonies both upriver into Syria and east to Susa. Possibly the Uruk people wanted a permanent relation with trading partners for stone and wood, which among other things were not available in southern Mesopotamia itself.[18] The settlements were abandoned toward the end of the period. Perhaps they were parts of a

trade diaspora, settlements established only for trade. But the evidence for imports from the outposts is weak. It seems that the Uruk people were the first to use the wheel, and this may have been connected to their interest in moving bulky goods.

The most amazing achievement of the period, one of which we are right now enjoying the benefit, is the invention of writing. This appears to have arisen as an aid to memory in connection with administration. As early as 3300 B.C.E. we begin to get what we call numerical notation tablets, small pillows of clay on which there are marks that seem to represent numbers. Sometimes someone will have rolled his cylinder seal over the tablet, as if signing for receipt of this many of something. What exactly was being received was not indicated, but if it was something important, as seems likely, the parties involved would remember. These kinds of tablets are found widely in the world of greater Mesopotamia, from Susa at the eastern edge of the Iraqi plain all the way up to Habuba Kabira, which now lies under Lake al-Assad in central Syria. Sometimes in addition to numbers and sealings the tablets had small tokens stamped in them. Perhaps the tokens made the numbers more explicit and told exactly what was being counted. It may be that scribes eventually found it helpful just to draw the tokens on the wet clay instead of trying to find the very one they wanted, and this may be the origin of writing.[19]

When we first see the writing system, in the southern city of Uruk, it is already highly complex and has a great many signs. We obviously have not yet found the earliest stage of the system.[20] The signs of the writing system are pictographic, that is, they are little pictures of what is meant, but they are inscribed on the same clay tablets as the numerical notation signs were, though some are bigger. We cannot understand everything in the texts, but we can see that the administration of the city of Uruk was listing and distributing a great variety of items, probably as salaries to people who worked for the administration.

We call this writing system cuneiform from the Latin term for "nail-shaped" because eventually the marks in clay came to resemble nails inscribed in the clay. The invention opened up vistas of self-expression, but probably not at first. For several hundred years writing was in all likelihood confined to the mundane efforts of administrators to record workers and the surplus they generated. Also from these earliest periods of writing we get what we call lexical texts, dictionaries that helped people to learn to write in the system.

At this early time it is still not possible to say with certainty what language was being written because the texts, mostly just lists, may be read in any language. But there is continuity in the numerical system and in the writing system, too, and so we assume that the language was Sumerian, the same as that in later texts. Sumerian is not related to any other language, and we know it

largely through later lexical texts provided with translations into better-known languages for people who were trying to learn Sumerian.[21]

The idea of writing was to check and control surpluses. And though accounting techniques did develop and become more explicit over time, the aim was not to check profit and loss but rather to control pilfering and decay.[22]

The Uruk period seems to flow without a break into the one hundred years of the Jemdet Nasr period, from 3100 to 3000 B.C.E., which, however, because it is traceable only in southern Mesopotamia, may be just a regional cultural style in pottery and art. In later Mesopotamian tradition the break between Jemdet Nasr and the next period, the Early Dynastic, was marked by the Great Flood, which destroyed almost all of humankind. Archaeology does not confirm that there was a flood at that time, although two sites have what were interpreted as flood layers. There does not seem to be any break at 3000, but the sources provided by later texts do get more interesting after that date.[23]

The Early Dynastic period is called that because we have a list of early kings who ruled Mesopotamian cities in the period. The list was compiled much later, probably around 1800 B.C.E., and is called the Sumerian King List. It lists rulers from various cities that existed after the flood, and the interesting thing about some of them is that their names make sense not in Sumerian but in Akkadian. Akkadian is the earliest known Semitic language, and although it is written in the same cuneiform system as Sumerian, it is similar in structure and vocabulary to other Semitic languages, including modern Hebrew and Arabic. The listing of kings with Semitic names so early probably shows that speakers of Akkadian were settled on the Iraqi plain very early and were significantly involved in the politics of the cities in which they lived. There is no indication that they formed a separate social group.[24]

The problem with the Early Dynastic period, though, is that little material comes directly from the earlier parts of it, and a lot more comes from the end. We usually divide the period into three parts, labeled I, II, and III. Early Dynastic I lasted from about 3000 to 2800 B.C.E., and our guesses about it, based entirely on later texts, include the idea that it may have seen a kind of primitive democracy in which notables made decisions by consensus, perhaps including even people from several different cities meeting in a central place like Nippur, which eventually became the religious capital of the plain.[25]

Earlier temples seemed to be important economic centers that organized much activity. And it is possible that in the Early Dynastic period we see the rise of a different class of exploiters whose power base was outside the temples; these became kings and eventually expropriated the lands and people of the temple. At Lagaš, where this development may be seen, the situation was actually more complex, the apparently secular power weakening at the expense of temples. But each city was different. Temples in Mesopotamia were always economic plums that rulers wanted, and usually kings managed to dominate them, even if they did not emerge from the temple hierarchy themselves. Temples were important in storage and redistribution of goods. Palaces certainly grew more elaborate, and yet it is clear that since the Ubaid at least there were buildings that looked like palaces. In spite of such architecture private houses did not really show status distinctions until the early Uruk period.[26]

Early Dynastic II lasted from about 2800 to 2500, and again we are limited almost exclusively to later reflections of the period. Kings from this time who appeared in the Sumerian King List were remembered in later poems as having had adventures involving long-distance travel at least into Iran and perhaps even Lebanon. Although the King List assumed that there was always only one preeminent king on the Iraqi plain, there are indications that some men in the list were contemporaries. The most famous of the heroic kings, Gilgamesh of Uruk, is not directly attested in contemporaneous texts, but we have found an inscribed mace with the name Enmebaragesi, the father of one of the other kings whom Gilgamesh reportedly confronted. The problem of finding the historic Gilgamesh is complicated by the fact that the name Gilgamesh is almost certainly a later epithet for the hero, not a name he bore in life; it may mean "heroic ancestor."[27]

SOCIETY AND ECONOMY IN
EARLY DYNASTIC AND EARLIER

With the Early Dynastic III period, which lasted from about 2500 to 2334 B.C.E., we get a flood of documents, almost all of an economic and administrative nature. This period yields the so-called pre-Sargonic texts from Lagaš-Girsu, about sixteen hundred of them, which give a picture of life in the temple administration during a disastrous war. We also have inscriptions from the city-governors of that city and a few others that show their goals if not the results of their policies. Inevitably we will draw to a considerable extent on these texts because there are simply more of them than texts from earlier periods.

The presence of speakers of a Semitic language is clear because of the names in texts, though texts appear to be intended to be read in Sumerian.[28] And by Early Dynastic III about half of the scribes in one archive had Semitic names. This implies early bilingualism and foreshadows the breakdown of bilingualism in favor of Akkadian, the Semitic language.

Ancient ethnicity is as slippery an issue as modern ethnicity is. Usually all we can say is how the person is described and whether his name makes sense in one language or another. But of course, as today, pure ethnic groups and cultures existed only in the minds of certain observers, not in reality.[29]

Around 2400 B.C.E. we begin to get texts from the site of Ebla in northern Syria in the same cuneiform system but intended to be read in a Semitic language we call Eblaite. We have found a royal archive of a small state involved in trade and relying for its wealth on its production of vast amounts of textiles deriving from herds of sheep.[30]

We must not be blinded by Early Dynastic III and think that if we can understand it, we can understand the origins of Mesopotamian social and economic life. The beginning of Early Dynastic III, around 2500, is one thousand years after the beginning of the Uruk period. That may be like trying to study the modern English-speaking world and draw generalizations intended to cover not only what could be observed at the end of the twentieth century C.E. but also English society before the Norman Conquest a thousand years earlier.

Surface survey reveals that between the end of the Jemdet Nasr period and the Early Dynastic many small village sites on the Iraqi plain were abandoned, and the larger villages grew into great cities. The cities sucked in population from the villages and left a depopulated corona of about fifteen kilometers, or nine miles, in all directions. Probably the people who lived in the cities themselves went out and worked these fields, and there were few villages left in the coronas. A similar expansion is seen in north Syria, but it is not clear if city growth there resulted from migration from outside the region or from the absorption of villages.[31]

People's motives for concentrating in cities may have been self-defense against depredations of other cities. It is in fact in the Early Dynastic period that archaeologists find cities with walls. Perhaps it became less safe for peasants to live in unprotected villages. Or administrators' increased skill in managing complexity may have led them to order people to relocate for defense, and this led to the increased specialization of labor and to increased stratification of wealth.

One physical manifestation of the standardization of the bureaucracy is the beveled-rim bowl, found widely in urban sites of the period. It is not known what the purpose of producing lots of similar-looking cheap bowls was, but it certainly shows large organizations wanted lots of people to have the same or similar quantities of something. Later literary texts see cities as the very matrix of civilization, representing the order needed for the development of organized existence. They appear in such texts at the beginning of creation and are closely connected to kings.[32]

After we begin to get texts, we cannot see any distinct social groups aside from those that we might have guessed existed before, the dominators and the dominated. There has been considerable discussion about ethnic groups being socially significant, but it appears that the differences between Sumerians and Akkadians at least were linguistic only by the time we can observe these groups in written texts. In other cultural and social aspects it is not possible to separate characteristics that are more typical of one or the other group.

The basic question of whether there really were social classes in this period will remain unanswered at least for the time being because of the lack of texts. One might guess that the Ubaid period may have known no particular class distinctions beyond that between leaders and followers, headmen and peasants. But in the course of the Uruk and later periods this initial distinction led to a more profound class division.[33]

The families of rulers are those we know best in the period, and they appear to be simple nuclear families, a father and mother and two or three children. It is not unlikely that more extended families existed that are unclear to us in art or writing. Peasant family size cannot be gauged from the Lagaš-Girsu archives, but we may guess that working families valued helping hands and had more children than the elites.

The fact that children are depicted on rulers' plaques seems to indicate that they were cherished. A woman likely would have had to bear between five and six children to maintain a stable population because only between one and three would survive to puberty.[34] Children who lived would usually be highly valued.

The inscriptions of rulers indicate that inheritance, at least among them, proceeded through the male line, though the eldest son did not necessarily inherit all power. Polygamy was probably an option for the rich, but in fact we have no instances of it. We do see in the Lagaš-Girsu ruler Uru-inim-gina's Reform Texts that in the past polyandry had been practiced, though the ruler clearly condemns it; there are no other references to the custom in the whole of Mesopotamian history, and the matter is doubtful.[35]

The Early Dynastic III texts show that the labor of lower-status women was exploited by the city-state in weaving sheep's wool. Women wove, perhaps because weaving was a job that could be interrupted and thus was compatible with child care. But women also appear as priestesses and seem to function as high officials at least in some temples at Lagaš-Girsu. The wife of the city-governor there was clearly someone to be reckoned with. Women bought and sold land, and they were legally capable persons.[36]

The sexual division of labor that dominates most societies also pervaded early Mesopotamian society. Some jobs were probably regarded as women's work, but this division did not keep women from exercising considerable freedom of movement in commerce and from dominating some institutions.[37]

We see that in great temple households labor was sometimes drawn from men and women who were called g u r u š and g e m e, terms that later refer to laborers who were doing forced labor, or corvée. Sometimes it appears that such work was a tax in labor on otherwise free peasants. We do not know how the labor was coerced, but we know that the laborers were given standard rations during the period of their work at least. Children were sometimes involved in forced labor.[38]

Because the foreign origin of some slaves is noted, we believe that most were of foreign origin. The free person, in contrast, is termed the native. Our definition of slavery is conditioned by subsequent experience, and not everyone would agree that freedom of movement, salability, legal rights, or status necessarily define a slave. I take the position that salability is the key feature of slavery, and yet many, perhaps most, slaves were not sold once they had entered a household. The earliest documented slave sales were in the southern city of Girsu around 2430 B.C.E.[39] Slaves were not held in large numbers and were not very important in supplying labor.

There are few traces of officials hiring laborers in the period, and some have taken that absence as an indication that there was no market in labor and even that all peasants were dependent on the great organizations of temples and palace. It now seems much more likely that officials did not usually resort to hiring. As posited for early modern Africa, some people did sell their labor, but before the rise of state organizations few did so, relying instead on community and family organizations.[40]

Agriculture flourished along canals and outside cities. Records of land sales show that communal consent to the sale was frequently needed, but sellers were few in numbers and buyers appeared alone. Actual communal ownership thus appears to be excluded. The northern part of Mesopotamia had more land sale texts selling larger fields than the south, and maybe this means that private ownership was more widespread in the north. This north-south contrast in sales persists in the Old Babylonian period (2004–1595 B.C.E.).[41]

Earlier students sometimes assumed that rulers had total control over land and could be said to own it, but there is no specific evidence to support that assumption. It seems much more likely that the government was merely one landholder, possibly the largest, among many. The idea of owning land probably involved the bringing together of various rights to use land and especially water and the appropriation of them by families and individuals. When texts become understandable at pre-Sargonic Lagaš, the state or temple had three categories of land: land belonging to the state and farmed by it, land given temporarily to officials and workers as part of their salaries, and land rented out to others.[42] The concern for canal building and maintenance that glows forth from almost every one of the inscriptions of city rulers derives from the elite's desire to keep as much land irrigated and thus cultivated as possible and to open up new land to agriculture.

The Iraqi plain might seem a forbidding environment in which to raise animals, but human beings brought down from the foothills many of the domesticates that they had there and learned to use their labor and their products in the plain, too. Sheep and goats especially could be pastured on the margins of the cultivated land and on fallow fields in ways that complemented the growing of plants. Children, who would not have been useful in the fields, may have tended the sheep and goats so that in terms of the human labor involved such herding was complementary to sedentary agriculture.[43] Doubtless too settlers on the plain exchanged products with nomads, people who followed their flocks from place to place where grass was to be found. Sometimes nomads were major sources of social tension, though that is not evident around 3100 B.C.E.

Some of the earliest cuneiform texts deal with the management of sheep and their products. These may have been annual summaries of flock productivity, perhaps produced as the sheep were being plucked or sheared in the spring and reassigned to shepherds.[44] This archive from Uruk derived from a government operation and may not be typical of what usually went on, but it seems to show some concern for the sex ratio of sheep, to assure that there were many more females than males to maximize reproduction. Humans consumed their milk products, and goats and sheep were plucked or sheared for hair and wool, slaughtered occasionally for meat—especially young males—and at death their skins were tanned and used for clothing and tents.

At pre-Sargonic Lagaš oxen and cows were managed to maximize herd expansion. Later texts show that archaeologically attested domesticates like oxen and donkeys were used by large households at least. Ducks and other birds were kept for their eggs and for food. Pigs also were herded, and their meat was eaten; the ambivalent feelings about pigs nowadays in the region were definitely absent in early antiquity.[45]

The archaeological record shows a high degree of specialization and considerable artistry in some areas of endeavor. The tiny cylinder seal called forth brilliant artists who depicted natural and mythological scenes for patrons. And cult expenditures may have inspired the exquisite small objects found in the Royal Graves at Ur from around 2700 B.C.E. as well as many less gorgeous objects that have reached museums through the antiquities trade.

In the Ur graves at least four important personages were buried with their retinues, including in one case more than forty women and men. All were gaily decked in gold jewelry, and the harp that the excavators found smashed by the weight of earth thrown in on it may have been playing as the group drank poison. This sort of opulent funeral sacrifice is unprecedented in the region and is unknown later in Mesopotamia, though there are examples from other cultures.[46] Usually Mesopotamian grave goods were limited to bits of jewelry and perhaps a cylinder seal and some pots of ointment.

Whatever the religious or political meaning of the Ur graves, they show that craftspeople were creating magnificent pieces. We assume that most of this magnificence was going into the households of the elite, and the pottery of the period does not show that poorer people enjoyed the material luxury.[47]

The Ur graves are an indication of a vigorous trade in raw materials for luxury items. The gold had to come from elsewhere, perhaps even from Egypt, and stone came from the Iranian mountains or Turkey. Some raw materials may have been passed along from village to village. But there are indications that some people in Mesopotamia were systematically trying to acquire foreign goods. When there are texts, we can read of the existence of people called d a m g a r, which we translate "merchant" because it is an Akkadian loanword understood as merchant in later related languages. The contexts for the work of these merchants are not clear in the archival lists of the earliest period, and we do not know if the merchants worked only for the city-rulers or if they also could execute private purchase orders. The crucial thing we do not know is whether the merchants themselves traveled anywhere to acquire goods or just took advantage of other people's travels to buy things.[48]

The trade in lapis lazuli, a semiprecious blue stone that is available in the Near East only in Badakhshan in Afghanistan, peaked in Early Dynastic III and then almost disappeared in later periods. Archaeology reveals that toward the end of the period there was contact with the Persian Gulf trade, which may have led ultimately to the Indus Valley in modern Pakistan. In later periods there are stamp seals, atypical for the period in Mesopotamia, that show affinities with seals found at Indus Valley sites. This may indicate that merchants from the Indus were bringing goods for exchange to the ports on southern Mesopotamian rivers. We do not find any Mesopotamian seals in Pakistan, and that may show that the merchants of the Mesopotamian texts did not get that far.[49]

But it is not just objects that were imported. Because they are attested in texts, we can be sure that resins and spices were also brought in, perhaps from Iran and perhaps from Syria and Turkey. Wood may have been imported, sometimes from a considerable distance, though there were stands of poplar and other scraggly trees in Mesopotamia itself. We assume that what Mesopotamia was exporting to acquire these goods was, as in later periods, textiles and grain.[50]

The evidence of trade does not uniformly show that contact with Mesopotamia generated growth in complexity in adjoining centers. Instead, there
were interactions that seem to have served the needs of elites in several areas for
semiprecious stones.[51]

In later times when the documentation improves, foreign trade was not a
major component of the southern Mesopotamian economy. Agriculture was
always and everywhere much more important. Northern Iraq, later called
Assyria, may have been more dependent on trade because it was less agriculturally productive. Nonetheless, trade allowed elites to acquire better material
possessions than they could have if they had relied only on kinship groups to
which they belonged.[52] At this time some modern theorists would see the transition from the so-called natural economy to the money economy, from the use
of barter for most transactions to the use of some symbolic commodity as a
replacement for things. Certainly economic life in cities must have been getting
more complex, but it is wrong to draw an exact line between barter and money
economies. Barter persists in predominately money-oriented modern
economies, and it no doubt played a role throughout Ancient Near Eastern
history.

The transition to a money economy may have been gradual and unnoticed.
Some things were habitually used to pay for other things, either because they
were available or because they became traditionally associated with such payments. The moneylike thing worked best if it was fungible, that is, could be
divided easily and each fragment of it was like other fragments of it. In later
periods not only precious metals were treated as money for payments, but so
was grain. Grain does not last so long as precious metal, but it does last a considerable time if stored in a dry place, and it is fungible.[53]

The precious metal that eventually came to the fore as money was silver, and
the etymology of the word for silver in Akkadian, *kaspum*, has led scholars to
guess that it was "broken" and then weighed on scales. We have silver rings
from later periods that appear to be ways of storing wealth, and it is possible
that coinage itself derives from cutting off the ends of such rings.[54] Coinage
came in only much later, and it can be understood as an effort to speed up the
weighing process by creating small units with weights guaranteed by some
authority.

We have few indications of the levels of prices, and much of the textual evidence comes from the temples.[55] Temples may have tried to be self-sufficient so
that they would not have to spend their money outside the household to get
what they needed, and thus they did not record many prices.

Can we speak in this time of an economic policy of any government? Yes,
insofar as we can regard the expansion of the canal and irrigation systems as

something in which the governments were interested. In Early Dynastic III the city-governor of Lagaš-Girsu, Uru-inim-gina, presented a program for economic change in his Reform Texts. The major concern seems to have been the alleviation of previous oppressive taxation and extensive government supervision. Uru-inim-gina promised that his relatively new administration—the texts date from his second year—would return fields formerly usurped by his predecessors to the temples and would not take unfair advantage of the weak. The political context of Uru-inim-gina's declaration was the deteriorating situation he was confronting in his war with the neighboring city of Umma, a war he would soon lose.[56]

The Uru-inim-gina texts were probably addressed not to the public at large but to the gods; they are preserved on votive plaques that he dedicated in temples. There certainly was a political purpose to his declarations in that he wanted to bolster support for himself among the oppressed. And he seems not to have hesitated at all in promising to tinker with economic life to assure that the poor got a better break. The attitude that the government ought to have an economic policy of some sort was probably older than Uru-inim-gina because he assumed it was reasonable, and, as we shall see, it continued to the end of the Ancient Near Eastern civilizations.[57]

On the other side of the known world, Egypt also was experiencing a revolution in human organization and economic development. These transformations seem to have happened later than in Mesopotamia and sometimes even to have been reactions to developments in Mesopotamia.[58] The domestication of plants and animals reached Egypt later than it did other centers in the Ancient Near East, and the earliest remains that show domestication probably do not predate 4000 B.C.E. Oddly, we do not find even indications that people were building permanent houses and so had settled down into agricultural villages until about 3500 B.C.E. in the Gerzean period, named after an important site in central Egypt. But to the west of the Nile in that period we already find elaborate burials that include fancy pots and jewelry.

The arts of agriculture diffused into Egypt, but Egyptians had been gathering intensively from their environment since 12,500 B.C.E. There have been dryer periods in the past, and the present arid conditions were probably established by the Old Kingdom, around 3000 B.C.E.[59]

In the deserts to the east of the Nile there were deposits of gold, and people living in Egypt mined them at least from 3000 B.C.E. It is possible that foreigners visited the deposits, perhaps coming in from the Red Sea. The agricultural villages in Egypt may have been dominated by headmen who came from the families with the best land, and some of these from the central part of the country may have been inspired by the visits of foreigners to the gold fields to try to control the fields themselves. As part of that effort they began conquering their neighbors, perhaps to reduce the competition for the gold.[60]

This explanation of how Egypt began to be politically unified seems too simple. There was a lot more to it, but it is an attractive idea and helps to explain the Mesopotamian elements one sees in the Gerzean period and in the Early Dynastic period in Egypt (3100–2686 B.C.E.), when the first two groups of kings dominated most of the land. The elements from Mesopotamia include cylinder seals found in Egypt, and also the habit of putting niches in building walls. This feature was helpful in strengthening the mud-brick walls in Mesopotamia, but the niches made little sense in Egypt, where lots of limestone was available for big buildings. So there definitely was a foreign influence, though it died out after the Egyptian Early Dynastic period.[61]

The major facts of Egyptian social life were well established by the Early Dynastic, and the headmen who had unified the land collected taxes from peasant villages but otherwise may have left them alone. The taxes supported bureaucrats who attempted to manage the surplus grain that Egypt produced thanks to the regular flooding of the Nile in the early summer. Such flooding meant that as the water receded peasants had only to plant the newly silted fields.[62]

Because of the administrators' ideology, which we see more clearly later, our attention in Egypt is usually focused on the king to the exclusion of most other Egyptians. The administrative ideology held that the king was a god, and all fertility and success came from him. Administrators strove to do his will, and presumably peasants did, too, insofar as they were aware of it. But this view of Egypt as a land of monolithic obedience, the ultimate Oriental despotism, is probably true for no period, and it ought not to be emphasized for the very early period. Local leaders continued to mobilize peasants for local projects, and there is some indication from later texts that in the Gerzean and Early Dynastic periods especially lowborn people could hope to reach great heights within the administration through diligence and brilliance. Perhaps in imitation of Mesopotamian principles, the Egyptians invented a writing system, now called hieroglyphic, "priestly writing," which in theory was like the Mesopotamian; but its forms remained much more pictographic for most of ancient Egyptian history, and none of them resembles any Mesopotamian forms. There does not seem to be an evolution toward writing in Egypt as there was in the greater Mesopotamian area, and that is why we think the idea of writing was borrowed.

Tombs show several apparent instances of polygamy, probably among unusually rich officials. But the number of polygamous officials was small compared to the number of preserved tombs.[63]

In all periods in which land prices are attested in Egypt, they seem very low, for example, two acres sold for a cow in the Old Kingdom. The explanation of this is that the purchased land was usually expected to be worked by peasants who had to be supported by it, and so the purchaser would get only a small part of the crop. It was thus not such a valuable investment. But land was privately owned and could be sold in all periods. Land transfers sometimes included people living on the land in the Old Kingdom, but people were not sold apart from land.[64]

Innovation in crafts is evident in the archaeological record. The crafts that are preserved were devised for funerals, but there may have been lots of other exciting things that were in wider use but that have not been recovered. The odd thing about craft production is that it was creative and innovative in the early period, but the major market for it was the government and people associated with the government. Once their tastes were accustomed to the brilliant jewels and trinkets of the period, the style for what was acceptable in Egypt was set at least until the end of the ancient world. Probably the government simply refused to pay for anything new in design, preferring the archaic instead. So there was an early stagnation after a brilliant time of craft innovation. Trade appears to have been dominated by the king, but Old Kingdom tombs do have market scenes, and this may indicate that our textual evidence is incomplete.[65]

The cliché social fact of the Egyptian Old Kingdom, that the pyramids were built by slave labor, appears to be false. It is much more likely that the pyramids were part of government make-work projects that used idle peasants in the off-season from agriculture in forced labor. The workers may not have wanted to participate, but they were not slaves. The point of the mammoth expenditure on death was not only to employ the unemployed but also to establish institutions that would perpetuate the fame of the current king. We call these institutions pious endowments, and the pyramids themselves are only one aspect of them.[66] The endowments also had temples associated with them and a professional priesthood whose duty it was continually to celebrate the life of the king and offer sacrifices for the well-being of his soul. The establishments were supported by fields and peasants who were assigned to the support of the endowments, and we know that at least two of the institutions did survive as working temple complexes for years after the deaths of their founders, Sneferu and Teti. Kings elaborated on the design of the bench-graves that officials had built for themselves and developed stepped levels to them, which then were smoothed into the pyramid shape.

These arrangements focus attention on the odd Egyptian attitudes toward death, which were not shared in the rest of the Ancient Near East. Egyptian kings believed that if their burials were proper and their mortuary cult maintained after death they would move to the west, like the sun, and live forever with the gods. It is not known if ordinary Egyptians shared similar hopes, but high officials may have.

Over time kings may have given more lordly titles to local worthies as a counterweight to the growing bureaucracy at the capital. It has been suggested that this eventually led to the end of the Old Kingdom as decentralization increased.[67]

It is anachronistic to speak of Israel in this period because the people of Israel came together much later, around 1200 B.C.E. But the region of Syria and Palestine, part of which eventually became the land of Israel, was much more a part of Mesopotamian developments than it was of Egyptian. There are sites that show the domestication of plants and animals and sedentarization in what became Israel, and there are pottery cultures later that have analogues and contacts with the Ubaid. The Early Bronze Age in the land of Israel lasts from about 3150 to 2200 and marks a time when new metal technologies were enriching life and new cities were being formed.[68]

The agricultural basis of life in Syria-Palestine was not dependent on rivers but on rainfall. The peasants of the region in all probability lived in small villages and sporadically paid taxes to nearby city-rulers who may have been trying to protect the peasants and their fields from other city-rulers. As in Mesopotamia no large states were formed, but villages formed coronas around the cities, supplying them with their needs. The class structure of the societies may have been like that in Mesopotamia, oppressors on top and the oppressed underneath. Because we do not have texts from the region, we cannot say much about social mobility or the economy.

Archaeology reveals that other parts of the Near East, including Anatolia and more eastern parts of Iran, had participated in the process of domestication and the formation of the patterns of village life. But nowhere else had cities formed at this early time, and we may guess that life remained on a fairly basic level for most of the world's population. The rhythms of the agricultural year brought surpluses from the efficiencies of domestication, and on the fringes of the Near East people were still discovering that domestication was advantageous for them, too. And we do not see that innovations from the periphery of the Near East made any impact on the central cultures. The Egyptians and Mesopotamians had contact with the periphery mainly to trade for or to seize raw materials, and in that contact they may have influenced the people they confronted. The effect of these confrontations is obvious in sub-Saharan Africa in what is now Sudan, where headmen began to imitate Egyptian crafts and even burial customs.[69]

In China, urban life did not generate dynasties of rulers remembered in later writings until around 1766 B.C.E., the traditional date for the founding of the earliest dynasty. Village farmers were established there earlier. We do not know when village life appeared or whether in some way it was indirectly influenced by distant Mesopotamian examples. The plant domesticates in China were ones that grew near to hand, although the Chinese had pigs and sheep, which were known earlier in the Near East.[70]

We will not go much amiss if we imagine that the places described and their societies and economies were the most interesting and brilliant that human beings had created up to that age. Parts of Europe were still learning about domestication, and the Americas were inhabited still by hunters and gatherers. The center of the human cultural world was between the Nile River and the Iranian uplands, in what is today the Near, or Middle, East.

T·W·O

THE RISE OF EMPIRES

2300–2000 B.C.E.

The young woman named Huda had gotten a message to come, and so she had dressed in her best cloak and done her hair, but really she had no idea why she had been summoned to the palace. Her husband, Pada, as usual, was away, supposedly doing the king's business in distant lands; he had left in the spring when the roads became passable, but now it was the ninth month, about December, and he still had not appeared.

One never knew about those things. Travel was difficult, and when he did come home, usually twice a year, he looked worn and tired and wanted to take a bath every single day for a while until he got to feeling clean. He was a small man with quick black eyes; she knew he was rarely beaten when it came to getting a really good deal. He had had a difficult childhood, had been abandoned as a child, and that was why he was called Pada "the one found," sometimes even Puta-Pada "the one found in a well," though he told her once that the kind couple that had picked him up had found him near a public building, not in a well at all. His foster father had been a farmer, but Pada had seen the merchants arrive, their donkey-packs bulging with goods with strange-sounding names, and especially he enjoyed the tales they told.

Mostly lies, what the merchants told him, she thought, as she moved along toward the city-governor's palace. Mostly lies like his. For surely no self-respecting woman could believe that he had seen forests where the trees were legion and taller than two temple-towers. Or a sea on which one had to sail for two months to find a port.

No doubt about it; Pada was a liar. But he provided well for her and the children, and his salary was paid whether he was in town or not. There were some advantages to an absentee husband, she thought, not that she would make use of them in the way it was rumored some wives did, not like those sluttish military wives whose husbands might never return from the endless battles on the northern frontier. But they might feel they had little to live for because their husbands might turn up dead, and, given how bad communications were, they might never even be told. She worried about Pada too, of course, but he assured her that the governor's merchants had never actually been harmed in their travels. But, oh, they had had some scrapes!

He would eventually turn up, though, dirty and smiling and with nice lit-

30

tle gifts for the children—the children, whom he sometimes couldn't even recognize because they had changed so much since he had gone. And he did seem
truly sad when she had told him, as she had twice already, though she was only
twenty, that the child he saw last winter had died. No, Pada was a good man,
even if he was unlike the men her sisters had married, who all worked out in
the fields and could be counted on to be home for supper as soon as it was
dark. Her sisters, though, were always pregnant.

The guards paid no attention as she entered the palace and found the merchants' court. It was bustling with the caravan that had just arrived, asses bray-
ing on all sides as workers tried to calm them and unload them. In the middle
of the court a table had been set up, and the boss was sitting at it making tiny
notations on a clay tablet as slaves and workers gathered around, calling out to
him quantities and prices of the loads. A group of bureaucrats, more restrained,
clustered behind the boss, waiting to pick up their deliveries. The asses smelled,
but the goods emitted their odors of spices and pine trees. So if you stood near
the right pile, you could imagine yourself in a very lordly house indeed.

She did not push her way to the front. It was unusual that she should be
summoned, and she was afraid that it was to receive bad news. Maybe Pada had
finally taken one risk too many. So she watched the record-keeping advance
and the parceling out of goods. And the silver, more silver than she had ever
seen, lay on the table; the boss used it to pay off the drivers. It was late after-
noon and the heat was abating; she edged toward the boss, but only when he
had finished with everyone else did he notice her.

"Huda," he called in his hearty, big voice, "I'm glad you came. Pada asked
me to call you in and give you this." He picked up a package from under the
table, wrapped in rags. She took it and opened it, and the smell enveloped her:
cedar, exuding coolness and distance. It was about three pounds of incense such
as would be suitable for scenting the house, and there was enough to offer some
to the gods too. It was a very opulent thing.

"But, sir," she asked, adjusting her scarf, painfully aware that she had never
spoken to anyone so important in her young life, "is Pada well?"

"Oh, of course he is!" the boss replied, almost laughing, as if concern for
Pada were the funniest thing he had heard about that day. "This is Pada's caravan, all right, but he'd heard about a good price on bitumen and just couldn't
resist looking into it; he sent his men on ahead and told them to tell me to give
this to you. He'll be home tomorrow or the next day."

She bowed and smiled, but before he would let her go, the boss wrote down
the entry at the end of his tablet: "3 weights of cedar resin, its cost in silver 54
grains, via Huda, Pada's wife." He read it off to her, and she was amazed. Fifty-
four grains of silver for her? That seemed an impossibly high sum to spend on

a woman. Or had it really been meant for her? Perhaps she had misunderstood. What did it mean, "via"?

"Do I have to take it somewhere and deliver it?" she asked.

"Don't be silly, girl," the boss said, smiling. "We simply have our accounting formulations, and they must be followed. Take it home and use it, starting right now. Pada will want his house smelling good when he rolls in."[1]

The period from 2300 to 2000 marks the beginning of political consolidations on the Iraqi plain and the start of imperialistic adventures like the one in which Pada was involved. The organizations that had arisen in city-states extended themselves to broader horizons with mixed results. Central Mesopotamia finally was unified, but the diversity of interest that had marked its cities continued, and it could not be suppressed for long by even the most vigorous of rulers.

Sargon, a northern Mesopotamian leader, united the north and then the south around his new capital city of Akkad around 2300 B.C.E. and founded a dynasty that held the river basin together politically. We call these kings Sargonic and the period the Old Akkadian. Unity dissolved around 2200, and outsiders from the east, the Guti, ruled parts of the plain. They were driven out by a king of Uruk, whose control was inherited by a dynasty from Ur, the third from that city in the Sumerian King List. They ruled a hundred years and succumbed around 2000 B.C.E. to Elamites from the east and were succeeded by Amorites, people from the west of Mesopotamia.

Surface survey reveals that during this period the large cities continued to grow to hitherto unparalleled proportions. Uruk, the best studied, probably had more than sixty thousand people, and other cities of the empire likely also blossomed.[2] But the countryside was not abandoned either. And this time must be seen as the ancient high point of irrigation development. Areas hitherto not reached by canals were reached, and villages grew along canals that marked the edges of newly created fields. The extent and sophistication of irrigation works were rivaled only once again in the history of Iraq until the modern period, and that was in the Sassanian period around 400 of our era.

Governments continued to spend money on canal maintenance and building, and rich private persons did too. In fact it may have been a quick way to political prominence for a rich man to sponsor canal works in his neighborhood. The benefits would be remembered by peasants and landowners for years to come. Oddly, there were only minor attempts to have a uniform calendar, and local traditions continued, even including when to intercalate lunar months so that the seasons would not progress.[3]

It seems likely that the absolute population of the Iraqi plain also reached a high, though what that might have been we cannot say. Hundreds of thousands of people lived there, and its agricultural productivity continued to make it the breadbasket and the wonder of the world.

Beyond the major division between the managers and the managed we find in texts a great many other designations that might refer to class or status. But texts do not explain how contemporaries viewed the social divisions. We are best informed about people who were involved in laboring for the government. The status of these persons, called usually g u r u š and g e m e "young men" and "girls" as in previous periods, was probably low, and we know how they were paid while they were working. But we do not know if they had to work all the time or if they had access to other land of their own or at least for their own use. A subgroup of the g u r u š were the e r i n ("squad"?) people, who at Lagaš made up a large part of the workforce; perhaps four thousand were attached to temples and another thousand to the city administration. Another subgroup of the g u r u š were the u n-i l, which etymologically means "bearers, carriers." The e r i n people may have been lower-status g u r u š because they got fewer rations. But there is no indication that all cities had people from this class, and the designation may not be a class name.[4]

The linguistic division between speakers of Sumerian and speakers of Akkadian continued in the period, though some scholars believe that Sumerian may have died out as a spoken language. The north spoke Akkadian, and the south Sumerian.[5]

Sargon was an Akkadian emperor who established a power-base in the northern part of southern Mesopotamia and then chipped away at city-state independence until he controlled almost all of the plain and perhaps a great deal more besides.[6] From his successors' reigns, about 2334–2192 B.C.E., we get texts written for the first time entirely in Akkadian, but Sargon did not impose the language anywhere, and local scribal traditions continued.

Other linguistically definable groups were the Amorites and the Hurrians. These groups acted on the northern and western periphery of the Iraqi plain, and they would later come to dominate parts of it. Amorites spoke a Semitic language related distantly to Akkadian, and some of them seem to have been nomads operating on the desert fringes around the Euphrates. Their name in Sumerian and Akkadian means "westerners," and they did come from the west, although they were to be found as well in what is now Iran. There were also Amorites who lived in southern Mesopotamia and held posts in the bureaucracy and may even have adopted or been given Sumerian names.[7] The linguistic distinction seems, in short, not to have been socially definitive for Amorites.

Hurrians appeared in northern Mesopotamia and in what is now Turkey;

their language was related only to the Urartian language, which was found later in that region. Hurrians were sedentary on the whole, and many of their rulers in the north must have adamantly opposed the advance of Mesopotamian imperialism because there were frequent wars. The Hurrians used the cuneiform writing system to write their own language, but they do not seem to have integrated themselves into southern Mesopotamia as much as the Amorites had. Much more obscure are other northerners known as Subarians, who were distinct from the Hurrians, though they lived in similar northern mountainous regions.[8]

Information about families becomes much more abundant, and the basic structure remains the same. Monogamy was the norm, and two or three children was average. Because we do not know much about contraception in any period in Mesopotamia, we can assume that infant abandonment and sales were not uncommon, as in medieval Europe. Breast-feeding may have lasted as long as three years, though, and that would decrease fertility.[9]

Because older brothers and maternal uncles were frequently mentioned, we think they were important in leading the family, and some might see in this aspect an indication of an older or a local emphasis on matrilineal inheritance. In the texts, though, there seems to be patrilineal inheritance in which the oldest son does not have any advantage.[10]

Kings and maybe other very rich men had polygynous families and recognized all progeny as legitimate, and in fact it is not clear that there was a category of illegitimate child anyway. In the case of Šulgi, second king of the Ur III dynasty (2094–2047 B.C.E.) we know of more than fifty children. Proverbs collections that were recorded later but go back at least to the Ur III period mention raucous polygamous marriages.[11]

Women in the Sargonic Empire (2334–2197 B.C.E.) occasionally reached high station, but usually because of the influence of their brothers or father. Free women had extensive business dealings. Royal ladies had access to wealth and were not sequestered. The most powerful was Enheduana, the first occupant of the post of high priestess of the moon god at Ur and of the goddess of love and war at Uruk; she is known to us through contemporary inscriptions and through several hymns attributed to her.[12] The hymns argue that the apparently Sumerian goddess Inanna had the same characteristics as the Akkadian goddess Ishtar. The hymns were part of Enheduana's father's and brothers' project to unify southern Mesopotamia culturally. One of them alludes to a rebellion in which Enheduana was a target of persecution, but the rebellion was apparently put down.

In the Ur III period (2112–2004 B.C.E.) we see that queens and princesses occasionally appeared in the archival texts that recorded the goings-on at the

royal cattle pen near Nippur. The first and last kings were apparently monogamous, but Šulgi had nine known wives. They were frequent beneficiaries of the
grants of goods and animals. None held a high administrative office, though,
and few female scribes are known in the whole period.[13]

The legal texts indicate that women could testify in court and make contracts and frequently did so. Doubtless we hear only about upper-class women
in court cases, and such cases almost always deal with disputes about expensive things and slaves, frequently as parts of inheritances. Daughters did not
inherit if there were sons, but they may have gotten gifts from the estate. Still,
at least once there seems to be a presumption that a widow would inherit.
Women and slaves appeared in court. Once a woman dissolved her marriage by
a one-sided declaration.[14]

Lower-class women were heavily exploited by administrators, especially
when they were helpless. Women who worked in the forced labor gangs always
were given fewer rations than men. In spite of the government's propaganda
concern for widows and orphans, there was no systematic welfare system. The
institution that dealt with the problem of young families bereft of a father and
husband is called the a-r u-a, meaning "dedicated." Women and children were
"dedicated" by relatives who could no longer support them or by themselves,
and they were employed especially in weaving and processing wool. Because we
have several detailed records of such persons, we know that they usually did not
live long after they had been dedicated, probably owing to the wretched conditions in which they lived and worked. Some men were dedicated too, but not
so many as women and children. Perhaps the men were somehow debilitated
members of poor families. Women weavers were exploited extensively at
Lagaš; their children no doubt died at a high rate: one group of 679 women
had only 103 children, though other groups had more. Women were important in wool processing in Ebla in North Syria. The queen mother there was
influential.[15] The women's ration system at Ebla shows male workers getting
twice as much as female, but royal women's rations were higher than those of
male overseers.

Lagaš-Girsu legal texts show children being sold into slavery, and this led
the texts' editor to posit a weak family bond. If, as seems likely, the parents were
choosing life over death for their children, one does not need to doubt their
devotion to the children.[16]

The organization of unfree labor was well documented. The g u r u š and
g e m e "young men" and "maids," got rations from the great households while
they worked for them, but we are not sure that they had to work year-round.
Perhaps some of the year they returned to their homes and farmed plots. These
dependent people seem to have included all sorts of statuses within the soci-

ety, and some lists show agricultural workers as well as scribes and bureaucrats getting rations.[17]

The caloric level of rations seems in general in early Mesopotamia to have been around the ideal three thousand a day, and that modern boundary was usually exceeded. But children did not get as much as they needed, and this probably made them more vulnerable to disease.[18]

The question of whether the ration system served the dependent persons all year long remains open, but there are indications that most people drew sustenance from other sources, including their own garden plots. At Ebla old people and children were not recorded as getting rations, as they were in southern Mesopotamia.[19]

In the Ur III period there were hired laborers, almost always men, who were only infrequently mentioned in earlier times. The work people were hired to do was usually agricultural and backbreaking. The existence of hired menial labor indicates that the government and its households were being forced to turn to the free labor force for some needs. In Ur III hired laborers were relatively rare at harvest times, indicating that they were probably working in their own fields then. Wages were standardized, just as rations were for the forced labor, although there were some fluctuations in what a hired worker was paid. And the hired laborer usually got exactly what a hired slave got.[20]

Slaves are not attested in great numbers, perhaps because prices for them were high. Slaves cost from six to twenty shekels of silver as compared to one to three shekels for about an acre, four-tenths hectares, of land. Unfree laborers were much more important to the Mesopotamian economy than slaves were. The origins of slaves in all probability were in foreign countries, and many were sold in Mesopotamia as a result of their having been captured in foreign wars. Slaves could appear in court in the Ur III period, and usually when they did so it was to protest their servile status. They were not held in great numbers; the largest number attested in any household is 220, but that number is unusually high, and most free persons probably had none at all.[21]

Slaves could marry and have families, and by definition they could be sold. We do not hear of the breaking up of families, but we do hear of runaway slaves. We also have records of runaway dependent laborers. Certainly the life of a slave was not a happy one, but it may not have differed too much from the lot of native Mesopotamians who had to do forced labor. Prisoners of war, few in number, were distinguished from slaves, and we do not know how the distinction was made because most slaves originated as prisoners or children of prisoners.[22]

Population distribution shows that there were likely more fields cultivated than in earlier times, and we know a little more about how they were managed.

Some, perhaps most, of the agriculturally productive land was in private hands. This we can see from the Stele of Manishtushu, Sargon's son (2269–2255 B.C.E.), who recorded in meticulous detail a series of land purchases he made and the families from whom he bought.[23] Actually it is not always clear what the relation of all the people mentioned was to the sale at hand, but a reasonable guess is that they were co-heirs who all had to agree before the land could be sold. The stele demonstrates eloquently that the idea that the king owned all the land is wrong; he had to buy some of it if he wanted it, and his estates, though they may have been the largest and most lucrative, were not the only holdings.

The existence of private landholding probably continued into the Ur III period, but, oddly enough, we do not have any records of sales of agricultural land from that time. We do know of some sales of house plot and of orchards, and it is not known why the otherwise rather full record lacks these kinds of documents. An inability to sell land does not mean that private landholding did not exist. One text, unfortunately broken, may speak of a sum "for buying a field," and the details are not preserved. Some have speculated that land sales had been somehow prohibited by governments, but it seems unlikely to me that any government of the period would have been able to enforce such a decree.[24] Perhaps feelings against selling productive land outside the family were great, or the government scribes were uninterested in recording such transactions between private persons; maybe the success of irrigation efforts meant that cultivable land was practically free, and people would not buy what they could take.

Fields could be rented, usually for a small fraction of the expected return at the time of the harvest.[25] Maybe this cheapness of rents derived from the abundant new land that the canal-building and -revamping programs had created. Fields became increasingly salty as they were irrigated, and the minerals that occurred naturally in the soil rose by osmosis to the surface, where the drying up of the waters may have deposited them in unnaturally high concentrations. Barley could survive this process better than wheat, and Mesopotamians are said to have gravitated to that grain. But it is clear that the Mesopotamian farmers knew about leaching the soil to remove salts, and the posited switch from wheat to barley is not unequivocally attested.[26]

The productivity of Mesopotamian agriculture appears to have been extremely high, compared to premodern European standards. But there was wide variation in the ratio of seed planted to crop produced.[27]

The administration of land by great households may have differed between north and south, corresponding to the geographic terms Akkad and Sumer. The northern system seems simpler and based on standard units, unlike that in the south. The Sargonic state attempted to introduce the northern system into the south.[28]

Quantitative study shows that the Ur III state did extensive surveys of fields three times at Lagaš-Girsu. These indicate that efforts were made to intensify cultivation.[29]

Information about how animals were managed is abundant, especially from the era of the Ur III kings. Earlier, too, Sargonic administrators showed that they were interested in developing the herds of goats and sheep that furnished the raw material for the textile and leather industries. At Ebla the palace must have had at least seventy or eighty thousand head of sheep to sustain the attested consumption.[30]

In his thirty-ninth year Šulgi of Ur founded an animal farm that was a center for receipt of tax contributions for the temples at Nippur, the religious capital of Mesopotamia. The scribes at the place, called Puzriš-Dagan, perhaps in honor of the previous owner, kept detailed records of incoming and outgoing animals along with records of many other sorts of things that were distributed to government agencies and court favorites. There was an elaborate system of traveling officials who visited officers in outlying regions and even villages to collect animals, which they then drove to Puzriš-Dagan. Other officials would record the take and assign the animals to immediate consumption, to fattening, or to later distribution. City-governors of big cities contributed large numbers of animals for one month each year.[31]

The tablets thus generated are the most common kinds of cuneiform tablets in almost all collections today. Most are small, no bigger than five centimeters square, and record only one delivery. Others are larger and summarize the activity recorded in many small tablets. The point of the detailed accounting was probably to avoid loss and pilfering, but it allows us to see not only how the officials worked but also how court favorites and royal family members benefited from the flow of taxes. Contributions came not only from within the area controlled by the empire but also from friendly princes outside it and from Amorite groups who might still have been nomadic. Because of the brief nature of the texts we rarely see why contributions were made, though sometimes we can understand where the goods and animals were being distributed and for what purposes. A goal of one early series of texts that predates the founding of Puzriš-Dagan may have been to supply animals as sacrificial victims to a cult devoted to the memory of soldiers who had died in battles on the northern frontier.[32]

The efforts to fatten sheep at Puzriš-Dagan were directed partly toward the king's table when he visited Nippur and partly toward supporting the numerous priests and their families who lived in the holy city. The sheep were fed grain and probably not allowed much exercise as they were prepared to be culinary delights. The practices involved can be paralleled in another interesting group of texts from the Middle Assyrian period around 1350 B.C.E.[33]

Most sheep, however, were kept for their wool. Textile exports were important in other periods and in all likelihood were a significant factor both for internal distribution and for foreign trade. Surprisingly we do not often hear of management of wool-producing sheep, though from Lagaš-Girsu there is an archive that shows how it was handled.[34] Centrally supervised shepherds were assigned a herd for a year and might be reassigned if they did a good job, though mostly the shepherds did not reappear in the archive, and this may mean that they preferred not to be burdened with the responsibility. At shearing the next spring they would be accountable for sheep that died during the year and also for maintaining a good ratio of male to female. Most male sheep were gelded because geldings give better wool, but a small number of males was kept as stud animals. The administration was trying to increase the size of the flocks by making sure that shepherds did not take too many newborn lambs for their own use, though shepherds clearly could take some of them.

The only records of what happened to animals came from agencies connected to the government. It is quite likely that most sheep and goats were not under government control and may have been handled differently. Ordinary people doubtless did not get to eat meat very frequently, and sheep were regarded as too valuable to kill for food.[35]

At Ebla in Syria exports of finished cloth goods were a major source of wealth. In the texts, the exports were evaluated in silver.[36]

Knowledge about crafts comes from the archives at Ur in the Ur III period. These archives were found in secondary use as fill under a threshold, and we are not sure how they were originally organized. They show that there were craftsmen working at the capital city on all sorts of projects, mostly involving the production of small art objects and statues. While working on official projects the craftsmen were given rations as if they were dependent laborers, and as usual we do not know if this was their exclusive means of livelihood.[37]

The Ur texts show that precious stones were mounted, and many different kinds of fancy objects in metals were fabricated. The destination of these productions was not usually indicated, but it seems likely that the royal administration absorbed most of this fancy stuff as rewards for lackeys and favorites.

Other sites in the Ur III period have archives dealing with work in reed and leather. Reed may seem a worthless commodity, but the archives show that many useful baskets and sieves were created and were regarded as valuable. Also, we know quite a bit about the activities of smiths in the various cities;

they worked alone on contract to the government agencies and in addition probably did work for other individuals.[38]

Under the Sargonic kings there seems to have been a preference for naturalistic representation of people and animals in relief sculptures and in cylinder seals. Those objects thus appeal to us more than the stereotyped depictions from earlier and later periods. We know nothing of the craftspeople who produced such pieces.

Trade brought metals and stones to almost every household in Sargonic Nippur. Merchants, though, are not attested bringing such things; they purchased only resins. They may have worked partly for the government and partly for others.[39]

River-borne trade dominates, and in Ur III especially we hear in detail about the boats that were necessary to maintain the trade. Grain and textiles moved within Mesopotamia most easily by water, and textiles at least may have been shipped abroad too. It is important to note, though, that foreign trade probably was not of great importance to the functioning of the Mesopotamian economy. Mesopotamia generated great surpluses of grain and wool in all periods. Though Mesopotamians clearly needed and wanted stone and wood and other goods like the resins that Huda received in the story at the beginning of this chapter, these did not constitute a significant proportion of the goods and services Mesopotamia used.[40]

Even though it may not have been economically crucial, merchants from the southern city of Umma produced detailed records of their procurement activities, frequently but not always on behalf of official bureaus. It is not clear that the merchants themselves traveled abroad, as I guessed they did in Huda's story above, but they had access to foreign goods in markets in Mesopotamia if they did not themselves travel.[41] Twice a year a merchant would receive silver and grain and wool and would be expected to sell the grain and wool and buy amounts of products that government agencies and others did not produce. The products include resins perhaps from Iran or Syria-Lebanon, some wood, bitumens and gypsums for constructing buildings and boats, honey, raisins, and precious metals. Some of the products were native to southern Mesopotamia, but others, like the resins and the honey, were not.

The merchant would distribute what he had bought as soon as he got it home, and scribes would sometimes write up a small tablet to show the receipt of the goods. Twice a year there would be an accounting in which the merchant had to show how he had spent the capital he had been given. The texts that record the accounting do not reveal how the merchant himself was paid, and the merchants do not appear frequently in their own texts as receiving anything; the mention of Huda, Pada's wife, is exceptional. Probably the merchants got rations like lots of others who worked for the government when they were at home, and on the road they must have been able to trade for their own benefit as well perhaps as to fill orders from friends and other people who did not work for the government.[42]

The most interesting aspect of the merchants' activity is that they were required to record the prices paid for goods in weights of silver, and these sums were then totaled for each fiscal period and compared with the sum of capital. Any unspent money was carried forward so the merchant could use it in the next fiscal period. Deficits rarely occurred. Some merchants were rich and owned slaves. Still, it is not so clear that the professional designation d a m-g a r really helped to define a class or even profession. In the Old Babylonian period it sometimes means "creditor."[43]

Although the Umma merchants gave us the best-documented trade system from the period, there are many other indications that trade was flourishing. Imported stones and metals are found in archaeological contexts, and although their origins usually cannot be pinpointed, they show that Mesopotamia was exploiting peripheral regions for luxury goods and sometimes for raw materials.[44]

At Ebla the travel of merchants was not documented, but the city was a center for the distribution of metals. Goods likely changed hands as tribute and ceremonial gifts between governments. Relations between Ebla and Egypt are documented by finds of datable Egyptian objects relating to the kings Chephren and Pepi, separated by two hundred years in their reigns.[45]

Two products, silver and grain, appear as money.[46] Grain in Ur III Lagaš-Girsu seems to have been the money of account in internal government operations; goods and animals were priced in grain, and rations were paid in grain. But silver there was reserved for dealings of the officials with people outside their households and outside the control of the government.

Modern economists say that a commodity used as money may have several different functions. It can be used as a unit of value, evaluating something else, though perhaps never being actually physically paid for it. It can be used as a unit of account, expressing overall activity in an accounting period. And it may be used as a means of payment, being given for the receipt of something else. This last does not mean that the thing paid really is a money in other senses because in a barter system almost anything can be used as a means of payment. But in Mesopotamia in the period under consideration both grain and silver, and in all probability some other things too, were used in all three of these ways.

As we noted before, silver was weighed and probably broken and weighed again if the chunk was too heavy. Grain was measured by volume and not usually weighed.

In their summation of activities the Umma merchants gave the prices of all
the products with which they dealt, both the ones that had been given them
as capital and those that they had bought. Their texts constitute the world's earliest price series and so the first reliable index of prices in any society. A price
series is a set of prices from one institution over time, and it is a good barome-
ter of the level of prices in a society because it shows the institution facing different prices over time while the institution can be assumed to have had relatively stable needs.

There was considerable stability in the level of prices in southern Mesopotamia.[47] There is some indication that resins and spices were becoming
slightly more expensive and that grain was becoming somewhat less valuable.
This may mean that there was a tendency to inflation because something the
merchants used as capital was getting cheaper while one category of things they
wanted to buy got more expensive. But there is no indication of rampant
inflation.

The Umma series ended before texts from Umma did, and the central government at Ur lost control of Umma at some point after the fifth year of the
last Ur king. At Ur itself, though, the political decay toward the end of that
king's reign was associated with inflation in the prices of dairy products, and
perhaps in other prices, though the evidence is less clear.[48] But this apparent
crisis looms in the king's years six through eight, and though texts do not fully
document it, the last Ur king reigned another sixteen years, so this crisis may
not have felled the dynasty.

The existence of prices shows again that the economy was a mixed one, in
which the government may have been an active participant. But it was not the
only participant; people produced and delivered goods to the government that
the government could not command, and the people wanted to be paid. As
usual, the extent of this ostensibly private economy is hidden from us, except
in certain instances.

The mound of the city of Nippur in particular has preserved a number of
documents that show loans with interest of silver and grain to and from private
persons. It could be that the accidents of survival of cuneiform tablets have
kept us from finding similar texts from other cities. The study of documents
recording sales shows an increasing uniformity of form, actually culminating in
the Old Babylonian period.[49]

The inscriptions of kings show that there was a continuing concern for economic matters, though there are no indications that governments had consistent economic policies. The earliest real law code is that of Ur-Nammu, trans-
mitted by his son Šulgi in the Ur III period, and it shows a concern for the
downtrodden and widows and orphans. Kings declared their interest in estab-

lishing uniform weights and measures, and archival texts show that the orders were in fact given to attempt to establish uniformity, although modern scholars are divided on what that may mean.[50]

Legal collections do not mention prisons, but a later hymn to a goddess of prisons implies that distraint was used only before sentencing. Punishments themselves tended to be monetary.[51]

The distinction between the army and the police was not clear. Both functions were carried out by the Ur III state.[52]

In Sargonic times in Mesopotamia and at Ebla governments appear to have been content to tax the free landowners, but the Ur III state may have farmed more fields directly, assuming more risk, and leaving more extensive accounting records; the Ur III state then also courted economic disaster when the centralized system failed. Productivity may have declined as peasants took less interest in their work for the state.[53]

The mention of economic measures in royal inscriptions shows that the kings thought that their population expected them to take measures to deal with crises and perhaps to regulate prices. There is, however, no indication that governments ever managed actually to control prices. There is the kernel of an economic theory presented in the literary text we call "The Curse of Agade," probably produced under the Ur kings but concerning the fall of Akkad. The supposed impiety of Naram-Sin was felt to have led to high prices, and consequently piety in general was felt to lead to low prices.[54] To demythologize this idea, one could say that righteous policies led to low prices.

The city of Ur was dominant politically but not, interestingly enough, economically. Texts show its influence reaching only about fifty kilometers, thirty-two miles, outside it. The reason for this limit may be the lack of good roads and canals suitable for boat traffic.[55]

The relation between temples and palaces in Ur III is quite confused. It is not clear that royal officials supervised temples in each city, but the king may have sometimes been trying to appropriate temple land. The temple of Inanna at Nippur seems to have owned less land than its southern counterparts and to have been dominated by a single family that ran it as a private preserve. Perhaps Šulgi had reorganized the temples and made them de facto state property under royal governors. Governors might be chosen from among local worthies, but the generals that accompanied them were definitely creatures of the king. Temples at Ebla seem to have been less important than in southern Mesopotamia, and they were places of treasure storage for the central administration, which had to support between twelve and eighteen thousand persons.[56]

Royal officials were the ultimate controllers of most of the public institutions of their cities, including the a-r u-a "dedicated" system for exploiting women and orphans mentioned above. The officials had an impact on the economy in many ways, and their texts expose only a small part of their activities. One presumably got to be an official mainly through inheritance; many officials were able to pass on their posts to their sons. This led inevitably to a lack of flexibility in the bureaucracy and eventually limited the kings' power over their supposed servants. It may be one cause of the breakdowns in the imperial systems at the end of the Sargonic period around 2197 B.C.E. and the end of the Ur III period around 2004 B.C.E.

It is still an open question whether these political breaks constituted general economic crises. The fall of the city of Akkad at the end of the Sargonic period was lamented in subsequent periods with explicit mention of the high prices that the fall engendered. And the end of the Sargonic dynasty was followed by a period of political confusion in which foreigners called Guti, perhaps from the Iranian hills, ruled.[57] Our archives for the period are scant. But we cannot be sure that a major break really occurred in the ways most people went about making their livings.

The same can be said for the fall of Ur. In literary texts composed and copied in later periods, the loss of the city was depicted as a major trauma.[58] But then there was no period of foreign rule, and though the states that emerged in the next century were not so strong or all-encompassing as the Ur state tried to be, there is no reason to imagine that important economic changes had taken place.

It does not appear that there was a move toward greater household autonomy in the whole period. And though the power of the market certainly varied, it probably never totally collapsed and caused people to turn more extensively to their own local resources.

The Old Kingdom in Egypt, about 2686 to 2160 B.C.E., was among the most brilliant of any age known to humans if one judges by its monumental remains. The pyramids, which still serve as a symbol of Egypt, were constructed then, apparently as burial mounds for kings. There are few contemporary inscriptions, however, and social and economic life is only sketchily known.[59]

We do have royal inscriptions that refer to a cattle census every two years, and such a census indicates a degree of centralized power and administrative acumen unparalleled elsewhere at the time.[60] But we do not know simple things like whether all of the cattle in Egypt were subject to the census and to the taxation that may have been the goal of the census.

Graves needed grave goods, and the crafts traditions that had developed earlier were perfected under Old Kingdom kings. It is likely that accomplished craftsmen were employed full-time by the kings and did not have to do any agricultural labor. This allowed the creation of wonderful work, but the dependence of craftsmen on administrators soon inhibited further development of their arts because the tastes for fancy goods that had been created were not easily changed.[61]

All four of the provincial towns excavated have walls around them.[62] This may show that internal security was not what the royal ideology would indicate it should have been. The king was felt to be divine, the giver of all good things and guarantor of fertility and success. But perhaps he could not keep the peace and protect cities from marauders.

The royal officials were frequently closely connected with and sometimes actually the same as religious officials. The king's men had concentrated most significant administrative power in their hands.

The later tradition sees the end of the period as an important break, and the subsequent First Intermediate period, 2160 to 2040 B.C.E., as a time of social upheaval and economic want. Inscriptions from nomarchs, the governors of regions, boasted of how they insured the grain supply for their nomes, or counties, while others suffered. The central royal authority broke down and the bureaucracy collapsed. There was no external threat that brought on that collapse, but perhaps the weight of regulation simply became unbearable. The local authorities took increasing control, and most Egyptians experienced a reversion to headman government of the sort known in the premonarchical period.

The Intermediate period ended with the rise of a new dynasty that again derived from Upper Egypt and was bent on forcing local potentates to recognize its authority. The scribes declared that the opening of the Middle Kingdom, which these new kings inaugurated, was a blessed and welcome event.

As usual we do not know what ordinary Egyptians may have thought because so many modern Egyptians are living exactly where the ancients did. Certainly for some, even those of peasant stock, the Old Kingdom was a time when considerable personal economic advancement was possible. For most, though, the centralization that created pyramids and fancy goods was a source of increasing oppression in an already difficult life.

In what later became Israel the cities founded earlier continued to thrive, but there are no written remains, and we are not well informed on social and economic developments.[63] There is a decisive archaeological break, however, around 2200 B.C.E., when the Middle Bronze I period begins, lasting to around 2000. The period corresponds to the First Intermediate period in Egypt, but the decline it represents was probably not directly related to events in Egypt.

A new social group arrived in the land of Israel after the old cities had been depopulated, or perhaps the new group was somehow the cause of the depopulation. The sites that the Middle Bronze I people occupied were much simpler than the earlier cities, and village agriculture was the major mode of organizing economic life. This is definitely a period of economic in-turning of households.[64]

The period has been of interest to biblical scholars because there is a possibility that the new arrivals in the land had something to do with the wandering patriarchs, who were depicted in the Genesis stories as being relatively rustic and perhaps nomadic. The patriarchs did not, however, wander through an empty land but had encounters with settled groups, though not with cities. Many researchers believe the patriarchal period cannot be dated with any precision, and though some figures like the patriarchs may have wandered into the land in Middle Bronze I, others must have come later.[65]

The transition from Middle Bronze I to Middle Bronze II about 2000 B.C.E. appears to have been abrupt.[66] We do not know why the Middle Bronze I culture ended and its bearers departed, if they all did. But Middle Bronze II is something totally different. It may be associated with groups called Amorite in Mesopotamia, who spoke a West Semitic language and were most likely settling down after pursuing a nomadic life on the Syrian and Arabian desert.

On the island of Crete and in the Aegean Sea there is an increased sophistication in metallurgy and in seaborne commerce.[67] There are trade connections to Egypt and probably to the Syrian coast. And the fineness of craft goods indicates that there was specialization of labor and that some people were acquiring greater wealth than others. But the region had no writing at this time.

Beyond these outposts affected by Near Eastern developments the earlier Near Eastern innovation of settled village agriculture appears to have spread, and the domesticated plants and animals on which it was based spread with it. The center of human innovation and achievement remained in the Ancient Near East.

But in South America this appears to be the period of the first florescence of cities in Peru, where agricultural surpluses were used by governors to create temples.[68] The New World had been reached by hunter-gatherers from Asia as early as 11,000 B.C.E. Sedentarization and the domestication of plants and animals occurred gradually in favorable ecological zones after 6000 B.C.E., of course completely independently from any Near Eastern model. The new Peruvian finds are the first indications of urban life. We do not know why the cities died, as they apparently did after a thousand years. Cities did not reappear in the hemisphere until our own era.

In general, the rise of imperial states formalized social and economic relations and forced some people to explain their acts to a central government, sometimes in writing. In Mesopotamia, cities continued to be self-conscious and proud, unlike in Egypt, where they were the creation of kings. The Mesopotamian kings usually succeeded in imposing an imperial order, even though details of social and economic life could not be regulated by the rudimentary state apparatus.

DISUNITY AND REFORM

2000–1600 B.C.E.

It was so hard to make a good impression, to maintain that proper balance between royal disdain and humane interest, as the people filed in. But it was clear to the king that he had to keep on trying to appear both haughty and concerned; otherwise he would seem less kingly, and to seem less kingly was to invite rebellion.

He felt personally secure. His guards were trustworthy, and he was, after all, the tenth of a series of long-lived kings to sit on the throne of Babylon, and his subjects knew that. Any grandeur that had accrued to his forebears could be called on, in a pinch, to make him seem more regal. But grandeur is no defense against a quick dagger thrust from a petitioner.

They filed in, men in capes against the winter wind, and as they came in, they made for the braziers that he had had set up in the great hall. One of them, though, walked right up to his chair and fell on the floor, full length, before the bailiff could even begin to decide who would be the first to present his petition to the king.

"My lord and king," the man moaned to the floor. He was wearing a dirty coat and had an unkempt black beard. Around his head, he had a sort of rag which had not recently been washed.

The king stared at him a moment, looked at the bailiff, then decided he had better seem to be in control of the situation. "Rise," he said, and the man slowly got up. "Speak; what is your petition?" asked the king.

The man got up, but only to his knees. Then he said, "My lord, I have never addressed you before, and none of my family has ever stood before you. But our situation has now become too horrible. We have borrowed grain for the last four years for seed, and we have not been able to repay the loan. We have borrowed also for food until the next harvest, and now our creditors have said that if they do not get their money this winter, they will take my children—and there are five of them, all willing to serve the king, your majesty, as my family has always done—and my wife and me and sell us as slaves."

The man stopped to measure whether his words were having any effect. The king nodded for him to go on.

"My lord, to you this may seem a minor thing, a very minor thing that a loyal subject of yours should lose his entire house and his family. And I would

not approach you in this way if it were not for an additional fact. My family
and I are not alone. Almost our entire village is in exactly the same condition,
and the creditors from Sippar are threatening us all. And I would not come to
you in this way if it were only one village which through luxurious living, perhaps, had gotten itself into trouble in this way. But my brother-in-law's village
is in the same situation, and in fact, everyone I have talked to on the way here
is facing similar menaces."

The crowd that had come in with the man had begun to focus on what he
was saying, less and less on the king with his curled black beard and long white
linen robe and golden necklace and rings on each hand.

"Is there nothing you can do for us?" the man cried, and fell on his face
again.

The king looked concerned, and whispered with his bailiff. Both smiled,
and the king turned to the man, indicating he should rise again; he did, this
time to his feet.

"My son," the king began, although it sounded odd since the man was probably forty-five if he was a day, and the king had just turned twenty. "My son,
because this is the first year of my reign, and my glorious ancestors have had
the custom of issuing an edict of freedom for certain debts and taxes, I will
issue such an edict in the near future. Until it is issued, and to make sure that
it applies to you, go with my secretary here who will write down your name
and make sure that your case is properly handled. I do not want my free subjects to fall into slavery by any means."

The king smiled benignly, and the man fell on the floor again, thanking him
with opulent blessings on his house and progeny. The secretary, a squat man
with a wispy gray beard, helped the man up from the floor and led him away.
As the bailiff was taking the names of the others and trying to line them up, the
king wondered if, in fact, anything would come of the edict he was working
on. Perhaps, given increasingly chaotic conditions, it would be ignored, even
by his own officials. But, he sighed to himself, it was traditional, and the man
was right; debt was plaguing lots of peasants these days, perhaps most of them.
Something had to be done, and kings were supposed to be able to do it, even
young ones like him.

The Edict of Ammisaduqa was promulgated around 1646 B.C.E. A modern
theory proposes that there were two kinds of decrees in it, one sort intended
to apply only to the immediate situation and to last for a few months, and
another intended as more general principles that might not be new at all but
were supposed to be valid for all time. The petitioner's debts might or might
not have fallen under the detailed stipulations of the edict.[1]

The time after the fall of Ur is called the Old Babylonian period, but that is a slight misnomer. In the early part of the period the city of Babylon was not an especially important city, but it became increasingly so late in the period, and its most aggressive king, Hammurapi, who reigned from 1792 to 1750 B.C.E., united all of Mesopotamia for a few years. His successors failed to maintain that unity. Modern scholars call the whole period after the city even though, before and after, dynasties from different cities dominated parts of the Iraqi plain.[2]

Surface survey results are ambivalent for the period because the pottery chronology does not reveal that there were many new styles that came in then. We guess that there was considerable continuity with the Ur III period in where and how people lived. The political disunity of the region may have impeded repair of the canals and irrigation systems, and there may have been somewhat less land available for agricultural use than in earlier times. The population may slowly have declined. But it is not a period in which people were aware of any decadence setting in, and many of the structures of economic and social life continued as before.

Mesopotamians may have been concerned about overpopulation and saw barrenness and infant mortality as necessary correctives to overpopulation.[3] Celibacy of some priestesses may have been thought of as a measure against overpopulation.

The city of Nippur allows one to study the density of occupation of rooms archaeologically preserved and also reflected in texts. One can say that, exactly as in modern villages, there were about 1.28 persons per room on average, but the rooms seem smaller than in modern villages that have been studied.[4] The extended family headed by a man was the norm, although smaller, nuclear family living units were known.

Nippur has textually attested neighborhoods that seem to be grouped by kinship ties, clientage, or occupation. It has been suggested that these groupings and the idea of private ownership of land came with rural peasants moving to the city.[5] The city of Ur can be studied similarly and has a greater area of domestic dwellings uncovered; there, neighborhoods, except for the area inhabited by temple administrators, seem not to have been united by any kernel institutions. Still, although Ur is ostensibly a modern excavation, it must be stressed that frequently the information recorded was so spotty that real reconstruction is impossible.[6]

The diet in the period as represented in the lavish banquets of the kings of Mari, a city on the Middle Euphrates River now near the border between Syria and Iraq, provided between 3,582 and 3,672 calories a day, more than enough for adult males. But average persons certainly survived on less.[7]

Class divisions appear to be between palace dependents and those independent of the palace, not between patriarchs and plebeians, at least at Mari. One scholar suggests a three-class division of exploiters, exploited, including slaves and what he calls helots, and those who were neither.[8] As usual, we know least about the latter.

Amorites, in origin tribal peoples from the west who may have sometimes been nomadic, continued to be an important part of the political process. Most of the kings of the period had Amorite names or were closely related to people who did. In the Edict of Ammisaduqa the king makes the distinction between Akkadians and Amorites, and he seems to include under these terms everyone in his realm. This may mean that in this period the Sumerian language died out, or people who spoke Sumerian were no longer a recognizable group. Presumably Akkadian meant anyone else who lived in southern Mesopotamia who was not an Amorite.[9]

We do not know if the Amorites were demographically important. People with Amorite names do not occur widely even in the royal correspondence of the period. But they were politically important, perhaps because army generals, and maybe the armies as a whole, tended to be Amorite; one term that we translate as "general" literally is "overseer of the Amorites."[10]

In the northwest itself Amorites were less important than Hurrians. In fact, the population of the Syrian plain appears to have been mostly Hurrian. Although we think of the time as one in which there was extensive travel, there seem to be rather few actual foreigners who appear in Old Babylonian Sippar, where they were mercenaries and merchants. There probably was continuous sedentarization of nomads. The absence of terms for nomads and sedentaries most likely indicates that the categories were fluid, and towns and tribes could share the same name.[11]

As noted in connection with Nippur, the structure of the family probably did not change much from that of the previous period, but because there is a proliferation of documents that deal with families involved in legal disputes, we are much better informed about some aspects of family life. Monogamy continued to be the norm, and divorce was possible, so there were serial marriages in which one man might have had several wives over the course of his life, and a wife might have had several husbands.[12]

It is in this period that we find words for the family units. We must be careful to note that these words may not correspond to our notions of what constitutes a family, that is, to lineages of persons all related to each other by blood or marriage and living in the same place. It is likely that slaves and others who were not related by blood or marriage were also felt to be part of family households. The word i m-r i-a is attested in Sumerian, but only in lexical texts in

Akkadian, which was becoming the dominant language of southern Mesopotamia. A *kimtu* in Akkadian was a kin group, which could include a woman's
brothers as well as her children and husband. There were houses referred to as
"family houses" using this word. The word *nišūtu*, which may etymologically
just mean "people," seems very similar in meaning to *kimtu*. Rather more general is *illatu*, which means a kinship group or clan, but also just confederates or
groups of people. Community elders, who may have been heads of extended
families, appeared in texts as judges and as representatives of communities.[13]

Families seem unimportant economically, even though we have more texts
not connected to government concerns than earlier. When individuals bought
land, they usually did not mention families. And in Eshnunna "Laws" paragraph 38 it is assumed that a brother must pay for part of a house held by his
family. In Old Babylonian Ur, on the other hand, an extended family has been
identified as living together and pursuing economic ventures together. The
structure of the Sumerian family might be a fratriarchy, in which an older
brother dominates. And it is remarkable that Akkadian lacks terms for fathers'
brothers and sisters, so widespread in other Semitic languages.[14]

Although there are many indications that nomads or people who had once
been nomads were influential in some parts of Mesopotamia, one does not see
many indications of tribes' being important to families, although they may
have been important to politics. At weddings and at divisions of inheritances
more distantly related relatives showed up, but on a day-to-day basis there was
not much interaction with such people.[15]

Older views held that Mesopotamian marriage was basically a commercial
arrangement in which the groom purchased the bride, and it is true that extant
texts are interested in the economic relations that were being forged by the new
union. But it is not helpful to see marriage as purchase because the bride's family too usually presented gifts to the groom's family; instead, marriage seems
more a change in status for both parties, like adoption. Polygamy was possible, but sources do not envision more than two wives. We do not know the
ages of persons at their first marriage. But because the economic burden falls
preponderantly on the female's family, we may guess that the situation may
have been similar to that in late medieval Europe, when the females' families
paid more and the brides tended to be extremely young, as young as twelve
years, and the grooms tended to be much older, over thirty. This disproportion
in ages may have precluded modern companionate marriage, in which friend-
ship and commonality of interests are assumed. And yet the attitude toward
children was not unlike ours, even though childhood as a time before one had
to work probably did not last long.[16]

Inheritance seems usually to have been equally divisible among all male heirs with an extra portion for first sons, but women too are attested as heirs. Regular rules were deviated from when there was an adoptive son.[17]

These customs led to the rise of an institution for assuring that some daughters of rich families did not reproduce and create heirs who would further dilute the inheritance. Daughters were sometimes dedicated to the service of a god and were called *nadītu,* which probably meant "fallow," a woman who was not usually supposed to have children.[18] In some cities these women, who have been compared to nuns in the Christian tradition, lived in cloisterlike buildings and may have been restricted in their communication with the rest of the world. We do not know anything about their religious duties, if any. But we are well informed on their economic roles because they continued during their lifetimes to control the land and wealth that they had as their inheritances. In the northern city of Sippar the *nadītu* seem to have been the most important source for loans of all sorts, and they were heavily involved in real estate deals.

There is an irony connected to the high status and great economic power of these women. And that is that they frequently managed to pass on their inheritance to heirs whom they chose, usually younger women from other rich families who had been dedicated as *nadītu* too. The *nadītu*' brothers would dispute such donations, which seemed to contradict the purpose of the institution of dedication in the first place, but the brothers never won in the preserved court cases. The power of the *nadītu* was simply too great for courts to overrule what they wanted.

Nadītu in Nippur were less prominent than in Sippar, but the institution was similar. It has been argued that freely alienable temple offices, in which *nadītu* were involved, eroded the feeling that family land should not be sold outside the family.[19]

Other women also had a certain economic clout, even if they were not so influential as the *nadītu*. Alewives were merchants who ran taverns that were social centers, and legal texts show that in addition they gave loans to farmers to get through till the next harvest and for seed.

In this period, in contrast to earlier ones, several women served as scribes. Some worked for the powerful *nadītu*. On the question of how one became literate, evidence from Ur shows that what scholars had thought was a school may not have been, and yet the text collections do show a "private" family interest in education, and that may be where the literate became literate. This period may have the highest rate of literacy in ancient Mesopotamia—not that that rate should be taken to include a large percentage of the population—on the basis of the fact that even some women were trained as scribes.[20]

Royal daughters sometimes found themselves being used as pawns in political games, even with scruffy nomadic tribesmen whom they were forced to marry. One archive from Mari shows that such daughters stridently complained about their plights and begged to be allowed to come home.[21]

At Mari, women owned land and participated in agriculture, although less frequently in the texts than men. Female civil servants were rewarded with land allocations. From the Code of Hammurapi it appears that only three types of women could marry as they wished: widows, divorcées, and abandoned women. Others appear to have been under male authority. Still, unlike the women of Greece and Rome, they could appear in court.[22]

Forced labor continued to be an important way in which public works projects were carried out, but it may not have been nearly so important as in earlier periods. Instead there was a group of persons who were crown dependents, called *muškēnū*, who may have gotten land allotments in return for an established number of days of work a month or a year. The term may refer in some contexts to all commoners, and so its use is not always clear in regard to the labor expected. But the legal texts were concerned that people who owed the king work not be interfered with in the exercise of their rights. Such crown dependents were not always poor and downtrodden: some parlayed their land and free time into small real estate empires that they rented out to others.[23]

The corvée under the Isin kings, who followed the fall of Ur and preceded Hammurapi's dynasty, may have consisted of ten days a month of work for unmarried men only, a kind of "national service," except for citizens of the city of Nippur, which was exempted. At Larsa some dependent laborers worked all year and had few resources except those given them for labor.[24]

We are well informed about hired laborers, who continued to be important. Wages could be paid in grain or in silver. A group of texts from the reigns of the kings of Babylon Hammurapi and Samsuiluna, 1792–1712, records the names of hired men and also of bricklayers who were to be paid for a long term, although other lists or dockets record workers who were hired on a daily basis.[25] These archives from governmental agencies show that the private economy could be tapped for labor in times of need.

Slaves were used mainly for household labor because of the difficulties of supervising them in the fields. Again, the numbers of slaves even in the richest households were not high, no more than three or four. The source for slaves was the northeast frontier, where the rulers, like those of Ur III, conducted preemptive raids and took prisoners, who were reduced to slavery. Slaves might also be made to wear a metal band on their arms. Both slaves and dependent laborers tried to escape, and lexical sources show that the learned elite saw the danger that might arise from widespread defections. There were special slave personal names that only slaves tended to bear, and these may have helped keep the problem of escape from slavery to a minimum, as did the typical slave haircut, called the *abbuttu,* which was apparently a knob of hair worn prominently on the top of the head.[26]

But study of slave names at Sippar shows that 60 percent of them were borne by free persons too, and this may mean that the persons entered slavery as adults and did not change names. As in other slave systems, the choice of servile name probably lay with the owner, but manumitted slaves did not change their names. Kinship terms diminished in frequency in slave names over the period, perhaps indicating that slaves may have been viewed less as members of families and more as objects.[27]

In this period we see the private sale of land more clearly than ever, and we can see even that some families in the city of Nippur actually took advantage of depopulation to build their real estate holdings. Sales of land must always be assumed to have been made under extreme economic duress because the family was dispensing with part of its means of livelihood. Prices for fields and houses dropped around the year 1740 in Nippur. Before this crisis texts about inheritances seem to show a fairly even distribution of wealth among the minority of inhabitants who had access to writing. Afterward, families bought up land, and within a few years the entire site, once the most holy city of Mesopotamia, was abandoned for three hundred years. This crisis probably saw the liquidation of small family farms and led to larger agribusinesses, created at the expense of peasants. We are not well informed on what was happening elsewhere, but some have argued that there was a major transformation in land ownership in the period. Land that previously had been owned by governmental bodies passed into private hands, perhaps unofficially at first as the elites simply treated as their own the fields that had been given them as part of their government salaries.[28]

Scholars who believe that land sales were prohibited in Ur III see the variation in land prices of 2000 percent as an indication that there was no general concept of the price of land. Fields could be sold only to relatives closely related through males, but houses apparently could be sold to persons less closely related. This may have been the motivation for some adoptions. When money gains were made in this way, natural heirs were slighted in favor of adoptive ones.[29]

There is regional variation in the preservation of land sale documents. There are only about a dozen from the south but 240 from middle and northern Babylonia. There may have been a restriction on sales in the far south, or the paucity of texts may derive from relative shortage of water because in Mesopotamia a field was unusable unless it could be irrigated. The south had a lower level of prices than the north; but field prices everywhere seem low, only three or four times the cost of grain produced in a year on the field. There was a distinction among house plots, gardens, and fields, which may derive from Ur III, where the first two categories could be sold, but perhaps not the third.[30]

We have an archive on canal digging in Old Babylonian Larsa. Contractors were given money by the state and expected to pay for all necessary work.[31]

The distinction between someone who worked for the government as an official and a private landowner is not easy to make. Many persons that seem to have been private actually had official connections with various enterprises sponsored by the palace. Also, people who were obviously officials may have been working in individual transactions for themselves or their families and taking advantage of their positions to gain more land and wealth. Some of these dealers were connected with temples, but the temple in the Old Babylonian period seems to have had no influence on politics.[32]

Shepherds were given government flocks each year and entered into written agreements with authorities about how much of the products of the flock and of the newborn lambs they could keep. The proportions of males to gelded male sheep and females in texts from northern Mesopotamia show that the shepherds were trying to pursue several goals in keeping the herds, not just intensive wool production.[33]

In the southern city of Ur texts reveal that the Nanna-Ningal temple controlled more than forty thousand sheep at one point. Accountants recorded the production of butter.[34]

Texts from Larsa, also in the south, record government flocks that were no doubt being kept for their wool. About two pounds, or about a kilogram, of wool could be expected from each of the sheep, compared to between 0.7 and 1.2 kilograms from modern sheep. Sheep were apparently entrusted to private persons during most of the year for pasturing. But once a year sheep were brought in to be sheared, and the central authority recorded how many had survived the year and how many had been born. Nongovernmental herds certainly existed, although the mention of them is much less detailed, and sometimes the private herders expected a slightly low productivity of about 0.75 kilograms of wool from each. Larsa texts show too that the royal palace had fishermen who worked for it, and their produce was sold by the palace.[35]

Letters reveal that sheep fattening differed from the intensive grain-feeding of Ur III. Sheep were grazed on pastures near the river and sometimes were led far afield. At Mari, nomadic groups brought sheep to sedentary workers to shear the wool because the textile industry there had more demand than raw material. Old Babylonian herding contracts generally allowed shepherds 8 to 20 percent of newborn lambs as payment.[36]

Archives from Isin in central Mesopotamia show that an organization was keeping detailed records of craft work in leather. The things produced ranged from shoes to sieves. The industry was dependent for its raw material on the animal herders, and it distributed goods to several organs of the government and to religious establishments. An interesting aspect of the texts is their close resemblance to Ur III leather texts from a few years earlier and from cities other than Isin. This underlines that the break that the ancients saw as significant for politics at the end of the Ur III period may not have been so important for other activities.[37]

The d a m-g a r, or merchant, might have worked for the government, but it seems likely that he also executed private commissions on his travels. In trade texts the merchants were not called d a m-g a r, perhaps because that title implied a royal commission. As before, though, the merchants may not actually have done any traveling, but they did buy foreign things in markets. The things they got were similar to things attested in the Ur III merchant texts. Spices and woods were brought from afar, and their prices were recorded. We have such texts from several merchants in Larsa, but we do not have so many that we can reconstruct the bureaucracy under which they worked, as we can in the Ur III period. There are other continuities, including even the usual price for wool.[38]

In this period also we have records of a very long-distance trade between the city of Assur in northern Mesopotamia and various cities in what is now central Turkey, where Assyrian merchants had set up trading depots. These texts, oddly enough, come mostly from Turkey, and there are few from Assur itself, which seems to have been the center for the trade.[39]

The goods traded were tin, which may have come ultimately from somewhere in Iran to the east, and textiles, which had been produced in Mesopotamia. Payment was usually in silver, but sometimes gold. Some textiles may have been imported into Assyria for transshipment west. Merchants would set out on two-month caravans to Turkey and come back with their profits in gold; profits of as much as 100 percent were not uncommon, so the trip was well worth the trouble. Some merchants stayed in Turkey, took local wives, and acted as agents for friends or family members who stayed in Assur. In Turkey the merchants in each city organized themselves into a kind of board of trade or Assyrian chamber of commerce; they called themselves the *kārum,* quay or market, and they had the power to punish wayward members and to try to negotiate with locals for favorable terms.[40]

The texts showing this trade range in date from 1900 to 1700, with some gaps, and we are not sure why it came to an end. It is true that people with Indo-European names, whom we will later call the Hittites, began to appear, but they were not particularly disruptive of trade contacts or unfriendly to resident foreigners like the Assyrians. Perhaps local rulers, with whom the Assyrians had been on good terms, were eventually unable to guarantee their safety. Although many of these so-called Old Assyrian texts are dated with an eponym, the name of the official designated at Assur to preside over the year, we cannot put the texts in order because we do not have lists giving the order of the eponyms. Scholars are working on grouping texts according to the persons involved, and we know the generations of some frequently occurring families, so we can place texts that have those persons in relative chronological order. But this aspect of the texts, their timelessness, renders them difficult to use in creating a theory of the ancient economy.[41]

The trade with the Persian Gulf continued, bringing merchants from perhaps as far away was India. The trade seems to end with the fall of the Larsa dynasty around 1763. The trade to Dilmun, perhaps the island of Failaka, broke off and resumed only in the 700s B.C.E. We know little of Larsa's internal trade, yet we can show what city people sometimes owned.[42]

Silver continued to be the dominant kind of money in the period, although some people still used grain as money for some purposes. We have references to payments in both, and they also served as moneys of account, used to evaluate other things for accounting purposes. Silver was not an elite currency, restricted to rich people and opulent transactions. It is quite likely that most adults had a little silver around the house. Various things, including sesame and wool, were used for payment in Larsa. The rate of interest was usually 33 percent for barley loans and 20 percent for silver. We do not know if the rate was paid per year or per month.[43]

In spite of the large number of texts preserved, there is nothing like the price series from Ur III, in which one set of people recorded prices over time. And even for a commodity as common as barley, there are few prices available, and these seem to show no overall trend.[44]

At Sippar there may have been a general cheapening of land, perhaps owing to a decline in productivity because of overirrigation and consequent salinization, although that issue is controversial. From late in Hammurapi's reign to about the tenth year of his successor there was relative prosperity. There were low prices and high wages, but under the king Abi-ešuh (1711–1684 B.C.E.) there were high prices, and wages went up then too. It may be that the military successes of Hammurapi caused the prices to be low, and the weakness of the later kings of Babylon may have contributed to the apparent inflation under them. But it seems as likely that much more complex processes of supply and demand affected the level of prices. And we do not know how political developments may have affected prices outside the area controlled by the city of Babylon.[45]

There were several efforts by various governments to regulate the economy. Most of the efforts probably failed, and most of them may have been inspired not by any analysis of economic and social life but by a need to be seen to be doing something about economic crises. The texts that tell us about these measures almost all come from royal chancelleries and reflect the king's desire to be seen as just and kind. Also, as usual, we have lots of texts from royal sources that cast a "documentary illusion" that the royal activities were all that was going on. The king and palace did not control the economy, and the roles of temples were negligible. The palace tended to farm out its business, satisfied to get a portion of the date harvest coming to it in exchange for not having to send its bureaucrats physically to collect it all.[46]

Clearest in regard to effects were the decrees, or *ṣimdātu*, which were issued by kings about kinds of loans that could be renegotiated.[47] Reference to decrees appears in several kinds of private legal documents, and so there is good reason to think that the people who had access to writing did pay attention to them. We do not have copies of any, though, and we cannot be sure if they were to be of limited application or applied only a limited time.

Another sort of text we call the edict. We have only two fragmentary examples, but there are references to such texts in the names that kings gave to the years, and more than thirty possible edicts are referred to in texts. The best-preserved example is from Ammisaduqa, king of Babylon 1646–1626. The king ordained that some kinds of loans be made temporarily illegal and some kinds of tax payments be suspended, apparently for a period of a few years. The king also issued rulings in the edict that called for much more general reforms, but these were either unenforceable or refer to already established community norms. Unfortunately, we have few texts from Ammisaduqa's reign and so cannot judge the practical effect.[48]

Kings alluded to prices in royal inscriptions, usually to show how well-paid and happy people were living under them. When we can compare contemporary prices with the prices quoted in royal inscriptions, we see that the royal inscriptions exaggerated the well-being of the subjects, saying that prices were lower and wages higher than the archival texts. Such lists, which we call tariffs, do show a general level of prices that must have been conceivable at least to royal scribes.[49]

Another kind of text closely related both to royal inscriptions with tariffs and the edicts is the so-called law code. Like the texts of Uru-inim-gina of the Early Dynastic III period and Šulgi's legal collection of the Ur III period, these texts usually were political in motivation. The oldest of them may be the fragmentary Sumerian text from Lipit-Ištar, a king of Isin from 1934 to 1924 B.C.E. That king attempted to regulate some marriage betrothal practices, but he did not address any issue over which his government might have had some control, like taxes. Slightly later may be the Akkadian texts called the Laws of Eshnunna; unlike Lipit-Ištar's code, these are not preserved only in school copies in later periods. The laws are found in two contemporary texts, and they are not obviously part of a royal inscription. There is a long section at the beginning that lists a tariff of prices and wages. Scholars have argued that the copies were really cribs for market supervisors of some sort. But the rest of the text deals with much more general situations, including at least one that appears in Šulgi and Lipit-Ištar too, the case of the bridegroom who was at first accepted and then rejected by the father of the bride.[50]

The most impressive of these texts is Hammurapi's code, which apparently comes from late in his reign. It includes both a tariff of prices and wages and many provisions dealing with social life, including the rejected bridegroom problem. The epilogue shows that the code, which is preserved on a seven-foot stone stele, was meant to be consulted for enlightenment about what justice was. But it was not intended particularly to be a collection of all kinds of provisions that were to be enforced in Hammurapi's domains; neither was it a reform of the various city legal systems that Hammurapi united politically. If the Code of Hammurapi is not really a code, it nonetheless gives us many impressions of the range of possible activities that people in Babylon might pursue and of the royal view of what was just.[51]

I have already used the social vision of the code in sketching aspects of Old Babylonian society, and any sketch of almost any aspect of that society must start with the code.[52] But the code treated interesting, not necessarily typical, cases. It shows that there were three large groups that might be thought of as classes. First was the *awīlū*, meaning "men" in many contexts. Injuries to them were to be punished with higher money payments than injuries to other classes. The code does not tell us how one qualified to be an *awīlum*; perhaps birth alone allowed one to be privileged. In contrast to this upper class were the *muškēnū* discussed above, who may have been common citizens or perhaps dependent persons working for the government. At the bottom of the code's scale of society and also of recompense for injury was the slave.

Codes were never referred to in judicial texts, and courts ignored them when it came to making decisions, which were probably based not on what the king believed was just but on what local tradition said was just. But the codes do show that there was concern for social and economic norms, and especially from Hammurapi's legal collection one gets the impression that the values of responsibility for one's work and of trying to insure justice for the weak were cherished, at least among Babylonian intellectuals. Royal power appears to have grown under Hammurapi, and there may have been a sort of secularization as temple and judicial officials began to identify themselves, on their seals at least, as servants of the king, not the temple.[53]

The Middle Kingdom in Egypt began about 2040 and lasted till 1786 B.C.E. and was marked by another political unification of the land by a strong dynasty from Upper Egypt, just as the first unification was. Many of the traditions of the Old Kingdom were carried forward, but because of the problems of the First Intermediate period, the triumphalism of kings was muted. Pyramids were still built, but they were small and cheaply made. And although the cult of the death of kings was the dominant cultural manifestation that we can study, there are indications that its trappings were available not just to kings but to the rich as well. This has been termed a democratization of death, but it is more likely that it is merely a democratization of the evidence for the death cult.[54] After all, people had been buried with fancy things in Egypt as early as the Gerzean period.

There is more evidence for social and economic history from the Middle Kingdom than from earlier periods in Egypt. We not only see that some of the pious foundations established around the pyramids of the Old Kingdom continued, but also get some glimpses of how life was organized. An earlier barter economy seems to settle on the use of several commodities as moneys, with silver predominating.[55]

Archaeology shows that Middle Kingdom Egyptians were making frequent trips to the desert to the east of the Nile, where they could find gold and other minerals. In addition, they expanded their influence up the Nile itself and set up trading posts and forts in what is now Sudan. Trade with Syria and Lebanon was resumed, especially with the port city of Byblos, which supplied wood and spices for the Egyptians and seems to have developed its own Egyptianate culture fostered by resident Egyptian tradesmen.

The first important king of the period, Amunemhet I (1991–1962 B.C.E.), was associated with developing the Fayyum Oasis, a natural swamp to the west of the Nile. His engineers built a canal between the oasis and the Nile, and they improved irrigation works to expand the amount of area under cultivation there.

The scribes of the Middle Kingdom perfected the administration of surpluses and tried to keep track of a great many things that previously had been dealt with only orally. Ration texts show what men got when they went into the Sinai Peninsula to mine minerals for the government.[56] Ordinary unskilled laborers received a basic allotment of ten units of bread and beer, and officials would get multiples of that basic ration. Because of the odd fractions that sometimes appear in these lists, like 5/6 and 23/30 of bread and beer (and there are also fractions of cattle!), it seems likely that people were not necessarily paid in real bread and beer, but in some other commodity used as money.

The preservation of documents allows detailed studies of the titles and functions of officials, but it has not till now given a general picture of life in Egypt in the period. A tomb at Assiut from the beginning of the Middle Kingdom has contracts that set up the cult to be paid perpetually to the man buried there, and these contracts show that the man, Djefe'-He'py, made a distinction between property that he held by virtue of his office and his personal property. Tomb depictions of the period suggest polygamy, and in the later New Kingdom, there are some nonroyal instances of it.[57]

Local rivalries among officials from different nomes, or counties, may have played a part in the slide toward the Second Intermediate period, 1786–1558 B.C.E. This time of disunity was dominated not just by local competition but by foreign invasion. People from southern Palestine and beyond came into the eastern delta of the Nile and set up their own kingdom, which at various times had control of the whole delta and parts of upper Egypt too. The later Egyptians referred to these people as the Hyksos, "kings of foreign lands," and the period was seen in later tradition as particularly barbaric and horrible.[58] The Hyksos themselves, though, tried to act like good Egyptian kings and in all likelihood shed most of their previous Amorite heritage in favor of Egyptian culture. The few Hyksos personal names we have show that there were Amorites and Hurrians among them, and probably other ethnic groups too.

Some scholars would date the invention of the Proto-Sinaitic writing system as early as the early Middle Kingdom. The evidence is ambiguous, but the graffiti in Sinai clearly deploy a simple writing system that has a separate sign for each consonant and thus was a precursor of the writing system we use today.[59]

In what later became Israel the period corresponds to the Middle Bronze II period, which, as we noted above, constituted a break from the squalid intrusion before it. The culture that took over lasts from about 2000 to about 1200 without notable breaks. In the early part of the period we have no contemporary texts from the land of Israel, but we do have an Egyptian text, the Tale of Sinuhe, that tells the story of how a courtier, upset by political disturbances around the death of Amunemhet I in 1962 B.C.E., fled to Lebanon or Syria and lived among the princes ruling small cities. Eventually this Sinuhe became a sort of Egyptian consul in the region, looking after traveling Egyptians and longing to hear the news from back home. Egyptian execration texts that list foreign place-names in order to put a curse on them also give us an Egyptian view of Israel-Palestine in the period, and some of the cities that flourished later were attested then too, including Jerusalem, Ashkelon, and Byblos.[60] A later group of execration texts shows that there were more cities to be cursed, and this may argue that there was an urban expansion. The names of all of the rulers mentioned are West Semitic, that is, somewhat like Amorite but clearly related to the later languages spoken in the area. There are statues of Egyptian noblemen and scarabs, little amulets shaped like beetles, found in many places in Israel, showing that Egyptians traveled in the region.

Occupation was resumed at many older sites that had been abandoned during Middle Bronze I, and new forts were built around the new cities. The Hyksos who ruled Egypt in the Second Intermediate period had cousins in the land of Israel. The ramparts with sloping glacis, or steep slopes, which defended the larger sites used to be attributed to the Hyksos, but these technologies were older than the advent of the Hyksos.[61] The Hyksos were chased from Egypt into southern Palestine, and they made their last stand and were defeated by the Egyptians at a place called Sharuhen, which may be the modern Tell el-Far'ah.

The largest site was Hazor in the Galilee, which expanded to include a lower mound that was home to tens of thousands of people. It is the only city in the region mentioned in the documents from Mari around 1760, where it was the destination of a shipment of tin.[62]

The Egyptians called the region Hurru, implying that the Hurrians that were among the Hyksos were also at home in the land of Israel.[63] Scholars have speculated that the Hurrians arrived with Indo-European invaders who imposed themselves on the West-Semitic-speaking population, but the existence of the Indo-Europeans here is attested only by the fact that the Bible later says some of the people of the land were called Hittites. There are destruction levels at various cities around 1550, and these may have something to do with Egypt's renewed interest in dominating the region.

In Asia Minor the newly arrived Indo-European speakers, the Hittites, established a kingdom in the center of the country. They learned cuneiform, probably from Syrian scribes whom they had kidnapped on raids south, and most of the texts they produced were for rituals. We are not in a position to describe Hittite society or economics in this period, the Hittite Old Kingdom, about 1770–1595 B.C.E. There are more texts from the Hittites in the next half-millennium, and I shall say more about them later.[64]

The first half of the second millennium saw at least two other centers outside the Near East where there were writing civilizations, but in each case we are still unable to decipher the writings, and our knowledge about their social and economic history is consequently minimal.

To the west on the island of Crete the civilization that we call Minoan, after the Greek name for the legendary pre-Greek ruler of the island, drew its wealth from seaborne commerce.[65] The rulers of the unwalled cities of the island did not form any unified empire and did not set colonies down elsewhere in the Mediterranean, but they certainly drew wealth from distant contacts by sea.

Their palaces attest to a great sophistication of building technique, and their wall paintings indicate that there was at least a class of full-time artists supported by the rulers through their appropriation of peasants' surpluses. Trade connections to Egypt are the clearest of any with the other centers of the Near East, but there is no indication that there were social structures like the Egyptian.

The script the Minoans used, called Linear A by modern scholars, looks as if it conveys pictures of objects and seems similar to the later Linear B script, which has been deciphered as a form of Greek. But attempts at seeing Minoan as a Semitic language have failed to convince scholars. The script might be an indirect borrowing of the idea, probably from Egypt, much as the Egyptians may have borrowed the idea from the Mesopotamians earlier. Although the Minoan documents cannot be read, it is clear that the administration depended on sheepherding.[66]

At the other end of the world, in what is now Pakistan and India, the Indus Valley civilization flourished. It can be dated partly on the basis of the trade goods found in Mesopotamia that are related in style; these occur in levels as early as 2500 B.C.E. and as late as 1500 B.C.E. Carbon-14 dates from the subcontinent show that the sites were occupied around 1900 B.C.E. At Lothal in Sind a great dock was built on what may have been a branch of the Bhogava River inland from the Gulf of Cambay apparently for berthing ships in an artificial channel.[67] There are only three large city sites, Harappa, Mohenjo-daro, and Lothal, but there are more than twenty-four other sites that must have been small farming villages that contributed to the maintenance of the cities by growing wheats and rice. Trade may have been of some importance because Indus Valley merchants journeyed to Mesopotamia to pursue it, but Mesopotamian objects are not found in Indus Valley sites.

The script, used on seals and on economic texts, was seemingly syllabic because there are many more signs than would be necessary for an alphabet. Some have proposed that the language depicted is Indo-European, and that the Indus Valley people were the progenitors of the Aryans who conveyed their religious traditions to later Indians, but there is no consensus yet on decipherment.[68]

We do not know how the Indus Valley civilization came to an end. Scholars have proposed that marauding tribesmen from the hills above the Indus plain swept down, but others look to internal factors for decay.

In China, as noted above, 1766 B.C.E. is the traditional date for the founding of the first dynasty, but archaeologically there seem to be no important changes toward city life that early.[69]

The disunity referred to in the title of this chapter is political; what we now

call the Old Babylonian period was one in which city-states in southern Mesopotamia again asserted their independence from centralizers. Hammurapi by
exception contrived briefly to unite most of Mesopotamia under his control,
but his son quickly lost most of the south, and the older pattern was reasserted.

Whether there was real reform may remain an open question. The edicts of
kings and their legal texts show a desire among intellectuals connected with the
courts to formulate their ideas about justice. But such people may not have had
access to the administrative apparatus and almost certainly had little access to
the local courts of elders who made decisions in real cases at law. So the reforms
may have been political propaganda and not something most people would
have experienced.

In Mesopotamia a Dark Age ensues, the length of which we do not know, and
the social and economic realities of which are obscure. In the middle chronology,
used widely by modern scholars, that age may have lasted from 1595 to 1375
B.C.E., as much as 220 years. Because all dates before this period are dependent
on the length of the period, they are all uncertain; there are no synchronisms with
Egypt that might help anchor the chronology before 1360 B.C.E.[70]

The Dark Age probably derived from both internal and external factors. We
know that at some point a raiding party led by a king of the Hittites raided
down the Euphrates and looted the city of Babylon. But it is not likely that this
or other raids from other quarters were the decisive element in the collapse of
governments. Much more likely is the idea that tax gathering was impeded by
rebellious peasants scratching a living out of fields watered by canals that were
less and less well maintained.

Still, there were continuities. We do not know where, but the cuneiform
writing system was still taught and learned, and it was not changed in any
major way after the Dark Age ended. With the system of writing must have
gone some texts, and later Mesopotamians did know about some of the major
figures in earlier Mesopotamian history.

However it happened, the Dark Age doubtless meant a turn toward household self-sufficiency and a diminishment of trade. Governments did not control much area, and they could not insure the safety of the people living under
them. Peasants tried to depend less on markets and to grow and make more of
what they needed themselves.

Economically, as well as politically, these times were full of variety and disunity. Access to writing was relatively broad, however, and so we see many
strands in community and economic life.

F·O·U·R

RETRENCHMENT AND EMPIRE

1600–1100 B.C.E.

Politically this period is one in which the old centers in the south of Mesopotamia found that others were competing for resources too. Southern
Mesopotamia was ruled by the Kassites, a dynasty of foreigners who preferred
to be known more for their building activities than for war. In the north of
Mesopotamia the Assyrians recovered from the uncertainty of the Dark Age
and extended their economic interests to the west, into Syria and Turkey, preferring to emphasize warlike accomplishments in their inscriptions. In Turkey
itself the Hittites again began looking to the south for luxurious goods and the
arts of civilization. In Egypt the new policy of involvement in Asia designed
to prevent a recurrence of the Hyksos invasion led to clashes with petty Palestinian states and eventually to warlike and then diplomatic contact with many
of the other great kingdoms, giving the historian synchronisms for the first
time, in which two persons from different cultures are attested in the same text,
showing that they were contemporaries. In spite of the break in some traditions
in society and economy during the Dark Age there seems to have been considerable continuity.

The old slave woman had begged her master repeatedly not to sell her, but
Kidin-Ninurta refused to listen to her pleas. "I sold you and your family some
time ago, with the understanding that you would be delivered later, when I
could more easily spare you," he yelled at the small old woman, a bit of spittle
already on his black beard. "You knew long ago this day would come. And here
it is. This is happening all over the place, people scaling back their staffs, and
you shouldn't be surprised that we do it too. If you want to tell me about how
you suckled my father and that sort of stuff, that is all very well, but a deal is a
deal; I needed the money back when I made it, and I'm going to carry it
through now, no matter what you want."

He left the courtyard and went back into his room. She sat there a moment
squatting, thinking how like his father he was. She would have to comfort her
children, certainly, for they had known nothing besides life in this household.
She, on the other hand, could still remember when her mother brought her up
to the great city of Dur-Kurigalzu, near the ruins of Babylon, because the
uncles could no longer support them, with her father dead. Her mother had

borrowed money to live, and then, when the debt came due and she had nothing to show for it but a couple of more years of life, both mother and daughter had been sold into slavery.

It had not been so bad as one might think, she mused. After all, she had not minded so much being the clandestine mistress of her young master, and look at the fine children she had had. If only they were not slaves too. The master could have acknowledged them as his own, but he never did, especially not after he had moved on to other slave-girls. And now all five of them were to be given over to this unknown fellow, Arad-Šamaš.

Later, when the transfer was actually made in front of the house, there were no other witnesses, but Kidin-Ninurta had called a scribe, who made a little reddish tablet on which the facts were set down in laconic style:

"The woman Usatuša who had been given to Arad-Šamaš instead of (another) slave, Ši-ina-mati, her daughter, Rišatum, her daughter, Umušu-limmer, her son, the brewer, Rimutum, her son, the weaver, Kidin-Ninurta, the son of Tab-ša-Dayyan, gave to Arad-Šamaš."[1]

Surface survey shows that there were fewer sites and that their size shrank between the Old Babylonian and the present period, called in the south the Middle Babylonian period or the Kassite (sometimes spelled Cassite) period, after the ethnic group that supplied the kings. There were fewer canals maintained and therefore less land cultivated. We do not have distinctive pottery; archaeologists attribute sites to the period when they have second millennium pottery and the sites are not obviously Old Babylonian. We do have a map of Kassite Nippur, which, along with textual evidence, allows one to argue that cities were divided by canals into neighborhoods.[2]

The new Kassite rulers apparently constituted only a small ruling class. They, like the Amorites before them, retained their own styles of personal names, but they accepted Mesopotamian traditions about what a good ruler should do and in general presented themselves as good Mesopotamian kings. The length and the stability of the dynasty show that their rule was widely accepted. There has been much discussion about how the Kassites were tribally organized, but they appear to have been mostly sedentary in this period.[3]

Toward the end of the era another ethnic group begins to impinge, the Aramaeans. These originated as nomads in the deserts to the west of Mesopotamia. Organized into competing tribes, they never formed a political unity, but they infiltrated around settlements to pasture their flocks and eventually settled down as farmers. Their language, which we classify as a West Semitic one related to Hebrew, came to be widely spoken in the first millennium as a first language throughout the Near East, even among people who had never been nomadic.[4]

Also, Hurrians took a leading role in northern Mesopotamia and across the Syrian plain. The site of Nuzi in central Iraq had a Hurrian-speaking society preserving archival texts about land deals. In southern Babylonia the Hurrians seem to have had low status and to have worked in servile jobs. A class called *maryannu* may have been at origin Indo-European chariot warriors. But in Alalah, in what is now Turkey near the Syrian coast, we know that some did not own chariots, and there and in Ugarit, near modern Lataqiah in Syria, kings could create persons *maryannu,* so the status became like any other in the control of the king.[5]

On the fringes of most of the writing civilizations a social group called the *ᶜapiru* or *habiru* or *hapiru* consisted of stateless persons who had withdrawn from peasant and city life and made their livings as robbers and mercenaries.[6] The term apparently means "dusty" or "crosser" and refers to desert travelers, and it is used as a designation for a social class of dissatisfied former city dwellers who had taken to a life of brigandage, preying on kings ruling small cities and their commerce.

Interest in the term *hapiru* has derived from the possibility that it is related to the word for Hebrew, *ᶜibrī* in Hebrew. The term does not refer to a self-conscious ethnic group. For one thing the term is attested even as early as the Old Assyrian trade in the 1900s B.C.E. and also in other parts of the periphery of Mesopotamia until around 1200 B.C.E. Although one can conceive of the later Hebrews as originating from among such groups, it does not seem that there was a direct connection.[7]

Village communities continued to fall under the influence of royal powers. From Alalah we know that villages varied in size between 3 and 180 houses or about 900 to 1,500 persons. The existence of rural communities as self-governing bodies in Syria is unclear, although the fact that land sales are disguised as adoptions or gifts of kings may imply that community sensibilities had to be respected.[8]

At Ugarit there may have existed village communities that owed taxes and one to five days of forced labor a month. The primary unit was the house or household, usually peopled by a family of modest size.[9]

We are ill-informed on families and family structures. The Middle Assyrian "laws" from shortly before 1077 B.C.E. in the north of Mesopotamia preserve older traditions, and they assume much the same monogamous marriage as we see in the Code of Hammurapi from the Old Babylonian period. The slave family in the text discussed above may have been atypically large given that it had four children surviving to adulthood. The absence of a male head of household was usual in slave families.

In the north the Middle Assyrian laws contain some of the most stringent

regulations ever seen in the Ancient Near East restricting the movements and
contacts of at least highborn women. They were to go about veiled, and lower-
class women who affected the veil were to be publicly humiliated. As usual, we
have no indication if these regulations reflected reality, but they were someone's
idea of how nice women were supposed to behave. There is no precedent for
this extreme restriction. From Nuzi we know that free women could sometimes
act as heads of families in extraordinary situations. They were said to "do the
fatherly duty." Such women were kept from remarrying and sharing their head-
ship and money with someone outside the family.[10]

Nuzi texts show the typical Mesopotamian interest both in bride price and
in dowry. This would indicate that it was a society in which both women and
men were valued for their labor in agriculture, and they also had inheritance
rights that were important.[11]

Royal women were used as pawns in international marriages to cement relations between far-flung sovereigns. The Egyptian king wed a Babylonian
princess, and a widowed Egyptian queen requested a Hittite prince as her
spouse. This second deal did not work out because Egyptians assassinated the
prince, whom his astonished father had dispatched south. We do not have
complaints from the women themselves about being packed off to the other
side of the world in order to reinforce their father's foreign policy, but their attitude, like that of the royal women at Old Babylonian Mari, was no doubt one
of fear and disgust. A Babylonian king asked for an Egyptian princess, but
admitted that any Egyptian would do! At Ugarit a text shows that in five of
twenty listed households there was more than one wife. And a married woman
could own and manipulate land. Although in Mesopotamia the *terhatu* was
usually a kind of dowry, at Ugarit the term meant money from the groom to
the father of the bride.[12]

Private persons acquired slaves by buying infants from their parents, although some were foreigners captured in battle or traded into Mesopotamia.[13]
Slaves cost in general more than in the preceding period, about ten shekels for
an adult male and seven or eight for a female. This rise may show that there
were fewer of them, and so they were in greater demand. Texts mention whole
families of slaves, who apparently lived together. There were fugitives as well.
Some texts speak of temporary slavery, in which the slave served only as a
pledge for his family's debt, and when the debt was paid off, the slave was again
free.

At Alalah in Syria there were relatively few slaves, not more than three in
private households. Most slaves there were defaulting debtors; fewer were prisoners of war. Children of a master and a slave girl were free there, but a special
act was needed to free the mother. The average price was fifty-four shekels of

silver, a comparatively high sum. Some slaves worked independently of their masters, as in the later Roman system. Contemporaneous Ugarit had households with one to twenty dependents. Some households had between six and thirteen slaves.[14]

Two lists of Ugaritic farm personnel show that laborers on them had been reduced from peasants to dependent laborers; their rations supported families of between two and three persons—hardly the size expected in a healthy premodern agricultural environment. Even some scribes were slaves of the palace at Nuzi.[15]

Hired laborers continued to be used in agricultural work too.[16] The Middle Assyrian laws paragraph 36 referred obliquely to sons' being hired by people outside the family. The paucity of references to hiring reinforces the idea that private households did not feel that they could turn to the market in labor to support themselves and had to rely upon what they themselves could produce.

At Nuzi there are few wage contracts, and corvée labor was required from some peasants. Slaves were few. Another source for labor was indenture, which involved a loan given against the pledge of the work of a person for a term. There is an Assyrian labor contract in which a man was to work for a person for ten years, after which he would take a wife from the household and be free; the parallels with the Jacob story in the Bible are clear, although it is not known if the specific wife had been picked out at the beginning of the contract.[17]

Unfree labor continued to be important to the Babylonian economy, and men were the backbone of the force, although they may have been more inclined to seek to escape than others. But escapees had to elude an "elaborate guard system."

Prisoners of war and deported persons were used as forced laborers also by the Assyrians, and they might be used for personal purposes by officials. In Syria there seems to have been a major increase in refugees of free status; perhaps an increase in nomadism resulted from the success kings had in finding sedentary refugees.[18]

Forced labor was important at Ugarit as elsewhere. In Syria there was a shortage of labor, and so kings were inclined to accept refugees from abroad. A treaty from Alalah asks that the Alalah king inform another king of the names of fugitives.[19]

A type of text that is identified with the period is the land-grant document called in Akkadian *kudurru*. It is known in numerous forms and usually consists of a large slab of diorite or other semiprecious stone that has astral symbols carved in the top and a text in Akkadian cuneiform around the bottom. The *kudurru*s show the king granting an officer or official a defined piece of agricultural land as a special honor for meritorious service. They were composed as official reminders of land grants and were solemnly deposited in holy places.[20]

These texts have given rise to the practice of calling the period a feudal one, by analogy to the situation in medieval Europe. Some aspects of the European situation are not to be found in the Middle Babylonian one. The person who was awarded a land grant could have the peasants on the land work it for him, but he did not have any judicial or civil authority over the peasants. On one occasion a king made a land grant from land he had previously purchased; this event clearly shows that the king did not own all land.[21]

Another problem with the European analogy is that we do not know if this was the only or the dominant way the king had of rewarding his servants. And even if it was a major way of dispensing salaries, it seems similar to the Old Babylonian custom of assigning land in return for *ilku* "service" to the king, in war or in administration. The land granted in this way in the Old Babylonian period was for a short time and was apparently routinely rotated among the king's servants. A similar custom may have existed in the Middle Babylonian period. The emphasis that some scholars have put upon the foreignness of the land practices represented in the *kudurrus* is probably misplaced, as is their suggestion that the customs reflected in the texts came from ethnic Kassite practices.

In Assyrian archives families of free peasants sold their land to rich people, and this means that impoverished farming families were trading the means of production, their land, for temporary monetary benefits because of the extreme poverty into which they had sunk.[22] This process may be seen as the extinction of independent peasant households. Perhaps the people whose households dissolved in this way were absorbed in the service of the Assyrian imperial administration as soldiers or as peasants.

Land sales consisting sometimes of whole villages are known from contemporaneous northern Syria. At Ugarit the people involved may have been well-connected high officials because the king frequently appeared confirming the deal. A couple of lists of farm personnel show that the royal economy had taken over the working of some land and was paying peasants for their work. And the peasants were suffering in the arrangement; the number of children was quite small, although the overall profit from the operations seems large. This system depended on the reduction of peasants almost to slave laborers, and there must have been an economic crisis going on among free laborers for them to submit themselves to such exploitation.[23]

Middle Assyrian texts show the king making land grants as in Babylonia. But even in private cases the king oversaw transactions and intervened. This kind of practice is the reverse of what would happen in a feudal system, in which decentralization of authority would be the rule. Instead, throughout the texts there was state intervention.[24] Some scholars believe nonetheless that all private land was held from the king on the understanding that an *ilku*, or service, was owed the king. But this land could be freely transferred, although the seller might retain the duty to do the service.[25]

At contemporaneous Nuzi there was a tendency for large landowners to increase the sizes of their holdings, sometimes for better exploitation of sheep. One set of texts shows a large landholder with many women and dependent children, who may have been slaves. The exploitation of the peasants may have been similar to the situation in Syria; in particular loans for grain come only from the later period of Nuzi texts, and this would indicate that peasants were unable to feed themselves. Nuzi land was not all irrigated, and in a good year rainfall agriculture was possible, so the yields of fields were generally lower than elsewhere in Mesopotamia. The most expensive fields to buy were those irrigated or near water. Prices were only about a year's crop from the field to be purchased, thus greatly favoring a buyer and showing that sales occurred in times of need for an owner sinking into poverty. Payment was made in silver, copper, barley, tin, sheep, or goats, and once an ox. Land prices at Ugarit were higher than in Babylonia and Assyria.[26]

Middle Assyrian texts reveal a system for fattening sheep for royal consumption that has analogues in the Ur III system.[27] Shepherds were assigned sheep and given the grain to feed them and were expected to report back with them within the year.

In Nuzi too there are texts that show in detail how shepherds dealt with sheep that were intended for wool production.[28] The Nuzi shepherds were using land that would not be productive agriculturally to pasture their sheep. And the central administration demanded an accounting of births and deaths and wool at the time of the spring shearing.

We are ill-informed about the organization and production of crafts, but because reedwork and leatherwork are known before and after the Middle Babylonian period, we may assume that there was continuity in the production of craft goods. Perhaps these activities were carried on mostly in small households and not in large workshops since they are not attested in the period.

Although we do not have texts directly from merchants, we do have references to their activities that indicate that there was at various times a lively trade between the great centers not only of southern Mesopotamia but also of Syria and Egypt. In the correspondence recovered at Amarna in Egypt, carried on in Akkadian cuneiform on clay tablets, the mode of international communication of the day, the king of Babylon complained about the quality of gold that the Egyptian king had sent him, which he clearly regarded as a payment for his gift of horses. The trade between monarchs had its irrational aspects in that a ruler on Cyprus, which has no naturally occurring ivory, was expected to send some to an Egyptian ruler, but it was prestige and friendly symbols that were being traded rather than goods. Still other goods, more consumable, were treated more as economic goods to be exchanged for advantages, not just to keep up good relations.[29]

Kings were interested in protecting the activities of their own merchants. Scholars have seen these texts as indications that the kings had a monopoly on foreign trade, but it is more likely that the royal nature of our sources skews the picture. Perhaps merchants were state employees in Assyria, but they probably acted in private capacities too.[30]

At Ugarit a text shows that some merchants were commercial agents of the king. They were given gold, or at least equivalents of gold, to make purchases. A document recounts that an assault on a merchant working for the king of Carchemish was to be tried at Carchemish itself. Being a merchant was in a list of services owed to the palace. Nuzi merchants may also have been government officials, and there is evidence that they actually traveled. Ugaritic ships visited many ports throughout the Mediterranean, and the king was assumed to be able to equip 150 ships, a substantial navy.[31]

It is likely that textiles continued to be exported from Mesopotamia, and precious metals and stones came in. Aside from their working for kings, we know nothing about the merchants' other activities or social status.

Silver was no longer the money of account as it had been earlier; rather, gold was the major currency. It could be that this preference for gold came from the increased availability of that metal because of closer connections with the gold-fields to the east of Egypt.[32] The use of gold is not to be understood as a conscious shift of currencies, but in an economic system in which several commodities could serve as money, it would not have demanded a conceptual adjustment for people to use more frequently a commodity that previously was too rare to use as a money but now was more widely available.

In an Assyrian trade text after 1150 B.C.E. a merchant was mentioned and tin and bronze were used for purchases that were recalculated in grain. Both Assyrians and non-Assyrians were involved in long-distance trade, and houses, slaves, and skins were acquired.[33]

The international correspondence of the period does not represent the conditions of trade that most people in the Ancient Near East of the period faced. And it is not possible to reconstruct prices for most items. But it is probable that the earlier system of market-driven prices recovered from the Dark Age and was again functioning, at least in cities and in areas affected by cities.

At Ugarit prices were given usually in silver, but sometimes in gold or copper. Real estate, livestock, lumber, food, stones, metals, vessels, wool, and clothes were paid for in silver, and there were only two cases of apparent barter, in which other materials are exchanged for goods. But we lack prices for common goods like wheat, barley, oil, and wine, which must have been widespread. Price levels of barley in Mesopotamia appear to have been double the Old Babylonian price.[34]

At Ugarit we see the king confirming sales, and his family was heavily involved in real estate deals in the farming hinterland around that Syrian city. There are no legal codes from the Mesopotamian plain in the period except for the Middle Assyrian, and that set of texts is not in the context of a royal inscription that tries to demonstrate the efficiency of government intervention in the economy. Its concerns focus on regulating the conduct of women. In Middle Assyria there seems to have been a tax in sheep flowing into Assur.[35]

In royal inscriptions we get only the most general indications of government intervention in the economy, vague references to the well-being of the people. In short, we are poorly informed about how the Middle Babylonian kings and their contemporaries elsewhere handled this aspect of their rule.

This period is called the New Kingdom by modern scholars of Egypt, and it is one marked by an increase in interest in court circles in what was happening in Asia and in Africa south of Egypt. Expansionist kings led Egyptian armies both north and south, and although they did not overthrow local rulers, they tried to impose some order and left behind garrisons and officials. We have a great deal more information from the period about life in Egypt itself, probably because of a greater interest in using scribal skills to smooth the administration of surpluses.

At Deir el-Medina in the hills to the west of the Nile there was a small village of the New Kingdom that allows us to recover many aspects of the lives of ordinary people. This village's people were not typical, however, because they worked full-time on decorating the pharaohs' tombs, and their involvement in the cult for the dead is why their village was perched out in the desert and why it has been preserved. The site shows that even an ordinary person was concerned for the afterlife, and burials included the tools of the person's craft. Monogamy was common, and divorce was possible. But freedom of movement was not; the administration wanted to keep track of these artists and their families.[36]

Polygamy occurred among kings, but much less among private persons. Kings also had brother-sister marriages, unlike commoners. Frequently, criminal penalties were extended from the perpetrator to his wife and children. Women appeared independently from husbands in legal proceedings, and thus can be thought of as having an independent legal identity.[37]

Stories that were copied over by young men learning to be scribes show the period to be one in which upward social mobility was possible. And yet when filiation was mentioned, the norm was for sons to inherit their father's trade and position. A market in luxury goods, at least, existed, and women took part in it. Trade agents were involved in water transport and worked for temples. And there was no shortage of land, but rather of laborers. Slavery had been rare or absent in earlier periods, but prisoners of war from Egypt's campaigns in Asia fueled an internal slave trade.[38]

When the administration dealt with people not directly under the control of the government, it had to pay money for goods, and these constitute an indication of price levels. There was stability in the prices recorded, followed by inflation toward the end. We have 1,250 prices of various commodities from the village of Deir el-Medina, and they are frequently given in weights of copper. Wages were never paid in that metal but only in goods. Silver, copper, and grain were used as units of account. There was a rise in the price of land between 1200 and 1085 B.C.E., and then a return to the cheap norm. Outside Deir el-Medina precious metals were used as currency, frequently in the form of rings, as in Old Babylonian Mesopotamia.[39]

Politically and religiously the New Kingdom was a time of upheavals, especially between 1363 and 1347 B.C.E., when the pharaoh Akhnaton tried to reform religion and direct it toward a single deity, in addition to himself.[40] This change, sometimes called the Amarna revolution after his new capital, must have had social and economic implications, but we are not sure what they were. Certainly during his reign the previously opulent temples of the god Amun, and perhaps temples of other gods, suffered from a lack of royal support.

The imperial effort may have created a standing army for the first time in Egypt. And there must have been foreign fortunes to be made in the imperial service. Still, because posts became hereditary, one should in all probability rule out extensive social climbing. The reason for the imperialism was on one level to avoid the repetition of the Hyksos domination of the Second Intermediate period, but it also gave access to raw materials. From Africa Egyptians wanted gold, ivory, and incense; from Asia the major thing mentioned was the wood that came from Lebanon and Syria.[41]

The New Kingdom ended not so much because of threats of foreign invasion but because of internal administrative ineptitude. There were some external threats, though, in the form of movements of people probably from the Aegean Sea and from Libya, people whom the Egyptians called sea peoples. They moved along the Egyptian coast and confronted the pharaohs in two waves; they managed to drive them out of the Delta and back into Palestine, where they made them settle.

The Egyptian archives from Amarna allow us glimpses of the constellations of Syro-Lebanese-Palestinian city-states that flourished in the period of Akhnaton's rule and those of his father and successors.[42] There were kings who ruled only the cities and their agricultural coronas, and they were constantly appealing to the pharaoh to send them paltry numbers of troops to protect them against their rivals. We do not hear, however, how the petty kings paid their own retainers or dealt with the common populace.

Archaeology confirms the textual record's impression of flourishing cities. The problem of how this world fell apart is one of the most vexing in scholarship because it involves the period of the Israelite invasions or conquest. These seem connected obliquely with the incursions of the sea people in Egypt, and around 1200 B.C.E. there was a great deal of movement of peoples in the Ancient Near East, which may have led to the decline of Palestinian city-states and the invention of new political and economic structures. These movements joined those of runaways seeking to get out of the palace-centered system.[43]

The Hittite Empire flourished as the Hittite rulers pushed down into Syria and blotted out the kingdom of Mitanni, on the Upper Balikh and Khabur Rivers, and came into conflict with the Egyptians, who were pushing north at the same time. The archives in cuneiform from the Hittite capital of Boghazköy show a great deal about politics and magic, but not much about social and economic life. Imperialism here, too, must have broadened the perspective of some servants of the state and may have fostered a spirit of individual initiative.

Land in the Hittite areas was owned communally, and the king's power over land was limited. Some land could be sold, while other categories of land probably could not. Land prices in the Hittite laws seem low. There was a tax in labor that the king could extract. Landholdings were dispersed among many fields. Several texts show the king granting land to individuals before witnesses, and the land granted sometimes came with the personnel to work it. But again it is a misnomer to call these arrangements feudal because there was no class of landowning lords.[44]

Perhaps one can see remnants of a tribal organization in the roles of elders among the Hittites, but the elders were limited to religious and judicial functions. Offering lists show the existence of nonbureaucratic worthies, and so of a private sector. Local assemblies may have functioned consultatively to the king.[45]

From the collection of Hittite laws we can see that the family was monogamous, although kings had concubines whose children had lesser status. A treaty mentions that marriage with sisters was forbidden, but we know that a Hittite king did marry his sister, apparently in order to concentrate power in their offsprings' hands and to eliminate the influence of brothers-in-law and their children in royal administration in the next generation.[46]

The laws show a concern for the downtrodden similar to that in the earlier Mesopotamian collections. These laws had two versions, an earlier one and a later, and the trend in the later version seems to be toward milder physical punishments and toward monetary punishments.[47] This updating of legal sections may indicate that these formulations were meant to be enforced and had to be kept current, unlike Mesopotamian collections.

Archival texts are few and brief, usually just lists of goods. The inventory texts show that iron and gold were available, but they are too laconic to allow a reconstruction of the Hittite economy.[48]

Forced labor was probably more important than hired or slave labor, if one may judge by the laws. Even draft animals were subject to the corvée.[49]

Internal trade is attested by the presence of metals in cities, even smaller ones. Herding was important in the economy of the Hittites, especially for wool production.[50]

In Crete, the Minoans gave way to Mycenaeans under unclear circumstances. The Mycenaeans, who wrote a dialect of Greek, learned much from Minoans and took over some, but not all, of their sites. The connection of the Minoan decline with the eruption of a volcano seems weak. In China, the legendary Shang Dynasty continued its putative reign until 1122 B.C.E., when it was thrown out by the Chou.

The unity of southern Mesopotamia at least had been maintained for centuries. But society was permeable, and new peoples made inroads into the land and into the power structure without basically altering the edifice of Mesopotamian society.

ASSYRIAN DOMINATION

1100–626 B.C.E.

After the political dissolution of the Middle Babylonian state, another earthquake shook Ancient Near Eastern society. We think of it as involving ethnic movements, and some have referred to it as the problems of the sea peoples, but it was probably much broader and deeper than a foreign invasion. The sea peoples were what Egyptians called the invaders from the north and from Libya, in the late 1200s and 1100s B.C.E. The contemporary kings of Egypt claimed to have beaten off the invaders, and some of the invaders may have been resettled as mercenaries in southern Palestine, where Egyptian administration still had influence.[1]

The sea peoples themselves were not a gigantic force and did not change the face of Egypt, but at the same time many other peoples were on the move. Recent theories suggest that movements may have been connected with a drying of climates, and people who had been able to eke out a living in Libya or in the Arabian desert now found that they could no longer do so and had to move elsewhere to maintain themselves.[2]

The Assyrians saw new peoples, called Aramaeans, moving into their fields, first as marauding nomads and then as farmers settling down. An Assyrian king fled Assur, but the dynasty did not end. In the west Ugarit and the Hittite Empire were destroyed by movements of peoples around 1200, though languages like Ugaritic continued to be spoken in the area, and even Hittite was preserved in small states south of the Taurus Mountains in Syria.

The most problematic and best-studied case of disruption after 1200 is the arrival of the Israelites. They saw themselves as related to the Aramaeans and traced their history back to Mesopotamia; their later traditions, however, affirmed a connection with Egypt also, though they entered the land of Israel from the east, across the Jordan River. The first extrabiblical reference to them came in 1209, when the Egyptian king Merneptah claimed to have destroyed them along with a number of cities in Syria-Palestine. Archaeology does not clearly show that they, or anyone, invaded the city-states and destroyed them. Surface survey shows a big increase in the number of people living in the hill country behind the areas that had long been farmed by people in the city-states. Not all of the new people could have come off the desert, but former nomads may have been joined by refugees from the city-states.[3]

The Bible derives entirely from later ages, and yet it does preserve a reason for Israel's movement that makes sense. Israel came from the desert seeking a more fruitful land, and its ideologues saw the land they got, for all its rockiness and difficulty, as a wonderful contrast to where they had been.

What began politically as a time of disruption ended in the most all-inclusive empire people had yet imagined, the Neo-Assyrian. The Assyrian state assimilated its new arrivals, and its leaders resumed their rounds of tribute collecting and administration, extending their control into Israel, destroying the northern kingdom of that name, and even taking Egypt for a short period.

The ideology that motivated Assyrians to fight for this new empire was apparently the same as that which has motivated more recent imperialisms, including Nazism: the center, the motherland, demanded obedience from the unruly, subhuman periphery, and those lucky enough to be born Assyrians had a duty to obey their leader and expand his domain. Naturally, people who might have wished to assert the importance of their own local traditions would not be happy to be assaulted physically and ideologically by the Assyrians, and probably the reaction of most of the politically aware people in the west was one of disgust and revulsion at being included in the empire.[4]

One of the causes for the revulsion was that the Assyrians, like some earlier Mesopotamian imperialists, practiced deportation, resettling opinion leaders from recalcitrant communities in other places, frequently in the heartland of Assyria itself. Perhaps 4.5 million persons were deported over three centuries, most in the period from 745 to 627 B.C.E. This kind of exile was intended to destroy the person's individuality and rebelliousness, and it seems to have usually worked in the short run.[5] But in the long run the Assyrians found themselves hated by important groups in almost every region that they had included in their empire and by some that they had not managed to enslave.

The rich simply did not understand. They could still smuggle in grain and apples from their estates, but someone who had to work as a potter all day did not have time or money to take advantage of what little they offered for sale. And so he sat on the wall impassively as the officials with their glorious cloaks and finely trimmed beards trooped down to meet with the Assyrian general. A city under siege is no place to get fat, and there is no time to waste on spectacles, but maybe these negotiations would bring an end to the matter. There had been talk that the city would have to pay a hefty tribute, but at least life could get back to normal, and there could be an end to these ridiculous shortages. Even now he could see the ripening grain down the ravines to the north of the city. The plain would have lots more, if the Assyrians had not already destroyed the grain along with the towns. There had been rumors.

From his position on the wall he could hear only words and phrases, but the officials seemed agitated. Then the general started yelling to the men on the walls, in Hebrew, no less. These Assyrians were pretty crafty to have generals with this kind of local expertise even if his accent was strange. He was saying something about how all of the gods had bowed down to Assyria, and now our god also wanted us to bow down to him too. Bow down to their strange gods? The potter found that a little hard to take. But a little submission might not be all that bad. And what if the Assyrians did exile a few people? They would not exile a simple potter. It would be people like that loudmouth prophet Isaiah, who had been saying we should sit tight. Might as well give in on this one, the potter thought. And yet in a broad sense the potter could see that the prophet had a point; this could not last forever. The only question was how long the potter himself could hold out without making any sales.

His friends on the wall seemed to be swayed by what the Assyrian was saying. You can't hold out against the kind of power the Assyrians could bring against us; you simply have to accommodate it, and that would cost money. Better than dying, though, and better, the potter thought, than sitting another day with nobody buying a single thing he made, though pots were breaking at exactly the same rate, if not faster, than usual. But people were running out of money and so were keeping it to buy food instead of pots.

The officials looked sheepish as the Assyrian kept on yelling. They let him finish, said that they'd have to discuss the matter, then scurried inside the walls and went up to see the king. Something had to give, the potter thought, and it had better be us because it clearly was not going to be the Assyrians.[6]

The Mesopotamian floodplain had a downturn in the number and area of sites after 1200 B.C.E. This decrease is part of the long decline coming after Ur III probably because of the decay of the canal systems. But in the late 700s the decline was reversed, and a long, slow pattern of growth emerged.[7]

Elsewhere, the hill country of Israel, which previously had never been occupied, now held a great many people. Two techniques not seen widely in the area before made this settlement easier.[8] People dug cisterns into nonporous rock and thus could keep the rain that fell only in the winter for their needs during the rest of the year. Also, farmers built terraces up hillsides so they could grow crops where previously only sheep and goats could graze.

Some argue that in the Assyrian worldview there were only two social groups, the oppressed and the exploiters.[9] Most of the civilized world at one time or another was oppressed by the Assyrians, but socially and economically such non-Assyrians were very different from one another and probably maintained their old social divisions.

Among important ethnic and linguistic groups were the Aramaeans, who may not have been a cohesive social group after settling down to farm. By the middle of the first millennium speaking Aramaic gave one no particular ethnic classification, and the Judahite officials who met the Assyrian general during the siege of 701 B.C.E. wanted to be spoken to in Aramaic, not Hebrew. Chaldeans were a separate group who spoke Aramaic in southern Babylonia and were more likely than Aramaeans to be sedentary, though both groups were divided into tribes. Chaldeans tended to settle along the Euphrates, Aramaeans along the Tigris.[10]

Assyrians may have seen their situation as Assyria versus the rest of the world, and yet Assyrians themselves seem not to constitute a self-conscious ethnic group.[11] A scholar has recently argued that the repeated phrase in royal inscriptions "I counted/considered [deportees] together with the people of the land of Assyria" shows that kings made no distinction between natives and deportees. The scholar suggests that a change happened under Sargon II (721–705 B.C.E.), whose military successes created a new Assyrian pride and self-consciousness, and the phrase "I counted . . . " was no longer used. To prove this interesting contention, one would need a clearer exposition of whether oppressive practices as attested in archival texts actually increased in frequency under Sargon. It is certain that in this or a succeeding period ethnic self-consciousness did arise, but one cannot be sure that it was among Assyrians first.

And yet we must suppose that the military families that gave the Assyrian army its strength did have a certain self-consciousness and pride in their tradition that set them apart at least occasionally from the people among whom they lived. Deportees included people from high status groups but others too.[12] And once resettled, they did not have any uniform or distinct status.

In Babylonia between 745 and 627 B.C.E. there may have been a growth of large family groupings as well as of an aristocracy that may have been hereditary. These (mār) rab bani "elitist class" people may have arisen in northern Babylonia from non-Chaldean urban dwellers; they did not appear in the south. We do not know how one got to be counted among the noble.[13]

The structure of the family seems a continuation of earlier models. Rich men, and kings especially, could afford more than one wife, but most people were monogamous. The families recorded in the so-called census lists from Harran, in southern Turkey, were nuclear ones headed by a father; on the average they had 1.43 children—not a high number compared to modern figures in the region. There was no preference in inheritance among sons; all inherited equally. The images of women in Neo-Assyrian literature are the same as those seen in earlier tradition. The alewife still gave loans, and the prostitute plied her trade, while the faithful mother continued to be the norm. Women were not involved in litigation to the extent that they were earlier. But they apparently acted as heads of families when widowed, and they had religious roles in the official cult. It is hard to see that the oppressive norms of the earlier Middle Assyrian Laws still had any reflection in custom. Some queens ruled as regents for their minor sons and were remembered for their efficiency, and there were some female scribes. Some texts show royal officers buying slaves for the purpose of marrying them.[14]

Two forms of labor continue to dominate. As usual, we are better informed about forced labor, called in the period *dullu ša šarri* "the work of the king," than about free labor for hire.[15] The great institutions turned to the free peasants for extra labor when it was needed during the agricultural year. If particular peasants traditionally worked for the crown as part of their tax burden, the government could demand their work. If not, the government had to pay.

The military was the most spectacular of the schemes for labor exploitation. Probably a large part of the upkeep of the troops came directly from the towns they looted, but when there was peace or duty that did not involve pillage, troops were paid with rations from government stores. These rations were the same for both officers and men.[16] That means that they were intended for basic upkeep while on noncombat duty, but it also shows that the army cultivated an ethic of egalitarianism, like the modern Israeli army, which allowed its officers to draw on comradeship in arms as well as the power of command and coercion to get their men to do ridiculously dangerous things.

Peasants in Assyria could sometimes be sold with the land, but they nonetheless had rights and remained free in some sense. They may be described as servile or slavelike, but they were not like slaves who could be sold apart from the land they worked.[17]

The census lists from Harran, in the west of the empire, show groups attached to the land that had been bought by large landowners who got their wealth by working in state administration. These men did not, however, put together large contiguous estates but owned many small plots scattered in various parts of the empire; they themselves lived in big cities. These census lists were lists of people who were exempt from taxation perhaps because of the influence of their owners at court. Small amounts of goods and animals were registered as "their own," indicating that most of the rest of the equipment and land belonged to the absentee owners. The lists indicate there was a two-year fallow cycle. The largest plot was not big, no larger than a square kilometer, about 250 acres. There were free laborers as well who worked for hire on those lands, though because of the royal source of the documentation, they were not frequently mentioned.[18]

The villages that dominated the early Middle Assyrian landscape had disappeared by this period. The landscape might have looked the same, but the
villages were peopled in the Assyrian heartland increasingly by exiles from elsewhere, brought there to break their political spirit. Elsewhere, the Assyrians
allowed old customary land relationships to continue and did not interfere
with the economy of regions that owed them tribute except to assign them to a
governor and an army to enforce tax contributions. Tax farming was not
known in the period, and the usual method of taxation was the use of the
threat of the governor's force against farmers. Royal officials built up large
estates from lands confiscated from defeated ruling classes.[19]

Assyrian cities grew too large to support their populations from the agricultural produce of the immediately surrounding regions. Temples too could not
exist on voluntary offerings, and so kings felt obliged to support them. It is
possible that kings regarded all land as in some sense belonging to them,
though this is not clearly stated and, as in earlier periods, may be a modern
interpretation.[20]

Kings in their royal inscriptions speak of the wonderful animals they captured or had brought from distant places for their menageries; still, we do not
know how the sheep industry in Mesopotamia fared. It may be assumed that
it continued much as before because we see it again in later periods. Shepherds
paid a fee in silver as they took care of government-owned sheep, though why
exactly is unclear. Private herds were probably kept by free villagers, and there
are a few sheep contracts.[21]

Crafts do not leave many direct traces in the records either, but the lexical
texts from the period, many of which go back at least to Old Babylonian models, show a lively interest in all kinds of leather and reed products as well as
finer metal work. The royal inscriptions gave anecdotes about kings' having
captured Phoenician artists working in ivory and wood, and we have found
some of the ivory. Some captured craftsmen were organized in units like military ones. They worked as if they were independent workers; the government
supplied their raw materials and expected a set amount of craft goods in
return.[22]

Babylonia produced timber from poplar and other local trees that was
prized for building palaces. Shortages of copper and tin to make bronze may
have led to the switch to iron in this period. The technology probably developed first in the Ancient Near East and then spread to Cyprus, which around
1000 B.C.E. made a superior blade.[23]

Kings had access to wonderful things from the west and presumably gold
from Africa via Egypt. Spices, precious stones, and gold were taken as booty
from nomadic Arabs on the desert fringes of Mesopotamia, and later were sent

by them as tribute to the Assyrian kings. We lack the texts about merchants that we have in earlier and later periods and so do not know how their work was organized. Some have argued that the lack of texts shows that all trade was a state monopoly, but that seems unlikely. In documents about other matters people called "merchant" frequently have non-Akkadian names. Though it has been suggested that the collapse of the empire came about because of its exploitative foreign trade policies, it may also be that the concentration of wealth in the cities of the empire created imbalances that alienated rural populations.[24]

Kings boasted of low prices, and there were few indications of what real prices were because most of the documentation for the period comes from royal archives intent on inventory control of rations. The dominant money in the 700s B.C.E. was copper, but in the next century silver became more popular. The invention of coined money in Asia Minor around 625 B.C.E. had no immediate impact on Babylonia.[25]

Grain prices varied widely, by as much as 100 percent depending upon how dry the year had been. Land prices ranged from a third of a shekel of silver per homer, about 1.8 hectare or almost 4.5 acres, to more than fifteen shekels; usually we cannot see why a given bit of land should be more valuable, but this kind of variation is also typical in the region today.[26]

Previous Mesopotamian governments spoke eloquently of the standards of economic justice, but they did not successfully intervene in the economy; neither did Assyrians. Certainly their policy of deportation disrupted economic life both at the sending and receiving ends, and it was designed for political purposes. The economic implications of deportation appear only occasionally to have been considered, as when a king settles people in previously uncultivated areas in hopes that they will be able to farm them.[27]

The court itself may have had to maintain as many as thirteen thousand people, and we are not sure exactly how that was done. There are no records of the king's own land, only of state and private land.[28]

In Babylonia, temples sometimes financed the intervention of anti-Assyrian Elamite armies and thus must have had considerable wealth and influence. Paradoxically, although Babylonia was the scene of frequent fighting, its economy seems to have prospered.[29]

The Neo-Assyrian kings apparently had a policy of laissez-faire, and there is no evidence for price controls. Many people owed the state *ilku*; in earlier periods that term represented a land grant in exchange for service, but in the Neo-Assyrian period it was a charge on the land that could sometimes be paid in cash. Tax rates on crops sometimes were 10 percent.[30]

The Assyrian state grew at the expense of village producers on its borders, and this meant in the long run that the agricultural base of the region became less sound. It was thus more vulnerable to outside attack than it would have been had autochthonous peasants been left to defend their fields. This may explain why, when the empire fell, it fell apart quickly and permanently.[31]

Though Egypt withstood the invasions of the sea peoples, it did not usually assert its former dominance in Asia. For most of the time Egypt was ruled by kings from sub-Saharan Africa and from Libya. Though neither of these groups was disliked as much as the Hyksos, and though the kings tried to present themselves as good and normal Egyptians, they were unable to recapture the glory of the imperial New Kingdom (1558–1085 B.C.E.), and the parts of Asia that they wanted in their spheres of influence drifted into independence under their own rulers.

These kings were apparently less respected than earlier Egyptian ones had been, at least in literature. And there was a new pattern of settlement in which cities built defensive walls. This development implies that in contrast to the New Kingdom the countryside was insecure. In addition, people were more likely to live within the cities than in a corona of villages, and this may have caused the lower prices for farmland.[32]

In the period when Assyria controlled Egypt, 663 to 609 B.C.E., the Assyrians do not seem to have disrupted economic life. There were no major deportations from Egypt, though a notable Egyptian was once a hostage at the Assyrian court.[33]

Around 1200 B.C.E. Israel had appeared in the land, and the flood of materials that is preserved in the Hebrew Bible begins. The writers of the Hebrew Bible, the Old Testament, were mostly not interested in social and economic issues except insofar as they believed that people ought to behave in certain ways to each other.[34] The light shed on our questions is thus almost always oblique and uncertain, and these questions are also not frequently examined in Bible study because the other, more obvious philosophical questions continue to be of concern to us as they were to Hebrew intellectuals.[35]

Early Israel apparently consisted of large immigrant groups living in hilly regions of limited agricultural productivity that had not been heavily occupied before. They appear gradually to have filtered from the hills down into the more fertile plains and in some cases to have assimilated the populations of previous cities. This process seems clear with the north-central city of Shechem, and some scholars speculate that Joshua 24 is a memory of the Shechemites' joining Israel, though it is itself a late text. The number of people living in central Israel in the period of Israelite political independence from 1000 to 587 B.C.E. may never have been more than 300,000 to 350,000.[36]

Surface survey indicates that the occupation of the land of Israel around

1200 began from the northeast and proceeded to the southwest. The areas occupied could be adapted to rainfall agriculture, but in drier years disaster could strike, so people settled where diversification in crops and herding was possible. Israelites exploited three technological innovations: terracing, use of iron, and cisterns, though these alone cannot explain their success at establishing themselves in the difficult hill environment. Terraces cannot usually be dated archaeologically because they are often not associated with datable remains like pottery, so many of the observed terraces may not have come from the period. Terracing was important, though, because it allowed people to farm hill slopes that otherwise would not have been arable. Cisterns are known from the Late Bronze period too, and iron is found in the hill country only in the 900s B.C.E. and then not in significant amounts.[37] Thus the initial Israelite occupation must not have depended on iron.

Israel was divided into tribes, usually twelve in number, which changed size and identity over time. Although in early periods the tribes seem to have had some political meaning, this faded during the monarchies of Saul, David, and Solomon and their successors, and tribal names became identical to region names. When the monarchy divided around 925 B.C.E., tribal leaders did not appear prominently in political or religious roles. The chiefs of the tribes presumably constituted a ruling class, but the judges, the leaders who arose in response to military threats to organize groups of tribes in defense, were not clearly tribal chiefs. And in fact tribal chiefs led a shadowy existence in the Bible. There is debate about the extent to which the earliest kings of Israel were tribal chiefs. Certainly Saul and David were connected to their tribes as later kings were not, but they may not have been leaders of their tribes before they become prominent beyond the tribes.[38] Our uncertainty about who was in charge of tribes may derive from the vagueness of tribes; they may have come together only for self-defense.

There are several Hebrew words usually translated "noble," sometimes in the moral sense. The occurrences of the words do not shed light on who may have been considered part of this nobility or what its relations might have been to the land. Perhaps they were loose terms that did not always have a concrete social meaning.[39]

Of military importance was the group of people called men of valor, which probably referred originally to especially courageous warriors but then to men who could afford to outfit themselves with armor for battle and were influential in community affairs. In some periods of Israelite history these may have constituted an upper middle class, and the term does seem to be used more broadly than in military contexts to show status, as in reference to Boaz in Ruth and to the "woman of valor" in Proverbs 31. Among such people the elders in all likelihood constituted the leaders; they decided local legal cases and served as a town council.[40]

At the bottom of the social scale, as elsewhere in the Ancient Near East, were the slaves of either foreign or local origin. Fifteen percent of those who returned from exile after 539 B.C.E. were slaves, and in earlier times probably even less of the population was enslaved. Ziba, Saul's slave, owned slaves himself, showing that the economic status of slaves could vary.[41] Biblical legal writers were interested in humane treatment for slaves who could be regarded as Israelites, but this concern shows as well that even such slaves could be treated poorly.

There were semifree statuses in Israel as elsewhere. Gibeonites were Canaanites, that is, people who preceded Israelites in the area, forced to work for Israelites. After the exile ending in 539 B.C.E. there were temple servants, who seem to have been very like Mesopotamian g u r u š "dependent laborers." The status of resident alien was, however, a protected one, and such a person seems to have been viewed as a defenseless client of a community.[42]

Levites were seen as a tribe without land and in some periods acted as religious experts for local religious centers like India's Brahmans. Priests had to be Levites, but not all Levites were priests, and some stories relate conflicts between priests and nonpriestly Levites.[43]

Free peasants must have constituted the largest group in any period. These persons were probably to be identified with the later rabbinic tradition's "people of the land," whom the Jewish teachers regarded as ignorant and morally worthless.[44]

The prophets of the 800s and 700s B.C.E. were agitated by social change they observed, and this change has sometimes been interpreted as a class struggle in which rich landowners took advantage of poor farmers and drove them into debt, finally dispossessing them. This conflict has frequently been seen as one between Canaanite exploitative practices and pristine desert feelings of equality, but the situation was much more complex than that. In dry years peasants needed credit to get from one harvest to the next, and dry years tend nowadays to come in dreadful clusters. Peasants could apparently sell land to kinsmen, as in Jeremiah 32, or go to nonkinsmen for grain or money, using their fields as security. If one fell into increasing debt, one could end up being enslaved for it, and this in particular angered the prophets. There had likely always been poor people in Israel, and prophets may not have been reacting to a new struggle but to poor people's more publicly being reduced to slavery or dependency.[45]

The rich, especially kings, had several wives, but otherwise monogamy was the norm. We have the impression that spring-fall marriages, in which the bride was much younger than the groom, were not uncommon, but the clear example in the book of Ruth implies that the woman, who was herself no nubile youth, had considerable latitude in seeking a spouse. Her eventual spouse says to her, "You are blessed to Yahweh, my daughter; you have done better with your last kindness than your first since you did not go after the young men, whether rich or poor" (Ruth 3:10). There are some indications that arranged marriages were not common, though the patriarchal stories deal only with arranged marriages. Again, arranged marriages may have been something the rich could afford but others could not. Also, the historicity of the patriarchal stories has been questioned, and the events they describe are basically undatable.[46]

In other cultures if families do not have to endow women with large amounts of goods and thus do not have to go out of their way to make them attractive to suitors, the women are likely to be more powerful and to be nearer the age of their grooms at first marriage. But we do not know much about dowries. Ruth did not need one, and Laban's daughters may have thought that he ought to give them a dowry, but he did not, so they stole his household gods.[47]

The rich man seems to have had many children through his several wives. But people of modest means in all probability succeeded in nurturing only a couple of children through the rigors of childhood disease to adulthood. The high mortality rate for children can be demonstrated in grave remains and probably was assumed in at least one text in which children over five years old had a higher valuation than younger ones. Nuclear families may have lived in four-room houses with bedrooms on upper stories. Most families had about four people.[48]

Unwanted children were sometimes exposed to the elements and thus killed. Selling children into slavery was a more attractive alternative because the parent knew that the children would survive and be taken care of. Weaning of children may have happened at age three, but when adulthood was felt to be reached is not clearly indicated. That a boy is *bar mitzvah* "subject to the commandment" at age thirteen derives from the rabbinic period, though its modern form is not found until the 1400s of our era.[49]

One would think that in a recently settled society the extended family would play an important role. We usually translate *mišpāḥāh* as "clan" or "family," and it occurs widely in the Bible in clichés like "according to their families" in Genesis 10:20. Stories do not, however, indicate that this was an important social unit, and most narratives concern only the nuclear family of father, mother, and children. Even grandparents are rarely mentioned, perhaps because of high mortality rates in advancing age. The clan was not mentioned after David, around 960 B.C.E., and is absent also from Deuteronomy, indicating that it may have fallen out of use.[50]

Some feminists have argued that Israelite women had little legal power and were thoroughly exploited by the men in their lives. Others have countered that freedom of movement was not restricted, veiling was almost unknown, and stories show that women could occasionally manipulate male institutions to get what they wanted, as Naomi did in the book of Ruth.[51] Tamar donned a veil in Genesis 38:14–15, covering her face like a harlot so her father-in-law would not know her; this story does not imply that most women or even most prostitutes were veiled. The only other reference to veiling is Genesis 24:65, in which Rebecca veiled herself on being told that a man walking in the fields was her groom, Isaac.

The distinction between legal stipulations and actualities is important in regard to women. In the case of Israel we have very few legal stories that might bear on legal stipulations and no other relevant contemporary documentation. But we do have indications that the law collections were unconnected with governmental authority and derived from piety-minded circles in opposition to the governments. The codes may have had some function as a guide to judges, but the fact that the inclusion of motive clauses increases in the biblical codes over time indicates that they increasingly served a teaching function.[52]

In Proverbs and elsewhere are indications that legal stipulations did not apply or were simply unknown among the population at large. For example, legal material attributed to the Holiness Code, which may date from after 539 B.C.E. but reflects earlier conditions, says that a woman's father or her husband could revoke her vows; that is, any agreement or oath she had entered into could be recalled by a male who had power over her. This stipulation seems to restrict the legal freedom of women to participate in commerce. But the view of the woman of valor, the upper-class woman in Proverbs 31, shows a woman who has considerable legal discretion; she could consider a field and buy it all by herself and was the main moneymaker of the household. Her husband sat honorably in the gate of the village to hobnob with other men, while she took care of the household. Proverbs were occasionally misogynistic, but they chose to personify their central concept, wisdom itself, as a woman who gave speeches in the street. With Proverbs we have the problem of not being able to date the book or the specific section, but even if it is mainly from a time after the exile to Babylon in 587–539 B.C.E., it is conceivable that it reflects earlier possibilities for women.[53]

Leviticus 27 has the relative evaluations of women and men, giving a list of prices for converting vows made by various age categories of people into money to pay the temple. The percentage paid by women was between 33 percent and

40 percent of that paid by men. This may show how much women contributed to food production, and this possible division of labor reflects a relatively egalitarian society. The age of marriage for women may have been as young as twelve, as in later Jewish practice, and death from childbirth in a woman's reproductive years was common.[54]

It was certainly more oppressive to be an Israelite woman than to be a modern Western one, but the society seems to have retained some of its putative egalitarianism and to have allowed some women to reach positions of authority. Whether these were vestiges of an earlier sexual arrangement or exceptional charismatic flukes is a matter for dispute. Women were excluded from religious offices, as they were not in most of the rest of the Ancient Near East. The origins of restrictions on women's sexuality and perhaps also participation in public affairs may lie in the need to populate the new land after the ethnic and perhaps plague-related upheavals around 1200 B.C.E. in the whole region. But there does not seem to be a trend in biblical materials toward greater exploitation of women.[55]

Some people were unfree laborers attached to institutions, and a few were household slaves, but the free peasantry did most of the work of the society. There was seasonally at least a market in labor because we hear of the hired man, and the legal texts wanted richer Israelites to be sure to pay him his wage promptly because to delay would be oppressive to him; the hired man was thus assumed to be very poor, living from hand to mouth.[56]

More is known about forced labor, a system by which free citizens worked on a royal project as part of their tax burden. It has been suggested that there was a distinction between the levy, Hebrew *sēbel*, and the corvée, *mas*, and this may explain why the northern kingdom would choose Jeroboam, formerly over the levy, to lead it while stoning Adoram, Rehoboam's official over the corvée (1 Kings 12). It is unknown how long and how frequently one would be called on to serve. But we do know that the institution was controversial and was seen by religious people as a dangerous innovation. Some even claimed that in the early monarchy it had been imposed only on Canaanites, the non-Israelites living in the land.[57] Because of the vacillation on the question, though, it seems much more likely that under David and Solomon forced labor was imposed on Israelites too, however one defined Israelites at that early period. The work done usually had to do with building fortifications and other structures. The felling and transportation of wood for the temple by foreigners aided by forced labor was lovingly described by a later author who himself probably never was subject to such a corvée (1 Kings 5:13–18).

Slaves may not have been numerous, even in rich households; Abigail had five slaves, and perhaps Nabal's whole household in the early monarchy had fif-

teen; Mephibosheth's slave Ziba himself had twenty, as noted above. But legal-
ists and other religious people were concerned about Israelites who fell into
slavery because of unpaid debts, when the creditor could simply appropriate
the person and his labor to pay the debt. The legal thinkers wanted a distinction between Israelites and non-Israelites, with non-Israelites suffering permanent slavery but Israelites serving only for a term of seven years.[58] No evidence
supports the idea that this was ever put into practice.

The conditions of agricultural labor were portrayed in Ruth's harvest scene,
though it is not clear if the reapers were hired or slave.[59] They included women,
and there was the danger than an unconnected young woman would be molested
in the field (Ruth 2:3–22). The work was backbreaking and ran from dawn to
evening, though there was a break for a meal, and when the work was done for
the day, the poor person who was gleaning after the reapers still had to beat out
her grain to get the edible kernels. Of course, the work lasted only as long as the
harvest, and the Israelite peasant would then have had a harvest festival, as in
Ruth 3, and then a slack period until work on the next planting began.

Most agriculturally productive land was apparently privately owned and
worked by individual families and their slaves, if any. But there was a feeling,
which the law collections and some stories reflect, that extended families had
some claims to land, so that when a person was forced to sell his land, the first
right to buy it went to someone who was of his near kin. This person was called
the redeemer because he saved the land from falling into nonfamilial hands.
Perhaps this function was a relic of an earlier time when communities owned
land in common.[60]

The prophets Isaiah and Micah, both speaking in the late 700s B.C.E., complained about what has been called, by analogy to Roman history, *latifundia*
"broad fields," large estates created by the dispossession of poor peasants. Both
of these men lived in the southern kingdom, which did not have such good
land as the northern. Apparently their complaints were directed against exiles
from the north who, after the region fell in 722 B.C.E., were trying to impose
northern land development on the south. Micah complained of those who

> covet fields, and seize them;
> and houses, and take them away;
> they oppress a man and his house,
> a man and his inheritance. (Micah 2:2)

And Isaiah said,

> Woe to those who join house to house,
> who add field to field,
> until there is no more room. (Isaiah 5:8)

Possibly sections of land had been divided so many times by inheritance that they were unworkable anyway. Landowners did not create big estates because there were more slaves available than before, as may have happened later at Rome. Prophets in general disliked the economy's becoming more complex in any way and worried about how changes would affect the poor.[61]

Another kind of land was royal land, but whether it was just land that the king owned as a private person or government property that he used is not clear. Certainly 1 Samuel 8 implies that the future king would be able to confiscate and to redistribute land to his officials as salary. Still, there are no traces of such a system in connection with a specific king. Once at the beginning of the monarchy King Saul ironically asked his supporters if his rival David would be able to give them fiefs, implying that it was inconceivable that he could. But could Saul himself award his subjects fiefs? In one instance David as king regulated the succession to land owned by a son of Saul, but maybe that was exceptional.[62]

The religious calendar describes the rhythm of the agricultural year, which began in the spring and had to get over the long, dry summer until the harvest in late September and October before the winter rains started again. Having the calendrical new year in the fall was probably an old custom associated with the end of the last harvest; later the new year began in the spring under Babylonian influence.[63]

Religious thinkers wanted to institute a sabbatical year in which no agricultural work would be done, to give the land a rest like that for persons every week, and some hoped in addition for a jubilee year every forty-nine years in which all debts would be remitted and land that had been alienated from its traditional possessors would be returned. It seems unlikely that any of these proposals was ever put into effect.[64]

Herding must have been a lucrative way for sedentary peasants to bank surpluses and insure against crop losses in bad years because herds would not be so directly affected by drought as crops. Herding may have been a way of avoiding taxes when the government was strong enough to collect them; one could drive the sheep away when word arrived that tax collectors were coming. Ethnographic parallels show that sheepherding can give as high as a 40 percent return on investment, a valuable source of profit for any farmer in a region where rainfall was problematic and irrigation usually unfeasible. As seen in Proverbs, one could buy goats to resell for land. Also, oxen were useful for plowing and for carrying large loads.[65]

The Jacob stories tell of one sheep-tending agreement through which a clever shepherd using now-doubtful knowledge about genetics managed to become rich in sheep. Jacob and his boss agreed that Jacob would keep the spotted and speckled newborns, but Jacob cleverly exposed rutting animals to speckled and spotted sticks of wood, and, on the theory that mothers give birth to something resembling what they see when they conceive, they gave birth to spotted and speckled offspring (Genesis 29:25–43).[66] The Bible is full of pastoral images, and no doubt many of the rocky hillsides of Israel were used to herd sheep and goats.

Two references imply that the court owned herds. Mentions of sizes of herds indicate only great wealth and do not show the normal sizes of herds.[67]

Weaving was the work of women, but there were male potters. It appears that these and other crafts were pursued only within households, large and small, though the kings may have had factories or work depots (2 Samuel 12:31 and 1 Chronicles 4:23). The metalworking site found by archaeologists at Ezion-Geber at the northern tip of the Gulf of Aqaba may have been one such depot.[68] The texts speak of the importation of foreign craftsmen, especially Phoenicians, to work on the temple and on Solomon's other ostentatious buildings (1 Kings 7:13–46, paralleled by 2 Chronicles 2:3–15 and 3). This correctly reflects the relatively backward state of crafts in early Israel.

Israel was located near major north-south trade routes, and its Plain of Esdralon in the north was an important thoroughfare for trade. We hear of trade as a major activity only under Solomon, about 965–925 B.C.E. The story in I Kings indicates that Solomon imported horses from Cilicia in southern Turkey and sold them in Egypt, buying chariots from Egypt in order to sell them further north. With Phoenician help he also established a trading fleet on the Gulf of Aqaba that dealt in spices. All this activity is presented as a royal monopoly, and we do not see who did the actual work or how it was organized. The trade was in luxury items, and it may not have had any far-reaching effects on the economy. The overall thrust of Solomon's efforts was detrimental to the Israelite economy because he was forced to cede cities to a Phoenician monarch to pay his debts, and so the money he was bringing in from trade was insufficient for his needs.[69]

Solomon's legendary wisdom may have derived from stories about his wealth. It has been observed that the stories that told of wealth and linked it with wisdom had a fabulous cast. Also, Solomon's trade has no support in archaeological finds.[70] So efforts to make sense of how goods were flowing may be futile.

In other periods there are casual references to merchants (sōhēr, rōkēl), although many of them refer to foreign merchants, and another word, kᵉnaᶜani "Canaanite" frequently means merchant. This seems to imply that trade, even local trade, was in some periods in the hands of non-Israelites, and these peddlers may have been distrusted.[71]

References to prices are brief and inconclusive; we are assumed to know that four hundred weights of silver is a lot of money for a field, even one with a cave in it, in Genesis 23, and prices for Solomon's chariots are meant to indicate high finance. But prices of normal items for normal people are rarely noted. Still, there are indications that almost everyone had a little silver, which was carried around in chunks tied up in bundles, and that expenses were frequently paid in weighed precious metals.[72]

Gold seems much less important than silver as a means of payment. Accounting techniques may be seen in Numbers 7, perhaps a very old list of offerings given at the dedication of a shrine by tribal leaders. The order of presentation of the items there conforms to a West Semitic accounting norm as opposed to a Mesopotamian one: the number comes after the thing counted, whereas in Mesopotamia the usual order is the reverse.[73]

The prohibitions against taking interest may have been directed at first only against oppressive loans to the very poor, but they may have been broadened in Deuteronomy 23:20–21 to include all Israelites. This is sometimes seen as a protest by pious thinkers against city practices. The prohibitions seem odd given people's penchant for taking interest on loans in the Ancient Near East, but they are not completely isolated in the first millennium.[74] There is no evidence that these prohibitions were observed, and their repetition implies that they were not.

The prophet Amos complained of "selling the needy for a pair of shoes."[75] The prophets were concerned about the oppression of the poor and especially about taking interest, and an increasingly complex money economy may have been one source of their unhappiness.

Though we lack royal inscriptions from Israel and so cannot usually see what the kings wanted their subjects to think they were doing, we do see occasionally that their economic roles may have been similar to those of other Near Eastern kings. Proverbs shows that they were involved in judicial decisions affecting poor people, though you would not know that if you read only the biblical legal material.[76]

Because the institution of kingship was seen as a late development, it did not have the prestige that other monarchies had, at least in Mesopotamia and Egypt. It was viewed with distrust by some religious people, who felt that concentrating power in the hands of a king was an intrinsically bad thing. We do not know if this attitude actually affected how kings thought about themselves, but it affects the ways in which kings' actions are reported because the biblical texts come mainly from the piety-minded opposition. Biblical texts ignored kings' economic policies and concerns or treated them as if they were part of the oppressive nature of kingship.[77]

Government expenditures under Solomon, especially for chariots and other defense purposes, must have imposed a tremendous burden of taxation, which can be seen as a major cause of the dissolution of the united monarchy after Solomon's death. Many would see the rise of the monarchy as a decisive social break with earlier Israelite history, and it is true that we get information of a different sort when there are kings.[78]

Taxation after Solomon was sporadic and inconsistent, including forced labor and tribute. In late texts there was a tax for the upkeep of the temple.[79]

The question of whether the kings, especially those of Judah, usually had control of the temples' wealth remains open. The kings did use that wealth in times of extreme hardship, but it is rash to see that use as devoid of hesitation and as a kind of standard operating procedure.[80]

David's apparently successful attempt at conducting a census of Israel, the first step toward a rational taxation and conscription system, was condemned by the religious (2 Samuel 24). Solomon's divisions of the land into twelve districts in addition to Judah (1 Kings 4:7–19) may have been as old as David. It seems strange that districts with different agricultural potentials were supposed to support the king's court for the same length of time, a month each year. But six of the districts may have depended on customs duties collected on important roads running through them.[81]

Josiah's religious reform in 622 B.C.E. tried to centralize most aspects of government in his hands, and he also wanted the temple gifts to flow only through his temple in Jerusalem.[82] The Book of Deuteronomy's concern for centralization may have predated Josiah's plans; it certainly conformed to them. Probably part of Deuteronomy was the book that Josiah found in the course of his temple renovations (2 Kings 22:8).

The prophets condemned mercantile activity and loan gouging. They had no consistent economic analysis or policy, but they generally opposed any growth in complexity or impersonality and argued for a return to what they saw as traditional village values of justice and equality in economic relations.[83]

A recent view holds that the prophets of the 700s and 600s B.C.E. were complaining not only about complexity but also about the imposition of a government-directed redistribution system, by which taxes were redistributed to government employees.[84] This does explain the prophetic concern about official wrongdoing, but the evidence for a complex bureaucracy is not widespread.

The ostraca from Samaria, archival inscriptions on potsherds, show a complex system for receiving wine, probably as taxes for a king of the northern kingdom. Some would see in these documents from the 850s B.C.E. an indication of the continuation of the tax districts attributed to Solomon in 1 Kings 4.

The ostraca might also be read as remains of the internal administration of royal vineyards and orchards.[85]

Populist measures attractive to prophets were not put into effect. Isaiah (745–705? B.C.E.) was the only prophet who clearly had access to kings, and the rest of the prophets were not mentioned in any book outside their own until after the exile ended in 539 B.C.E. This may mean that the words of prophets were not influential in determining royal policy, though they did constitute one dissident political group that kings took into consideration. A recent study argues that the development of free-market capitalism might have been accelerated in ancient Israel if the prophets had had a better understanding of the benefits of such a system.[86] Probably no one could have foreseen the economic takeoff of the Industrial Revolution so long ago because of the difficulty of communication and of movement of goods in the ancient world. Though scarcity always played a major role in how human beings behaved economically, the benefits of a broad market can be imagined only when the benefits of a limited market are clear.

The picture one can draw of Israel's social and economic life using the Bible is surprisingly complex, in spite of the dearth of contemporary documentation. A predominately tribal society settled down and dissolved its tribal loyalties, developed fairly complex governmental institutions, and resolved itself into two polities that were eventually destroyed by dint of international pressure. But the society that had been created continued to function on a local level for several hundred years, and of course the moral vision of the society's religious thinkers continues to be important down to our own day, as does the continuation of the society of Israel in the land and abroad.

The national self-consciousness that may have arisen among Assyrians certainly took root in Israel, though we cannot be sure that it appeared before the end of the kingdoms. And it makes sense to place its first flourishing during and after the exile, which we will consider in the next chapter.

Economically conventional wisdom indicates that Israel's political unification under David and Solomon led to a flowering of international trade and of economic life in general. Archaeology shows that this flowering may actually have been later than the united monarchy period, but certainly sometime in the 800s B.C.E., when large military structures were being built on foreign models. Prophets from the next century condemned the oppressions that resulted from an increased economic complexity, the exploitation of the poor by the rich. Though sources do not give details about these developments, perhaps during the 700s, as Assyrians pressed harder on both kingdoms, economic life deteriorated and class differentiation increased. The deportations eliminated the northern kingdom as a political and eventually even as an ethnic element, but they did not basically affect the southern kingdom, the elites of which continued to think of themselves as Judahites, or Jews, even though they later lived abroad and looked toward Israel only as their spiritual home.[87]

Phoenician inscriptions from the Lebanese coast may date from as early as 1100 B.C.E., and the maritime expansion of Phoenicians into the Mediterranean was apparently a later development. Eventually Phoenician colonies grew up as far away as Spain.

The Phoenicians' development of the syllabary has been related to their needs to record trade, and the spread of the syllabary to Greece led to the Greeks' developing a true alphabet in which all significant sounds of their language could be represented. Whether there was a close link between a more sophisticated gold-using economy, proverbial wisdom expressed in writing, and the alphabet remains a question for speculation. Peasant attitudes about justice seem to have been similar in Israel and in archaic Greece if one can judge the latter from Hesiod's "Works and Days" from around 760 B.C.E..[88]

Farther south, remnants of the sea peoples who had afflicted Egypt installed themselves on the coast of Palestine, the name of which derives from theirs. The Philistines around modern Gaza are the best known, but there were apparently people known as Tjekker farther north. They had come from the Aegean area, and they brought a Mycenaean kind of pottery found earlier in Greece, which they then reproduced in their new homes. The Philistines had five major cities, each of which was ruled by a despot, though they may have cooperated in some ways. The Bible sees the Philistines as aggressively trying to control the hill country, where they may first have come as Egyptian mercenaries.[89]

Archaeology has recently shown that the Shang Dynasty, remembered in later tradition, actually did have some claims to ruling central China. The writing system seen earlier in the oracle bones continued, no doubt mostly on perishable material, because there is continuity with the later writing tradition. Shang economy and society were probably divided like the Ancient Near East between the managers and the oppressed. Trade may have been an important element in supplying luxury goods for the court but was not likely to have been the basis of wealth; that was farming. Although iron was smelted as early as the 1100s B.C.E., a systematic technology for it arose only later, in the 600s B.C.E. in China. There is evidence that ownership of land in China shifted from lords to independent farmers between 722 and 222 B.C.E; the term for noble comes to connote moral, not political, worth.[90]

In Southeast Asia in what is now northeast Thailand, society had developed skill in metallurgy, perhaps inspired by Mesopotamia or China or perhaps entirely by itself.[91] Carbon dating puts metallurgy in this period, while excellence in crafts implies leisure for specialization of labor. Therefore peasants must have been creating surpluses.

Because the Indo-Europeans probably had invaded India sometime between 1700 and 1100, we may assume that the period from 1100 to 626 marks the elaboration of the caste system, which may have arisen from the alienation of the conquering people from the conquered.[92] This system, which still dominates Indian society, divided people who traditionally did different kinds of jobs from each other, not in all social interaction, but only in eating and marriage. There was a scale of uncleanness of jobs based on the ritual purity associated with the work, so that warriors, though frequently actually dirty, were regarded as more pure than leather workers, who had to deal with things that were dead. Though there are tendencies toward occupational social divisions in all societies, the Indian carried it to the furthest limit of complexity.

Elsewhere in the world archaeology shows that Indo-Europeans most probably had established themselves in most parts of Europe. And in America some hunters and gatherers had in some places settled down to village life, domesticating local flora and fauna, not in imitation of developments in the Old World but through their own initiative.[93]

The Ancient Near East had already seen two thousand years of written history. But the rest of the world remained to a large extent illiterate and unable to describe in any detail the societies and economies that gave people life and work.

Societies old and new had been disrupted by imperialism, and the entire Near East had been united in trade and in war. We glimpse in the Bible some of the agonies such events entailed. For most people political events were distant and unreal except in times of acute terror. And yet the union, however brief, did open the possibilities of wider contacts and wider consciousness of the world.

1. An artist's reconstruction of an Early Dynastic temple shows the ample space not devoted to religious purposes, for sheep-herding, storage, and community life.

2. Ur's ziggurat, an imposing mud-brick mound, was a center of royal economic organization during the Ur III dynasty and may have had a temple on top, which has since eroded.

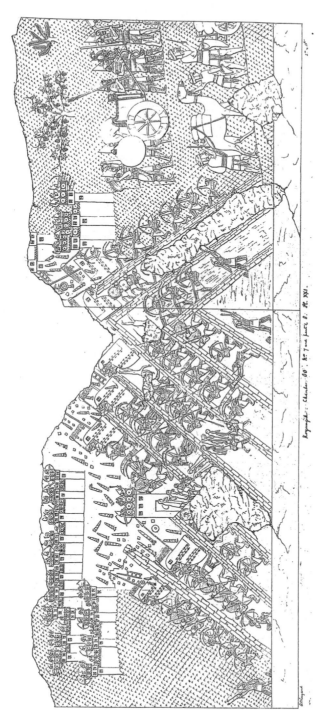

3. This Neo-Assyrian relief shows the attack on Lachish, in central Israel-Palestine; the Assyrian army sought to protect its soldiers with shields and tank-like battering rams.

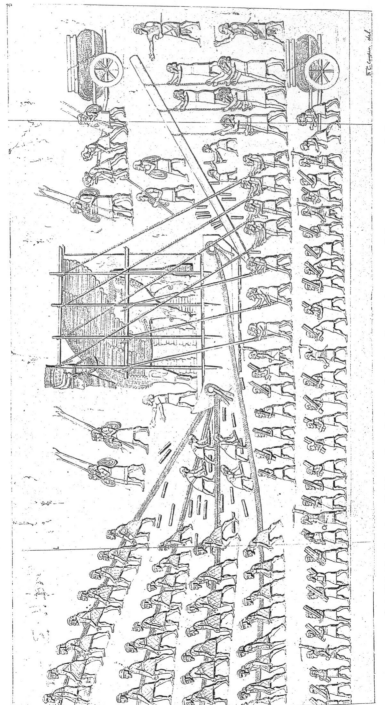

4. This Neo-Assyrian relief shows the techniques of moving a large sculpture on a sledge; manpower was the key.

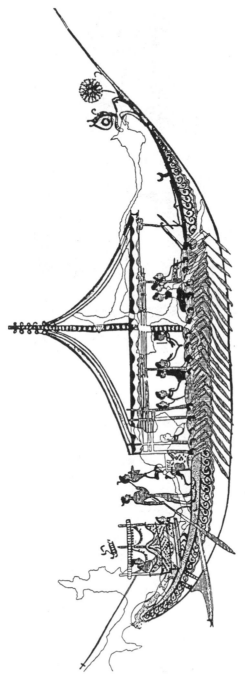

5. A Minoan boat from a wall painting in the Aegean around 1500 B.C.E. shows the technology that made seaborne trade possible, though the use of paddles instead of oars indicates that the procession depicted was ceremonial.

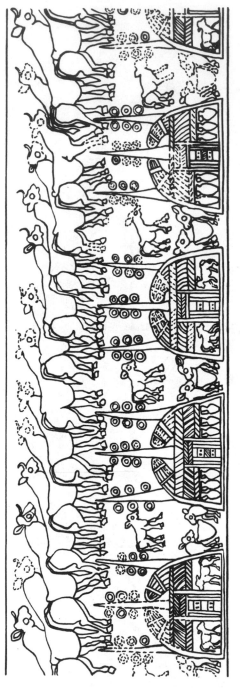

6. A cylinder seal impression from the late Uruk period may show community herds in front of sheep barns storing daily production. The posts with rings were symbols of the goddess Inanna.

7. The most common type of cuneiform tablet is the Ur III receipt for a delivery of animals to the royal cattle pen of Puzriš-Dagan near Nippur.

8. Irrigation techniques are illustrated on this New Kingdom tomb painting from Egypt.

9. The solemn gaiety depicted in this painting from a tomb in Egypt may have been usual in family gatherings, but it was rarely shown.

10. This woman living in a village in modern Syria may face some of the same problems as her ancient sisters.

BABYLON AND A PERSIAN WORLD

626–332 B.C.E.

Politically the Persians took over from the Babylonians in 539, but socially and economically this date does not seem important. One can nonetheless argue that the Babylonian idea of empire was much more like the Assyrian idea than the Persian was. The Babylonians wanted to insert themselves at the tribute-receiving end of the crumbling Assyrian system, and Babylonian leaders did not calculate the considerable costs they might have to pay in animosity from the subjected peoples and eventually even from their own people by continuing Assyrian precedents.

Assyria fell in a prolonged crisis starting perhaps in 627 B.C.E. or earlier and culminating in the assertion of the Babylonian king in 604 B.C.E. of his right to control the lands to the west of Mesopotamia. This king, his descendants, and their followers ruled most of Mesopotamia and the southern part of the Near East until 539 B.C.E. Persian kings based in what is now Iran had joined with the Babylonians and many others in ending Assyrian rule, and between 600 and 539 they ruled the northern part of the Near East, what is now Iran, northern Iraq, and Turkey. But around 539 they turned south and snuffed out the Babylonian rule, inheriting all of the former Assyrian domains. This Persian empire lasted until the conquest of Alexander the Great from Macedonia in 331 B.C.E.

The Persians may have perceived from the beginning that they did not have the aptitude or organization for oppressing vast stretches of the civilized world, and they left most local traditions intact. They did not try to impose Persian values or bureaucracy, but they did want the subject peoples to accept their propaganda, which they themselves may have believed, that the Persians came to bring peace and to foster local heritages, as long as those heritages could be made to support Persian hegemony. Hence the apparent generosity to the Jews, which was probably paralleled elsewhere.[1]

But they were different from the earlier Mesopotamian political structures in another way: they were not centered in either of the great river valleys. They could conform to how kings should behave in Mesopotamia and later in Egypt, but they did not think of themselves as only Mesopotamian or Egyptian kings. They were first and foremost Persians. This situation differs from the closest analogous one, that of the Amorites in the Old Babylonian period, in that the

Amorites never won a united empire that included both their homeland in the west and the cultural centers. That is just what the Persians did. We can see that they were different kinds of kings in their royal inscriptions, which do not conform to earlier cuneiform models even though they are written in cuneiform. Their most famous imperialistic adventures, the attempts to conquer the Greek mainland in 490 and 480 B.C.E., can be understood as efforts to impose the Persian peace on Greek-speaking Ionia, which, the Persian operatives saw, would never be subdued unless influence from the cousins on the Greek mainland could be subdued.[2] What to the Greeks—and to most subsequent Western thinkers—seemed to be the very embodiment of Oriental despotic imperialism appears from the Persian side to be an unsuccessful police action to extend the peace.

In a way this broader Persian view of the subjected territories, their concern for their homeland, which previously had been a cultural periphery, and for the imposition of peace, is the model for the Macedonian expansion begun under Alexander the Great in 334 B.C.E. The Persians had no complex cultural agenda, but it is clear that many elements of Hellenism had precedents in Persia.

In spite of politics, the continuities in Babylonian and Egyptian society of the period seem greater than the discontinuities. And the real breaks for both appear to come two hundred years after the Greeks got control of both places. Those breaks may be more apparent than real, however, because what happened was that traditional ways of record keeping were gradually replaced by Greek written on perishable papyri and skins. In Egypt such things are preserved for us, giving us the most detailed picture of social and economic life in Egypt yet, but in Mesopotamia papyri and skins decayed, and as the cuneiform record dwindled, we know less and less about later Mesopotamian life.

Herodotus, the Greek historian, found it so confusing arriving in a foreign city, even though he had done it many times before. A place to stay, a place to eat— ah, that is the real problem here, something to eat besides that execrable lamb and onions the Babylonians seemed to like so much along with that strange spice, garlic, they had, which they vastly overused—these were the essential problems a traveler faced after weeks on the dusty road. But then, if one didn't know the language—who knew the language?—and if there weren't enough Greeks around, one needed a good guide, and this fellow said he came from a priestly family and seemed to know a lot of things and could make himself understood passably in Greek. Overpriced, of course, but the traveler knew he would end up paying one way or another, either in real cash or in failing to see the really interesting things.

So Herodotus and his guide were off early this morning into the temple precincts of Babylon, where there seemed to be no problem at all about allowing a foreigner to enter and ask stupid questions. And who *were* all of these women? They were sitting out in the temple square dressed in what must have been their most alluring attire, and they seemed to be talking to passersby with considerable freedom. Certainly in a Greek town, even in liberal Ionia, these women would have been regarded as whores.

He asked the guide if they were harlots. And the guide obliged him. Yes, these women were whores in a way. They came to fulfill a vow, or rather, women of a certain class all had to come once in their lives, usually before they were married, to fulfill the vow. And were they whores? he persisted. Oh, yes, exactly that; they had to have sex with at least one passerby for the honor of the goddess, and then they would contribute their fee for sexual services to the goddess's treasury. Herodotus was amazed. The sexual license linked to religious duty was unprecedented in his world. He did not question the guide further about the matter, but they moved on to where some sick people had come apparently to seek the blessings of the goddess for their infirmities.[3]

Herodotus did not believe everything he was told, and he seems frequently to have been in a state of wonderment over the un-Greek practices he observed and heard of; and he was much more interested in what we would call religious history than social and economic history. His observations about the women of Babylon are controversial still because there is no other evidence for such a practice, and certainly not as a prelude or prerequisite to marriage.[4] And yet whenever Herodotus writes of anything, it is of interest even if demonstrably wrong, for he is a foreign traveler in that world who asks questions like those that we might ask and to which we cannot always trust the answers.

The regions that have had surface surveys show a spurt in settlement activity. The growth in southern Mesopotamia may have begun before the Neo-Babylonian era, but it took off as Babylon again became an imperial capital.[5] When the political center moved after the Assyrian demise to southern Babylonia there was a surge in building activity around Babylon and in other southern cities, and their sizes increased.

There were ethnic groups that became important in the period, but probably not any new classes of people that were socially significant. Chaldeans, Aramaic-speaking city dwellers in southern Babylonia, came to prominence under the Assyrians as members of their armies. From them came the Babylonian rulers. The dynasty is sometimes called the Chaldean dynasty, and in older books Aramaic is even called Chaldean or Chaldee after them. There were

Aramaic-speaking nomadic tribes in southern Babylonia, too, and the Chaldeans were adept at marshaling their support.[6]

The Persians themselves were a new ethnic presence in Mesopotamia, Indo-European in language, recently sedentarized, and only gradually detribalized. The distinction between Persians and Medes, a tribal group who were usually associated with them, was apparently clear to them and to people who dealt with them for several generations, but it is not clear to modern students. Though the impact of their administration was considerable on the Near East, the actual presence of Persians in Babylonia and points west was minimal. Persian names appeared rarely in Mesopotamian texts before Darius I had to put down rebellions in the west at his accession in 521 B.C.E., and there were few Persian names even after that.[7]

The recording of names makes us think that the Persian administrative presence was usually lightly felt. Native officials were employed for most tasks, including military ones, and although taxes flowed to the capital in what is now Iran, little in the way of cultural influence flowed the other way.

The unifying of the civilized world under a single suzerain led to the creation of a vast and relatively accessible market, and this attracted other ethnic groups in small numbers to take advantage especially of the labor markets. We are particularly well informed about Greek mercenaries who came to fight for the Persians.[8]

In Babylonia a status of *mār banê* "son of people of quality" may have been the highest and may indicate that a person was free and independent. At the other end of the social scale the temple slave, called "dedicated one," *širku*, could be born free or slave but could not be sold.[9]

As before, the nuclear family was the norm. Study of Neo-Babylonian marriage contracts reveals what we had suspected for earlier periods, that men in middle age married very young girls. Divorce was usually not initiated by women, although Egyptian custom, seen in Aramaic papyri and in two odd texts perhaps from an Egyptian community living at Susa shows women starting divorces.[10]

If women married young, they also tended to survive older husbands. Legal texts show women manipulating property among their children. There was little freedom of choice for women in marriage, and sons too were subject to a father's direction. Women could apparently not appear as witnesses, and it is not clear whether they could inherit.[11]

Another aspect of how some exceptional families thought about themselves is revealed in the families of scribes. Although the practice may begin as early as the Middle Babylonian, it is in the Neo-Babylonian and Persian periods that we have increasing evidence that scribal families traced themselves back to an eponymous ancestor and called themselves "sons of" that ancestor.[12] Usually we cannot say exactly when or whether that ancestor lived, but the ancestors did tend to have long Akkadian names that were stylish in the Middle Babylonian period five hundred years before. This consciousness of distant tradition makes sense for scribal groups, and perhaps this kind of family name was becoming popular elsewhere in the society. We have no other indication in any period of the use of family names. Most people probably identified themselves by reference to their parents or to their places of origin if there was confusion. And although there is much confusion for us because many periods are dominated by common names, there probably was little confusion for the scribes who kept the books.

Herodotus's extravagant tales about the power of queens and lesser women at the Persian court may document what had been going on for a long time in Mesopotamian courts. He told stories of queens acting as regents for minor sons dispatching armies, although they did not lead them. Women in all likelihood were not regarded as capable of being really good rulers, but there is no contemporary evidence of their being rejected out of hand. The Mesopotamian omen tradition docs see in the antediluvian reign of the queen Ku-Bau an unlucky omen. But courtly women were capable of exerting influence and did so, in Herodotus's view, especially in favor of their sons, working behind the scenes to affect the world of politics, which usually belonged to men. Adad-guppi, the mother of the last Babylonian king, for example, lived to be 104 years old, and her piety may have inspired her son's.[13]

The hiring of workers in a market for labor seems more important in this period than use of semifree workers, but there were still taxes to be paid in labor. And there was at least one class of persons, the temple servants, who were not free to leave their jobs. They were paid in fixed rations, and although they were able to marry, have families, and leave small estates to their heirs, they did not enjoy the rights of free peasants.[14]

Actual slaves may not have been numerous, although there probably were more of them than in earlier periods. In contrast to earlier periods, most were of local origin, and natural reproduction, not capture in war, was the source of most slaves. And we see that they could hold a great many different statuses.[15] Their major work continued to be as household servants, but ones who knew a trade or were otherwise clever were allowed to set up their own shops and pay their owners a rent for the use of their time, keeping the rest of the money they made in their businesses. Some of the slaves became quite rich in this kind of setup, and some bought other slaves, who ultimately were seen as belonging to the owner of the slave-artisan. A few slaves became famously wealthy and even made themselves useful as financiers to governments, but such persons could still be sold, for a great deal of money, of course.

We do not know why rich slaves did not simply purchase their freedom. But the status of being a slave bore little stigma and had some advantages, including the ability to count on one's master's political and economic support should fortune turn and perhaps an immunity to being sued directly.

Although these statuses of workers are interesting because they seem anomalous in later human experience, they were not economically important. The free peasants, still largely undocumented because they were beyond the direct control of governments, did most of the essential work in society, paid the taxes, and suffered most when crops failed and armies passed. Free laborers frequently worked for hire and were paid the same as the hire for slaves. But the free hirelings struck when they were not promptly paid.[16]

One kind of hired worker that we have not seen much of earlier was the mercenary, the soldier, frequently from abroad, who was paid to sit in a garrison or to fight in a battle. Mercenaries about whose lives we know most were the Jews who guarded the entrance to Upper Egypt for the Persians at the First Cataract of the Nile on Elephantine Island at Aswan. Letters and contracts in Aramaic written on papyrus have been preserved from these people, and aspects of their land dealings and their intermarriage with locals are revealed. Their connections with Jews in Israel were tenuous, and their religion was polytheistic, although it included worship of the god Yah, who was the Bible's Yahweh, the personal name of Israel's god, usually translated as "The Lord." The Jews complained that their temple at Elephantine had been destroyed, and they asked Persian authorities for the right to rebuild it; naturally, if Jews were concerned with Deuteronomy as we know it, they would have hesitated to have a temple anywhere but in Israel. But theological niceties were not of concern to these soldiers and their families.[17]

The Jewish mercenaries at Elephantine claimed to have arrived before the Persian conquest of Egypt in 525 B.C.E., and their outpost may have been destroyed when native Egyptians threw the Persians out around 400 B.C.E.[18] The Elephantine Jews may have been anomalies in Egypt; still, the scope of the Persian Empire probably scattered other groups across it, far from their homelands but doing the work of empire.

Private agriculture may have continued to be the most productive way of organizing the land. But we have much better documentation about the actions of large corporations manipulating land that ultimately belonged to the government. King Darius around 518 reorganized royal land in Mesopotamia, giving it out to Persians who owed him service. The House of Murašû was a family that for a hundred years in the Persian period leased government land and then rented it out to small producers.[19] And it managed to force the farmers to buy seed and agricultural equipment exclusively from the house. Because the land was highly productive, this arrangement was basically a license for the house to make money, and it was exercised with no concern for the fate of the small farmers. These frequently went into debt to the house and not infrequently were sold into slavery to recover the debt. This kind of oppressive capitalism was possible only with the collusion of governmental authorities, and it seems that the house was well connected with Persian governors, who indirectly may have shared in the profits.

As usual, we do not know how representative the house's activities were, but they let us see how creative middlemen could flourish in the Persian economy. The Persian kings were becoming more dependent on mercenaries and less on people who owed them service, which could be commuted to money anyway.[20]

Another set of cuneiform texts, but from the Neo-Babylonian period, annually gave estimates of a commission sent out by royal authorities to estimate date production before making a tax assessment. Smaller orchards seem to have been the most productive in these estimates.[21]

Private landholding is not well documented, but it continued to be important and perhaps even to predominate. The field plans from the early Persian period appear to be mostly of private plots; land held as fief does not appear. Inheritance texts show that land tended to be divided up among all heirs, leading to smaller and smaller plots.[22]

Flocks belonged to large temple estates in the cities of Sippar and Uruk. Annual summaries show that chief shepherds employed by the estates took in charge thousands of sheep, undoubtedly at the time of the spring shearing. The chiefs then redistributed the flocks to several shepherds who did the actual tending. We are not sure how the shepherds were paid and what their cut of lamb and wool production was, and the matter may have been treated as a private deal between the chief shepherds and their underlings. It is not clear that fishing was a royal monopoly, and it seems unlikely that it was.[23]

Textile production continued to be a major source of export goods and of wealth in general, although texts do not elucidate how it was carried out. Probably there was a mix of government-sponsored workshops and small producers. A labor contract from the Persian period shows goldsmiths agreeing to work exclusively for a temple. It has been proposed that the craftsmen were organized in a guild, but the consensus of modern scholars is that the smiths worked in small groups that were not further organized.[24]

Archaeological remains from Persepolis indicate that Persian kings employed foreigners, particularly Greeks, to create their columned halls and adorn their friezes.[25] Perhaps these artists were slaves, but others may have been attracted to work for the Persian court by the scale of building that was being done and the opulent rewards they could expect.

A small group of texts shows traders from Uruk buying goods to ship to the west to trade for woods and spices and precious metals.[26] Oddly, given Babylonia's continued wealth in wool, the merchants also bought cotton from the west. The texts are few, but because of their standard form they imply an ongoing routine of contact with the west under the Neo-Babylonian kings. And just like the Ur III merchant documents these texts evaluate the goods bought in silver. The merchandise came from Egypt and Lebanon and probably Cyprus and Asia Minor. The merchant received a compensation for his troubles and in addition a payment that was termed a tenth, but in fact his share was much less than 10 percent of the total. Perhaps the trader could sell his share at a profit on the Babylonian market. Metals were the largest items of the consignments, and there were chemical dyes, spices, honey, and wine.

The overland trade texts do not mention merchants by title, *tamkārum*. But several persons with that title are mentioned, perhaps as royal agents buying dates and garlic and importing alum from Egypt.[27] Other texts present agreements to finance trips for trading purposes. Profits may have been as much as 40 percent of capital per year.[28]

From the Persian period we lack merchant texts, but anecdotally we know that similar kinds of trade persisted on an even wider scale because more of the world was under Persian control than had been under Neo-Babylonian. Herodotus narrated the wonder of the roads that the Persians had built to expedite their spy networks from Sardis to Susa.[29] A fast messenger could travel the sixteen hundred miles, he said, in two weeks. But good, safe roads allowed merchants less interested in speed to move from one end of the empire to the other with light and valuable goods.

The traditional economy in weighed silver continued, but it was supplemented by the invention, sometime around 625 B.C.E., of coinage. Coinage was at first merely a way to speed up weighing transactions. Someone in Lydia, a small realm in south central Asia Minor, stamped a design on lumps of metal and thereby meant to certify that it was one unit of the usual weight.[30] This practice led, perhaps immediately, to abuses, as people scraped metal off the coins and tried to pass them off as full weight, but canny traders continued to weigh the coins anyway and to test their quality. The invention of coinage thus seems initially a waste of a government's time, but it apparently soon took on political meaning. The city that could issue its own coinage was asserting its fiscal if not political independence, and its designs could tout its own traditions. The practice of issuing coins spread to Ionia and Greece, and the Persians picked it up when they conquered Asia Minor.

Coinage did not drive out other forms of money, and the political import of the designs on coins was irrelevant to most of the people using them; the weight in precious metal was still the important thing. Gradually, though, coins began to be accepted, even though everyone knew adulterators and forgers abounded. The right to coin was not limited under the Persians to particular cities or even to governments in any way, but the Persian gold darics, so named after Darius I, who authorized them, became the most important large denomination of money in the region, and the Persian silver drachma (from the Greek for "handful") was the most common form of money by the end of the period.[31] Coins issued by other entities, including even the recalcitrant Greek cities across the Aegean Sea, were widely used in the Persian realm. Most of these early coins have been lost because they were later recast into other coins.

Although there are no price series, there are many prices attested, and the general trend of these was upward. Prices for dates, a major product of southern Mesopotamia, for example, doubled from the Neo-Babylonian to the Persian period, and barley too rose in price. But metals, except for gold, became cheaper over time, perhaps because of better smelting or mining techniques or new sources. There also was an inflation in land prices and in rents. The most abundant prices attested are those for slaves, and they rose from forty shekels a slave in the early 500s B.C.E. to fifty before 539 B.C.E. to sixty and ninety shekels before 522 B.C.E.[32]

Why would the opening up of distant markets because of the security of the Persian peace cause prices to rise? It is possible that the costly wars of Persia contributed to the inflation. It is also possible that the fact that foreign trade was made easier and cheaper was not important for the economy as a whole because the things that came from a distance were mainly luxury items.[33]

In spite of the major political transition of the coming of the Persians, it is not clear that there is any change in the governments' attitude toward the economy. The fragmentary Neo-Babylonian legal texts do not mention tariffs or interventions in the economy, and the study of prices does not reveal any government interference.[34]

The Persians seemed willing to rebuild and partially to endow temples, but there are indications that they regarded temples differently from the way most earlier Mesopotamian rulers had. They wanted to tax these pious endowments that in the past had accumulated wealth partly because they owed the government only religious support.[35] Persian administrators were posted within the southern Mesopotamian temples to ensure that the government got its cut. This change in the way governments thought about Babylonian temples dated back to the Neo-Assyrians, who thought of the Babylonian temples as representing a different, if not altogether alien, tradition from their own. The Assyrians and then the Persians had concluded that the large temple estates were productive units and ought to be taxed just like other units, and they may not have appreciated the cultural importance of the temples as repositories of wealth that might be drawn upon in emergencies and for purposes of social welfare. The reactions of Babylonians to the Assyrian and Persian fiscal incursions into temples are unknown: there is a possibility that this change in tax status led eventually to the decline and neglect of Mesopotamian religion. The analogous modern change would be a decision in the United States to tax churches, synagogues, and universities; these are large and sometimes economically productive institutions that loom large on the cultural landscape, but most of them owe their ability to continue to function to their tax-exempt status.

The royal economy is known only indirectly because texts from royal archives remain unpublished. But there seems to be a close connection between the kings and temples. The temple archives known are from the temple of Eanna in Uruk and Ebabbara in Sippar, and both end before 484 B.C.E.[36]

The Persian period was in most places one of economic growth, and some elites in many places may have enjoyed the benefits of the worldwide market, even if peasants everywhere noticed little change. Conditions may nonetheless have been deteriorating around Nippur, about which the Murašû texts give us so much information.[37]

In the relative freedom brought on by the fall of Assyria an Egyptian dynasty that had been fostered by the Assyrians came to the fore. It was centered in the city of Sais in the Delta, and the Saites managed not only to unify Egypt but also to assert Egyptian interests again in Western Asia, resisting the Babylonians for some years and managing for many more to tinker in Palestinian politics and to form a counterweight to the Babylonian interest. Curiously, it appears that the Egyptian attitude toward these pharaohs and successors was not so uncritical as earlier.[38] Kings were seen as fallible, and it was possible that kings could actually go against the will of the gods. The independence of these kings persisted till 525 B.C.E., when the second Persian king, Cambyses, imposed his rule even in Egypt. Another Saite dynasty threw out Persian rule in 404, and independence was maintained till 343, when the Persians reconquered, briefly holding Egypt until Alexander's advent ten years later.

As before, a large proportion of Egyptian wealth was locked in temple estates, and Cambyses, noticing this, tried to curtail temple incomes.[39] Three Persian kings used temple treasuries for their own political purposes, but popular opinion condemned them, as it did the one native Egyptian who is remembered as having done something similar.

There were four classes mentioned in contemporary texts: officials, priests, warriors, and commoners, and the first three frequently overlapped.[40] Besides commoner peasants there were some slaves.

The petition of a certain Petiese, the major source for social history for the period, argued that he should be appointed priest because his father was a priest. Herodotus asserts that Egyptians always did what their fathers did. If that tradition had been unbreachable, Petiese would not have had to petition. Priests were paid well in agricultural products, and many had land allotments from the lands of the temple estates, which they could rent out to make more money. Some priests had multiple priesthoods, presumably because each post involved few official duties. Petiese used a priestly stipend to try to bribe a court official; he had a few spare stipends. Officials continued to combine what we would see as priestly and civil authority.[41]

Warriors may often have been Libyan in descent, and each was granted an eight-acre (3.2-hectare), tax-free fief, officers perhaps being given more land than ordinary infantrymen. Contracts from the Saite period show temple land being rented to cultivators and to ladies and scribes, who planned to work the land with slaves.[42]

Marriage contracts reveal that women had a measure of independence, and most marriages were monogamous. The brother-sister marriages known from the royal house are not found outside it.[43]

Divorce was easy: one party could simply repudiate the other. Fathers had a right to the property and labor even of sons who were grown, and sons had to support parents in old age, although they could avoid it if they could prove that the parents had failed in their own duties. Women apparently had to support parents regardless of how the women had been treated. Every child, whether male or female, had a claim on the parents' estate, and each transaction required that all texts relating to a piece of property be transferred to the new owner. Families therefore kept their own archives, some of which survive.[44]

Because of such archives we know quite a bit about serfs and slaves in the period. A serf was someone who was born into the status, was a prisoner of war, or had been condemned to the status for a crime. A serf was, however, distinct from a slave: whereas the slave owned nothing at all, a serf could own things, though he was bound to the land and required to work for the landowner or his tenant.[45] Although some foreigners were treated as serfs, others were treated as Egyptians simply because they had adopted Egyptian culture. Intermarriage was widespread, as we see in the documents from the Jewish garrison at Elephantine.

Most big settlements, as mentioned before, were surrounded by fortifications, and the congested towns sometimes had houses with more than two stories. The view of Egyptologists is that the economy of the period is "a classic example of the storage and redistribution type" in which the palace organized the whole economy.[46] There were, however, village markets that were not controlled by the state. Such markets dealt in locally produced agricultural goods. We assume that all land theoretically belonged to the crown, but others got grants of the land. In fact, information on the crown lands themselves is slim in the period. The Saites did try to open up more productive land in the Delta, and they seem to have made Egypt somewhat more productive than before. They may also have perfected the use of dikes to keep the Nile back until it was high enough to flood the fields in a controlled way.

Payments seem mainly to have been made in kind. But emmer wheat and silver were used as media of exchange, the silver being weighed as elsewhere, as were Greek and Persian coins. Toward the end of the period there were Egyptian silver coins stamped with both the traditional hieroglyphs and the schematized version of them that we call demotic, or "popular."[47]

An early Saite ruler encouraged foreign trade in order to get timber and incense from Western Asia.[48] And he encouraged Greek seagoing traders to settle in the Western Delta at the city of Naucratis. The first iron smelting found in Egypt was found there, and so it may have arrived with the Greeks.

When the Persians took over, Darius opened a great canal from the Nile to the Red Sea in 497 B.C.E., functioning like the modern Suez Canal. We do not know if it really had any economic impact.[49] Otherwise, the coming of the Persians did not affect the internal administration. Persians used Egyptian administrators for all but the highest posts. The administration continued to be swayed by bribes and overwhelmed with paperwork.

In Israel the coming of the Neo-Babylonians was disruptive of social and economic life. King Josiah of Judah hoped to use the fall of the Assyrians as a springboard to independence, but he was caught in the grinding of international power politics and was killed in 609 B.C.E. by a Saite Egyptian king who was going north through Megiddo to try in vain to support the Assyrians. Judahite kings after that were puppets first of the Egyptians and then of the Neo-Babylonians, who got control of the West after 605 B.C.E. But Judahites viewed the Babylonians as oppressive successors of the Assyrians and rebelled unsuccessfully. In 597 the Babylonians exiled a number of opinion leaders to Babylon, and in 587 they took even more away and destroyed the temple and defenses of Jerusalem.

This exile was the pivotal event in Jewish history because it caused religious thinkers to question their previously land-based religion and to assert eventually not only that the worship of Yahweh could happen anywhere, even in Babylon, but also that Yahweh was the only god there was, and he had a plan that included even non-Jews. Unlike the exiles of the northern kingdom of

Israel in 722 B.C.E., the Judahites were kept more or less together in central Babylonia. Prophets could address them as a group, and they may have brought with them earlier books that they recopied and edited with a view to their present plight. Some of them remained conscious of their heritage and hoped for a return to the land and the old relationship to their national god. Contemporary cuneiform texts show that a Judahite king, Jehoiakin, and his family received rations from the Neo-Babylonian king and was apparently treated with honor and respect. Other Judahites were set up as small farmers in the vicinity of Babylon and began to make new and productive lives for themselves.[50]

Theoretically the exile lasted only till the Persian conquest in 539 B.C.E., and the first Persian king, Cyrus, was remembered in Jewish scripture as having permitted a return to the land of Israel. Few Jews took advantage of the opportunity, perhaps because the exiles and their children—forty-eight years had passed, after all—had established good lives in Babylon and were not eager to give that up. But some did return, and gradually a small community of returned exiles established itself in the ruins of Jerusalem. These Jews lacked political independence, attaining it only in a rebellion under the leadership of the Maccabee family against the Seleucids, a Greek dynasty of successors to Alexander, in 164, and giving it up to the Romans in 63 B.C.E.[51]

The Neo-Babylonian and Persian periods were thus ones in which Israel's institutions, society, and economy were forcibly torn down and gradually and self-consciously rebuilt by those who returned from exile. It is probable that many more Jews remained in the land than were exiled, but the returners always viewed them with suspicion and thought that they had not been so faithful to the old traditions as the exiles had been. This suspicion may underlie the stories in the books of Ezra and Nehemiah about "Samaritans" wanting to help rebuild but being denied the privilege.[52] These persons may not have been quite so alien to the returnees as they were depicted, but they were seen as having given in to the religious forces around them and having intermarried. Even if they have good Yahwistic names, like Tobiah (Nehemiah 4:3 and following = Hebrew 3:35), the returnees believed they could not trust them.

It is important to underline that the sources for this entire period are sketchy and heavily influenced, perhaps more than usual in biblical texts, by later analyses. The books of Ezra and Nehemiah were filtered through the editorial process of the Chronicler, who may have written around 300 B.C.E. with a special interest in Levites and temple singers, a marginal and odd group from whom to get our only view of the history of the time. It is as if the history of New York City were to be written from the point of view of the Radio City Music Hall Rockettes; you would learn some important things from such a narrative, but you might miss some essential elements. As usual, in Israel there is no contemporary documentation, and the prophets who may have been contemporary to events usually cannot be dated. Even the careers of Ezra and Nehemiah cannot be securely dated because the dates of the Persian king with whom Ezra was linked are ambiguous, depending on whether Artaxerxes I or II is meant. Both Ezra and Nehemiah probably worked between about 450 B.C.E. and 398.[53]

The books of Ezra and Nehemiah do allow us a rather gritty view of problems of the returners and furnish a portrait of the society and economy and the efforts of officials to regulate them that is not paralleled earlier. Nehemiah, a Persian governor of Jewish descent, faced the problem of the unequal distribution of income, and the poor complained to him that they were indebted to the rich to pay their taxes to the Persians, and they began to sell off their children as slaves.[54]

Nehemiah lacked policing power to regulate abuses, and he appealed to the consciences of the richer Jews. He said that he personally lent money to the poor without interest, and he appealed to the rich to leave off charging interest. This is the earliest reference to the application of the interest prohibition, known already from the early collection of legal material in the Covenant Code, Exodus 22:25–27. Nehemiah wrote to preserve his own good name, not to show that his policies were effective, and we do not know whether rich people in general accepted his advice.[55]

Nehemiah was more forceful and perhaps more effective in trying to impose the Sabbath prohibition. He had his soldiers close the gate to Jerusalem and forced merchants to move away from it on the Sabbath. Probably Nehemiah saw this prohibition also as a means of giving the poor a better life.

Both Nehemiah and Ezra dealt with intermarriage, and both approached the problem in the same way. Intermarriage apparently meant the marriage of returnees from exile, or rather, descendants of families that could be proved to have returned from exile, with locals who may have been in some sense Jewish but who could not prove that they had been exiled. The pious people led by Nehemiah and Ezra saw this as a problem because of the cultural dissolution that might come if the children of such unions could speak only the language of Ashdod and not the language of the Jews; we do not know how these languages may have differed at the time. And the religious were concerned by the older Deuteronomic texts, which they did not quote exactly but which were clearly known in principle; these texts argued that Israelites should not marry the people they found in the land, or Yahweh would take away their inheritance.[56]

Ezra dramatically prayed in a driving rainstorm to get the Jews to repent of their ways. When some did so, he convened a court that reviewed all marriages in which the spouses could not prove descent from exiles and in a lengthy process that is not described dissolved some marriages. This must have been a traumatic procedure, and even persons of priestly descent opposed it as unnecessary. It was the act of a leader who felt his people threatened with dissolution and believed that only by radical measures would it be preserved. Ezra's acts may not have been popular, and it has been speculated that the Persians recalled him or otherwise ended his authority because of these marriage trials.[57] But Ezra did set the tone for later Jewish exclusivism, one that was to prove effective in preserving the Jewish people as a self-conscious entity. Ezra and Nehemiah were the first persons we see trying to attack the question of who is a Jew, and their answer to the question was clearly the beginning of national self-consciousness in a modern sense, though it had earlier roots.

The glimpses we get of the economy of the Jews in the period—which is usually called the Second Temple period after the rebuilt house of Yahweh, completed in 520 B.C.E., and sometimes the Second Commonwealth—show that it was again predominantly agricultural. The poor borrowed against the next harvest. And although there were traveling traders, they tended to be foreigners who did not understand Jewish traditions as the religious leadership did. Defaulting on loans could lead to enslavement. The preserved stories give no indication about the use of coinage; perhaps it was not widespread in the backwaters of the Persian empire like Jerusalem.[58]

The sources boast of the political support that the Persians gave to rebuilding Jerusalem and even stress that they allowed private contributions and made the Persian treasury available to pay for some temple expenses. But the Jews in the land also had to pay a tax to the Persians. And they continued to resent the political dominance by foreigners even though they did not participate in the few rebellions against Persian rule.[59]

The ending of Persian rule in 333 B.C.E. passed unnoticed in the Bible, although some chapters in Zechariah may refer obliquely to Alexander. The condition of the Jews did not change markedly with the change in governments; taxes still had to be paid to foreign rulers. And Hellenism initially made no impression at all on Jewish thinkers, although it eventually became an important issue for those concerned about the danger of assimilation of Jews to neighboring peoples.[60]

Greece by this period had emerged from obscurity and learned to use the syllabary borrowed from the Phoenicians as an alphabet to write all kinds of texts, but not, unfortunately, many that bear directly on the society and economy. A syllabary reflects consonants with vowels, but an alphabet tries to depict all the sounds of the language that can occur independently of each other.

Archaeology shows that in the preceding two centuries Greek cities had dispatched colonies throughout the Mediterranean. Perhaps initially these were viewed as temporary trading bases, like some of the earlier-founded Phoenician colonies, which tended to be built on easily defensible peninsulas. Phoenicians too had set up agricultural colonies, the most successful of which was Carthage in North Africa.[61]

Greek colonies soon became full-scale farming communities and may have been seen as population pressure valves to which mother cities could send excess people but at the same time retain their allegiance. Marseilles in France, Cádiz in Spain, and several cities in Italy were founded or refounded in this way by Greeks. Thus for some time many Greek cities, even rather small ones, had international networks for trade and were interested in the fates of their overseas relations.

Two of these mainland Greek cities came to prominence in wars against the Persians, and they were seen by later Greeks as embodying elements worthy of emulation, although they seemed in some ways to be opposite.[62] Athens, on the Attic Peninsula, saw herself as a democracy in which all free males could vote on policies and officials. Sparta, in the Peloponnesian Peninsula, was a military aristocracy that required rigorous monastic training for its leaders. The two united against the incursions from Asia, and their success against the Persians led to the creation of two rival leagues, one centered on Athens and one more loosely on Sparta; the competition between the leagues deteriorated after 431 B.C.E. into the Peloponnesian War, which Sparta eventually won. But intellectually Athens continued to be dominant, and Athenian thinkers of the period, Socrates, Plato, and Aristotle, though not originally Athenian, have set the themes for Western thought ever since.

Although documentation on social and economic life is sparse from this time, some aspects of it are known through references in texts copied later. The first and most basic is that all the Greek cities were slave societies and relied much more heavily on slave labor than any of the societies we have previously examined. We must underline the irony of Athenian concern for freedom and that of the other cities in opposition to Persia when citizens' lives were based on the exploitation of human beings they owned. This irony frequently is ignored in modern celebrations of the achievements of Greek reasoning and historiography. Slaves came into Greek society partly as war booty, although there seems to have been a feeling that one should not enslave other free Greek-speakers. Slaves who came from lands to the north of Greece were preferred, and we know of Syrians and other Asiatics who ended up in Greece. At Athens slaves could not testify in court unless they had been tortured; the idea was that slaves were inherently untrustworthy and would lie unless they had given their testimony under pain.[63]

The brutality of the slave system was rivaled by that of the peculiar Spartan class of helots; these were technically not slaves, but they were subject peoples, perhaps descended from the pre-Greek inhabitants, who owed service to the Spartan state.[64] The helots had families and village organizations, but they were distrusted by the Spartan nobility and were subject to arbitrary murder to keep them in their place.

Demographic estimates are more slippery in Greece than elsewhere, but from texts we get the impression that as many as a third of the inhabitants of Greek cities were slaves, a percentage that rivals that in the American South before the Civil War.[65] Many slaves may have had paternalistic masters who were not oppressive, but in Greece alone of the societies we have studied slaves were used in mass work projects, including agriculture and, most notoriously, mining. Private Athenian citizens sent their slaves to the nearby silver mines, where they worked in close quarters under sadistic overseers; the citizens would get a cut of the mines' production and the slaves would get an early death. Why slaves were exploited so extensively by Greeks and less so by others may have to do with the nearness of deserts and wastelands into which slaves could escape in Western Asia and Egypt. They were harder to control there, and so they were not used so much.

Another aspect of classical Greek society that has parallels elsewhere is the increasing racism. From of old there had been a feeling that people who did not speak Greek were barbarians, and yet as late as the Homeric poems from around 700 B.C.E. there was a respect for the Trojans and their allies. But later not only the barbarians were to be despised: even people who were not born in one's own city were regarded as second-rate. The Athenian leader Pericles passed ethnic legislation in 451/450 B.C.E. that denied citizenship to children of marriages between free Athenians and citizens of other cities. This occurred when tensions with Sparta were high, and patriotic fervor was on the rise. Still, a large proportion of the people who lived at Athens were resident aliens, frequently rich merchants, who were barred by the legislation (at least in theory) from entry into Athenian families and the rights of citizenship. As in the Jewish case under Ezra, leaders may have been responding to outside pressures that they saw threatening their traditional culture. It seems doubtful that there was any direct contact on these or other matters between Jewish and Athenian leaders, but they may both have been swept up in a contemporary quest by many peoples for what would eventually be called national identity, something that had not previously existed or had existed only in an embryonic state.[66]

Aristotle was the first to describe the economy as a separate aspect of human society.[67] Aristotle's reactions to what he saw are controversial because they form a basis for Karl Polanyi's idea that the market economy did not exist before Aristotle's time, as we shall see in the Appendix below. Aristotle observed that especially in the Piraeus, the harbor of Athens, resident aliens had taken to speculating on the delivery of goods, to hoarding and playing distant markets to make a profit. And Aristotle disliked the outsiders and especially their ways of making money. So he condemned them and their efforts and advised that a cultured gentleman should seek only what was sufficient for him and his household and not be greedy about making more money. Aristotle's concern was parallel to that of the eighth-century Israelite prophets who condemned the rich and disliked increasing economic complexity.

Further afield, on the fringes of the Greek world the Etruscans had a writing civilization in central Italy. Interpretation of their achievements is limited by the lack of progress in understanding their language, which they wrote in a Greek alphabet. A union of twelve cities developed around 550 B.C.E. and controlled the village of Rome. The traditional date for the founding of the Roman Republic was 493 B.C.E., after Etruscan kings had been expelled from Rome. Greeks were scandalized that Etruscan women participated in banquets with men, and so they must have been relatively liberated.[68]

In northern Greece a new political power arose in the fourth century B.C.E. as a tribal union leading to a monarchy. The family that led the union in Macedonia began to meddle in Greek politics and to take on a patina of Greek culture. The ultimate expression of that culture was that Aristotle, the most popular teacher of his day, was hired to tutor the prince Alexander. His father, Philip, took advantage of the disunity of Greek city-states to install himself as protector first of northern Greece and then of all of it. The son used the fierce devotion of the old warrior families in his court to organize an army of hoplites from the Greek cities, and he was fired by a vision of world union that led him into Greek-speaking Ionia and then on a campaign of vengeance against the Persian Empire beginning in 334 B.C.E.[69]

The Persians did not at first take Alexander seriously, and he was met only by local militias, which he easily swept aside. A battle in western Turkey at Issus did pit more substantial Persian forces against him, but his hoplites carried the day. Alexander marched south, leaving garrisons along the coast, took Egypt, where he portrayed himself as an Egyptian pharaoh, and then headed back through Syria toward Iraq, where in 332 at a place called Gaugamela on the upper Tigris the Persians concentrated their forces. These too he beat, and the Persian emperor fled into Iran, where he was eventually assassinated.

Alexander had vanquished Persia, but he pressed on further east in search of adventure and more booty for his troops. He established garrisons and formed new towns supposedly modeled on Greek city-states: little Greek-speaking islands of soldiers and veterans in the sea of native populations all the way to the Indus River in Pakistan. The world-conquering prince returned to Babylon in 323, fell ill from a fever, and died.

The empire he had founded so quickly fell apart as his generals fought each other for control. The Near East eventually came under the sway of two generals, Ptolemy, who controlled Egypt and Israel and sometimes parts of Syria, and Seleucus, who had the rest of Syria and Iraq. Practically this arrangement obtained from the late 320s, but the Seleucid era of year numbering began only in 312 B.C.E.[70] Alexander's adventures and legacy are a classic case of a peripheral cultural and political power seeking to emulate and then to replace an older and supposedly greater power.

The philosopher Karl Jaspers argued that this period, and the times slightly before and after it, constituted a special time in human history, an Axial Age, as he called it, in which human history turned on its axis to face new directions.[71] Jaspers was pointing out the fact that the seminal thinkers that still affect human thought about the ultimate things all lived at the same time. These persons were not aware of each other, and they came to rather different conclusions about how life should be lived. But Jaspers underlined that they all radically criticized previous traditions in their regions and came to new syntheses. He included the Hebrew Bible prophets, the philosophers of Ionia in the 500s B.C.E., the Iranian prophet Zoroaster, the Buddha in India, and Confucius in China.

There is no way of knowing why they were inspired to act and teach as they did at roughly the same time, but there is the possibility that slight dislocations in climate, perhaps desiccations, led thinkers to worry about whether traditional life could continue as they had known it under current conditions. These thinkers are of interest to social and economic history because they reacted to their contexts but also because they pose questions about the possibility of renewal of institutions that might otherwise be in decline.

Inevitably the Axial Age figures lead one to wonder about cultures in which such figures did not arise, like Egypt and Mesopotamia. Perhaps there were such thinkers, but they simply did not gain a following, or an understanding and sympathetic following, as the other figures of the Axial Age did. For example, the last king of Babylon, Nabonidus, was practicing a new kind of devotion to the moon god, one that alienated the Marduk priesthood of southern Babylonia.[72] He was seen both in Babylonian and later in biblical tradition as a madman partly too because he spent the last eleven years of his reign in central Arabia, building a little Babylonian city there. From Babylonia it did look like insanity, but perhaps it was connected with moon worship or securing southern trade routes when the Persians had the northern trade routes. We will never know the full explanation for Nabonidus's behavior, for he had no disciples. Disciples, of course, might not know the full explanation either, but they might have had a more positive explanation of what was going on than we get from Nabonidus's enemies.

The failure of the oldest cultures to produce Axial Age figures may be attributed ultimately to the rigidity that some observe in the cultures.[73] Access to scribal lore in Egypt was in some periods self-consciously limited to an elite. This may have been less the case in Mesopotamia, but cuneiform writing certainly never became widespread, even though it may not have been hard to learn, if it was depicting one's native language. Scribal elitism was linked to the very ancient organs of culture in library and administrative practice, and these were tied to actual governments and temples. When the governments fell and the temples faltered, fewer and fewer persons felt it in their interest to take the time to cultivate the old skills and the associated values.

These observations ought not to be taken as sufficient explanations of why something did not happen to revivify Egypt and Mesopotamia. We rarely can explain what did not occur, and we have enough trouble with what did. But we can note that maybe it was the very age and grandeur of those two centers that kept their descendants from searching for new answers.

There is no indication that Egyptian intellectuals were conscious of a decline in their civilization in spite of centuries of foreign domination, and the same is true of Mesopotamian intellectuals. Both probably had the view that foreign domination would pass; had not the Hyksos, had not the Guti, eventually been driven out? And do not these foreign kings, wherever they come from, try to behave like pharaohs or kings of Sumer and Akkad? The cultures that did produce Axial Age figures had been shaken by setbacks; those that did not may not have seen their setbacks as significant. Overconfidence may have stopped creative change.[74]

S·E·V·E·N

TRENDS AND IMPLICATIONS

When one surveys so vast a span of human endeavor as we have, one might doubt if there are any trends to be discerned. Most observers have thrown off the simpler nineteenth-century idea that there was linear human progress from ancient times to the present, that human societies and economies have gotten better over time. And yet there is the residual feeling that things have usually gotten better, perhaps only in spurts and unevenly, but in general.[1]

The terminology we sometimes use in characterizing archaeological ages implies some such sort of progress, as one moves from the Stone Age to the Bronze Age to the Iron Age.[2] The idea here is that the "most advanced" elements of the societies had access to the better and more efficient material. And yet archaeology shows that stone materials continued to be used right into the present century, probably because more advanced material was unavailable or too expensive for peasants. So it is only in a rather diluted sense that such peasants could be said to be living in the Iron, or now the Nuclear, Age.

Marvin Powell has argued that the development of technology does change societies.[3] And yet the societies we have surveyed, though they include ones from the Bronze and the Iron Ages, appear to have changed little in response to technological change.

Of course Powell would not argue that this kind of change would be quick and unequivocal and clear in the records. Still, only a couple of possible examples of it come to mind, both from the first millennium B.C.E.: Israel's ability to eke out a living in the hill country that previously had been ignored was eventually if not originally due to improved terracing and to improved techniques of hewing cisterns from rock, the latter perhaps thanks to the availability of iron tools; and the persistence of the Assyrian and Persian empires seems to owe something to the maintenance of roads or at least way stations that allowed messages to pass relatively quickly from distant provinces to the imperial centers.

It may seem paradoxical to argue that technological change was not a major force for economic or social change in that part of the ancient world we have considered in which there was such startling innovation. But this idea is in line with the suggestion that our culture, which fosters the collection and dissemination of knowledge, is the result of the workings of patent and copyright laws that reward an individual for innovation. In ancient times and later, innovations obviously occurred and were sometimes broadly adopted as they proved

119

useful to individuals and societies. But there was no incentive to make one's invention widely known, and as in all societies conservative forces preferred the status quo. In some places this conservatism persisted; elsewhere it dissipated. For example, M. I. Finley traced the lack of enthusiasm in the classical world for adapting technical innovations like the watermill and suggested that in societies in which labor was abundant, innovation was not.[4] We have seen that there were labor shortages but not consistently enough to fuel innovation.

There is a discontinuity between our own societies, in which technological change affects everything rapidly, and earlier societies, in which such change was slower. The Industrial Revolution after 1750 is usually taken as a watershed between the premodern and the modern. Why technological change should have become so decisively denser after 1750 cannot be resolved here.[5] The many societies that still partake to a lesser extent than the Western in the drama of rapid change are by no means premodern in a technological sense, but they do share some aspects with the ancient societies, more perhaps than we do. And so understanding how ancient societies and economies worked may produce some practical benefits as we try to understand non-Western groups.

I. Hahn argued that the brilliance of the cities of the ancient world never penetrated the hinterland, and so the fact that previously thriving centers of civilization like the Near East are now part of the less-developed world is for him not a problem.[6] The cities never were able to export to the countryside the technological advances they had generated, and so the so-called third world has simply emerged from the countryside. This idea is plausible, but it too ought not to blind us to the possibility that the countryside in ancient and modern times did change, even if it changed slowly and imperceptibly to contemporary observers.

Here I want to survey the various social and economic subjects we have looked at to see if there are trends or generalizations to be drawn from them. I do not want the findings of this section to be treated as a sketch of Ancient Near Eastern society as a whole because inevitably telling details will be omitted. But it seems useful to bring together in brief the overall findings in the various periods.

Mesopotamia showed a vast alteration of the landscape because of the use of irrigation. From the invention of writing to the Ur III period around 2000 B.C.E. there was a gradual increase in the sophistication of irrigation and in the extent of land opened up by it.[7] After 2000 B.C.E. the canal systems gradually deteriorated and with them the available arable land until in the Neo-Babylonian period or a bit earlier sites proliferated again, culminating during the Sassanian period, 243–635 C.E., in new and more grandiose efforts to perfect irrigation. The Ur III and Sassanian periods were also most probably the heights of population on the Mesopotamian plain.

We are obliquely informed about the political considerations that led to the expenditures on canals in the Ur III period, but not in the Sassanian period. It is clear that the political unity of the Ur III period deteriorated in succeeding periods, and this may have diminished governments' efforts to maintain canal systems. But probably more complex factors than what governments could do were at play.

The population of Egypt may slowly have grown throughout the period considered. And the central portion of the Near East knew dislocations and advents of people, like the arrival of the Israelites in the hill country around 1200 B.C.E.

A bewildering role call of ethnic groups and social groups has passed before us. In Mesopotamia there does seem to be a trend for seminomadic groups to come from the west down the Euphrates and to establish themselves first on the fringes of the cultivated areas and then to infiltrate, usually peacefully, into the settled land. The Guti, the Amorites, the Kassites, and the Aramaeans probably all conformed to that pattern, although with different political results. The first three groups came to constitute ruling elites in central Mesopotamia, but the Guti were thrown out as soon as possible and regarded as horrible foreigners. The rest were apparently assimilated with minimal pain. The Aramaeans never constituted a ruling elite, although their language permeated everywhere and eventually replaced older languages in the region.

The terms for social groups changed over time, but it is not clear that the basic structure of society really changed. At the top stood the rulers and their cronies, the exploiters of the other groups. Sometimes they arose from a warrior aristocracy, but at other times they owed their power to their connections to priestly families who had control of temple resources. In Egypt there usually was no distinction between what to us seem to be secular and religious power bases, at least before the Third Intermediate period around 1085 B.C.E., and the same may have been true elsewhere.

The nuclear family remained the basic structure of families in the Ancient Near East, though always very rich and very powerful men could coerce families into providing them with extra wives to form polygamous unions. It stands to reason that the extended family of aunts, uncles, and cousins was of importance, especially in the countryside. But the evidence for its importance is surprisingly slim, even in places where inhabitants had only recently settled down from a nomadic life, as in Israel. The connection to larger units, clans and tribes, was probably always fluid and flexible in importance; clan leaders would call putative members together to face a threat, but they might not be heard from otherwise.

It is not clear that there was a deterioration of the status of women over time.[8] The most oppressive conditions about which we know were those legislated for courtly women in the Middle Assyrian period (1400–1070 B.C.E.). The Middle Assyrian noblewomen were not to be seen in public, were always to go veiled, and were to be strenuously punished for deviance. The evidence for these practices comes from a legal collection, and that may not directly reflect reality.

In contrast, rich women in the Old Babylonian period owned land, appeared in court, and gave loans. Some were trained as scribes, although this appears to be the only period in which female literacy is widely attested. In Israel the ideal housewife labored longer and harder than her husband, but she too appears to have had certain legal rights and could take the initiative in economic and personal matters.

The Ancient Near Eastern attitude to women in positions of power was uniformly negative. A queen was a bad omen in Mesopotamia, and the queens regent of the Neo-Assyrian empire went to unhappy fates in later thought, if not in real life. In Egypt, Hatshepsut's inscriptions were defaced, perhaps less because she was a woman than because she inhibited the young king for whom she was regent. And Athaliah, the only queen to rule in Israel or Judah, was remembered for her ruthless purge of her relatives when she came to power.

And yet in Israel Deborah was a noted judge, and Huldah the prophetess was consulted by King Josiah of Judah. Female leadership was not the norm, but it was not impossible. Probably this was the case elsewhere, and no doubt matriarchs were important in the societies of the Ancient Near East, as they still are, in making the really important familial decisions, such as who comes home to dinner and who marries whom.

All of the societies we have looked at used forced labor. It was seen by administrators as a way of taxing peasants without having to resort to forms of money, and sometimes it was used to concentrate labor resources on a magnificent scale and to accomplish in a few years projects that otherwise might have taken generations.

The Mesopotamian irrigation system was at least partly maintained in this way, and the pyramids most probably were built with forced labor. Peasants did not leave records of how they felt about forced labor, except in Israel, where it was controversial; later writers asserted that it was such a brutal means of taxation that it was imposed only on non-Israelites, even in early times. But there are other indications that in Israel too all peasants were subject to forced labor.

Ancient Near Eastern societies also had classes of persons of low status who were not slaves but were also not free laborers. The Ur III g u r u š may have been the most important source of agricultural labor. And we do not know what such persons could do with their free time, if any. It is also conceivable that they were only g u r u š from the government's point of view when they were working as forced laborers, and other times they may have been free peasants. These serflike laborers also show up in Israel, where the *netînîm* of the Second Temple may have been temple-servants who were semifree.

Beyond the semifree were the free peasants, who were important in all societies, although their activities usually were not documented except when they impinged on the governments'. We do not know how free peasants were organized; in almost all periods we catch glimpses of them as the government and the rich attempted to disenfranchise them. Probably the clearest picture of this comes from the Middle Assyrian period (1400–1070 B.C.E.), when well-connected landowners bought out whole families of peasants.

Another clear indication of the importance of free peasants is the existence of hired laborers. In Mesopotamia these are not well attested before the Ur III period, probably because the governments did not need supplemental labor for agricultural work. But during and after Ur III, hired laborers did many jobs connected with canal maintenance and agriculture. They were usually paid no better than the rations of a semifree laborer, and that provided enough calories for a worker barely to subsist.

Slaves, people who could be bought and sold, were not economically important in any Ancient Near Eastern society. Police power was minimal, and these societies were not prepared to adopt the constant vigilance necessary for a slave society to flourish. Slaves came from abroad, brought in as booty in wars or as merchandise by merchants, and they frequently tried to escape or, where legal institutions allowed, to prove their free status. Most rich households probably had from one to five personal slaves who served the needs of the owners within the house, but rarely did the number of slaves owned go above fifteen. Because of their propensity to run away, slaves could not efficiently be used for agricultural work, and few attempts were made in that direction, although there may have been some in the Middle Babylonian and later periods. It is still controversial whether there were slaves in Egypt in all periods, but the indications are that in many periods there were small numbers of persons who could be bought and sold.

The debate over how one defines a slave in the Ancient Near East is not over. Some scholars would assert that the semifree really were not free and ought to be regarded as slaves. It is probable that ancient societies were not interested in precise definitions of social groups, and the loose usage of the term g u r u š "young man, laborer" in Ur III Sumerian may be taken as an example of this. Still, most Ancient Near Eastern languages had a word for "slave," and they made distinctions about what could be done to a slave and what could not be done to someone else.[9] If one wishes to say that the most important categories of laborers in most Ancient Near Eastern societies had a very oppressive existence, that can be easily accepted. But I believe that it needlessly obscures possible ancient distinctions to say that all of these persons were slaves. The term "serf" is probably too imprecise also because it conjures up a European feudal system in which peasants were not only attached to the land and had duties and taxes to render to a lord but also could count on the lord's political and military protection.

In spite of various efforts to find feudalism in the Ancient Near East, no one has demonstrated anything like the European reciprocal relationships in any Ancient Near Eastern society.[10] What has been documented is that in many periods soldiers and other government officials were paid at least in part by being given allotments of land by the government, not necessarily in perpetuity. The officials did not then have judicial authority over the peasants who worked the land. From the point of view of the government such a practice was extremely attractive. Taxes did not have to be collected, and yet the soldiers were fed.

From the point of view of the soldiers, the system involved tedious fleecing of peasants and took time and effort, but if you were assigned a good area, you could count on getting a good living from the effort. Peasants uniformly suffered because they could not easily appeal to the government about injustices, and in a good agricultural year or if they worked harder, they would simply lose more than usual to the rapacious soldiers. Strong kings would insist on reallocating a plot of land assigned as part or all of a salary for government officials and soldiers on the death of their officials.

There was continuity in the way the Mesopotamian plain was farmed over time, given the constraints of the changing irrigation system and population. Even field names used in the Old Akkadian period (2334–2195 B.C.E.) showed up in records from the same cities in the Ur III period (2112–2004 B.C.E.), and it is frequently tempting to use texts from one period to illuminate practices in another.[11] As far as we can now see, this practice is usually legitimate in Mesopotamian agricultural history.

One possibly important discontinuity is increased salinization. Irrigation brings salts and minerals in its water, and as the water evaporates, the salts are deposited on and near the soil surface. If these are not flushed away with a deep flooding periodically, the salts will build up and begin to affect plant yields. In the Ur III and Old Babylonian period (2112–1595 B.C.E.) administrators were aware that salinization was happening; there is mention in literary texts of "white fields." In other periods there was no reference to the problem, and there was no gradual decline in the crop yields. In Mesopotamia the seed-to-grain ratio ranged from 1:12 to 1:20. In contrast, later Palestine's and Rome's seed-to-grain ratio was usually 1:8 or worse, and early modern Europe managed from 1:5 to 1:8, so Mesopotamia was comparatively productive.[12]

It appears that there was private ownership of land in all periods and places, although the Egyptian case is not clear. Perhaps there was a royal ideology that placed all land in the hands of the king, as in the story about the origin of the Egyptian system in the Israelite sources seen in Genesis 41. Other attempts to find evidence that the king was felt to own all land appear to be rooted in later European idealizations of feudalism and not in the Ancient Near Eastern sources. Kings had to buy land, just like other persons, although they had soldiers and money that other people did not have.

The private or public status of the king's land is linked to the problem of whether temple revenues were seen as distinct from royal ones. In a number of instances kings appropriated temple funds for their own purposes, but this usually happened in emergencies. And the fact that the appropriations were remembered may indicate that they were seen as unusual and contrary to the community's sense of what was right. The king could do such things, but he was not supposed to. Does that mean he regularly had access to temple revenues? I doubt it, though I would not rule out close connections between temple and state leaders, especially in Egypt and probably in other times and places.

In the Ur III period there are no land sales. But it seems more prudent to posit a gap in record keeping than to imagine that the Ur III state managed against all Mesopotamian example to impose so far-ranging a decree as the abolition of private land sales. This in itself would be a glaring exception to the general continuities observed in Mesopotamian agriculture. Maybe the efforts of the state to increase irrigation meant that land was available for the taking, and so land would not be sold when it could easily be homesteaded. Land could be rented in all periods, and the rents were low compared to the yields that could be expected.

It appears that many times rich people bought up land held by poor people and destroyed an old agrarian order, replacing it with their own farms. This agglomeration of land, sometimes wrongly called latifundiazation by analogy to the process in Rome, was not made possible as at Rome by the extensive use of slaves in agriculture. And the "broad fields" thus created probably did not remain together for many generations, and neither were they necessarily individually broad because at least in the Neo-Assyrian period large landholders held many small plots scattered over several districts.

Social critics in Israel protested against what they saw as a depersonalization and a rejection of old values inherent in establishing new farms at the expense of old ones. Other peasants similarly disenfranchised probably had similar reactions.

The farming of agricultural taxes, that is, the king's selling to the highest bidder the right to collect taxes from districts, is a feature of first-millennium Mesopotamian administration, though not in Assyria. This led inevitably to abuses as the entrepreneur tried to milk the land in order to increase his profit, and peasants had no appeal to a government that had in effect sold them for the fiscal period. It was likely a source of discontent within the Neo-Babylonian empire, although it was continued by the Persians too, who masked the discontent with more effective propaganda.

The animal resources of Mesopotamia were managed in much the same way in most periods. Sheep and goats were of dominant importance because of the textiles they made possible. And we have similar texts about sheep fattening for food in the Ur III (2112–2004 B.C.E.) and the Middle Assyrian periods (1400–1070 B.C.E.). In both periods small numbers of sheep were isolated by government bureaucrats, fed with grain, and not allowed to reproduce or to exercise. The ultimate destination of the animals in the Ur III period was the temples of Nippur and the royal table; the destination was less clear in the Middle Assyrian period, but presumably the government distributed the animals to its functionaries.

Wool production necessitated the maintenance of large herds composed of gelding males and reproducing females because the geldings bore more and better wool. Wool production did not require the close supervision that fattening did, and such sheep were assigned to independent shepherds who had to report to the government about the progress of their flocks only once a year at shearing time. Ur III Lagaš-Girsu had an archive detailing these activities, which were continued and made more explicit by the northern Old Babylonian herding contracts stating how many sheep a shepherd could keep for himself and how he could make up losses. The story of Jacob as a crafty shepherd in Genesis 30–31 is an Israelite reflection of this practice, placed in an Aramaean milieu in North Syria.

Sheep intended for wool production could be grazed on the fringes of the arable land and in winter could even be driven deep into the desert to take advantage of the vegetation there. Sheep herding was in many ways complementary to settled agriculture, and small children and adolescents may have been frequently used to oversee sheep, as in modern societies.

Other animals attested in the Ancient Near East were probably not so economically significant as sheep and goats. Oxen were expensive to maintain, but their strength was useful for plowing and for clearing land. Keeping them from reverting to a wild state may have been a continuing problem, if one judges from the legal material.[13]

In the Old Akkadian and Ur III periods (2334–2004 B.C.E.) leather work and textile work were carried out on a large scale in government-run workhouses using semifree labor. Indigent women and children especially were used to process textiles, always a major source of Mesopotamia's wealth because they were relatively light, valuable, and easy to export. In other periods it is not clear how these crafts were pursued, but we can guess that when there was a strong government concerned with getting the poor off the streets, the government resorted to workhouses. There is also evidence in the early periods that craftsmen did not work full-time for the government and probably spent their free time working on commissions from individuals; this situation likely persisted later too.

Other crafts were practiced outside government control. Varied products of reed, ever-present in southern Mesopotamia, from sieves to baskets to belts, are attested in lexical lists starting in the Old Babylonian period and continuing to the end of the cuneiform record and to our own day. Craftsmen whose work required a high degree of training and skill—for example, those who made cylinder seals from semiprecious stones—may have worked on commission.

Regions specialized in crafts partly on the basis of the availability of raw materials. Syria, which had more forests and more elephants than it does today, was known for its woodwork and for its ivory carving in the first millennium B.C.E. And Egypt's gold deposits allowed its craftsmen to specialize in that metal.

One might think of crafts as an area of endeavor in which technological progress would be apparent, but this seems not to be the case. The fineness of the craftwork preserved in stone seems to be related to the amount of time the individual craftsman took, not to improved tools or techniques. The two naturalistic revolutions in sculptural depiction in the Ancient Near East, that associated with the late Old Akkadian kings (around 2250 B.C.E.), and that associated with the heretic king Akhnaton in Egypt (1366–1346 B.C.E.), appear to be related to shifts in official ideology, although that is less clear in the Old Akkadian case. Suddenly in both instances the old artistic conventions were replaced by an interest in natural depiction of the human body and of animals. These revolutions had few direct inheritors, and the traditional styles reasserted themselves, though traces of naturalism continued. The Old Akkadian seals were treasured in later ages and not disliked because they were more naturalistic. But in Egypt, because Akhnaton's religious views were rejected, his art was too.

Long-distance trade was almost always a factor in Ancient Near Eastern economic life, but it was rarely if ever a matter of great economic importance. The
amount of goods that moved was always small because of the limitations of
donkey caravans and of small boats, and the number of persons who had access
to the goods when they arrived at their destinations was also small. Usually
only elites had the chance to enjoy fine goods from distant lands. The profit
from participating in such trade was likely to be enormous; the risks of loss
were great, but the prices that could be fetched by rare foreign goods were far
out of proportion to the trouble importing took.

A similar long-distance trade in resins and spices, probably to the west and
to the east into Iran, is attested from the Old Akkadian period in Mesopotamia
(2334–2195 B.C.E.), and the Ur III and Old Babylonian periods (2112–1595
B.C.E.). Although the text genres in which merchants' bosses recorded this
activity cease, merchants were active in the Middle Babylonian period
(1400–1100 B.C.E.), and the international trade among Egypt, Mesopotamia,
and Hittite lands is well documented in Akkadian letters preserved in Egypt.
Also in the Neo-Babylonian period (625–539 B.C.E.) a few merchant texts
show continued importing from Syria and Lebanon.

The Ancient Near East was crisscrossed with natural trade routes, and,
except for the Zagros Mountains between Mesopotamia and Iran and the great
Arabian desert to the south, it had no natural barriers to trade. This ease of
movement allowed the sharing not only of trade goods but also of cultural elements, which propelled the region into urban life faster than other places. If
cities thrive on learning to replace imports with imitative goods of local manufacture, it follows that cities must have imports to replace in order to thrive.[14]
This process was easier in the Ancient Near East than in Greece, Europe, the
rest of Africa, and the vast distances in Asia may have impeded it. So trade may
have been economically unimportant to the centers involved, but in the long
run it may have been a seminal element in cultural change.

It is hard in this connection not to use the language of advance and
progress, and one does sense that some innovations, like the wheel, the seeder
plow, and the composite bow, made of several kinds of wood and thus stronger
than previous weapons, did make things easier for the people who used them.
And the most important innovation of all was the invention of irrigation,
which made settled life not merely possible on the Mesopotamian plain but
actually much more productive than unirrigated agriculture elsewhere. Later
innovations do not seem to have made similar differences. The domestication
and use of the camel in trade, which became widespread in the first millennium, was potentially revolutionary in that it opened up the deserts to trade.[15]

But otherwise, technological innovations that derived from trade contacts seem unimportant.

Precious metals and grain were used as money in the Ancient Near East, and metals were usually weighed and chipped into pieces that would approach the correct price. There was in most places a general agreement as to what things would be used as moneys in what situations. In Ur III Lagaš-Girsu, for example, grain was used as a money for keeping internal accounts by government agencies, but silver was used to pay debts incurred outside the government. Silver was the commonest kind of money in early periods in Mesopotamia, and it remained dominant down to the Middle Babylonian period (1400–1100 B.C.E.), when gold became the most important medium of exchange. We are not sure why this change took place; it may have had to do with the relative unavailability of silver, which must have come from the Iranian hills and from Anatolia. Certainly commerce with Egypt was brisk in the period, and Egypt had ready resources of gold. Late in the Middle Babylonian period and in subsequent periods silver again was the most important money.

In Asia Minor small states began to regularize the lumps or coils of silver around 625 B.C.E. by stamping images on them as if to guarantee that they were equivalent to one of the standard weights. This practice did not eliminate people's distrust of bad metal and the practice of weighing it when it was to be used as money. But it may have made small transactions easier, and it was good political propaganda for the issuing cities. Coinage caught on not only in Asia, where the Persian king issued coins, but especially in Greece, where Athenian coins were valued for their fine workmanship as well as their purity, which was made possible by the silver mines near Athens.

Prices showed considerable stability in early Mesopotamia, and some staple items, for example, the wool that Mesopotamia produced in abundance, carried the same price from the Ur III period (2112–2004 B.C.E.) to the Neo-Babylonian (626–539 B.C.E.).[16] This stability in some prices has led scholars to assert either that such prices were set by governments or otherwise had been traditionally established and were not responses to shortages in a price-making market. Other prices did change, and the mere fact that they were considered worth recording indicates that scribes were aware that they might change.

The world's earliest price series, from the Ur III period around 2030 B.C.E., showed stability. But there are indications from the capital city of Ur toward the end of the period that scarcity was sending prices skyrocketing. Prices from Old Babylonian times did not come from a series, but there seems to be a long-term inflationary trend, especially toward the end of the period.

We can say little about price trends again until the Neo-Babylonian and Persian periods (626–332 B.C.E.). Prices in the intervening periods have never been systematically collected and studied, and most of the Middle Babylonian texts remain unpublished in museums. In later times we find a general inflation in price levels that may have derived from the expenses of Persian frontier defense or other costs of empire. It seems to be paralleled, however, by inflationary pressures in Greece, which may have arisen when former colonies and trading partners of Greek cities learned to replace Greek imports with goods of local manufacture.[17]

It is not possible to compare ancient prices to modern ones because prices depend on the whole economy of which they are a part. Setting a standard of what a worker is paid for a day's labor may be helpful, but, as we know from our own experience, this varies widely in modern economies even for workers doing the same work, sometimes depending on whether the worker is female or male.

Ancient inflations, like modern ones, probably most affected the poor and made life even more difficult for them. We do not get frequent descriptions of economic crises in the Ancient Near East, and it is possible that people did not perceive them in the same way we do.[18] But it seems likely that decisions about abandoning village sites and associated arable land frequently were made as responses to such crises, just as decisions about opening up new irrigation projects can be seen as expressions of faith in the economic system's ability to accommodate expansion.

The introduction of coinage apparently did not affect inflation or deflation, but it may have made economies that became dependent upon coinage a bit less flexible than they were before. If there was a shortage of silver in multimoney systems, one could switch to grain or something else that had been less used before. But if one came to expect coined precious metal, and there was a shortage of it, inflation could quickly result, although other imbalances could cause inflation too. The existence of multimoney systems may explain why in normal times there was little inflation: if there was a shortage of one currency, people would use another.

Throughout Mesopotamian history rulers claimed that they intervened in the economy to make it more just for the poor, and they boasted of low prices. The ruling elites believed that the government should be concerned for the general economic well-being. But there is no evidence that kings actually managed to right economic wrongs or to regulate prices.

One possible exception to this generalization is the decrees of the king in the Old Babylonian period (2004–1595 B.C.E.). References to these decrees in sales and loan documents imply that some contracts were to be made fairer to a weaker party on the basis of the decrees.

All kings gave commands, some of which had economic implications. But usually Ancient Near Eastern rulers lacked mechanisms to enforce their wills in the marketplace or to interfere with other kinds of exchanges. The fiscal powers of the governments to direct their purchasing in ways that might encourage certain sectors of the economies were exercised, as when the Ur III kings encouraged sheepherding. In no Ancient Near Eastern society, it seems, was there an office like that of the Hellenistic *agoranomos* "market supervisor," whose functions were filled by what the Arabs called a *muhtāsib* "auditor."[19]

It is not clear when the royal authority could call on the police to help patrol economic crimes. The police may have been indistinguishable from the military, as their shared title shows, Sumerian a g a-u s, perhaps etymologically "crown follower," which in Akkadian is equated to *rēdû* "follower," frequently translated "private soldier."[20]

In the Old Assyrian trade of the 1900s B.C.E. in Asia Minor the *kārum* "quay," a board of merchants that supervised trade, had authority to declare unjust deals void and to insure that their home city's interests were served. And its leaders did use force as well as persuasion to enforce their views. But was the *kārum* a government? It acted like an Assyrian consul in each city in which Assyrian merchants were established, and it seems to have been sensitive to directives from home. Its activities cannot help us extrapolate customary governmental intervention back in Assur.

In some periods there was a tension between the state or the king and temples. This tension was mostly absent in Egypt, where secular and religious offices were held simultaneously by the same person. But in Mesopotamia when Sargon appointed his daughter Enheduana to run two major southern temples around 2300 B.C.E., he used the economic power of those institutions for his own political ends. Also under Hammurapi around 1760 B.C.E. there may have been an effort to get temple officials to define themselves, in their seals at least, more by their relation to the king than by their relation to the gods.

When scholars believed that temples owned most land in early Mesopotamia, they thought that the kings gradually usurped authority and land from the temples. Now that we know we have only a partial view of early landholding, we cannot be so sure about this trend, but it still seems likely that rulers did try to assign members of their family and their lackeys to priesthoods and to assure that the economic policies of the temples coincided with their needs.

In later Mesopotamian history there was a shift in the way governments dealt with the temples. Until Neo-Assyrian times most rulers viewed the temples as pious foundations that served both a public need in taking care of the

indigent and the unemployed and a spiritual need in assuring fertility and success. Temples were thus worth spending money on and were not directly taxed.
Their clergy were usually exempt from taxes and from forced labor. But the
Neo-Assyrian kings saw some of the temples as large estates that were generat-
ing profits and began to tax them. This process was carried to greater extremes
by the Persians, who had, as foreign rulers, no special affinity for Mesopotamian religion, and they stationed commissars within the temples to assure
that the king was getting his share of revenues. At the same time a feature of
Persian propaganda was the provision for rebuilding of temples and their maintenance, ostensibly from the royal coffers. But these initial expenses for rebuilding would have been minimal compared to the taxes collected. This may mark
a major shift in the taxing policy of the government and may have over the
long run led to the decline in the practice of Mesopotamian cults; they were no
longer being officially encouraged in the way they had been for millennia.

The sources for the social and economic history of Egypt in most of its first
two millennia of writing are so scanty that it seems cavalier to try to spot
trends. An early period of technical innovation, inspired obliquely by models
from Mesopotamia, led to the creation of a market for luxury goods, which
after that did not much change. In the Old Kingdom (2700–2200 B.C.E.) society knew great social mobility and perhaps ferment, but after that, creativity
seems not to have been valued in any field. The internal breakdown of the First
Intermediate period (2200–2000 B.C.E.) encouraged local leaders to take
responsibility for their regions, but the period ended with one leader imposing himself as king. This appears to have happened again after the Second
Intermediate period (1800–1600 B.C.E.), although the cause of collapse is usually attributed to foreign invasion. Egyptian society presented itself as unchang-
ing, and in some senses it may have been; sons did usually succeed fathers in
professions in all periods. Social mobility and economic creativity may have
been discouraged after the Old Kingdom.

This is certainly not the vision one gets, however, from the papyri that
reflect Egypt in the Hellenistic period (333–30 B.C.E.).[21] These show a striving,
self-conscious group of capitalistic exploiters renting out their land to peasants
for profit. Slaves and former slaves were able to climb the economic and the
social ladders. It is unlikely that this bustling society was the creation of the
Greeks. It is much more probable that our official Egyptian sources for earlier
periods ignored what did not fit into the old paradigms, and so we are only
partially informed.

The society of the people of Israel began as a collection of nomads who were
in the process of sedentarizing, who infiltrated into the hill country and lived on
land that previously had been considered worthless. But they must also have

been joined by sedentary peoples from elsewhere because they had the technology of terracing and of cistern building, which made the land more habitable. These peoples gradually loosened emotional bonds to tribes and allowed one tribe, first Benjamin and then Judah, to dominate the others and to form a state in reaction to external threats. This state was unstable, and within little more than a century it fell apart. Israelite self-consciousness was probably a result of that state's success along with the critiques by religious intellectuals of its failures.

It is unclear whether the Israelite state under the second king, David, actually controlled a larger empire. The archaeological glories that used to be interpreted as Solomon's may be better seen as signs of prosperity in the next couple of centuries.

The political dissolution of the united monarchy did not lead to a fissure in the society, as the activities of prophets in north and south show. Relative prosperity came to the north at least in the 700s B.C.E. perhaps because of the proximity of trade routes and of the Assyrians' diminishing interest in the area. This prosperity heightened class differences and led prophets to condemn oppression of the poor by the rich.

Perhaps because the northern kingdom succumbed earlier to Assyrian exile, the southern piety-minded elite became more self-conscious about traditions. When Babylonians deported opinion leaders in 597 and 587 B.C.E., some were ready to assert the importance of the tribal past, seen as a simpler and juster order of things.

When Persians decreed that return to the land was possible, few Israelites, now properly Judahites or Jews, did return. Life was too good for most in Mesopotamia. But those who did return attempted to reconstruct a pre-exilic society. The surrounding population was seen as being hostile to Jews, and this led religiously minded leaders to try to enforce prohibitions against intermarriage, work on the Sabbath, and taking interest. The leaders were not successful in recreating an earlier utopia, but they did contribute to the body of tradition that allowed Jews to maintain their identity regardless of where they were and what social positions they might find themselves in.

In the rest of the world, the complexity and variety of social structures increased. As far as we can tell, China began somewhat like Mesopotamia as a string of despotisms along the major rivers and became a rambunctious, competitive society dominated by great landholders, some of whom politically united the whole sedentary population within their control.

In India, the Harappan civilization had perhaps borrowed the idea of writing from Mesopotamia and created complex docks and cities to profit from seaborne trade. Invading Indo-Europeans about 1700 B.C.E. transformed the society they found in the Indus basin into one with rigid classes defined by heredity since the invaders disdained intermarriage with the locals. These classes were seen as castes or breeds of people and were further defined over time as occupational categories.

Greece had also been touched by Indo-European invasions but emerged much less quickly than India into complexity. Large landowners slowly ceded some of their power to their neighbors and created a society in which some cities were more or less democratically governed by members of old families. Newcomers and foreigners were allowed to enjoy the fruits of the cities in marketplaces but had no voice in politics (etymologically "city-matters"). Also slaves, on whose labor the society grew to depend, were excluded from decision making.

On the fringes of the Greek world Macedonians shed some of their tribal organization and by military force managed to unite Greece and then quickly around 333 B.C.E. to conquer Egypt and most of Asia. This conquest did not lead to political unity, but it did spread Greek culture to some cities, which were populated with veterans of the Macedonian armies. The contacts between such cities led to a continuation of the Persian world-economy, which spread beyond the areas formerly dominated by the Persians themselves.

Human beings outside of the areas we have considered here were probably at least slightly touched by developments in the Ancient Near East, India, and China. Gradually, coins appeared and were treated at first as luxury goods and eventually as money. Other technological innovations, especially the plow and the wheel, also filtered out to the fringes of the civilizations and made work slightly easier and more productive for peasants who had never heard of Babylon.

Earlier I expressed the hope that a survey of social and economic history might generate a new scheme for periodization of Ancient Near Eastern history that was not exclusively political. But it now appears that further work will be required to argue that there were larger unities that ought to be treated separately.

It does seem sensible to see in trade a possible indicator of openness to markets and a general out-turning of economies, even if interregional trade did not have major economic importance directly. In this view the Old Akkadian through the Ur III periods, 2334–2004 B.C.E., constitute a unit, although it might be argued that in at least some of the Old Babylonian kingdoms this trade continued, so that the date for a break ought to be lowered to 1595 B.C.E. or a bit earlier. We have only unsystematic records of trade from 1595 through to the Neo-Babylonian period around 624 B.C.E., and that is a very long time to posit an in-turning of economies, and it is much too long a period to be a meaningful one.

Others have proposed that a decisive break in economic life occurred in the

Early Old Babylonian period, when private ownership of land becomes much clearer in the record. But I am less sure that the change in availability of records really marks a major change.[22]

IMPLICATIONS FOR THE FUTURE

Our considerations lead us to wonder about questions of ultimate importance, questions that do not have clear answers. Here we will consider three of them and hope that on the basis of the sketch and the bibliography provided other students will be able to examine questions that come to light in new research. The questions we will study are (1) What can be learned by looking at traditions that last a very long time? (2) What causes ultimate declines? and (3) How did societies and economies manage to endure such a long time?

Beginning with Marc Bloch and Lucien Lefebvre and others associated with the journal *Annales* in the 1930s, French historians called attention to the benefits to be gained by studying phenomena that last a very long time to elucidate the long-term rhythms of life. This works particularly well in studying agricultural and economic phenomena, like the impact of climate on economic life as perceivable in the French grape harvest, for which records exist over several hundred years.[23]

This approach involves looking for underlying causes of events or conditions surrounding them and necessarily neglects unusual events of short duration that may have no direct physical result, for example, a change in the way people thought about the stars or about political freedoms. Some students of long duration, to translate the French *longue durée*, might argue that phenomena that do not last a long time are not so important as ones that do and would slight intellectual for other kinds of history. Others have criticized the search for phenomena of long duration as prejudicing the question of whether there was fundamental change even in areas in which the physical determinants do not change, such as farming in France before the revolution; people who study the long duration mostly assume that there was no real change, but it can be shown that in that assumption they were wrong.[24]

In the Ancient Near East we have phenomena of much longer duration than the French *Annales* school usually studies. At best, its series of data may cover seven hundred years, but more usually only three hundred. In the Ancient Near East individual series of texts and prices run for less than a hundred years, but phenomena can frequently be studied over periods of five hundred years and sometimes even for the whole length of cuneiform culture, as in the case of sheep management. The advantages of studying phenomena of long duration ought therefore to be magnified in the Ancient Near East, although the disadvantages also will be.

One disadvantage, that studying things of long duration ignores intellectual developments, is exacerbated by the fact that people in the Ancient Near East rarely wrote down reflections about how they thought. There seems to have been a continuing gap between the workaday world and the world of the scribe with its maxims and dictionaries, omens and hymns. And it must also be admitted that Assyriologists have rarely addressed questions of long duration except along broad and synthetic lines similar to what I am doing here. Comparative sheepherding over the long duration has not been studied, though sheep fattening has. Certainly other aspects of economic and social life deserve to be addressed in a way that will use data from several different periods and keep open the possibilities both of change and of continuity; trade, nomads, and bureaucracy, for example, deserve to be studied in that way.[25]

The advantage of studies that focus on phenomena of long duration is that we will be able to see how similar institutions respond to crises and other, more subtle changes. It may well be that we will not be able to generalize and to seek rules that explain the behavior of institutions, and we will probably find that apparently commensurable sets of texts are not really so similar as they seem. But when we discover that there are similarities in responses to change, we will be able to factor out brief and unrepresentative texts reflective of odd developments.

The sweep of Ancient Near Eastern history raises starkly question 2, Why do civilizations decline? This question becomes acute for us living in the West today because of the pervasive feeling that somehow our way of life is in decline, even while millions in the world aspire to emulate it or to appropriate parts of it without destroying their own traditions. A recent book has argued that imperialisms always overextend themselves, take on too many responsibilities in distant places that the home country cannot really afford.[26] It is not clear that that is the lesson to be drawn from the history of the Ancient Near East. Empires expanded, sometimes beyond reasonable limits, and yet the results are not always what might be expected. The Assyrians may have been overextended in taking Egypt, and yet at the end it was the Egyptians who tried to shore up the empire, unsuccessfully. And although it may have been the long distance to Egypt that tried the resources of the empire, it appears that political opposition from nearer home, from Babylonia and from Iran, was what toppled the state.

Some decline may be traceable to a change in the way temples were financed. Through most of Mesopotamian history temples were seen as pious foundations that served a community purpose and as such were exempt from taxes and other governmental interference. But the desperation of the Neo-Assyrian and Neo-Babylonian leaders and the indifference of the Persians to Babylonian tradition led to government taxation and supervision of temples. This did not immediately lead to a decline in interest in them, to the extent that the populace at large was interested in the state's religious observances — always a moot point in Ancient Near Eastern history. But it did mean that fiscal weight had been thrown against their continuance. The traditions that temples purveyed did not immediately die out, but as employment in them became less lucrative, bright young Babylonians must have turned elsewhere for employment, and the intellectual capital of the temples declined. This fiscal decision is not a sufficient cause for decline, but it does seem to be one factor of importance.[27]

States may decline, but such decline may not say much about the fates of economy and society. These are more closely linked to what one might call culture, and culture is, however defined, much more persistent and long-lasting. A rough-and-ready definition may include writing systems, and yet writing systems are not all there is to any modern or ancient culture. To use a modern and radical example, when Atatürk abolished the old Arabic writing system for Turkish in 1928 and chose a modified Roman system, he was self-consciously hoping that his culture would turn its back on its past. And, although many things have changed in Turkey since 1928, it cannot be said that he entirely succeeded; religion, for example, is still a force even though the political elite might wish it were less so. In the ancient world, too, culture is sticky to define and elusive. But it is likely to be much more important to society and economy than states.

Did the bright and young turn to Hellenism as a cultural alternative? Certainly not early in the Persian period, and probably not later either. As recent study has shown, even the adoption in a family of Greek personal names did not necessarily mean that the family members stopped appearing in cuneiform documents and behaving traditionally in their economic wheeling and dealing.[28] This implies that we really do not know what it was to be Hellenized and that there must have been many degrees of assimilation to Greek culture. At any rate, the Hellenization of Ancient Near Eastern cities may always have been superficial, affecting only the educated few at the top of the social pyramid. It is important to remember that on the level of popular culture Greek probably was not widely spoken outside the cities, and Syriac, the later form of Aramaic, was always more widespread than Greek.

What seems to have happened is that the culture slowly moved away from old norms. Having foreign rulers helped, but it was hardly an important aspect of the changes. Instead, the rise of alternative cultural norms, embodied in

Christianity in the West and Zoroastrianism in the East, eased out some of the old ways of acting. But this is the old intellectual argument, as old as Gibbon, that Rome fell because Christianity weakened it. In society and economy the new religions were not innovative. Instead, the religions underscored language change that reflected cultural change. A corollary in the economic sphere might be coinage, but we ought not to see coinage as an important innovation affecting masses of people in ancient times.

If we do not know the precise combination of forces that led to decline and ultimately to people's forgetting how to read Egyptian and cuneiform, we can still ask question 3, How did these civilizations manage to endure as long as they did? Certainly there is a self-conscious steadfastness in the intelligentsia, especially in Egypt, that was an important force for cultural continuity. The conservatism of Mesopotamian scribes was also a source of strength for the old ways of doing things. Less clear but still important was a willingness to adapt to new situations, especially political ones, when new rulers arrived from the hinterland and had to be taught how to behave as Egyptian or Mesopotamian monarchs. It seems clear that Egyptian intellectuals in the late period did not at all feel that their civilization was in decline.[29] Some things had changed; the kings were no longer so consistently seen as good as they had been in earlier ages, and perhaps there was a sense that the moral man could be moral even outside government service if he conformed to right order. But serious Egyptian scribes never thought the Greeks would in any sense replace the grandeur of Egyptian tradition. And the Greeks did not do so directly; they merely opened Egypt up to a new writing system and a new religious tradition that eventually replaced the old.

In both Egypt and Mesopotamia the process of decline of culture, the forgetting of the local written traditions, was one that went on for centuries. A contemporary might well not have noticed that it was happening, whatever the political order of the day.

We may conclude for our own times, in spite of the obvious discontinuities in access to literacy in the modern and ancient worlds, that our modern Western concerns for literacy are serious ones, but probably only if they continue for generations. A civilization endures, or appears in the written record to endure, only if it replicates its written traditions through education.[30] There is a certain obviousness and oversimplification in focusing on writing systems, and a certain ease because they are easy to detect, and yet for the ancient world the writing systems do seem to embody something important in the cultures.

Beyond these broad questions, which will always be of interest and will never be resolved, there are some trends we can observe in Ancient Near Eastern societies that may indirectly have contributed to the decline in the literate traditions. In the societies there may be an increasing openness to new peoples and to peoples from lower classes in positions of power. Most people probably continued to inherit their jobs and their status from their parents, especially in Egypt. But the social flexibility that allowed even slaves in the Neo-Babylonian period to wield power may have appeared elsewhere. Such openness contributed to decline if the new power brokers failed to assimilate old values sufficiently and brought in too much of their own previous traditions. But it might also contribute to cultural resurgence if the newly enfranchised accepted and asserted old values. What is too much of the new was, of course, a culturally determined decision that only local snobs could make.

In economic life there appears to be development toward more reliance on and trust in markets.[31] And the markets especially of the Neo-Babylonian and Persian periods in Mesopotamia seem to have been much better informed and more responsive to shortages and gluts than earlier. To some extent the markets may have been better and more reliable because of the political union of the civilized world created by the Persians.

If, as appears to me, we can assume among the ancients a great deal of economizing behavior even if markets in their modern-day trappings are not always present, we can use the insights of modern economists to illuminate aspects of this distant past. This does not exempt us from close study of the particulars in the Ancient Near East, but it does suggest that the mastery of our long durations may, if properly studied and presented, have more than passing interest for others who study other places and times.[32]

EPILOGUE

The young man's Grandpa insisted that he do it, so he did: make another copy of the same astronomical text, until he got it right. "And if you see Venus rising with a blush, it means misfortune. . . . " Seriously, there were so many little signs in each line that it was easy to get a couple wrong, and then the old man would be roused from his studies and look at him fiercely and jabber on about how important this all would be in his future.

He knew it had been important in the past. He knew his family had been famous and had made its living from drawing up cuneiform tablets for people. Later, its members simply supplemented their income from managing farms by being secretaries occasionally, but the problem was that it took the same amount of time to learn the writing system as it had before, when it was more lucrative. Nowadays no one came to ask Grandpa to make up a document.

His cousins, he knew, were not learning cuneiform at all. Grandpa was upset with their father, but their father said there were more important things for young men to do. They could go to the gymnasium and practice their wrestling; they could memorize Greek poetry instead of this silly old stuff that nobody cared about any more. Nobody but Grandpa.

During the Seleucid era, this, perhaps, was the dilemma facing generations of several families in the southern Mesopotamian city of Uruk, where, as far as we now know, cuneiform writing had begun. Their city and their families were confronted with Hellenism, a feeling that Greek things were better, more coherent, and more worth pursuing because they allowed entry into a much broader world than the traditional learning did. True, the Seleucid kings themselves did not control all of the Near East, but if one knew Greek, one could read things current in all the other Near Eastern kingdoms as well as the classical literature from Greece itself. Being able to write in Greek opened to the young man the possibility of rising in the government hierarchy or even becoming a world-famous writer in his own right. And it appears that Seleucid rulers did insist that some taxes be paid—and recorded—in the Greek manner, on papyrus, rather than in cuneiform fashion.[1]

Some non-Greek writers sought to put their local traditions into Greek for the Greek-reading public.[2] The earliest of these may have been Berossos, said to have been a priest of Babylon, whose work is preserved in fragments quoted in the Christian historian Eusebius. We also have part of the work of Sanchunjathon, a Phoenician, preserved in the same way. And most famous and latest of all is the work of Flavius Josephus, a rich Jew who wrote Greek histories of his people that were intended to show how their traditions were old and wonderful and ultimately compatible with Greek ideas.

Hellenism is an elusive thing to define, and in any particular time and place it may have meant little. And yet those who advocated it thought of things Greek as offering an international medium of understanding throughout the civilized world that Alexander had connected. Local traditions that were resistant to inclusion were mostly ignored except in those rare cases in which political rebellion followed cultural resistance, as among the Jews in the Maccabean revolt of 167–164 B.C.E., and more subtly when Iranians accepted Greek art but clung to their own religion.[3] Though Hellenism did not vanquish all other cultural forms anywhere, it did present to intellectuals a self-conscious alternative against which they sometimes felt forced to justify their own traditions.

In a sense Hellenism can be compared with the force of Western and particularly American popular culture in the world. Americans may not be calling Islamic or Hindu values directly into question and may not even be aware of the smaller local traditions affected, but jeans, Coke, and rock 'n' roll permeate places where the theory of capitalism has never been heard, and everywhere they offer a potentially threatening alternative to the older traditions. People imbued with old, self-conscious traditions may reasonably conclude that this, too, shall pass, but their adolescent children may not be so easy to convince. Naturally Hellenism lacked the mass media as a conduit for teaching its values, but its effects seem similar to those of westernization.

Everyone in the civilized world had in one way or another to come to terms with it, and what usually happened was that elements of it were everywhere assimilated, though not always the same elements. We have as the millennium turns a great many traditions, perceptible especially in art, that might be called Graeco-X traditions, certainly not mainland Greek traditions but reflecting the concern for naturalism or athleticism that Hellenism advocated.[4] And these traditions existed in places where Macedonian political power had never stretched, apparently because of the feeling that this was the new wave, that any ruler who was really up-to-date would have a few Greek-trained artisans on hand, along with the scribes, soldiers, acrobats, and what-not, whose presence is harder to document but was probably a lot more impressive for those at court.

From the societies we have studied emerged others about which usually much less is known because cuneiform writing on clay was abandoned. The exception to this rule is Egypt, where we begin to get masses of papyri that record in detail the vicissitudes of Egyptian agriculture. Elsewhere only archaeology and later tradition hint that the Parthians who came from Iran to overwhelm the Seleucids in Mesopotamia in 143 B.C.E. were devoted to Zoroastrianism. Parthian rulers were replaced in 226 of our era by other Iranians, the Sassanians, who came from Fars in southern Iran and saw themselves as preaching a more pure form of Zoroastrianism.[5] It was the Sassanians who brought the irrigation system to perfection, opening up more land to occupation than had been tilled even in the Ur III period twenty-three centuries earlier.

We have oblique views of Sassanian society and agriculture in the debates preserved in the Jewish Talmud, an extended commentary on the Jewish law as formulated around 215 of our era in Israel itself. But the rabbis who participated in those debates assumed that their listeners knew what life was like in Sassanian Mesopotamia and usually did not elaborate.[6]

A later political and religious development in the region was the advent of Islam, a monotheistic creed borne by city dwellers from central Arabia who felt great kinship with Judaism and Christianity, although those traditions were seen as flawed, early versions of Islam, which translates as "submission" to the will of the one God. The Muslim conquests scared peasants out of northern Syria; in other places, however, the Muslims did not displace old social and economic orders but merely placed themselves and their tax demands atop the old pyramid, thereby guaranteeing stability and beginning a long process of social change as Arabs became sedentary and native populations assimilated to Muslim norms. Muslims did not demand conversion—later popular ideas notwithstanding—because Muslims paid lower taxes than non-Muslims, and conversions would have shrunk their tax revenues. But gradually Islam did become a dominant cultural force, certainly by 850 C.E., when probably half the people in the central Near East had converted to Islam.[7]

Islam did not reject old traditions as a matter of course. Thinkers valued stories about the past for their intrinsic interest and the insight they might provide into the geography of the areas now dominated by Muslims—but scholars were much more concerned with understanding and elaborating Muslim traditions, almost all focused on the life of the Prophet, his revelation, and his companions.[8]

The last dated cuneiform tablet we have is an astronomical text dated to 74–75 of our era; the last text written in Demotic, the late Egyptian writing system, is from around 400 of our era. In Mesopotamia the languages that had been written in cuneiform had been replaced perhaps in the 600s B.C.E. by Aramaic as the spoken language. In Egypt the language of the pharaohs evolved and was passed down for centuries as Coptic, the language of Egyptian Christians, written in a Greek-based system with some additional letters; Coptic died out as a spoken language probably by the 1200s of our era.[9] The old traditions did not die out because of Islam, but Islam gave sanction to ignoring them.

And in Egypt, Christianity had already given new themes and concerns to writers in the language.

The societies and economies we have been studying did not die, but the texts that documented them ceased, their rulers changed, and they became slowly the societies and economies of the region today. It would be wrong to overemphasize the continuities with the past of those societies, which are themselves far from static, but it would be equally wrong to ignore that the geographical realities of the Near East are similar to conditions in ancient times. And so in the river valleys irrigation is still a crucial problem, and everywhere sheep in variable safety graze.

To have studied the distant past of these places does not give us keys to policy questions for people of the region today, and it does not answer questions about our own societies and economies. But it gives pointillist detail to a very long and important part of the human past and helps us see some of the variety and triumphs of our now dead fellows.

APPENDIX

THEORIES OF ANCIENT ECONOMIES
AND SOCIETIES

There is today no generally accepted theory of ancient economies and societies. Scholars working in various countries with various ideologies make contributions to the understanding of ancient realities, but they do not agree on what in general those realities mean or what implications they might have for understanding our own societies.[1]

The lack of a general theory is not an impediment to important work, as it might be in some other fields. An anthropologist without a clear theory would feel at sea without a rudder, and an economist without one would not know what to begin to measure. But in ancient studies we have so much important groundwork to do that the lack of theoretical agreement does not keep the work from being useful.[2]

EARLY THEORIES

There has been no study on the Mesopotamian views of social and economic life as such, although there has been some consideration of the biblical views on such matters.[3] But scholars have used the emerging data from the ancient world to present general ideas about how economies and societies worked. And even though their ideas cannot be said to be dominant in the field today, it is worthwhile to examine what they proposed.

Probably in the long run the most influential thinker about ancient economics and society was Karl Marx. He was trained in the classical tradition and had read primary materials from Greece and Rome. His analysis of the rest of the ancient world was necessarily sketchy because he was living at the same time as the implications of the decipherments began to be felt. And it is clear that he assumed that the ancient world was much more a unity than scholars today would allow. In particular, he believed that all of it could be classified as a slave society, that is, one in which the labor of slaves constituted the most important single factor in the production of goods and services. He did not always maintain that ancient slave societies led inevitably to feudalism as practiced in medieval Europe, but his friend and disciple Friedrich Engels did claim exactly that in works published after Marx's death in 1883.[4]

Marxists continue to be influenced by Marx's definition of the ancient world as one dominated by slave labor, but scholars, while seeing the insight as true for Greece and Rome, regard it as only of limited applicability to the rest of the ancient world. Slaves were not present in great numbers outside Greece and Rome. Marxist scholars admit that, but they propose that the forced labor seen in Egypt and Mesopotamia constituted essentially the same thing as a slave society. Even though the laborers could not be bought and sold, their lives were directed from above and they had limited freedom, at least when they were working on state-supervised projects.[5]

Marx insisted that classes and class feelings were the engine that drives change in any human society. His model is an attractive one, but it has usually been difficult to identify social classes in ancient documents. Most scholars now admit that there are two broad classes in ancient societies, the exploiters and the exploited, but ancient terminology does not usually conform to this division.[6] And there is a question about how much class self-consciousness there was among the downtrodden. If such people lacked self-consciousness, they presumably would not act collectively in a revolutionary manner.

A corollary of Marx's idea that slave society did not change much is what he called the Oriental mode of production.[7] Marx suggested that alongside the ways of organizing labor and capital that he had isolated in European history there was another way of doing the same thing, and this was found particularly in Asia. The European modes of production that Marx proposed were the slave, the feudal, the capitalist, and eventually the socialist. Marx felt that there was a logical, historical progression through these modes in Europe. But outside these the Asiatic mode might persist for a very long time without change. Marx never wrote much about this possible mode of production, but he seems to have been thinking of the economics of small Indian villages when he hit upon the idea.

Some modern Marxists find Marx's ideas about the Asiatic mode repugnant because they imply that there is no inevitable progress through the various modes.[8] The problem then becomes that perhaps Marxism has no particular analysis of how change might occur in societies dominated by the Asiatic mode. This possibility was problematic to those who would see in Marxism a scientific and universally applicable method of analysis.

More recent students have returned to the idea of an Asiatic mode with a view to extending the analysis of it and perhaps exploring ways in which it might be adapted to explain ancient evidence. The most famous of these attempts is Karl Wittfogel's *Oriental Despotism*, which sees the Soviet Union as a country dominated by the Asiatic mode and the centralized despotism associated with it. Wittfogel argued that the need for irrigation calls forth centralized control, and that this control increases over time. The archaeologist R. McC. Adams doubts one can see a single direction in Mesopotamian irrigation history, and in fact there is a change in direction: irrigation peaks around 2000 B.C.E., then declines, climbing to a peak again under the Sassanians, who ruled Mesopotamia from 226 to 636 of our era. Adams feels that Wittfogel's model is general and not based on testable processes, and many observers concur.[9]

Others have attacked the problem from a standpoint less involved with modern politics. The Assyriologist Carlo Zaccagnini has suggested that societies that are dominated by the Asiatic mode have the following characteristics:

1. Property is held in common at the village level;
2. A despot is the ultimate owner of the land;
3. The despot demands a large part of the product of labor as tribute or as forced labor;
4. The village is autonomous as an economic producer and even as a manufacturer;
5. The city and country are not differentiated.[10]

Zaccagnini argues that the Asiatic mode probably is seen in very early texts from Mesopotamia, but over the course of the second millennium B.C.E. the power of independent villages declined, and we see despots and friends of despots transferring whole villages among themselves.[11] Zaccagnini also proposes that the Assyrian imperial organization from the end of the millennium made the villages marginal to the main business of production.

And so Zaccagnini suggests that in the course of the second millennium we see the demise of independent villages, and thus the mode of production did not last into later antiquity. If it did reappear, it had to be reinvented after the centralizing states' decline.

Another Marxist approach is that of Emmanuel Wallerstein, who posits the creation since 1500 C.E. of a world system centered on Europe and the United States in which resources are extracted from the periphery for the use of the centers. It is attractive to see some Ancient Near Eastern systems as analogous.[12]

From a Marxist perspective the Assyriologist I. M. Diakonoff developed a typology of the monarchies of Ancient Western Asia, wishing to distinguish the irrigation-dependent from the dry-farming states. He sees the growth of royal estates in the Ur III period as leading to stagnation, which was replaced in the subsequent Old Babylonian period with more dynamic economies in which private enterprise was possible on royal and community lands alike. More recently, Diakonoff extended the typology to the rest of Western Asia, suggesting that Mesopotamia had a two-sector economy with both a vibrant public and private sector. Egypt, on the other hand, saw the state sector engulf the private community sector. Elsewhere, especially in Syria, there were lands that lacked river valleys, and consequently no centralized irrigation system had to be maintained there and no centralized despots arose, states being always confederations of different groups. Diakonoff's views are sensible, but the American Assyriologist A. L. Oppenheim attacked them as being uselessly general and not connected enough to the landscape in which people lived.[13]

Another strand of theory stems from Max Weber, who was interested in the institutionalization of social movements. This strand is less clearly traced in later students of the ancient societies and economies, probably because Weber was not ideological and never led or inspired revolutionary movements in contemporary politics. Weber's dense book on the agrarian relations in antiquity seems remarkably well informed on Mesopotamia (at least for 1909), and he sees that household organization was basic. His concern for the fall of Rome led him to suggest that the end came there because civilization became rural in character. In that work he opposes general schemes and suggests, "The aim should, rather, be the opposite: to identify and define the individuality of each development, the characteristics which made the one conclude in a manner so different from the other," and only then to compare differences. Weber saw conflict of forces in every aspect of society, and this seeking for conflict may be his most useful legacy to modern ancient historians.[14]

A further set of ideas arises from the study of an Ancient Near Eastern archive, that of the temple of the goddess Bau at the southern Mesopotamian city of Lagaš. Father Anton Deimel at Rome began the exploitation of the texts of the archive in the early part of this century, and his student Anna Schneider published a small book in which she argued that almost all of the economic activity in this period in Lagaš was in the hands of the temple authorities.[15] Schneider generalized from that archive and proposed that in other Mesopotamian cities and in earlier periods the temple-state, as she called it, had been the most important source of economic organizing power.

The temple-state theory was extended by other students to cover the periods they were studying. But because of the subsequent dominance of royal-centered collections of texts students asserted that there was a progression from temple domination of society and economic life to a situation in which the kings wrested more and more power from the temples. Rivkah Harris called this process secularization, although she meant nothing particularly about religious thought in the period. Power, she felt, moved from the temples to the kings' palaces. The motive for this change was probably to be sought in the greed of kings. But then, because later archives concern private matters, the idea was posited that there was a development in the second millennium B.C.E. toward more private ownership and power. The ambition of a rising middle class was presumably the source of this change. These developments have been characterized as beginning with a temple-state and leading to a statist economy and then to something like a capitalist economy.[16]

Although traces of the temple-state theory persist in textbooks, the theory relies on a fundamental error. Deimel and Schneider were generalizing from a single group of texts, which certainly did derive from a temple and so, quite reasonably, showed the concerns of the temple's leaders and staff members. Benjamin Foster has shown that the earlier scholars ignored clear indications of the partial coverage of the archive with which they were dealing. In particular Foster showed that the secular leader of Lagaš had power independent of temples in the period, and also that there was a group of private persons who manipulated wealth. H. J. Nissen has suggested that the temple-dominated state may have arisen not in the earliest periods of Mesopotamian history, but in Early Dynastic III, just before imperial expansion began around 2300 B.C.E. in opposition to the centralizing secular state.[17]

In short, the development that Schneider traced was one in record-keeping but not one that really was observable as a change in the economy or society. It is easy to see why Schneider and others were misled, but their error does not lead clearly to a new and better theory of what was happening.

Karl Polanyi, the late Hungarian-American economist, suggested that all economies that had not been directly affected by Europe and European development behaved differently from the economies that are familiar today. He thought that the major way goods were exchanged was by custom; that is, one family had from time immemorial supplied the village with eggs, and it did so on the understanding that its needs for other things would be met in a traditional way by the other families. This kind of arrangement Polanyi called "reciprocal trading."[18] The hallmark was the absence of markets. By markets he meant not only open places where trading could be carried out, but ways of exchanging goods that made the price given for them subject to their availability. That is, Polanyi envisioned societies in which supply and demand did not usually play a major part, and certainly not in the way most goods and services were exchanged.

To support his idea in the ancient world Polanyi noted a story in Herodotus in which a Persian king upbraids the Greeks with whom he was dealing by saying that the Persians, in contrast to the Greeks, did not set aside places in their towns where they could cheat each other, referring to the Greek *agora,* or marketplace.[19] Polanyi thought the remark implied that Persians did not have markets, although it might also be interpreted to mean that the Persians did not cheat so much as the Greeks did.

Polanyi also asserted that Aristotle in his day decried buying and selling, which did not create new products but just took advantage of price differences to make money. Polanyi thought Aristotle was observing and deploring something brand new, not just in Greece, but in human experience. Polanyi pointed out that archaeologists had not found any indication of large open spaces suitable for a marketplace within early cities in the Ancient Near East. Polanyi also studied the translations of texts from the Old Assyrian trade between central Turkey and northern Iraq from the early second millennium B.C.E. and argued that they showed a system of traditionally accepted trading relations in which the prices were set by official agreements and were not subject to fluctuation on the basis of how much of a product was available when a given transaction took place.[20]

Polanyi's ideas have been attractive to some students of Greece and Rome and to a small number of Assyriologists partly because Polanyi was saying that modern economics, with its plethora of formulae and graphs, is irrelevant to the study of ancient life. Also there is something romantic about believing that back in historical time there were more humane ways for persons to relate to each other economically. Polanyi thought that his study of the past might revive some paradigms of behavior that could eventually be imitated as modern people discovered how bad capitalism really was for them. In addition, there is a tendency among modern social sciences to search for the evolution of whatever subject is studied, and it seems reasonable to suppose that at some point economies were considerably simpler than they are now. Thus anthropologists in particular have felt at home with the idea that the peoples they study live in a simple economic system.

In some fields Polanyi's views still carry weight, but the empirical evidence does not support them. Klaas Veenhof subjected Polanyi's analysis of the Old Assyrian trade to a vigorous analysis that showed that Polanyi really had not understood the documents from that trade. Veenhof showed that there were fluctuating prices in the period. Wolfgang Röllig found that there were in fact several words for *marketplace* in the languages of the Ancient Near East. And Röllig suggested that markets were usually held at the city gate. Other scholars have questioned whether the contemporary anthropological evidence on which Polanyi relied could be trusted. After his death, some of Polanyi's students admitted that the application of his model worked only in fairly simple societies and certainly not in modern societies touched by the Western economies.[21]

The Assyriologist Johannes Renger has argued that Polanyi's posthumous book *The Livelihood of Man* is less adamant about the absence of markets and allows "market forces" to have been an important factor in the ancient world. I have argued that this amounts to a capitulation to more standard economics, in which supply and demand loom large, and I have also shown that the series of prices from the southern Mesopotamian city of Umma really were prices, most of which fluctuated, and not equivalencies, what Polanyi called exchange rates set by treaty or custom.[22]

Polanyi's theory has had the salutary effect of calling into question our assumptions about how economies normally work. But Polanyi was unable to demonstrate that he was right by using actual ancient texts. Douglass North pointed out that Polanyi's reciprocity and redistribution are "inherently changeless," while in fact change is important and did happen; North calls for theories that explain change, not stasis.[23] He also writes that the "lower the costs of specifying and enforcing contractual agreements to trade the greater are the gains to trade from price-making markets." Thus, when governments wax in strength and court systems are stronger, it may be easier to enforce agreements, and thus more people may be encouraged than previously to enter into such agreements, thereby stepping up competition and comparison pricing.

Timothy Earle has argued that Polanyi's approach—called by its practitioners substantivism because it tries to study the substance of exchange—is not really incompatible with analyses that look at how humans are optimizing benefits, as in the formalism of classical economic analysis. Earle suggests that substantivism studies the social constraints in which people act, while formalism looks at how people come to decisions within those constraints.[24] This seems to me to be a useful formulation and to pose clearly the question of what social and economic history does. We want to understand the social constraints of all sorts, not just economic, on ancient people. And in so doing we may be struck by how unlike us they were in their thinking. But we also wish to see how they maximized benefits for themselves, both socially and economically. And in that task we may be more struck with our similarity to them than our differences.

Zaccagnini has suggested that usually exchange can be seen either as redistributive or as commercial; the difference is not factual but in the point of view of the observer.[25] Some benefits are always being maximized, but one may choose not to see them as commercially remunerative.

The following statement of R. H. Tawney is helpful: "Capitalism in the sense of great individual undertakings . . . is as old as history. Capitalism, as an economic system, resting on the organization of legally free wage-earners . . . and setting its stamp on every aspect of society, is a modern phenomenon."[26]

With Polanyi, it is prudent to question if capitalism touches "every aspect of society."

Adams noted that anthropologists who are cultural evolutionists, persons committed to the idea that cultures change slowly over time more because of internal developments than outside impacts, in general cannot deal with entrepreneurism, with conscious decisions that may lead to violent change. The economist Donald McCloskey has labeled the belief in the absence of markets except in the West a historical mistake from which "arose the fairy tales of lost paradises for aristocrats or peasants and a reason for ignoring bourgeois virtues." McCloskey calls for a conscious return to the morals of fair dealing and friendly exchange.[27] It is not likely that getting ancient history right can directly contribute to such societal changes as McCloskey envisions, but neither can it be seen as irrelevant.

RECENT PROPOSALS

More recently a number of students have made suggestions about trends in the ancient economy and society, though none has written a major treatment of the problem.

Marvin Powell in 1978 published a paper that attempts to take up where Marx and Polanyi left off and to propose a new theory of how the ancient Mesopotamian economy changed. In the earliest periods he sees a persistence of private economic power alongside temple and state power, and then a gradual increase in the amount of land controlled by the state. But he refuses to endorse Deimel and Schneider in saying that the king dominated everything and thinks the Mesopotamian economy presents "a unique mixing of Polanyi's redistribution economy and capitalist principles." The key to change Powell sees in better technology for producing metal. He asserts that the market economy is not a development of the nineteenth century C.E., as Polanyi guessed, but one that was bound up with technological advance. Technology introduced the possibility of increasing differences between rich and poor, and the solution to this inequality was a stronger king, who could arbitrarily resolve disputes about the limited resources. Maybe disputing parties would not be satisfied, but at least all were in the same boat as subjects of the king.[28]

Powell wishes, then, to salvage Polanyi's views on redistribution systems and apply them to the government-sponsored welfare and exploitation systems. He is vague about how exactly new technology forces change. Powell's essay is only a sketch, however, and it is possible that he or others will be able in the future to be more precise about why societies and economies change.

J. Gledhill and M. T. Larsen reject the usefulness of Polanyi's analysis while welcoming his insight that our view of the economic sphere is relatively recent. They draw attention to cycles of centralizing and "feudalizing" that ancient empires suffered.[29] They call for attending to how structures recentralize after a period of decentralizing. Their idea can be fruitfully combined with others for a more dynamic view of ancient economies, and I will try to do that below.

In 1984, Mario Liverani returned to the idea of Marx's Asiatic mode of production and noted that the idea does have the advantage of distinguishing between village-level life and the life of the great state organizations; but it is problematic because it does not allow for any change, although change is observable. Liverani proposes two modes of production in the Ancient Near East, two ways of organizing economic activity, and he calls them the Palace and the Family. The first dominated the second, but the Family was more productive in absolute terms, and the Palace presupposed this Family productivity. Change arose because of the pressure from Palace workers' families to be supported; the Palace gave land allotments instead of direct rations. Another motive for change was that there was pressure for the Palace to accept the son of the Family as successor to the father as a worker for the Palace. This eventually undermined Palace land ownership and made it hard to dislodge the family.[30] Also, land might be granted and exempted from service, but this too undermined Palace control. In the first millennium B.C.E. there was in addition a process in which income or labor benefits previously enjoyed by the Palace were diverted to individuals; this too weakened Palace control in the long run.

Conversely, Liverani proposes that the Palace influenced the Family. When the father died, families, instead of resorting to communal ownership, tended to divide up land so that each son had some. Also, there may have been a diminished preference for the eldest son so that the whole family could benefit from Palace employment. There was further an idea that inheritance itself could be earned by merit, as in Palace activities. The father tried to protect a second wife from the sons of the first wife through adoptions or disinheritance; a sense of individual responsibility may have arisen. Finally, land might be sold outside the family; as a result, some families acquired lots of land and others none. In early Mesopotamia this kind of alienation of the land was seen as abnormal and reprehensible, but by the first millennium there was no restraint on it.

Liverani in his article does not fill in his theory with many details, and he may be able to do so in the future. Still, it is clear that the tensions between the Family and Palace are important in almost all periods, and they may be the motivating factors for important changes.

Morris Silver in his book brings the tools of a student of the modern American economy to the ancient world and suggests that the key to a proper understanding is to concentrate on transaction costs as a motivating factor for ancient trade; that is, he wants to look at what it costs to exchange goods and services. Silver suggests that classical economic theory, which relies on the power of supply and demand, is sufficient to explain the Ancient Near East as well as modern economies. Communication costs were especially high in the ancient world, and this limited the endeavors of people interested in trade and led them to diversify their efforts. If they had made a long, expensive trip to a source to acquire a valued product, they were especially ready to trade in other products that could be found there. Silver rejects Polanyi's emphasis on redistribution in the Mesopotamian economy, although he does admit that people stored much more than we do because the start-up costs for travel were so high.[31] Silver sees interregional trade as the important element that changes the ancient economies. But Silver does not demonstrate that Mesopotamians frequently thought in terms of transaction costs. In spite of his interesting insights, Silver has not provided a new theory of the ancient economies.

The distinguished lexicographer Miguel Civil has not been so rash as to put forward a new theory of ancient economies and societies. In an article written in 1980, however, Civil underlined a major problem with ancient texts: "There are bits of information, frequently essential for the solution of our problems, which do not occur in the texts, not because there were not *perceived* by the scribes, but completely on the contrary because they were *too well known* by the scribes."[32]

Civil's insight is especially relevant to theories of society and economy. It means that although some of our modern questions may eventually be answered, many of the most important ones were simply too familiar to ancient scribes to be explicitly mentioned. From ancient Western Asia and Egypt there is no equivalent to the discursive essay that explains basic cultural assumptions. Herodotus may be untrustworthy as a witness, but an earlier equivalent of his inquiring mind would be very helpful to us now.

A BASIC MODEL

Let us return to Gledhill's and Larsen's idea about centralizing and feudalizing periods and to Liverani's insight that there were two centers of production, the Family and the Palace. I would like to formulate their views slightly differently and propose that in any society, including ancient societies, we have two institutions that are sometimes in tension, the household and the market.

A household may be defined as a group of persons who think of themselves as a social unit and sometimes also as a producing unit. Inside a household gifts may be exchanged, and there can be exploitation of some household members by others, especially on the basis of gender. But the essential aspect of the household is that its members have on the whole a noneconomic, nonmonetary relation to each other. Nobody pays them for their work within the household. They get status, they get love, but they do not get commensurate goods and services. Alterations in ability to do work do not lead to basic changes in the household. Today when a working spouse is sick, she or he does not cease to be a member of the household merely because of sickness: the role played may change, but it is not eliminated. In ancient households sick slaves counted as members. Although their status was defined by the ability of other members of the household to exploit their labor, they did not lose their membership immediately as part of the household merely by becoming sick.[33]

The other term in the model I suggest is the market. With Morris Silver, I see the market as a system of information about what is available for purchasing at what price, in what place, under what conditions.[34] The household stands in opposition to the market. What is household is not market, and what is market is not household.

But the relations between households and markets can vary. At one extreme may stand the relatively self-sufficient Ancient Near Eastern household in times of economic stagnation when what we might anachronistically call medievalization sets in, when the household attempts in as many things as possible to be self-sufficient. I dislike Gledhill's and Larsen's term *feudalization* because it conjures up rather too precise images of soldiers holding land and having judicial authority over it, and these images do not clearly have a place in most periods of ancient history.[35]

In a medievalizing household what cannot be produced at home is done without. Although social relations may be cultivated across household boundaries, exchanges of goods may be infrequent and even hostile.

On the other extreme may be the modern Western household, in which most things consumed by the members are not produced by the household but are instead acquired with money that they have earned by participating in a labor market. The behavior of individual households and their members even under such conditions can vary a great deal with regard to the degree to which they choose to exploit the information about market conditions that is potentially available. There are housespouses who read food advertisements and clip coupons, who zip from store to store to hit the bargains, and there are others, not exclusively husbands, who choose the convenience of shopping in one place over the savings they might realize by taking advantage of market conditions.

The quality of information about market conditions varies. Insiders may know valuable things about mergers among corporations that make stocks valuable in unobvious ways. And bottlenecks, shortfalls, and, in our day, advertising campaigns may change the availability and attractiveness of commodities. In the ancient world it seems that the information varied in plentifulness and quality too, and on the whole was much worse than it is under modern conditions.

Let us try to fit Liverani's Palace into this picture. The government today views itself as being independent of any higher secular power. But in the Ancient Near East governments originally were households ruled by rich lords. They extended their exploitation in the historical period over some aspects of most of the other households of their areas and even over some aspects of markets, that is, of the ways in which the households interacted. But the governments never managed to eliminate all other households or to control very many markets. And, as Liverani points out, they would have been foolish to have tried because they depended on the productivity of the households.[36]

Governments may have been originally households writ large. But a modern government does not seem like a household. It has employees who are paid in money and must buy what they need in the market. In the past there have been other variations on how salaries were paid that made governments look like conglomerations of households, for example, land-grant systems in which soldiers and officials were paid by being given land or the right to collect tax from land, for limited or for indefinite terms.[37]

This simple model of the economy may allow us to say something useful about Gledhill's and Larsen's concerns about forces that tend to draw groups together and those that tend to pull them apart. Withdrawal from the market arises because the households have trouble filling their usual needs and desires in the market. As markets fail to fulfill their tasks, as they become less good, the households turn in on themselves and fulfill more of their own needs while neglecting other, nonessential desires. And when markets improve their ability to meet needs, the households, probably slowly and tentatively at first, adapt to the availability of goods and services from outside the household and seek more of what they need from the markets.

It does not seem that the quality of household productive capacity significantly changed over the course of Ancient Near Eastern history. Technological innovations like the advent of the plow helped the household to be more efficient and productive. But, as far as we can see, these innovations did not lead to a basic strengthening of the household's capacities. A plow helped the household produce more, but it did not increase surpluses in an individual household so much that many persons could be freed from agricultural work.

If households did not much change, markets in contrast seem to have been volatile. It is usual for historians not to be able to explain why prices varied, but it is obvious that they did, and that their doing so affected how households lived. If we view markets as the way in which households interact, we can see that they are likely to be affected by a great many factors exterior to themselves. The primary inhibitor of market activity in the Ancient Near East is certainly distance between households and the difficulties of crossing that distance with goods. This is what Silver means by transaction costs. War and raids may affect markets much more easily than they decimate households because people apparently felt, as they still feel now, a general fondness toward their household, but they did not feel anything much for the market they used. Hence the market was socially unstable and in fact fragile whenever it was afflicted by hardship.

There may be some ways to study what factors acting in the markets and on the households could precipitate or make more likely a withdrawal into medievalization, or, as Renger suggests calling it, autarchy. The drying up of the market for labor is an important sign that all markets were contracting and that households which previously had gotten extra goods from the labor of their members as wage earners would be signaled to withdraw into themselves; one could see this happening as large landowners eliminated the practice of hiring seasonal workmen to deal with agricultural needs. In modern terms we would say that a rise in unemployment might trigger experiments in self-sufficiency. The problem with taking changes in the labor market as especially significant of withdrawal from markets in general is that in the earliest periods of the Ancient Near East we have no data on labor markets, and hired workmen are attested only rarely before the Ur III period (2112–2004 b.c.e.), when they become fairly common.[38] This might mean that markets were weak, or it might mean that organizations with access to writing did not hire outsiders or did not consider such hiring worth recording.

Like the market in labor, the market in land is not widely attested early, and, oddly, it is absent from the massive number of texts preserved from the Ur III period. One would imagine that when markets in commodities collapsed, the market in land would soar because it could be used by households to produce more goods that could not be bought in the markets. At some stage only rich people could take advantage of the increased value of land, and they might in the process throw formerly effective households off the land. These sorts of acts, which end up being the dismemberment of peasant economies, are in fact attested in the Old Babylonian period and in the Middle Assyrian period, but the assembling of large amounts of land did not necessarily presage medievalization. The debate on the process and meaning of Roman *latifundia* ("broad fields") may show that such a correlation may not be assumed, that is, the collecting of broad fields did not precede a period of household medievalization.[39] Also we should not assume that all "dark ages" or periods in which central governments lose power are necessarily periods of household medievalization.

It is important to remember that the household-market model probably expresses only some aspects of ancient realities, and it may help us to see more clearly some of those features. But no period is likely to be one in which there were no markets at all or in which households turned to markets for all goods and services they needed and wanted. There was no such purity in the past, as there is none in the present. And we must be prepared for messy variety. This variety may be the reason that we have so few interesting theories, and it may limit our ability to generalize about Ancient Near Eastern social and economic life. But it seems crucial to attempt a description now, even if new models and new data will inevitably modify what we have to say.[40]

The basic proposal is that economies are best understood as collections of individual households in which members are sustained socially and economically with little regard to their abilities to produce. The ways those households interact are markets, networks of knowledge about what is available and at what cost. Both the household and the market have existed as far back as we can see, but the household was more stable, and the ways in which households interacted changed constantly.

NOTES

INTRODUCTION

1. J. M. Sasson, "Thoughts of Zimri-Lim," *Biblical Archaeologist* 47 (1984): 110–20, reconstructs the reflections of the Mari king; Sasson suggests, "It is a common verity of the profession, . . . that when it comes to reconstructing moments from Mesopotamian life, modern historians have largely failed to invest their narratives with the vision necessary to persuade and command attention."

2. On this method, see the work of its pioneer, R. M. Adams, *The Land behind Baghdad,* and, with H. Nissen, *The Uruk Countryside* and *Heartland of Cities,* and M. Gibson, *The City and Area of Kish.* The disadvantages of surveys have been stressed by Kay Kohlmeyer, "'Wovon man nicht sprechen kann.' Grenzen der Interpretation von bei Oberflächenbegehungen gewonnenen archäologischen Informationen," *Mitteilungen der deutschen Orientgesellschaft* 113 (1981): 53–79, emphasizing the possible unrepresentativeness of samples derived from surfaces of tells. Compare also the more historically oriented critique of J. A. Brinkman, "Settlement Surveys and Documentary Evidence: Regional Variation and Secular Trend in Mesopotamian Demography," *JNES* 43 (1984): 169–80, esp. 171–72, noting especially that surface survey is inherently imprecise because it distinguishes blocks of four or five centuries, when even ancient historians are concerned usually with change over decades.

3. But they probably never matched the characteristics outlined by P. A. Sorokin, "What Is a Social Class?" in *Class, Status and Power* (1947; reprint Glencoe, Ill.: Free Press, 1953), ed. R. Bendix and S. Lipset, 87–92, including the criterion that a class is "solidary, . . . antagonistic to certain other groups." Sorokin underlines that in his definition the phenomenon is limited to the eighteenth to twentieth centuries in Western societies, and the essence is occupational and economic identity. See also N. Gottwald, "Social Class as an Analytic and Hermeneutical Category in Biblical Studies," *JBL* 112 (1993): 3–22, opting, 4, for a definition based on the relation to the means of production.

4. See, in general, *Iraq* 39 (1977), reviewed by N. Yoffee, *Explaining Trade,* and A. Archi, ed., *The Circulation of Goods in Non-Palatial Contexts in the Ancient Near East.*

5. For an earlier approach, see Joyce O. Hertzler, *The Social Thought of the Ancient Civilizations* (New York: McGraw-Hill, 1936).

6. The name *Egypt* derives apparently from metonymy, using for the whole land the name *ḥk Pth* "house of Ptah," the chief god of the city of Memphis, near modern Cairo. The ancient Egyptians had no single term for Egypt, though other ancients called the land *Miṣru* "boundary," presumably the edge of the civilized area. Here I mean not the modern state, which is much wider, but just the Nile Valley and the oases controlled by people from the valley south into modern Sudan. See in general B. Trigger et al., eds., *Ancient Egypt: A Social History.*

7. On the need for hemispheric interregional history, see M. Hodgson, "Hemispheric Interregional History as an Approach to World History," *Cahiers d'Histoire Mondiale* 1 (1953–54): 715–23, brilliantly illustrated by his posthumous *Venture of Islam.* It may nonetheless be argued that Islam almost from its beginnings entered an arena limited

only by the oceans of its hemisphere. The spread of influence was probably usually a much slower process in the pre-Islamic world.

8. J. J. Finkelstein, "Mesopotamia," *JNES* 21 (1962): 73–92, showed that the Greek term that we still use translated ʿabr nahrain "the river land," referring to the land inside the big bend in the Euphrates in what is now Turkey and Syria. Here I mean the parts of the modern states of Iraq and eastern Syria and of Iran, Turkey, and Saudi Arabia that are drained by the Tigris and Euphrates rivers.

9. See on his work A. Parrot, *Archéologie mésopotamienne: Les Étapes* (Paris: Albin Michel, 1946), 176–207, and *Techniques et Problèmes* (1953), 46–47, and the appreciation in L. Cottrell, ed., *The Concise Encyclopedia of Archaeology* (New York: Hawthorn, 1960), 263–64.

10. See E. G. Kraeling, *The Old Testament since the Reformation* (New York: Schocken, 1955), and H. H. Rowley, *The Old Testament and Modern Study* (Oxford: Clarendon, 1952).

11. On Champollion, see J. Friedrich, *Extinct Languages* (New York: Philosophical, 1957), 16–26. Note that P. Daniel has argued that the same principles were used earlier, in 1754, by Jean-Jacques Barthélemy, the decipherer of Palmyrene, an Aramaic dialect written in the first few centuries of our era; see " 'Shewing of Hard Sentences and Dissolving of Doubts': The First Decipherment," *JAOS* 108 (1988): 419–36.

12. See, in general, J. Friedrich, *Extinct Languages,* 50–68, on cuneiform, W. A. Budge, *The Rise and Progress of Assyriology* (London: Hopkinson, 1925), and S. Pallis, *Early Exploration in Mesopotamia* (Copenhagen: Munksgaard, 1954), and his *The Antiquity of Iraq* (Copenhagen: Munksgaard, 1956), 99–103.

A modern squeeze was taken at Besitun by George Cameron, described in his "Darius Carved History on Ageless Rock," *National Geographic* 98 (1958): 825–44, with wonderful pictures, which make one appreciate Rawlinson's athletic achievement.

See for the decipherment "Comparative Translations by W. H. Fox-Talbot . . . of the Inscription of Tiglath Pileser I," *Journal of the Royal Asiatic Society* 18 (1861): 150–212.

13. M. Liverani, "Problemi e indirizze degli studi storici sul vicino oriente antico," *Cultura e scuola* 220 (1966): 72–79, seems sensible to me when he points out that the inevitable long philological training tends to make us neglect real historical problems, 72; he calls for new ideas and explorations of problems, and there is no question that the years since he wrote have seen a proliferation of valuable contributions that do address real historical problems. I fear that this has not yet meant that our studies have been paid much attention by our culture as a whole, as, in fact, they deserve, 79.

14. E. Said, *Orientalism* (New York: Pantheon, 1978). Among the numerous critiques, see esp. V. Brombert, *American Scholar* 48 (1979): 532–42, and A. Hourani, *New York Review of Books* 26 (March 8, 1979): 27–30.

15. See especially on the problem for the history of Israel F. W. Golka, "Die Königs- und Hofsprüche und der Ursprung der israelitischen Weisheit," *Vetus Testamentum* 36 (1986): 13–36, 35–36. I shall use the so-called Middle Chronology, which for Mesopotamia is summarized in J. A. Brinkman's appendix to A. Leo Oppenheim, *Ancient Mesopotamia,* 335–48.

16. See, in general, Peter Novick, *That Noble Dream: The "Objectivity" Question and the American Historical Profession* (Cambridge: Cambridge University Press, 1988).

17. See the symposium on the supposed crisis in historical thought because of the realization that we cannot be absolutely objective, *American Historical Review* 94 (1989); a later

response is J. Appleby, L. Hunt, and M. Jacob, *Telling the Truth about History* (New York: Norton, 1994). See also, in general, O. Carerro, *History of the Near Eastern Historiography and Its Problems, 1852–1985,* part 1 (Neukirchen: Neukirchen-Vluyn, 1989).

18. For a later view of the fall of Ur, see the Ur lament in T. Jacobsen, *The Harps That Once . . .* (New Haven: Yale University Press, 1987), 447–74.

19. As seen by M. T. Larsen, "The Tradition of Empire in Mesopotamia," in *Power and Propaganda,* M. T. Larsen, ed., 75–103, 88.

CHAPTER 1
THE ORIGINS OF CITIES

1. R. M. Adams, "Die Rolle des Bewässerungsbodenbaus bei der Entwicklung von Institutionen in der alten Gesellschaft," in *Produktivkräfte und Gesellschaftsformationen in vorkapitalistischer Zeit,* ed. J. Herrmann and I. Sellnow, 119–40, 122–23, suggests that cities offered protection for surpluses from raiders.

2. So C. Larsen and G. Evans, "The Holocene Geological History of the Tigris-Euphrates-Karun Delta," in *The Environmental History of the Near and Middle East since the Last Ice Age,* ed. W. Brice, 226–34. For a sketch of the Mesopotamian river area, see Adams, *Heartland of Cities,* 3–14, 52, on the Persian Gulf. For an overview of the sedentarization and urbanization process from an archaeological and anthropological perspective, see C. K. Maisels, *The Emergence of Civilization from Hunting and Gathering to Agriculture, Cities, and the State in the Near East.* See also M. B. Rowton, "The Woodlands of Ancient Western Asia," *JNES* 26 (1967): 261–77, and B. Brentjes, "Klimaschwankungen und Siedlungsgeschichte Vorder- und Zentralasiens," *AfO* 40–41 (1993/4): 74–87.

3. J. Harlan, "A Wild Wheat Harvest in Turkey," *Archaeology* 20 (1967): 197–201. K. Flannery, "Origins and Ecological Effects of Early Domestication in Iran and the Near East," in *Prehistoric Agriculture,* ed. S. Struever, 50–79, stresses that nobody was starving when the move toward domestication was made, but it was an innovation on less favorable land near an area of population growth, 70. Compare too T. C. Young, Jr., "Population Densities and Early Mesopotamian Origins," in *Man, Settlement and Urbanism,* ed. Peter Ucko, 827–42; E. Boserup, *Population and Technical Change* (Chicago: University of Chicago Press, 1981), 41, and F. Hole, "Environmental Instabilities and Urban Origins," in *Chiefdoms and Early States in the Near East,* ed. G. Stein and M. Rothman, 121–51, showing that dislocations may have arisen in the sixth through the fourth millennia, when cities arose.

4. R. Braidwood, "Prehistoric Investigations in Southwestern Asia," *Proceedings of the American Philosophical Society* 116 (1972): 310–20, 318; on obsidian's distribution, see M. Roaf, *Cultural Atlas of Mesopotamia,* 34.

5. Ann L. Perkins, *The Comparative Archeology of Early Mesopotamia,* gives the major pottery periods.

6. P. Kohl and R. Wright, "Stateless Cities: The Differentiation of Societies in the Near Eastern Neolithic," *Dialectical Anthropology* 2:4 (1977): 271–83, esp. 280. C. Peebles and S. Kus, "Some Archaeological Correlates of Ranked Societies," *American Antiquity* 42 (1977): 421–48, esp. 432. This appears to be the case in Mesopotamia at least until the Ubaid. Gil Stein, "Economy, Ritual, and Power in 'Ubaid Mesopotamia," in *Chiefdoms and Early States,* ed. G. Stein and M. Rothman, 35–46, notes that early Ubaid

lacked trade ties, but public buildings probably show elites gaining control of community finances.

7. Easy conceptually, but not physically; for a graphic illustration of the backbreaking work of irrigation, dam building, and canal maintenance, see *Cross Creek,* a movie with Rip Torn and Mary Steenburgen depicting Florida in 1928. Compare Adams, *Heartland,* 53.

8. R. M. Adams, "Historic Patterns of Mesopotamian Irrigation Agriculture," in *Irrigation's Impact on Society,* ed. T. Downing and M. Gibson, 1–6, and R. Adams, "The Mesopotamian Social Landscape: A View from the Frontier," in *Reconstructing Complex Societies,* ed. C. Moore, 1–20, 3.

9. Adams, *Heartland,* 59, notes that the density of first settlements declines as one moves north from the gulf. Neutron activation analysis, which allows the identification of origin of pottery, shows that the Ubaid pottery found on the coast of Saudi Arabia comes from Mesopotamia, closing out the possibility that the Ubaidians came from Arabia initially. J. Oates et al., "Seafaring Merchants of Ur?" *Antiquity* 5 (1977): 221–34.

10. R. M. Adams, and H. Nissen, *Uruk Countryside,* 9; one site in that region may be pre-Ubaid.

11. R. Adams, *Heartland,* 27–28; on the method and its limitations, 47–51. Even in rainfall agricultural areas there may have been irrigation to improve crop yields; so T. McClellan, "Irrigation and Hydraulic Systems in Syria," *Syrian Archaeology Bulletin* 2 (1990): 12–13, on the Habur River basin.

12. F. Safar et al., *Eridu,* 45. Oddly, Eridu ceased to be a village with an agricultural community at the end of the Ubaid period, but priests kept on living there, and the site continued to have cultural meaning, 46.

13. Note R. M. Adams's comparison of early Mesopotamia with early Meso-American urban developments, *The Evolution of Urban Society,* and see G. Stein, "Economy."

14. On the history of the question, especially on whether Sumerians existed as a separate language group, see T. Jones, *The Sumerian Problem.*

15. Adams, *Heartland,* 69. For the Jemdet Nasr-Early Dynastic I explosion of population, see R. M. Adams and H. Nissen, *The Uruk Countryside,* 17.

16. H. Frankfort, *The Art and Architecture of the Ancient Orient,* 20.

17. See the studies in *Seals and Sealings in the Ancient Near East,* ed. M. Gibson and R. Biggs, and L. Gorelick and A. J. Gwinnett, "The Ancient Near Eastern Cylinder Seal as Social Emblem and Status Symbol," *JNES* 49 (1990): 45–56. Compare also on stamp seals M. Rothman, "Sealing as a Control Mechanism in Prehistory: Tepe Gawra XI, X, and VIII," in *Chiefdoms and Early States,* ed. G. Stein and M. Rothman, 103–20, noting that sealings were not needed in small kin-based communities but did become important as a system of control in more complex societies, 118.

18. G. Algaze, *The Uruk World System: The Dynamics of Expansion of Early Mesopotamian Civilization,* 110, and his "The Uruk Expansion: Cross-Cultural Exchange in Early Mesopotamian Civilization," *Current Anthropology* 30 (1989): 571–608, esp. 571, 588, 598, 601.

19. G. Buccellati, "The Origin of Writing and the Beginning of History," in *The Shape of the Past: Studies in Honor of Franklin D. Murphy,* ed. G. Buccellati and C. Sperioni, 3–13, argues that writing is a proper symbol of the urban revolution because it allows more efficient communication, even over time, 4. Buccellati also emphasizes the impersonal approach to knowledge that writing represents, and he sees writing as an effort to get around the fact that the memory of the human brain cannot expand its capacity, 11. On

tablets, see A. Lebrun and F. Vallat, "L'Origine de l'Ecriture Suse," *Délégation archéologique française en Iran, Cahiers* 8 (1975): 11–59.

See also D. Schmandt-Besserat, *Before Writing*, vol. 1, *From Counting to Cuneiform*. The numerical tablets are found in Eastern Iran, Susa, Uruk, Khafaje, and Jebel Aruda and Habuba Kabira in central Syria. D. Schmandt-Besserat, "From Token to Tablets: A Re-evaluation of the So-called 'Numerical Tablets,'" *Visible Language* 15 (1981): 321–44, esp. 324. And see the critique of S. Lieberman, "Of Clay Pebbles, Hollow Clay Balls, and Writing: A Sumerian View," *American Journal of Archaeology* 84 (1980): 340–58.

20. M. W. Green and H. J. Nissen, *Zeichenliste der archäischen Texte aus Uruk*, list 771 signs. See, in general, H. J. Nissen et al., *Archaic Bookkeeping*.

21. M. Powell, "Sumerian Area Measures and the Alleged Decimal Substratum," *ZA* 62 (1972): 165–221, esp. 172, and M.-L. Thomsen, *The Sumerian Language*, 15–20.

22. G. E. M. de Ste. Croix, "Greek and Roman Accounting," in *Studies in the History of Accounting*, ed. A. C. Littleton and B. S. Yamey, 14–74, esp. 32, on classical period accounting, but doubtless true of the earlier periods considered here.

23. *Ǧamdat Nasr: Period or Regional Style?* ed. U. Finkbeiner and W. Röllig, esp. the discussion 367–80. M. Mallowan, "Noah's Flood Reconsidered," *Iraq* 26 (1964): 62–82. M. Gibson, "Violation of Fallow and Engineered Disaster in Mesopotamian Civilization," in *Irrigation's Impact on Society*, ed. T. Downing, M. Gibson, 7–19, argues that governments had encouraged farmers to violate alternate-year fallow to increase short-term yields and thus brought on disaster, 15.

24. T. Jacobsen, *The Sumerian King List*, 140–41, argues that it is from the early Ur III period, but for the lower date, see D. O. Edzard, "Königslisten und Chroniken," *RlA* 6:8–81. T. Jacobsen, "The Assumed Conflict between Sumerians and Semites in Early Mesopotamian History," *JAOS* 59 (1939): 485–95.

25. The approximate dates for the periods I take from W. W. Hallo and W. Kelly Simpson, *The Ancient Near East: A History*, 37 n. 16. T. Jacobsen, "Early Political Development in Mesopotamia," *ZA* 52 (1957): 91–140.

26. J. Oates, "Urban Trends in Prehistoric Mesopotamia," in *La Ville dans le Proche-Orient ancien*, 81–92, 89, notes that Eridu suggests slow development from founding into the third millennium. K. Maekawa, "The Development of the E_2-MI_2 in Lagash during Early Dynastic III," *Mesopotamia* 8–9 (1973–74): 77–144, esp. 138–42. J. Makkay, "The Origins of the 'Temple Economy' as Seen in the Light of Prehistoric Evidence," *Iraq* 45 (1983): 1–6. J. Margueron, "L'Apparition du Palais au Proche-Orient," in *Le Système palatial en Orient, en Grèce et à Rome*, ed. E. Lévy, 8–38. J. Oates, "Mesopotamian Social Organisation: Archaeological and Philological Evidence," in *The Evolution of Social Systems*, ed. J. Friedman and M. J. Rowlands, 457–85, 472–73.

27. Jacobsen, *The Sumerian King List*, 165–67. D. O. Edzard, "Mebaragesi," *RlA* 7:614. See the short bibliography in M. G. Kovacs, *The Epic of Gilgamesh*, xi, but translating "The old has become young," xxvii, following A. Falkenstein, "Gilgameš," *RlA* 3:357–63, 357.

28. R. Biggs, "Semitic Names in the Fara Period," *OrNS* 36 (1967): 55–66, 57–58.

29. K. Kamp and N. Yoffee, "Ethnicity in Ancient Western Asia during the Early Second Millennium B.C.: Archaeological Assessments of Ethnoarchaeological Perspectives," *Bulletin of the American Schools of Oriental Research* 237 (1980): 85–104.

30. I. J. Gelb, "Ebla and Lagash: Environmental Contrast," in *The Origins of Cities in Dry-Farming Syria in the Third Millennium B.C.*, ed. H. Weiss, 157–67, esp. 165.

31. Adams, *Heartland,* 81–94. Robert C. Hunt, "The Role of Bureaucracy in the Provisioning of Cities: A Framework for Analysis of the Ancient Near East," in *The Organization of Power,* ed. M. Gibson and R. Biggs, 161–92, stresses that the cities need their hinterlands, 163, and that in the Near East land was not in shortage, but labor and water were, 169.

      H. Weiss, "The Origins of Tell Leilan and the Conquest of Space in Third Millennium Mesopotamia," in *The Origins of Cities in Dry-Farming Syria and Mesopotamia in the Third Millennium B.C.,* ed. H. Weiss, 71–108, 91–92, sketches the growth between the equivalents of Early Dynastic I and III. The collapse of this site may be due, oddly, to volcanic activity, according to H. Weiss et al., "The Genesis and Collapse of Third Millennium North Mesopotamian Civilization," *Science* 261 (1993): 995–1004.

32. G. Buccellati suggests that the bowls were for drying salt cakes, "Salt at the Dawn of History: The Case of the Beveled-Rim Bowls," in *Resurrecting the Past: A. Bounni A.V.,* ed. P. Matthiae et al., 17–32, following D. Potts, "On Salt and Salt Gathering in Ancient Mesopotamia," *JESHO* 27 (1984): 225–71, esp. 268–69, and there have been many other suggestions, including that they were used for making bread; see A. R. Millard, "The Bevelled-Rim Bowls: Their Purpose and Significance," *Iraq* 50 (1988): 49–57. Note that sedentaries needed salt for their animals and may have had to resort to nomadic gatherers to get it. D. Potts, "Salt of the Earth: The Role of a Non-Pastoral Resource in a Pastoral Economy," *Oriens Antiquus* 22 (1983): 205–15. F. Brüschweiler, "La Ville dans les Textes littéraires sumériens," in *La Ville dans le Proche-Orient ancien,* 191–98, 197–98. Compare on archaeology H. P. Martin, *Fara: A Reconstruction of the Ancient Mesopotamian City of Shuruppak.*

33. I. M. Diakonoff, "Socio-Economic Classes in Babylonia and the Babylonian Concept of Social Stratification," in *Gesellschaftsklassen,* ed. D. O. Edzard, 41–52, 47–48, suggests that there were three classes, one owning land and living on the work of laborers, one owning land but living on their own labor, and the coerced laborers.

34. D. Engels, "The Use of Demography in Ancient History," *Classical Quarterly* 34 (1984): 386–93, 392. Compare S. Dunham, "Beads for Babies," *ZA* 83:2 (1993): 236–57, showing that dead children were valued. S. Shahar, *Childhood in the Middle Ages,* contests the idea that children in that period were not cherished, as advanced by P. Ariès, *Centuries of Childhood,* 39.

35. J. Asher-Greve, *Frauen in altsumerischer Zeit,* 183, suggests that the legal material shows monogamy was normal in late Early Dynastic. The legal texts were assembled by D. O. Edzard, ed., *Sumerische Rechtsurkunden des III. Jahrtausends,* but without a synthetic discussion of their contents. J. Cooper, *Sumerian and Akkadian Royal Inscriptions* 1:77–78.

36. J. Asher-Greve, *Frauen,* 169. See, in general, E. W. Barber, *Women's Work,* 29. And see I. J. Gelb et al., *Earliest Land Tenure Systems in the Near East: Ancient Kudurrus,* 17. A female scribe may once be attested, as noted by S. Meier, "Women and Communication in the Ancient Near East," *JAOS* 111 (1991): 540–47, 541.

37. Compare from an anthropological cross-cultural perspective J. Moore, "The Evolution of Exploitation," *Critique of Anthropology* 8 (1977): 33–58.

38. K. Maekawa, "Collective Labor Service in Girsu-Lagash: The Pre-Sargonic and Ur III Periods," in *Labor in the Ancient Near East,* ed. M. Powell, 49–71, suggests that we see a slow invalidation of the principle that an institution should conscript labor only from people to whom it gave land for service.

39. I. J. Gelb, "Terms for Slaves in Ancient Mesopotamia," in *I. M. Diakonoff A.V.,* ed. J.

Postgate, 81–98, though he does not discuss the "blind" who seem to be slaves, noted in
D. O. Edzard, *Gerichtsurkunden,* 86; Edzard gives slave prices, 87. Gelb's etymology of
the sign ARAD as Man+Foreign Country now seems unlikely. The "Foreign Country"
seems in early texts itself to be a status term. See A. Uchitel, "Women at Work," *Historia* 33 (1984): 257–82, esp. 262, and J. Krecher, "/ur/ 'Mann,' /eme/ 'Frau' und die
sumerische Herkunft des Wortes urdu(-d) 'Sklave,'" *Welt des Orients* 18 (1987): 7–19.

   I. J. Gelb, "Definition and Discussion of Slavery and Freedom," *Ugaritforschungen* 11
(1979): 283–97, esp. 294, prefers to stress the use of the person in service and the lack
of a family life. Gelb opposes Diakonoff, especially "Slaves, Helots and Serfs in Early
Antiquity," *Acta Antiqua* 22 (1974): 45–78, who tends toward a broad definition of slavery, including others that Gelb would term serfs. More recently, I. M. Diakonoff, "Slave-
Labour versus Non-Slave Labour: The Problem of Definition," in *Labor in the Ancient
Near East,* ed. M. Powell, 1–3, maintains this position. It may help to clarify the background to this assertion to note that in Russian history serfs could be sold, as pointed
out in Peter Kolchin, *Unfree Labor* (Cambridge and London: Harvard, 1987), 41–42.
For a brief survey of slavery throughout Ancient Near Eastern history, see I. Mendelsohn, *Slavery in the Ancient Near East.* For Girsu, see H. Neumann, "Einige Erwägungen
zu Recht und Gesellschaft in frühstaatlicher Zeit," *Šulmu,* 211–24, 219, to *RlA* 5:491.

40. Tiumenev, *Gosudarstvennoe Khozyaystvo drevnego Shumera,* 217, 228. P. Bohanan and P.
    Curtin, *Africa and Africans,* 130.
41. I. J. Gelb et al., *Kudurrus,* 17, 25. Gelb, "Household and Family in Early Mesopotamia,"
    in *State and Temple Economies in the Ancient Near East,* ed. E. Lipiński, 1–97, 69–71,
    notes that before Sargon there are no single sellers of land, but in the Old Akkadian
    period half the sellers act alone.
42. I. M. Diakonoff, "The Structure of Near Eastern Society before the Middle of the 2nd
    Millennium," *Oikumene* 3 (1982): 7–100, esp. 16. Compare K. Cuno, "The Origins
    of Private Ownership of Land in Egypt: A Reappraisal," in *The Modern Middle East: A
    Reader,* ed. A. Hourani et al., 195–228, referring to the nineteenth century C.E. I. M.
    Diakonoff, "Kuplia-prodazha zemli v drevneishem Shumere i vopros o shumerskoi obsh-
    chine," *VDI* (1955 4): 10–40, 10, positing that beyond this system lay the communi-
    ties of more private persons organized by large families, 30. See also in English his "Sale
    of Land in Pre-Sargonic Sumer," in *Papers Presented by the Soviet Delegation to the XXI-
    IId International Congress of Orientalists,* 5–32. P. Steinkeller, "Grundeigentum in Baby-
    lonien von Uruk IV bis zur frühdynastischen Periode II," in *Grundeigentum,* ed. B. Bren-
    tjes, 11–27, shows a temple administrator buying land toward the end of the period he
    considers, 24–25; this demonstrates the existence of land belonging neither to the tem-
    ple nor to the state.
43. R. M. Adams, "Strategies of Maximization, Stability and Resilience in Mesopotamian
    Society, Settlement, and Agriculture," *Proceedings of the American Philosophical Society*
    122 (1978): 329–35, esp. 331, stresses that sheep were more prevalent than today
    because marginal steppe land was used for grazing. He also guesses, "Since [central
    archives] have little to say about routine herd management, . . . this may well have been
    the almost exclusive province of traditional kinship groups."
44. M. Green, "Animal Husbandry at Uruk in the Archaic Period," *JNES* 39 (1980): 1–36.
45. J.-M. Kientz and M. Lambert, "L'Élévage du gros bétail à Lagash au temps de Lugalanda
    et d'Urukagina," *Rivista degli Studi orientali* 38 (1963): 93–117, 198–218, esp. 117,
    and M. Müller, "Ein neuer Beleg zur staatlichen Viehhaltung in altsumerischer Zeit,"

L. *Matouš A. V.*, 2:151–66. And see E. Firmage, "Zoology," in *Anchor Bible Dictionary*, 6, ed. D. N. Freedman, 1109–67, esp. 1133–35.

46. K. Maekawa, "Female Weavers and Their Children in Lagash—Pre-Sargonic and Ur III," *ASJ* 2 (1980): 81–125, M. Lambert, "Recherches sur la vie ouvrière: Les Ateliers de tissage de Lagash au temps de Lugalanda et d'Urukagina," *Archiv Orientální* 29 (1961): 422–43, and B. Hruška, "Zur Verwaltung der Handwerker in der frühdynastischen Zeit," in *Gesellschaft und Kultur im alten Vorderasien*, ed. H. Klengel, 99–115. L. Woolley, *Excavations at Ur*, 52–90, and C. J. Gadd, "The Spirit of Living Sacrifices in Tombs," *Iraq* 22 (1960): 51–59.

47. H.-J. Nissen, "Zur Frage der Arbeitsorganisation in Babylonien während der Späturuk-Zeit," *Acta Antiqua* 22 (1974): 5–14, shows that even in lists of professions before the Early Dynastic period some status differences were clear, implying a differentiated system of craftspersons.

48. M. Lambert, "Ur-Emush, 'Grand marchand' de Lagash," *Oriens Antiquus* 20 (1981): 175–85.

49. G. Herrmann, "Lapis Lazuli: The Early Phases of Its Trade," *Iraq* 39 (1968): 21–57, esp. 49, 57. Contrast on the role of the northern site of Gawra, Y. Majidzadeh, "Lapis Lazuli and the Great Khorasan Road," *Paléorient* 8 (1983): 59–69. See E. C. L. During Caspers, "Harappan Trade in the Arabian Gulf in the Third Millennium B.C.," *Mesopotamia* 7 (1972): 167–91, esp. 169.

50. H. E. W. Crawford, "Mesopotamia's Invisible Exports in the Third Millennium B.C.," *World Archaeology* 5 (1973): 232–341.

51. C. C. Lamberg-Karlovsky, "Patterns of Interaction in the Third Millennium: From Mesopotamia to the Indus Valley," *VDI* (1990–1): 3–21, with English summary.

52. W. F. Leemans, "The Importance of Trade: Some Introductory Remarks," *Iraq* 39 (1977): 1–10, and 6 on Assyria. L. Marfoe, "Cedar Forest to Silver Mountain: Social Change and the Development of Long-Distance Trade in Early Near Eastern Societies," in *Centre and Periphery*, ed. M. Rowlands, 25–35, 34. Marfoe suggests, 35, that attempts at conquest were indications that favorable trade situations could not be maintained by peaceful means because they were unstable. Compare for the literary evidence for Early Dynastic trade negotiations, all in texts available only in Old Babylonian copies, C. Zaccagnini, "Ideological and Procedural Paradigms in Ancient Near Eastern Long Distance Exchanges: The Case of Enmerkar and the Lord of Aratta," *Altorientalische Forschungen* 20 (1993): 34–42.

53. See the unpublished thesis of R. Sweet, "On Prices, Moneys, and Money Uses in the Old Babylonian Period" (Ph.D. diss., University of Chicago, 1957), considered in more detail below. Compare on the process by which prices given in iron bars but actually paid in cloth bolts gave way gradually to European currency in Senegambia between 1665 and 1752 C.E. P. Curtin, "Prices and Market Mechanisms of the Senegambia," *Ghana Social Science Journal* 2 (1973): 19–41.

54. W. Eilers, "Akkad. *kaspum*, 'Silber, Geld' und Sinnverwandtes," *Welt des Orients* 2 (1957): 322–37, 4(1959): 465–569, 322. M. Powell, "A Contribution to the History of Money in Mesopotamia prior to the Invention of Coinage," in *L. Matouš A. V.*, 2:211–43.

55. D. O. Edzard, ed., *Sumerische Rechtsurkunden*, 87, lists slave prices, and compare the prices of barley and other commodities given as additional payments in land sales, I. Gelb et al., *Kudurrus*, 1:287–90. See M. Powell, "Identification and Interpretation of

Long Term Price Fluctuations in Babylonia: More on the History of Money in Mesopotamia," *Altorientalische Forschungen* 17 (1990): 76–99, esp. 88–89.

56. For a translation, see J. Cooper, *Sumerian and Akkadian Royal Inscriptions*, 1:70–77.

57. Care for widows and orphans was a continuing theme through Mesopotamian history and indeed may be a constant in human society. F. C. Fensham, "Widow, Orphan, and the Poor in Ancient Near Eastern Legal and Wisdom Literature," *JNES* 21 (1962): 129–39, and, arguing that this is an anthropological universal, I. Weiler, "Zum Shicksal der Witwe und Waisen bei den Völkern der alten Welt; Materialien für eine vergleichende Geschichtswissenschaft," *Saeculum* 31 (1980): 157–93, esp. 193. The potential for loss of status at the death of a husband and father derives from patriarchal family structure, but also from the growth of the nuclear family as opposed to the extended family. Presumably when the extended family functions well and prosperity allows, such extra people would be easily absorbed; see Weiler, 158–59, 191–92.

58. This sketch is dependent on B. Trigger et al., eds., *Ancient Egypt: A Social History*.

59. K. Butzer, *Early Hydraulic Civilization in Egypt*, 107, 11. K. Butzer, "The Late Prehistoric Environmental History of the Near East," in *The Environmental History of the Near and Middle East since the Last Ice Age*, ed. W. Brice, 5–12, 11.

60. Trigger, *Ancient Egypt*, 48–50.

61. P. R. S. Moorey, "On Tracking Cultural Transfers in Prehistory: The Case of Egypt and Lower Mesopotamia in the Fourth Millennium B.C.," *Centre and Periphery*, ed. M. Rowlands, 36–46, noting that Mesopotamian goods reached Egypt already in the Gerzean period.

62. Note that what I call the Early Dynastic in Egypt does not correspond in time to the Mesopotamian Early Dynastic. For the periodizations, compare the listing of periods mentioned above in W. W. Hallo and W. K. Simpson, *The Ancient Near East: A History*, with the Egyptian appendix there, 299–302. For tribal organization around Memphis only, which developed away from kinship groups, see Ann M. Roth, *Egyptian Phyles in the Old Kingdom*, esp. 207–08.

63. Naguib Kanawati, "Polygamy in the Old Kingdom of Egypt," *Studien zur altägyptischen Kultur* 4 (1976): 149–60, 159–60.

64. Klaus Baer, "The Low Price of Land in Ancient Egypt," *Journal of the American Research Center in Egypt* 1 (1962): 25–43, esp. 25, 33, 44–45. Abd el-Mohsen Bakir, *Slavery in Pharaonic Egypt*, 8.

65. W. Helck, *Wirtschaftsgeschichte des alten Ägypten im 3. und 2. Jahrtausend vor Chr.*, 114.

66. Trigger, *Ancient Egypt*, 85–92, and D. A. Warburton, "Keynes'che Überlegungen zur altäyptischen Wirtschaft," *Zeitschrift für altägyptischen Sprache und Altertumskunde* 118 (1991): 76–85 (reference courtesy of Daniel Nevez). On the continuation of cults, see Trigger, 95–96. On the evolution of pyramid design see Kurt Mendelssohn, *The Riddle of the Pyramids*. Our word for the structures derives from what Herodotus called them, *pyramis*, and he was using the name for a similarly shaped Greek cake, though in fact we do not know what the cake looked like, as noted by H. Liddell, R. Scott, *A Greek-English Lexicon*, 1555b. The native term was *mr*.

67. Trigger, *Ancient Egypt*, 92–96, and see the still useful sketch of H. Frankfort, *Kingship and the Gods*, 15–212. K. Baer, *Rank and Title in the Old Kingdom*, 30–302.

68. See Y. Aharoni, *Archaeology of the Holy Land*, 35–47, and V. Fritz, *Einführung in die biblische Archäologie*, 89–95.

69. Trigger, *Ancient Egypt,* 40–43, 61–63.
70. K. C. Chang, *The Archaeology of Ancient China,* 135, 305, 55.

CHAPTER 2
RISE OF EMPIRES

1. The line from the tablet is the Morgan Library Collection text 2600, column 5, line 11, now housed in the Yale Babylonian Collection and quoted by permission of its curator, William W. Hallo. The text was part of my study *Ledgers and Prices,* where it is given the designation AS7ixPd.
2. R. M. Adams, *Heartland,* 136–55.
3. See W. W. Hallo, "The Coronation of Ur-Nammu," *JCS* 20 (1966): 133–41, 135, and compare the fact that Thomas Jefferson first came to local prominence for his advocacy of clearing the Rivanna River near his home in western Virginia so that it could be used to transport goods to the coast; see D. Malone, *Jefferson, the Virginian* (New York: Little, Brown, 1948), 115–16. R. Whiting, "Some Observations on the Drehem Calendar," *ZA* 69 (1979): 6–33, and F. Pomponio, "The Reichskalendar of Ur III in the Umma Texts," *ZA* 79 (1989): 10–13.
4. K. Maekawa, "The Erin₂ People in Lagash of Ur III Times," *RA* 70 (1976) 9–44, 13. See also M. Sigrist, "Erin₂ Un-il₂," *RA* 73 (1979): 101–20, and 74 (1980): 11–28, and Dsh. Scharaschenidze, "Die "Träger" in der Zeit der III. Dynastie von Ur," in *Gesellschaft und Kultur im alten Vorderasien,* H. Klengel, ed., 229–33.
5. B. Foster, "Ethnicity and Onomastics in Sargonic Mesopotamia," *OrNS* 51 (1982): 297–354, chart, 299. W. Heimpel, "Sumerische und akkadische Personennamen in Sumer und Akkad," *AfO* 25 (1974/77): 171–74, comments on J. Cooper's earlier suggestions of language death. Heimpel thinks Sumerian was still living in the Ur III period, but B. Kienast suggests that Sumerian died by the rise of the Old Akkadian period on the basis of linguistic evidence, which seems to show old grammar rules slipping badly, "Ist das Neusumerische eine lebende Sprache?" *AfO Beiheft* 19 (1982): 105–11. On the phenomenon compare N. Dorian, *Language Death* (Philadelphia: University of Pennsylvania Press, 1981), on the death of a Gaelic dialect. D. Charpin, "Le Sumérien, langue morte parlée," *N.A.B.U.* (1994–1): 7 #6, suggests that school texts show that Sumerian was spoken in the Old Babylonian school, probably not as a first language, but rather as a scholarly language, like Latin in medieval universities.
6. The use of the word *emperor* implies imperialism, and the use of this word has reasonably been questioned for the ancient world by Elisabeth Erdmann, "Römischer 'Imperialismus'—Schlagwort oder Begriff?" *Geschichte in Wissenschaft und Unterricht* 28 (1977/8): 461–77. Clearly in Latin it carries none of its modern negative baggage. And it is very imprecise. I will nonetheless continue to use it because it does conjure up a negative response, as the phenomenon usually did in ancients who were oppressed by outreaching states. Sargon called himself king of the land and king of the four quarters, referring to the directions; see W. W. Hallo, *Early Mesopotamian Royal Titles* (New Haven: American Oriental Society, 1957), 151–52.
7. C. Wilcke, "Zur Geschichte der Ammuriter in der Ur-III-Zeit," *Welt des Orients* 5 (1969): 1–31, 28. See G. Buccellati, *Amorites of the Ur III Period,* 334–39, on sedentary Amorites and their high status.
8. See, in general, G. Wilhelm, *Grundzüge der Geschichte und Kultur der Hurriter,* and *The*

Hurrians, the English translation, and the review of the latter by M. Astour, *JNES* 53 (1994): 225–30. And see I. J. Gelb, *Hurrians and Subarians.*

9. See H. Limet, "La Condition de L'Enfant en Mésopotamie autour de l'an 2000 av. J.-C.," in *L'Enfant dans les civilisations orientales,* A. Théodoridès et al., eds., 5–17, 7, though legal texts show one family with five. On breast feeding, see 5.

Compare the rich and interesting material in J. Boswell, *The Kindness of Strangers: The Abandonment of Children in Western Europe from Late Antiquity to the Renaissance* (New York: Pantheon, 1988), which argues that in medieval to early modern Europe most abandoned babies lived and thrived with adoptive families, until, ironically, children's homes were instituted, which turned out to be breeding grounds for fatal diseases.

10. The basic study is still Å. Sjöberg's, "Zu Einige Verwantschaftsbezeichnungen im Sumerischen," *Heidelberger Studien zum alten Orient . . . A. Falkenstein,* 201–31, and H. Limet, "L'Enfant," 6.

11. Šulgi's offspring are listed in W. W. Hallo and W. Kelly Simpson, *The Ancient Near East: A History,* 85. See E. Gordon, *Sumerian Proverbs,* 302–04, but in fact proverb 1.160 could as well refer to serial marriages.

12. B. Foster, "Notes on Women in Sargonic Society," in *La Femme dans le Proche-Orient antique,* J.-M. Durand, ed., 53–61, "Notes," 53–54, referring to Ama-e$_2$, the distaff side of the Ur-Šara archive, *Umma in the Sargonic Period,* 77–78, his Group B. See W. W. Hallo and J. J. A. Van Dijk, *The Exaltation of Inanna,* 1–11.

13. M. van de Mieroop, "Women in the Economy of Sumer," in *Women's Earliest Records,* B. Lesko, ed., 53–66, 56–61, listing the kings' consorts and the earlier literature. Add, too, J. Klein, "Šeleppūtum, a Hitherto Unknown Ur III Princess," *ZA* 80 (1990): 20–39. N. Schneider, "Der dub-sar als Verwaltungsbeamter im Reiche von Sumer und Akkad zur Zeit der III Dynastie von Ur," *OrNS* 15 (1946): 64–88, lists no women, but compare A. L. Oppenheim, *Eames Collection,* 21–22, C1, column vii 10 (note that in printing the reverse and obverse were switched), as noted by S. Meier, "Women and Communication in the Ancient Near East," *JAOS* 111 (1991): 540–47, 541.

14. A. Falkenstein, *Die Neusumerischen Gerichtsurkunden,* 1:113. On widows, see D. Owen, "Widow's Rights in Ur III Sumer," *ZA* 70 (1981): 170–84, esp. 174–75, and Falkenstein, *Gerichtsurkunden* 1:69, 81.

15. Gelb, "The Ancient Mesopotamian Ration System," *JNES* 24 (1965): 230–43, 233. I. J. Gelb, "The Arua Institution," *RA* 66 (1972): 1–32, and D. Foxvog, "A Third Arua Summary from Ur III Lagash," *RA* 80 (1986): 19–29. K. Maekawa, "Female Weavers and Their Children in Lagash—Pre-Sargonic and Ur III," *ASJ* 2 (1980): 81–125. Note, though, that women and men were divided by gender for corvée labor, and it can be shown sometimes that specific women were married to specific men listed elsewhere; see A. Uchitel, "Women at Work," *Historia* 33 (1984): 257–82, 272–73.

M. Biga, "Frauen in der Wirtschaft von Ebla," in *Wirtschaft und Gesellschaft von Ebla,* H. Waetzoldt, H. Hauptmann, eds., 159–71. M. Biga, "Donne alla corte di Ebla," *La Parola del Passato* 46 (1991): 285–303. V. Davidović, "The Women's Ration System in Ebla," *Oriens Antiquus* 26 (1987): 299–307.

16. A. Falkenstein, *Gerichtsurkunden,* 1:85, but Limet, "L'Enfant," 16, disagrees.

17. For a camp of prisoners of war near or in Iran, see B. Foster, *Umma in the Sargonic Period,* Group A, 46–50. For a sketch of one group of workers of low status, but with families and land allotments working for government only part of the year, see P. Steinkeller, "The Foresters of Umma," in *Labor,* M. Powell, ed., 73–115. Contrast V.

Davidović, "Guruš in the Administrative Texts from Ebla," in *Wirtschaft,* H. Waetzoldt, H. Hauptmann, eds., 199–204, since the term seems to mean man in general there.

18. R. Ellison, "Diet in Mesopotamia: The Evidence of the Barley Ration Texts (c. 3000–1400 B.C.)," *Iraq* 43 (1981): 35–45. On the system of rations, consistent from the Pre-Sargonic to the Kassite, see I. J. Gelb, "The Ancient Mesopotamian Ration System," *JNES* 24 (1965): 230–43, and for a history of it, culminating in Ur III, see L. Milano, "Le Razioni alimentari nel vicino oriente antico: per un'articolazione storica del sistema," in *Il pane del re: Accumulo e distribuzione dei cereali nell'oriente antico,* R. Dolce and C. Zaccagnini, eds., 65–100.

19. See H. Waetzoldt, "Compensation of Craft Workers and Officials in the Ur III Period," in *Labor,* M. Powell, ed., 117–41, guessing the number of persons on rations might be more than three hundred thousand! L. Milano, "Food Rations at Ebla: A Preliminary Account of the Ration Lists Coming from the Ebla Palace Archive L. 2712," *M.A.R.I.* 5 (1987): 519–50, esp. 549. R. Englund, "Hard Work—Where Will It Get You? Labor Management in Ur III Mesopotamia," *JNES* 50 (1991): 255–80, argues that the women workers he examines were "wholly property of the state," 256, but this is not true of many dependent workers, though he is probably right when he guesses, 280, that only flight or death absolved the worker from the obligation.

20. See the studies in *Labor in the Ancient Near East,* M. Powell, ed., and A. I. Tiumenev, *Gosudarstvennoe Khozyaystvo Drevnego Shumera.* Dj. Sharashenidze, *Formy ekspluatatsii rabochei sily v gosudarstvennom khoyaystve Shumera II pol. III tys. do n. e.,* 38, 35 n. 254. V. V. Struve, "Naëmnyi trud i sel'skaya obshchina v iuzhnom Mezhdurech'e kontsa III tysacheletia do n. e.," *VDI* (1948–2): 13–33, 21.

21. I. J. Gelb, "Social Stratification in the Old Akkadian Period," *25th International Congress of Orientalists,* 1:225–26, esp. 226. See I. J. Gelb, "Quantitative Estimates of Slavery and Serfdom," in *S. N. Kramer A.V.,* B. Eichler, ed., 195–208. Falkenstein, *Gerichtsurkunden,* 197–98; texts 1–12 there concern slaves' protesting their status.

22. Falkenstein, *Gerichtsurkunden,* 86–87. The importance of runaways was underlined by A. Tiumenev, *Gosudarstvennoe Khozyaystvo,* 367–68. Note that, for example, in the great labor ledger I edited, "The Lager Texts," *ASJ* 11 (1989): 155–224, 182–200, esp. 198–200, each work group had a few runaways, including even the city governor's policemen. I. J. Gelb, "Prisoners of War in Early Mesopotamia," *JNES* 32 (1973): 70–98.

23. The importance of private land was seen independently by I. J. Gelb, "On the Alleged Temple and State Economies in Ancient Mesopotamia," *Studi in Onore Edouardo Volterra,* 6:137–54, and by I. M. Diakonoff, *Obshchestvennyi i gosudarstvennyi Stroi drevnego dvurech'ya. Šumer.* For the stele, see I. Gelb et al., *Earliest Land Tenure Systems in the Near East: Ancient Kudurrus,* 116–40.

24. See H. Neumann, "Zum Problem des privaten Bodeneigentums in Mesopotamien," *Jahrbuch für Wirtschaftsgeschichte* (1987/5): 29–49, esp. 85 and n. 81, referring to D. Owen, *Neo-Sumerian Archival Texts Primarily from Nippur,* text 906. See the reasonable treatment of J. N. Postgate, *Early Mesopotamia,* 95, 183, 292. Steinkeller, *Sales Documents of the Ur-III-Period,* 128. Compare M. I. Finley, "The Alienability of Land of Ancient Greece; A Point of View," *Eirene* 7 (1968): 25–32, 30–31, arguing that even in Athens it is unlikely that land really was inalienable. Legislated restrictions indicate that land was being sold more, not that it really was not being sold, 32.

25. P. Steinkeller, "The Rent of Fields in Early Mesopotamia and the Development of the

Concept of 'Interest' in Sumerian," *JESHO* 24 (1981): 113–45, though the term that later means "rent" may have meant "irrigation fee" in Ur III.

26. M. Powell, "Salt, Seed, and Yields in Sumerian Agriculture: A Critique of the Theory of Progressive Salinization," *ZA* 75 (1985): 7–38. Even the idea that productivity declined is not sustained by careful analysis, 38. So also K. Butz and P. Schröder, "Zu Getreideerträgen in Mesopotamien und dem Mittelmeergebiet," *Baghdader Mitteilungen* 16 (1985): 165–209. Northern harvests were usually less good than southern, 198, and although no decline can be seen between Early Dynastic and Ur III, there may have been declines by the Neo-Babylonian because of lack of water, not increase in salt, 197–98. M. Liverani, "Il Rendimento dei Cereali durante la III Dinastia di Ur. Contributo ad un approcio realistico," *Origini* 15 (1990): 359–68, finds crop yields in Ur III between 1 : 13 and 1 : 16, comparable to the ratio of 1 : 10 known from Egypt and Middle Babylonian Nuzi, 365–66. And M. el Fariz argues, "Salinité et histoire de l'Irak pré-Islamique," *JESHO* 33 (1990): 105–13, that peasants in medieval times abandoned only fields that were very heavily salted, implying that in the ancient period not much resettlement was due to salting.

27. K. Maekawa, "Cereal Cultivation in the Ur III Period," *Bulletin of Sumerian Agriculture* 1 (1984): 73–96, esp. 86; L. Milano, "Barley for Rations and Barley for Sowing," *ASJ* 9 (1987): 177–202.

28. B. Foster, *Administration and Use of Institutional Land in Sargonic Sumer.*

29. M. Civil, "Ur III Bureaucracy: Quantitative Aspects," in *The Organization of Power,* M. Gibson, R. Biggs, eds., 213–53.

30. See especially the classic article by I. J. Gelb, "The Growth of a Herd of Cattle in Ten Years," *JCS* 21 (1967): 64–69. A. Archi, "Allevamento e distribuzione del bestiame ad Ebla," *Studi Eblaiti* 7 (1984): 45–81, 76.

31. On nonanimal items, see M. Sigrist, "Le Trésor de Drehem," *OrNS* 48 (1979): 26–53. See, in general, M. Sigrist, *Drehem,* summarized 408–09. English readers will prefer to turn to T. Jones, J. Snyder, *Sumerian Economic Texts from the Third Ur Dynasty,* 212–38. And compare M. Zeder, "Of Kings and Shepherds: Specialized Animal Economy in Ur III Mesopotamia," in *Chiefdoms and Early States in the Near East,* G. Stein, M. Rothman, eds., 91, and her monograph *Feeding Cities.* See W. W. Hallo, "A Sumerian Amphictyony," *JCS* 14 (1960): 88–114. For a different view, see P. Steinkeller, "The Administrative and Economic Organization of the Ur III State," in *Organization,* M. Gibson, R. Biggs, eds., 19–41, 29, and M. Sigrist, *Drehem,* 339–56, who sees the "turn of office" as a tax on the empire's upper classes. For a possible forerunner of Puzriš-Dagan, see C. Wilcke, "E-saĝ-da-na Nibru^ki: An Early Administrative Center of the Ur III Empire," in *Nippur,* M. Ellis, 311–24, perhaps, 324, the source of the "Early Series."

32. P. Michalowski, "The Neo-Sumerian Silver Ring Texts," *Syro-Mesopotamian Studies* 2/3 (1978): 1–16. On the "Early Series," see Jones and Snyder, *Sumerian Economic Texts,* 203–08; the memorial aspect was suggested in personal communication by Marc Cooper.

33. J-M. Durand and D. Charpin, "Remarques sur l'élévage intensif dans l'Iraq ancien," in *L'Archéologie de l'Iraq,* M.-T. Barrelet, ed., 131–56. See, too, K. Maekawa, "The Management of Fatted Sheep (udu-niga) in Ur III Girsu/Lagash," *ASJ* 6 (1983): 81–111.

34. See H. Waetzoldt, *Untersuchungen zur neusumerischen Textilindustrie,* and for a brief overview in English, T. Jacobsen, "On the Textile Industry at Ur under Ibbi-Sîn," in *Stu-*

dia Orientalia Ioanni Pedersen dedicata, 172–87. D. Snell, "The Rams of Lagash," *ASJ* 8 (1986): 133–217.

35. For the declining dairy production in Ibbi-Sin's years 6–8 in Ur, see T. Gomi, "On Dairy Productivity at Ur in the Late Ur III Period," *JESHO* 23 (1979): 1–42, 35–36. For the fishing industry, see R. Englund, *Organisation und Verwaltung der Ur III-Fischerei.*

36. See A. Archi, "Wovon Lebte man in Ebla?" *AfO Beiheft* 19 (1982): 175–88.

37. See, in general, about Ur D. Loding, "A Craft Archive from Ur," (Ph.D. diss., University of Pennsylvania, 1974), and on all the cities, H. Neumann, *Handwerk in Mesopotamien.*

38. A. Goetze, "Umma Texts Concerning Reed Mats," *JCS* 2 (1948): 165–202, and see J. N. Postgate, "Palm-Trees, Reeds and Rushes in Iraq Ancient and Modern," in *L'Archéologie,* M.-T. Barrelet, ed., 99–109, though not specifically on this period. Neumann, *Handwerk,* 75–86, 97–106, 113–27.

39. A. Westenholz, "The Sargonic Period," in *Circulation,* A. Archi, ed., 17–30. B. Foster, "Commercial Activity in Sargonic Mesopotamia," *Iraq* 39 (1979): 31–43.

40. W. F. Leemans, "The Importance of Trade," *Iraq* 39 (1977): 2–10, and compare D. Snell, "The Activities of Some Merchants of Umma," *Iraq* 39 (1977): 45–50, for a sample comparison of foreign and domestic goods in three texts. See H. Limet, "Les Schémas du Commerce néo-sumérien," *Iraq* 39 (1977): 51–58.

41. D. Snell, "The Allocation of Resources in the Umma Silver Balanced Account System," *JESHO* 31 (1988): 1–13; most recipients cannot be identified according to what government bureau, if any, they represented. For a reconstruction of the system, see D. Snell, *Ledgers and Prices,* 55–75.

42. B. Foster, "Mercantile Activity in Sargonic Mesopotamia," *Iraq* 39 (1977): 31–43.

43. Snell, *Ledgers,* 32, 103–08. For a different perspective on one merchant, see H. Neumann, "Zu den Geschäften des Kaufmanns Ur-Dumuzida aus Umma," *Altorientalische Forschungen* 20 (1993): 69–86. Some of the merchants at least appear to be government officials. H. Neumann, "Handel und Händler in der Zeit der III. Dynastie von Ur," *Altorientalische Forschungen* 6 (1979): 15–67, esp. 36, though others might be less official; see also 37, 48.

44. For literary references to trade, see G. Pettinato, "Il Commercio con l'Estero della Mesopotamia meridionale nel 3 millenio av. Cr. alla luce delle fonti letterarie e lessicali sumeriche," *Mesopotamia* 7 (1972): 43–166. M. van de Mieroop, "Turām-ilī: An Ur III Merchant," *JCS* 38 (1986): 1–80, has an archive from an unidentified site.

45. A. Archi, "Trade and Administrative Practice," *Altorientalische Forschungen* 20 (1993): 43–58. The relation between the cities of Mari and Ebla was the most important trade link in the area. A. Archi, "Les Rapports politiques et économiques entre Ebla et Mari," *M.A.R.I.* 4 (1985): 63–83, 67, 69, and the exchange may have been unequal, to Mari's profit. See, in general on imported lapis and other semiprecious stones, F. Pinnock, "About the Trade of Early Syrian Ebla," *M.A.R.I.* 4 (1985): 85–92, and with greater detail, "The Lapis Lazuli Trade in the Third Millennium B.C. and the Evidence from the Royal Palace G of Ebla," in *Insight Through Images . . . E. Porada,* M. Kelly-Buccellati, ed., 221–28. Trade was probably essential for Ebla's flourishing, as shown by J. Renger, "Überlegungen zur räumlichen Ausdehnung des Staates von Ebla an Hand der agrarischen und viehwirtschaftlichen Gegebenheiten," in *Ebla 1975–1985,* L. Cagni, ed., 293–311, arguing that the immediate area could not grow enough food for the posited population.

On Egyptian objects, see G. Scandone Matthiae, "Les Relations entre Ebla et l'Egypte au IIIme et au IIme Millénaire av. J.-Chr.," in *Wirtschaft,* H. Waetzoldt, H. Hauptmann, eds., 67–73.

46. See H. Limet, "Les Métaux à l'Epoque d'Agadé," *JESHO* 15 (1972): 3–34, and M. Lambert, "L'Usage de l'Argent-Métal à Lagash au temps de la 3e Dynastie d'Ur," *RA* 57 (1963): 79–92, 193–299. Ebla seems to have had more silver available than any other third-millennium site, so much so that workers and dependent people were often paid in silver; see A. Archi, "Prices, Workers' Wages and Maintenance at Ebla," *Altorientalische Forschungen* 15 (1988): 24–29, esp. 25, 29.

47. Snell, *Ledgers,* 189–96.

48. T. Jacobsen, "The Reign of Ibbi-Sîn." T. Gomi, "On the Critical Economic Situation at Ur Early in the Reign of Ibbi-Sin," *JCS* 36 (1984): 211–42, arguing that barley shortages were made up by issuing oils to dependent workers, 224, 242. K. Maekawa, "Rations, Wages and Economic Trends in the Ur III Period," *Altorientalische Forschungen* 16 (1989): 42–50, 50, sees general stability at Umma until Ibbi-Sin's third year. Old Akkadian and Ur III prices of barley in silver are slight declines from the earlier period, as seen by M. Powell, "Long Term Price Fluctuations," 88.

49. H. Neumann, "Zur privaten Geschäftstätigkeit in Nippur in der Ur III-Zeit," in *Nippur at the Centennial,* M. Ellis, ed., 161–76. P. Steinkeller, *Sale Documents of the Ur-III-Period,* 117. Lack of uniformity is seen also in the documents recording loans. H. Lutzman, "Die neusumerischen Schuldurkunden" (Münster: Diss. Erlangen, 1976).

50. The identification with Šulgi has been assured by S. N. Kramer, "The Ur-Nammu Law Code: Who Was Its Author?" *OrNS* 52 (1983): 453–56. I. Finkel, "An Issue of Weights from the Reign of Amar-Sin," *ZA* 77 (1987): 192–93.

51. G. Komoróczy, "Lobpreis auf das Gefängnis in Sumer," *Acta Antiqua* 23 (1975): 153–74, and M. Civil, "On Mesopotamian Jails and Their Lady Warden," in *W. W. Hallo A. V.,* M. Cohen et al., eds., 72–78. And compare P. Steinkeller, "The Reforms of Uru-KA-gina and an Early Sumerian Term for 'Prison,'" *Aula Orientalis* 9 (1991): 227–33.

52. For the army, see M. Civil, "Les Limites de l'information textuelle," in *L'Archéologie,* M.-T. Barrelet, ed., 225–32, 231, and for police, see D. Katz, "A Computerized Study of the AGA-Uš of the Ur III Period" (University of Minnesota Master's Thesis, 1979).

53. B. Foster, "Agriculture and Accountability in Ancient Mesopotamia," in *The Origins of Cities in Dry-Farming Syria in the Third Millennium B.C.,* H. Weiss, ed., 109–28.

54. Snell, *Ledgers,* 204–07. J. S. Cooper, *The Curse of Agade,* 54–55, 58–59.

55. H. Limet, "Ur et sa région à l'époque de la 3e dynastie," *Altorientalische Forschungen* 20 (1993): 115–22, 122.

56. See H. Limet, "Le Rôle du palais dans l'économie néo-sumérienne," in *State and Temple Economy in the Ancient Near East,* E. Lipiński, ed., 235–48, 247, on Šulgi's possible land grab. Compare J. N. Postgate, "The Role of the Temple in the Mesopotamian Secular Community," in *Man, Settlement, and Urbanism,* P. Ucko et al., eds., 811–25, 814, noting that the temple served in effect as a "joint company" to pool resources for the community. R. Zettler, *The Ur III Temple of Inanna at Nippur,* 234, 209, and his "The Genealogy of the House of Ur-Me-me: A Second Look," *AfO* 31 (1984): 1–14. P. Steinkeller, "The Administrative and Economic Organization of the Ur III State: The Core and the Periphery," in *Organization,* M. Gibson, R. Biggs, 19–42, 20–21, 25. A. Archi, "Ebla: La formazione di uno Stato del III millenio a. C.," *La Parola del Passato* 46 (1991): 195–219, 197, 219.

57. W. W. Hallo, "Gutium," *RlA* 3:708–20.

58. S. N. Kramer, *Lamentation over the Destruction of Ur*, and P. Michalowski, *The Lamentation over the Destruction of Sumer and Ur*.

59. See Trigger, *Ancient Egypt*, 71–116.

60. Ibid., 82–83.

61. Ibid., 50–51, 63–68.

62. Ibid., 96–104.

63. Y. Aharoni, *Archaeology of the Land of Israel*, 49–89.

64. Ibid., 80–89, and compare W. Dever, "Funerary Practices in EB IV (MB I) Palestine: A Study in Cultural Discontinuity," in *Marvin Pope A.V.*, J. Marks, R. Good, eds., 9–19.

65. See J. Van Seters, *Abraham in History and Tradition*, 104–12, though his conclusions are not universally accepted.

66. Aharoni, *Archaeology*, 86–89, and V. Fritz, *Einführung in die biblische Archäologie*, 108–11, 113.

67. See, in general, A. B. Knapp, *The History and Culture of Ancient Western Asia and Egypt*, 198–200.

68. The new finds in Peru were reported in the *New York Times*, October 3, 1989, III, 1.

CHAPTER 3
DISUNITY AND REFORM

1. The edict was edited by F. R. Kraus, *Königliche Verfügungen in altbabylonischer Zeit*.

2. For the political history of the period, see D. O. Edzard, *Die Zweite Zwischenzeit Babyloniens*.

3. R. McC. Adams, *Heartland*, 164–65. The fact that the Old Babylonian cannot be distinguished from the Kassite period, which follows, leads to a tendency among archaeologists to overestimate the Old Babylonian; see R. McC. Adams, *Land behind Baghdad*, 53. See A. D. Kilmer, "The Mesopotamian Concept of Overpopulation and Its Solution as Reflected in the Mythology," *OrNS* 41 (1972): 160–77.

4. See E. Stone, "Texts, Architecture and Ethnographic Analogy: Patterns of Residence in Old Babylonian Nippur," *Iraq* 43 (1981): 19–33, 32 on family size.

5. See E. Stone, *Nippur Neighborhoods*, 7, 22.

6. So M. van de Mieroop, "Old Babylonian Ur: Portrait of an Ancient Mesopotamian City," *JANES* 21 (1992): 119–30, 129–30, and his *Society and Enterprise in Old Babylonian Ur*. I. M. Diakonoff, *Lyudi goroda Ura*, which does, however, give reconstructions of houses and even clothes, 33–61.

7. L. Milano, "Alimentazione e regimi alimentari nella Siria preclassica," *Dialoghi di Archeologia* 3 (1981): 85–121, 109.

8. See J.-R. Kupper, "Mari," in *La Ville dans le Proche-Orient ancien*, 113–21. Diakonoff, *Lyudi*, 20.

9. See I. J. Gelb, "An Old Babylonian List of Amorites," *JAOS* 88 (1968): 39–46, studying a list perhaps for a census of men from near the Persian Gulf. M. Heltzer, *The Suteans*, studies the largest group of Amorites, seen especially at Mari. On nomadic-sedentary relations, see J.-R. Kupper, *Les Nomades en Mésopotamie au temps des rois de Mari*, and V. Matthews, *Pastoral Nomadism in the Mari Kingdom*. See Kraus, *Verfügungen*, 308, for instances.

10. On the *wākil Amurrim*, see Edzard, *Zwischenzeit*, 37 and n. 157, and in general M.

Anbar, *Les Tribus amurrites de Mari*, arguing, 213–14, that Amorites had once lived in the Syrian desert because Jebel Bishri was called the Mountain of the Amorites. Kassites in the Old Babylonian period are known only from the middle Euphrates and Alalah in the far west, J. A. Brinkman, *RlA* 5:465a.

11. See Wilhelm, *Grundzüge der Geschichte und Kultur der Hurriter,* 9–26, on the period, but consult the helpful review of the English edition by M. Astour, *JNES* 53 (1994): 225–30; on the Hurrian factor, see P. Michalowski, "Mental Maps and Ideology: Reflections on Subartu," in *The Origins of Cities in Dry-Farming Syria and Mesopotamia in the Third Millennium B.C.,* H. Weiss, ed., 129–56. Subarians "northerners" are referred to in the period, especially as making good slaves, but lists of names show they were not a linguistic group and probably not an ethnic one either. See J. Finkelstein, "Subartu and Subarians in Old Babylonian Sources," *JCS* 9 (1955): 1–7.

See J. M. Sasson, "Hurrians and Hurrian Names in the Mari Texts," *Ugaritforschung* 6 (1974): 353–400, showing that Hurrians at Mari are known through 487 personal names, and the Hurrians were not limited to lower-level jobs, 356.

R. Harris, "On Foreigners in Old Babylonian Sippar," *RA* 70 (1976): 145–52. See also N. Yoffee, "Outsiders in Mesopotamia," *VDI* (1989–2): 95–100, noting that most people identified as foreigners actually had good Akkadian names and thus already had begun to assimilate.

M. B. Rowton, "Autonomy and Nomadism in Western Asia," *OrNS* 42 (1973): 247–58, 255–56.

12. See, in general, R. Westbrook, *Old Babylonian Marriage Law.*

13. See the discussions in the *Chicago Assyrian Dictionary,* under the Akkadian words. Many students have worried about whether Sumerian aspects can be distinguished from Akkadian, but because we see almost all Sumerian culture through the prism of Akkadian culture, we probably will not be able to resolve questions like that. In general, see the symposium *Aspects du Contact suméro-akkadien.*

C. Wilcke, "Familiengründung im alten Babylonien," in *Geschlectsreife und Legitimation zur Zeugung,* E. Müller, ed., 213–317, 219, observes that the distinction is not always clear in the sources.

The very general word É = *bītu* "house" also is a normal term for family, though such a "house" can obviously include many kinds of kinship. See F. Kraus, *Vom mesopotamischen Menschen der altbabylonischen Zeit und seiner Welt,* 47.

At Dilbat, texts seem to show a shift from families as economic centers to bureaucracies, perhaps as a response to Hammurapi's attempts to centralize authority; see M. J. Desroches, "Aspects of the Structure of Dilbat during the Old Babylonian Period," (Ph.D. diss., UCLA, 1978), esp. 479.

See H. Klengel, "Zu den *šibūtum* in altbabylonischer Zeit," *OrNS* 29 (1960): 357–75.

14. W. F. Leemans, "The Family in the Economic Life of the Old Babylonian Period," *Oikumene* 5 (1986): 15–22.

See I. M. Diakonoff, "Extended Families in Old Babylonian Ur," *ZA* 75 (1985): 47–65, though note that elsewhere in Ur such family groups are not found; see M. van de Mieroop, "Old Babylonian Ur," *JANES* 21 (1992): 119–30, 129.

Wilcke, "Familiengründung," 219–20, and D. O. Edzard, "Sumerer und Semiten in der frühen Geschichte Mesopotamiens," in *Aspects,* 241–48, 255–58. Compare J. Renger, "*mārat ilim*: Exogamie bei den semitischen Nomaden des 2. Jahrtausends," *AfO*

24 (1973): 103–07, suggesting that a "daughter/son of a god" was a person belonging to a group within which members had to marry, 107.

15. See J. Renger, "Who Are All Those People?" *OrNS* 42 (1973): 259–73. Note Oppenheim's complaint that it is usually easier to learn about unfree persons in Mesopotamian history than free ones, who were not closely monitored by the authorities, "A New Look at the Structure of Mesopotamian Society," *JESHO* 10 (1967): 1–16, 2.

16. This is Westbrook's argument, summarized with earlier literature in *Old Babylonian Marriage Law,* 58, and 103 on polygamy. Compare for things changing hands, frequently slaves and garments, S. Dalley, "Old Babylonian Dowries," *Iraq* 42 (1980): 53–74. For rites, see S. Greengus, "Old Babylonian Marriage Ceremonies and Rites," *JCS* 20 (1966): 55–72.

    See the analysis of D. Herlihy, *Medieval Households,* 112–14, and see again H. Limet, "L'Enfant."

17. See E. Ebeling, "Erbe, Erbrecht, Enterbung," *RlA* 2:458b-60b. See F. R. Kraus, "Zum ab. Erbrecht," *Archiv Orientální* 17 (1949): 406–13, but in Kutalla near Larsa inheritance was settled by casting lots, as seen in D. Charpin, *Archive familiale et propriété privée en Babylonie ancienne: Études des documents de "Tell Sifr,"* 176.

18. See the extensive studies by R. Harris, including "The Naditu Woman," *A. L. Oppenheim A.V.,* 106–35, 109, and "The Organization and Administration of the Cloister in Ancient Babylonia," *JESHO* 6 (1963): 121–57, showing male officials administered the "cloister." And see her "Biographical Notes on the *Nadītu* Women of Sippar," *JCS* 16 (1962): 1–12, and also her study of the city, *Ancient Sippar,* and the review by M. Gallery (Kovacs), *JAOS* 99 (1979): 73–80.

19. E. Stone, "The Social Role of the *Nadītu* Women in Old Babylonian Nippur," *JESHO* 25 (1982): 50–70.

20. Harris, *Sippar,* 196–97, has assembled the evidence for thirteen attested at Sippar. On schools, see D. Charpin, *Le Clergé d'Ur au siècle d'Hammurabi,* 482–86.

21. See, in general, B. Batto, *Studies on Women at Mari,* and J.-M. Durand on the pre-restoration interlude, "Les Dames du Palais de Mari à l'époque du Royaume de Haute-Mésopotamie," *M.A.R.I.* 4 (1985): 385–436, and B. Lafont, "Les Filles du Roi de Mari," in *La Femme dans le Proche-Orient antique,* J.-M. Durand, ed., 113–23.

22. See B. Batto, "Land Tenure and Women at Mari," *JESHO* 23 (1980): 210–32, 237, 239, and J. M. Sasson, "Biographical Notices on Some Royal Ladies from Mari," *JCS* 25 (1973): 59–78.

    See, too, G. Cardascia, "Le Statut de la femme dans les droits cunéiformes," *Recueils de la Société Jean Bodin* 11 (1957): 79–94, 89, 93.

23. Finkelstein believed, "Ammisaduqa's Edict," *JCS* 15 (1961): 91–104, esp. 96–99, that it referred to crown dependents, while Kraus, *Verfügungen,* 329–31, gives recent literature, arguing that it means all commoners. His earlier discussion is *Vom mesopotamischen Menschen,* 95–117. And see G. Buccellati, "A Note on the Muškēnum as a 'Homesteader,'" *Maarav* 7 (1991): 91–100, that is, someone with limited title to land. In the Neo-Assyrian period the term became synonymous with "poor," in which meaning it entered Aramaic and then Arabic and French, and Spanish, where the meaning is "miser."

    B. Landsberger, "Remarks on the Archive of the Soldier Ubarum," *JCS* 9 (1955): 121–31, though the entrepreneur may have actually owned only one field himself, 128.

24. See D. Evans, "The Incidence of Labour-Service in the Old Babylonian Period," *JAOS* 83 (1963): 20–26. See N. V. Kozyreva, *Drevnyaya Larsa,* 27.

25. Code of Hammurapi, paragraph 273. See M. Weitemeyer, *Some Aspects of the Hiring of Workers in the Sippar Region at the Time of Hammurabi.* See, in general, H. Klengel, "Non-Slave Labour in the Old Babylonian Period: The Basic Outlines," in *Labor,* M. Powell, ed. 159–66.

26. Compare Harris, *Sippar,* 335–36, and the summary on Old Babylonian slavery in I. Cardellini, *Die biblischen "Sklaven"-Gesetze im Lichte des keilschriftlichen Sklavenrechts,* 31–117.

   Renger, "Flucht also soziales Problem in der altbabylonischen Gesellschaft," in *Gesellschaftsklassen,* D. O. Edzard, ed., 166–82. See R. Harris, "Notes on the Slave Names of Old Babylonian Sippar," *JCS* 29 (1977): 45–51, and the *Chicago Assyrian Dictionary* under the word *abbuttu.*

27. R. Harris, "Slave Names." R. Harris, "On Foreigners in Old Babylonian Sippar," *RA* 70 (1976): 145–52, 146.

28. See I. M. Diakonoff, "On the Structure of Old Babylonian Society," in *Beiträge zur sozialen Struktur des alten Vorderasien* 1, H. Klengel, ed., 15–31, 18. For Mari, see J. de Kuyper, "Grundeigentum in Mari," *Jahrbuch für Wirtschaftsgeschichte* (1987/s): 69–78, where all sales involved a single official.

   E. Stone, "Economic Crisis and Social Upheaval in Old Babylonian Nippur," in *Mountains and Lowlands,* L. Levine and T. C. Young, eds., 267–89.

   See the sketch by H. Klengel, "Einige Bemerkungen zur sozialökonomischen Entwicklung in der altbabylonischen Zeit," *Acta Antiqua* 22 (1974): 249–57, 250, seeing it as part of a trend toward individualizing that may have begun among Amorites.

29. See V. A. Jacobson, "Some Problems Connected with the Rise of Landed Property (Old Babylonian Period)," in *Beiträge,* 1, H. Klengel, ed., 33–37. H. Klengel, "Einige Bemerkungen," sees the private economy expanding and greater mobility in land rights and in labor. Compare J. Renger, "Interaction of Temple, Palace, and 'Private Enterprise' in the Old Babylonian Economy," in *State and Temple Economy in the Ancient Near East,* E. Lipiński, ed., 249–56, 250–51. E. Stone and D. I. Owen, *Adoption in Old Babylonian Nippur,* 2:33. Compare S. G. Koshurnikov, "A Family Archive from Old Babylonian Dilbat," *VDI* (1984–2): 123–33, 125.

30. J. Renger, "Das Privateigentum an der Feldflur in der altbabylonischen Zeit," *Das Grundeigentum,* B. Brentjes, ed., 49–67, 58, 62, 60, 53. Compare on the paucity of land sales in Larsa, N. V. Kozyreva, *Drevnyaya Larsa,* 118. On the villages surrounding Larsa, see N. V. Kozyreva, "Sel'skaia okruga v gosudarstve Larsa," *VDI* (1975–2): 3–17.

31. S. Walters, *Water for Larsa,* 147–51.

32. N. Yoffee, *The Economic Role of the Crown in the Old Babylonian Period.* See Oppenheim, "New Look," 13, and J. Renger, "Zur Bewirtschaftung von Dattelpalmgärten während der altbabylonischen Zeit," *F. Kraus A. V.,* 290–97, noting that the palace preferred to let entrepreneurs carry out exploitation of dates and other commodities; see also his "Patterns of Non-Commercial Exchange in Ancient Mesopotamia at the Beginning of the Second Millennium B.C." in *Circulation,* Archi, ed., 31–123, 38.

33. J. N. Postgate and S. Payne, "Some Old Babylonian Shepherds and Their Flocks," *Journal of Semitic Studies* 20 (1975): 1–21.

34. K. Butz, "Konzentrationen wirtschaftlicher Macht im Königreich Larsa: Der Nanna-Nungal-Tempelkomplex in Ur," *WZKM* 65/66 (1973/4): 1–58.

35. F. R. Kraus, *Staatliche Viehhaltung im altbabylonischen Lande Larsa;* for the wool expected, see 18.

N. B. Kozyreva, "Nekotorye dannye o chastnom skotovodcheskom khozyaystve v starovavilonskom gorode Larsa," *Peredneaziatskii Sbornik* 3 (1979): 135–41, and compare her *Drevnyaya Larsa,* 35–40.

Koschaker, "Zur staatlischen Wirtschaftsverwaltung in altbabylonischer Zeit, insbesondere nach Urkunden aus Larsa," *ZA* 47 (1942): 135–80. Compare M. van de Mieroop, "Sheep and Goat Herding according to the Old Babylonian Texts from Ur," *Bulletin of Sumerian Agriculture* 7 (1993): 161–82.

36. Jorge Silva Castillo, "Tribus pastorales et Industrie textile à Mari,"in *Nomads and Sedentary Peoples,* J. Silva Castillo, ed., 109–22, 121–22.

    See J. J. Finkelstein, "On Old Babylonian Herding Contract and Genesis 31:38f.," *JAOS* 88 (1968): 30–36, and J. N. Postgate and S. Payne, "Some Shepherds."

37. See M. van de Mieroop, *Crafts in the Early Isin Period,* on 920 texts in thirty-five years. Craftsmen were bound to the state and supplied by it, 86–87, but they worked only half the time, n. 88. The rest of the time they must have worked on their own accounts. For craftsmen in Old Babylonian letters, see J. Renger, "Patterns . . . " in *Circulation,* Archi, ed., 86–89. For Ur crafts, see M. van de Mieroop, *Society and Enterprise in Old Babylonian Ur,* 183–87.

38. W. F. Leemans, *The Old Babylonian Merchant, His Business and Social Position,* and *Foreign Trade in the Old Babylonian Period,* and see Hallo's review of Leemans, *Trade, JCS* 17 (1963): 60. Centralization under Hammurapi may have diminished the influence of merchants, and his sacking of Mari and Eshnunna probably ruined the east-west trade, Leemans, "Handel," *RlA* 4:76–90, 85; Leemans, "The Trade Relations of Babylonia and the Question of Relations with Egypt in the Old Babylonian Period," *JESHO* 3 (1960): 21–37, 34, notes that towns mentioned in Old Babylonian trade are on the fringes of the Mesopotamian plain, and there is no clear trace of direct contact with areas beyond that. Note G. Dossin, "La Route de l'Étain en Mésopotamie au temps de Zimri-Lim," *RA* 64 (1970): 97–106, on tin coming from the east to Mari and being sent west. On merchants working for the palace and others who did not, see D. Charpin, "Marchand du palais et marchand du temple à la fin de la Iʳᵉ Dynastie de Babylone," *Journal Asiatique* 270 (1982): 25–65, 60.

    The price of wool was eighteen grains of silver per mina, about a pound, just as in Ur III; see my discussion in *Ledgers,* 203. For Mari's shipping of wine, oil, spices, and honey, see J. Sasson, "A Sketch of North Syrian Economic Relations in the Middle Bronze Age," *JESHO* 9 (1966): 161–81. On demand for trade goods in outlying areas, see J. Renger's sensitive reading of the letters from the period, "Patterns . . . " in *Circulation,* Archi, ed., 108–12, and compare C. Zaccagnini, "On Gift Exchange in the Old Babylonian Period," in *Studi . . . F. Pintore,* O. Carruba et al., eds., 189–253.

39. See M. T. Larsen, *Old Assyrian Caravan Procedures* and *The Old Assyrian City-State and Its Colonies,* and K. Veenhof, *Aspects of Old Assyrian Trade and Its Terminology.* Still valuable as an overview is P. Garelli, *Les Assyriens en Cappadoce,* updated in his "Marchands et Tamkārū assyriens en Cappadoce," *Iraq* 39 (1977): 99–107, noting that capitalization for the journeys could have come from loans from Assyrian temples, 100. For a few texts actually from Assur, see V. Donbaz, "Four Old Assyrian Tablets from the City of Assur," *JCS* 26 (1974): 81–87.

40. M. T. Larsen, "Early Assur and International Trade," *Sumer* 35 (1979): 349–47 (*sic*). K. Veenhof, "Some Social Effects of Old Assyrian Trade," *Iraq* 39 (1977): 109–18, 115. For the route, see K. Nashef, *Rekonstruktion der Reiserouten zur Zeit der altassyrischen Han-*

delsniederlassungen, 62–76, arguing that the merchants mostly went north over the mountains as soon as they could instead of up the Euphrates. The *kārum* has been discussed, especially in M. T. Larsen, *City-State,* 368–73.

41. Karl Polanyi especially used these texts, available to him only in translation, as the basis of his interpretation in "Marketless Trading in Hammurabi's Time." Note that other centers may have fed into this trade; see S. Dalley, "Old Babylonian Trade in Textiles at Tell el Rimah," *Iraq* 39 (1977): 155–59.

For mechanisms of trade, see M. Trolle Larsen, *Old Assyrian Caravan Procedures,* showing that each shipment had three types of documents, transport contracts, notifying messages, and caravan accounts; rarely are all three preserved for one caravan, 6–7. On chronology, see M. T. Larsen, *The Old Assyrian City-State and its Colonies,* 80, 375–82 for the order of eponyms. N. B. Yankovskaya, "Wholesale Trade in the Near East before the Formation of Empires," *VDI* (1985–3): 3–8, emphasizes that age classes formed mutually supportive groups among the Assyrians.

42. W. W. Hallo, B. Buchanan, "A Persian Gulf Seal on an Old Babylonian Mercantile Agreement," *B. Landsberger A.V.,* 199–203. A. L. Oppenheim, "The Seafaring Merchants of Ur," *JAOS* 74 (1954): 6–17. N. V. Kozyreva, *Drevnyaya Larsa,* 56, 139 on trade, and her innovative survey of what people had, 100–39.

43. R. Sweet's dissertation, "Money and Prices in the Old Babylonian Period" (University of Chicago, 1957), is a valuable resource for the period. Sweet wrote that he believed he had come to no firm results about price movements and that his work was thus inconclusive, but his study of kinds of money remains essential to understanding ancient economic life. On the imprecise techniques of weighing, see F. Joannès, "La Culture matérielle à Mari (iv): Les Méthodes de Pesée," *RA* 83 (1989): 113–52, 140.

See Sweet, "Money," 177, 13. See also N. V. Kozyreva, "Nekotorye produkty tovorodenezhnyx otnoshenii v starovavilonskoi Mesopotamii," *VDI* (1984–2): 3–14, 4. Compare also her "The Use of Silver as a Means of Payment in Old Babylonian Mesopotamia," *VDI* (1986–1): 76–81. On Ur, see van de Mieroop, *Society and Enterprise at Ur,* 248. See W. F. Leemans, "The Rate of Interest in Old Babylonian Times," *Revue internationale des Droits de l'Antiquité* 1/5 (1950): /–34, 12, 15, 25.

44. Sweet, "Money," 11, 73.

45. H. Farber, "An Examination of Long Term Fluctuations in Prices and Wages for North Babylonia during the Old Babylonian Period" (M.A. thesis, Northern Illinois University, 1974), 51, 78, 85, and *JESHO* 21 (1978): 1–51. And see M. Powell, "Identification and Interpretation of Long Term Price Fluctuations in Babylonia: More on the History of Money in Mesopotamia," *Altorientalische Forschungen* 17 (1990): 76–99, 88, 92; barley prices in the Old Babylonian period were substantially higher than in Ur III. For prices and references to "cheap" and "expensive," see Renger, "Patterns . . . ," in *Circulation,* Archi, ed., 89–113. Compare N. V. Kozyreva, "Serebro kak odno iz sredstv vyplaty naloga i ekvivalent trudovoi povinnosti v starovavilonskoi Mesopotamii," *VDI* (1984–2): 3–14, with English summary, and her *Drevnyaya Larsa,* 133.

46. See D. Charpin, "Le Rôle économique du palais en Babylonie sous Hammurabi et ses Successeurs," in *Le Système palatial en Orient, en Grèce et à Rome,* E. Lévy, ed., 111–26, 125.

D. O. Edzard proposed that there never was real reform in a modern sense, and we are mostly misguided by the topos of the virtuous ruler. "Soziale Reformen im Zweistromland bis 1600 V. Chr.: Realität oder literarischer Topos?" *Acta Antiqua* 22

(1974): 145–56. J. Renger, "Zur Bewirtschaftung von Dattelpalmgärten während der altbabylonischen Zeit," *F. Kraus A. V.*, 290–97, 290.

47. See M. deJ. Ellis, "*ṣimdatu* in the Old Babylonian Sources," *JCS* 24 (1972): 74–82.

48. See Kraus, *Verfügungen,* 16–123. See also J. Bottéro, "Désordre économique et annulation des dettes en Mésopotamie à l'époque paléo-babylonienne," *JESHO* 4 (1961): 113–64, 160. He notes the existence of peasant revolts, 163, but these were unsuccessful and apparently easily put down. Compare also from Mari references to *andurārum* "freedom (edicts?)" (my translation) under three kings, D. Charpin, "L'*Andurârum* à Mari," *M.A.R.I.* 6 (1990): 253–70. Earlier Charpin had argued that *andurārum* should be translated "return to the original status," "Les Décrets royaux à l'Epoque paléo-babylonienne," *AfO* 34 (1987): 36–44, 38.

Ammisaduqa's is the measure announced in the opening section of this chapter. Note that in Old Babylonian Nippur there is no trace of royal administration in the texts preserved from Rim-Sin's time; J. Robertson, "The Internal Political and Economic Structure of Old Babylonian Nippur: The Guennakkum and His 'House,'" *JCS* 36 (1984): 145–90; see also his "The Temple Economy of Old Babylonian Nippur: The Evidence for Centralized Management," in *Nippur at the Centennial,* M. Ellis, ed., 177–88.

49. For a list of the prices from these royal tariffs, see E. Sollberger, *Ur Excavation Texts* 8/II, 16, and for Anatolia compare M. Marazzi, "Tarife und Gewichte in einem althethitischen Königserlass," *OrNS* 63 (1994): 88–92.

50. The literature is vast, but a good place to start is F. R. Kraus's study "Ein zentrales Problem des altmesopotamischen Rechtes: Was Ist der Kodex-Hammurabi?" in *Aspects,* 283–96. A. Goetze, *The Laws of Eshnunna,* 14, saw that collection as a set of cribs for supervisors.

The problem of the broken engagement is treated in Ur-Nammu/Šulgi paragraph 12, Lipit-Ishtar paragraph 29, Eshnunna paragraph 25, and Hammurapi paragraphs 159–61; the texts are available in J. Pritchard, ed., *Ancient Near Eastern Texts* (Princeton: Princeton University Press, 1969).

51. The date of the stele may be deduced from the list of places he has already conquered and the year names in which he celebrated those conquests; see, in general, H. Klengel, *König Hammurapi und der Alltag Babylons,* 188–89.

Kraus, "Was Ist," thought the stele was to serve enlightenment. This view is not universally shared, though it seems right to me. For instances in which practice does seem to conform to the code, see R. Harris, "The *nadītu* Laws of the Code of Hammurapi in Praxis," *OrNS* 30 (1961): 163–69, and H. Petschow, "Die [Paragraphen] 45 und 46 des Codex Hammurapi. Ein Beitrag zum altbabylonischen Bodenpachtrecht und zum Problem: Was ist der Codex Hammurapi?" *ZA* 74 (1984): 181–212. Compare R. Westbrook, "Cuneiform Law Codes and the Origins of Legislation," *ZA* 79 (1989): 201–22, suggesting that codes may have been built up from practical decisions, like omen collections. Note, however, that it is not absolutely clear that omen collections derived necessarily from experienced omens; see my "The Mari Livers and the Omen Tradition," *Journal of the Ancient Near Eastern Society* 6 (1974): 117–23. On the connection between the code and later texts, see R. Westbrook, *Studies in Biblical and Cuneiform Law,* 134–35.

52. Consequently, the preliminary sketch by F. Peiser, *Skizze der babylonischen Gesellschaft, Mitteilungen der Vorderasiatischen Gesellschaft* (1896:3): 1–31, penned before the discovery of the code, lacks the detail of subsequent treatments and relies heavily on mate-

rial from the seventh and sixth centuries B.C.E. Some aspects of the society that Peiser sketches appear similar to Old Babylonian norms, however, including the freedom of women, 12–13.

53. Kraus discusses two texts that may refer to consulting a stele, "Was ist," 292, and compare C. Wilcke, "*CT* 45, 119: Ein Fall legaler Bigamie mit *nadītum* und *šugītum*," *ZA* 74 (1984): 170–80. But it is clear that reference to the code is atypical.

On taxation, see M. deJ. Ellis, "Taxation in Ancient Mesopotamia: The History of the Term *miksu*," *JCS* 26 (1974): 211–50, studying land taxes. See also her useful *Agriculture and the State in Ancient Mesopotamia*, showing the distinction between assigned crown lands, for which service had to be done, and other lands, where the producer had to pay a share of the harvest. F. Kraus's scathing review, *BiOr* 34 (1977): 147–53, questions the existence of these two posited systems.

R. Harris, "On the Process of Secularization under Hammurapi," *JCS* 15 (1961): 117–20. But note J. Oelsner sees no trace of centralizing power in the legal texts from Old Babylonian Nippur, "Neue Daten zur sozialen und wirtschaftlichen Situation Nippurs in altbabylonischer Zeit," *Acta Antiqua* 22 (1974): 259–65. F. R. Kraus, "Der 'Palast,' Produzent und Unternehmer im Königreiche Babylon nach Hammurabi (ca. 1750–1600 v. Chr)," in *State and Temple*, E. Lipiński, ed., 423–34, argues that the palace made possible ostensibly private enterprise. And for the concentration of power under Hammurapi's predecessor, see M. van de Mieroop, "The Reign of Rim-Sin," *RA* 87 (1993): 47–69, 61–67.

54. Trigger, *Ancient Egypt*, 114–15, 176–77.

55. E. S. Bogoslovsky, "Drevneyegiptskaya ekonomnika na puti k vozniknoveniiu deneg," *VDI* (1982–1): 3–12.

56. D. Mueller, "Some Remarks on Wage Rates in the Middle Kingdom," *JNES* 34 (1975): 249–63.

57. O. D. Berlev, *Obshchestvennye otnosheniya v Yegipte epoxi srednego tsarstva*. Note D. Mueller, "Some Remarks," cannot distinguish rations from wages. A. Spalinger, "A Redistributive Pattern at Assiut," *JAOS* 105 (1985): 7–20. See W. K. Simpson, "Polygamy in Egypt in the Middle Kingdom?" *Journal of Egyptian Archaeology* 60 (1974): 100–05.

58. Trigger, *Ancient Egypt*, 149–74, and W. Helck, *Wirtschaftsgeschichte des alten Ägypten im 3. und 2. Jahrtausend vor Chr.*, 197.

59. See B. Sass, *The Genesis of the Alphabet and its Development in the Second Millennium B.C.*, 135.

60. See Aharoni, *Archaeology*, 80–89, 91–92. The tale is translated by M. Lichtheim, *Ancient Egyptian Literature*, 1:222–35.

61. Aharoni, *Archaeology*, 99–100, 102, and D. Redford, J. Weinstein, "Hyksos," in *Anchor Bible Dictionary*, 3:341–48.

62. Aharoni, *Archaeology*, 94–104, and G. Dossin, "La Route."

63. Aharoni, *Archaeology*, 103–15.

64. On the Hittite Old Kingdom, see O. R. Gurney, *The Hittites*, 21–26.

65. On Minoans, see M. Hood, "Minoan Civilization," in *Oxford Classical Dictionary*, N. G. L. Hammond and H. H. Scullard, eds., 690–92, and R. Castleden, *Minoans*.

66. On the script, see, in general, John Chadwick, "Minoan Scripts," *Oxford Classical Dictionary*, 692. J. T. Hooker, "Minoan and Mycenaean Administration: A Comparison of the Knossos and Pylos Archives," in *The Function of the Minoan Palaces*, R. Hägg, N. Marinatos, eds., 312–15.

67. S. R. Rao, *Lothal and the Indus Civilization*, 7, 70.
68. Compare J. V. Kinnier-Wilson, *Indo-Sumerian: A New Approach to the Problem of the Indus Script*, and I. Mahadevan, "Terminal Ideograms in the Indus Script," in *Harappan Civilization*, G. Possehl, ed., 311–17. See also D. O. Edzard, "Indusschrift aus der Sicht des Assyriologen," *ZA* 80 (1990): 124–34.
69. K. C. Chang, *The Archaeology of China*, 135.
70. The problems of the Dark Age have been helpfully summarized by M. Rowton, "Ancient Western Asia," *Cambridge Ancient History* I:1, I. E. S. Edwards et al., eds., 193–217, 231–33, and although progress is being made on chronology through the help of astronomy, the question of the length of the Dark Age has not been definitively solved. Compare M.-H. Gates, *Alalakh Levels VI and V: A Chronological Reassessment*, arguing for a lower date for the first dynasty of Babylon, 37, and the inconclusive symposium, *International Colloquium on Absolute Chronology: High, Middle or Low?* P. Åström, ed.

CHAPTER 4
RETRENCHMENT AND EMPIRE

1. The text has been preserved on a small clay tablet as part of the E. A. Hoffman Collection of the General Theological Seminary of New York City, now on permanent loan to the Yale Babylonian Collection, Number 183, quoted with the permission of the curator, William W. Hallo.
2. Adams, *Heartland*, 174. Compare on the long-term decline from Ur III to around 750 B.C.E. J. Brinkman, "Settlement Surveys and Documentary Evidence: Regional Variation and Secular Trend in Mesopotamian Demography," *JNES* 43 (1984): 169–80. See, in general, F. Baffi-Guardata and R. Dolce, *Archeologia della Mesopotamia: L'Età cassita e medio-assira*. E. Stone, "The Spatial Organization of Mesopotamian Cities," *Aula Orientalis* 9 (1991): 235–42.
3. See, in general, J. A. Brinkman, "Kassites," *RlA* 5:464–73. For political history, see K. Jaritz, "Quellen zur Geschichte der Kaššû-Dynastie," *Mitteilungen des Instituts für Orientforschung* 6 (1958): 187–265, and his "Die Kulturreste der Kassiten," *Anthropos* 55 (1960): 17–64, and J. A. Brinkman, *Materials for Kassite History* 1. For a possible homeland in the Mahi-Dasht area of Iran, see J. E. Reade, "Kassites and Assyrians in Iran," *Iran* 16 (1978): 137–43. On the remains of their language, mostly in lexical texts and lists of names, see K. Balkan, *Kassitenstudien I. Die Sprache der Kassiten*. H. Freydank, "Untersuchungen zur sozialen Struktur in mittelassyrischer Zeit," *Altorientalische Forschungen* 4 (1976): 111–30, defines terms for military contingents.
4. See my brief sketch in *From Ebla to Damascus*, H. Weiss, ed., 326–29. Compare the Sutians' being overrun or absorbed by Aramaeans, discussed by J. N. Postgate, "Nomads and Sedentaries in the Middle Assyrian Sources," in *Nomads and Sedentary Peoples*, J. Silva Castillo, ed., 47–56.
5. J. A. Brinkman, "Hurrians in Babylonia in the Late Second Millennium B.C.: An Unexploited Minority Resource for Socioeconomic and Philological Analysis," in *Studies on the Civilization and Culture of Nuzi and the Hurrians*, D. Owen, M. Morrison, eds., 27–35, 33.
      H. Reviv, "Some Comments on the *Maryannu*," *Israel Exploration Journal* 22 (1972): 218–28. See also M. Dietrich and O. Loretz, "Die soziale Struktur von Alalah und

Ugarit," *Welt des Orients* 3 (1964–5): 188–205, 5 (1969–70): 57–93, a listing of the apparent classes.

6. A helpful summary is M. Greenberg, *Hab/piru.*

7. On the term and its apparent Hebrew analogue, see M. Greenberg, *The Hab/piru,* and G. Buccellati, "ᶜApiru and Munnabtūtu—The Stateless of the First Cosmopolitan Age," *JNES* 32 (1977): 145–47.

   For a summary of attestations, see J. Bottéro, "Habiru," *RlA* 4:14–27, 15–20. O. Loretz, *Habiru-Hebräer,* 181, notes biblical references are all from postexilic texts.

8. M. Liverani, "Communautés de village et palais royal dans la Syrie du IIe millénaire," *JESHO* 18 (1975): 146–64. See also M. Liverani, "Communautés rurales dans la Syrie du IIe millénaire A.C.," *Recueils de la Société Jean Bodin* 41 (1983): 147–85.

9. M. Heltzer, *The Rural Community in Ancient Ugarit,* 24–30 and 102.

10. The restrictiveness of the Middle Assyrian Laws has been emphasized by G. Lerner, *The Creation of Patriarchy,* 117, 122.

    E. Ebeling, "Familie," *RlA* 3:15b. G. Cardascia notes the sexism but argues that individual responsibility and adaptation of punishment to the crime were features of the Assyrian laws in "Les Valeurs morales dans le droit assyrien," *Acta Antiqua* 22 (1974): 363–71. And note that women did occasionally appear in the official cult in the later Neo-Assyrian period, B. Menzel, *Assyrische Tempel,* 1, 295–96. See E. Cassin, "Pouvoirs de la femme et structures familiales," *RA* 63 (1969): 121–48.

11. K. Grosz, "Dowry and Brideprice at Nuzi," in *Studies . . . Nuzi,* D. Owen and M. Morrison, eds., 161–82, 182.

12. See, in general, W. L. Moran, *The Amarna Letters.*

    See F. Pintore, *Il Matrimonio interdinastico nel vicino oriente durante i secoli ix-xii a.C.,* and W. Röllig, "Politische Heiraten im Alten Orient," *Saeculum* 25 (1975): 11–23, surveying all periods, but this is the high point, 23 and 17, and Moran, *Letters,* 4:7.

    A. L. M. Muntingh, "The Social and Legal Status of a Free Ugaritic Female," *JNES* 26 (1967): 102–12, and P. Manassini, "Note sugli Apporti patrimoniali in occasione del Matrimonio nella Siria de II. Millennio," *Geo-Archaeologica* (1984–2): 65–75.

13. M. I. Murzoev, "O rabstve v kassitskoi Vavilonii," *VDI* (1988–4): 109–131.

14. H. Klengel, "Zur Sklaverei in Alalah," *Acta Antiqua* 11 (1963): 1–15, 14. Compare I. Mendelsohn, "On Slavery in Alalah," *Israel Exploration Journal* 5 (1955): 65–72. M. Heltzer, "Raby, rabovladenie, i rol' rabstva v Ugarite xiv-xii veka," *VDI* (1968–3): 85–95, with English summary. I. S. Shifman, *Ugaritskoe Obshchestvo, xiv-xii vv. do n. e.,* 163–88. M. Heltzer, "Private Property in Ugarit," in *Circulation,* Archi, ed., 161–93, 193.

15. See M. Liverani, "Economia delle fattorie palatine ugaritiche," *Dialoghi di Archeologia* 1(1979): 57–72. And see W. Mayer, *Nuzi-Studien I. Die Archive des Palastes und die Prosopographie der Berufe,* 135–37.

16. *CAD* under *agru* "hired man," *agrūtu* "hire, wages," and *agāru* "to hire."

17. See G. Dosch, "Non-Slave Labor in Nuzi," in *Labor,* M. Powell, ed., 223–35. See also B. Eichler, *Indenture at Nuzi,* and G. Jordan, "Usury, Slavery and Land-Tenure: The Nuzi *tidennūtu* Transaction," *ZA* 80(1990): 76–92. And see J. N. Postgate, "On Some Assyrian Ladies," *Iraq* 41 (1979): 89–103, 93.

18. J. A. Brinkman, "Sex, Age, and Physical Condition Designations for Servile Laborers in the Middle Babylonian Period: A Preliminary Survey," in *F. Kraus A.V.,* 1–8. G. F. Del Monte, "Razioni e classi d'età in Nippur medio-babilonese," in *Stato Economia Lavoro*

nel Vicino Oriente antico, A. Zanardi, ed., 17–30, systematizes ration texts. J. Brinkman, "Forced Labor in the Middle Babylonian Period," *JCS* 32 (1980): 17–22, 17. See P. Garelli, D. Charpin, "Rôle des prisonniers et des déportés à l'époque médio-assyrienne," in *Gesellschaft und Kultur im alten Vorderasien,* H. Klengel, ed., 69–75, 73. M. Liverani, "Il Fuoruscitismo in Siria nella tarda età del Bronzo," *Rivista Storica Italiana* 77 (1965): 315–36.

19. M. Heltzer, "Labour in Ugarit," in *Labor,* M. Powell, ed. 237–50, 237–38. M. Liverani, "L'Estradizione dei refugiati in AT 2," *Rivista degli Studi Orientali* 39 (1964): 111–15.

20. See J. A. Brinkman, "Kudurru," *RIA* 6:267–74, and J. Oelsner, "Landvergabe im kassitischen Babylonien," in *I. M. Diakonoff A. V.,* J. N. Postgate, ed., 279–84.

 For example, see L. W. King, *Babylonian Boundary-Stones and Memorial Tablets in the British Museum,* with four Middle Babylonian Texts, and Franz X. Steinmetzer, *Die babylonische Kudurru (Grenzsteine) als Urkundenform.*

21. K. Balkan, *Studies in Babylonian Feudalism of the Kassite Period;* E. Cassin, "Techniche della guerra e strutture sociali in Mesopotamia nella seconda metà del II millennio," *Rivista storica italiana* 77 (1965): 445–55, makes the argument that feudal-style land distribution derived from demands of persons who could afford to maintain their own chariots, which became important in wars in the period. Note that the term *feudalism* was coined in the eighteenth century C.E. by scholars looking back to the European middle ages; J. R. Strayer and R. Coulborn, "The Idea of Feudalism," in *Feudalism in History,* R. Coulborn, ed., 3–11, 5, say in summary that for them under feudalism "political power is personal rather than institutional." This definition seems very broad.

 For the varieties of feudalism in Europe, see M. Bloch, *Feudal Society,* 1:176–89, and compare S. Reynolds, *Fiefs and Vassals: The Medieval Evidence Reinterpreted* (Oxford: Oxford University Press, 1994), who questions the evidence for a uniform feudalism, 476–82.

 J. Oelsner, "Zur Organisation des gesellschaftlichen Lebens im kassitischen und nachkassitischen Babylonien: Verwaltungsstruktur und Gemeinschaften," *AfO Beiheft* 19 (1982): 403–10, 405, and compare on "feudalism," 408 n. 1.

22. C. Zaccagnini, "Modo di Produccione asiatico e Vicino Oriente antico," *Dialoghi di Archaeologia* 3 (1981): 3–65, and, in general, I. M. Diakonoff, *Razvitie zemel'nyx otnoshenii v Assirii.*

23. M. Heltzer, *The Rural Community In Ancient Ugarit,* 48–51. Compare M. Liverani, "Economia delle fattorie."

24. So P. Garelli, "Le Problème de la 'Féodalité' assyrienne du xvᵉ au xiiᵉ siècle av. J.-C.," *Semitica* 17 (1967): 5–21.

25. J. N. Postgate, "Land Tenure in the Middle Assyrian Period: A Reconstruction," *Bulletin of the School of Oriental and African Studies* 34 (1971): 496–519.

26. G. Wilhelm, "Zur Rolle des Grossgrundbesitzes in der hurritischen Gesellschaft," *Revue hittite et asianique* 36 (1978): 205–13. See C. Zaccagnini, "The Yield of the Fields at Nuzi," *Oriens Antiquus* 14 (1975): 181–225, 218. C. Zaccagnini, "The Price of Fields at Nuzi," *JESHO* 22 (1979): 1–32, 6–7, 15, 4–6. For the social geography of the region, see his *The Rural Landscape of the Land of Arraphe.* Compare also his "Transfers of Movable Property in Nuzi Private Transactions," in *Circulation,* Archi, ed., 139–59. M. Heltzer, "Private Property in Ugarit," in *Circulation,* Archi, ed., 161–93, 163.

27. J.-M. Durand and D. Charpin, "Remarques sur l'Élévage intensif dans l'Iraq ancien," in *L'Archéologie,* M.-T. Barrelet, ed., 131–56.

28. M. Morrison, "Evidence for Herdsmen and Animal Husbandry in the Nuzi Documents," in *Studies . . . Nuzi,* 1, M. A. Morrison and D. I. Owen, eds., 257–96.

29. For the participants' differing perspectives on the exchanges, see M. Liverani, "Dono, Tributo, Commercio: Ideologia dello Scambio nella tarda età di Bronzo," *Istituto Italiano di Numismatica. Annali* (1979): 9–28. See, too, M. Liverani, "Elementi irrazionali nel commercio amariano," *Oriens Antiquus* 11 (1972): 297–317, and compare C. Zaccagnini, *Lo Scambio dei Doni nel Vicino Oriente Durante i Secoli xv-xiii.*

30. See C. Saporetti, "La Figura del *Tamkāru* nell'Assira del xiii secolo," *Studi micenei ed egeo-anatolici* 18 (1977): 93–101.

31. M. Liverani, "La Dotazione dei Mercanti di Ugarit," *Ugaritforschung* 11 (1979): 495–503, 495 n. 2, who points out that trying to distinguish between the public and private employment of merchants is anachronous. See also M. Astour, "The Merchant Class of Ugarit," in *Gesellschaftsklassen,* D. O. Edzard, ed., 11–26, and, summarizing Soviet approaches, M. Heltzer, "Tamkar i ego rol' v Perednei Azii, xiv-xiii vv. do n.e.," *VDI* (1964–2): 3–16. C. Zaccagnini, "The Merchant at Nuzi," *Iraq* 39 (1977): 171–89. J. Sasson, "Canaanite Maritime Involvement in the Second Millennium B.C.," *JAOS* 86 (1966): 126–38; compare M. Heltzer, "The Metal Trade of Ugarit and the Problem of Transportation of Commercial Goods," *Iraq* 39 (1977): 203–11.

32. D. O. Edzard, "Die Beziehungen Babyloniens und Ägyptens in der mittelbabylonischen Zeit und das Gold," *JESHO* 3 (1960): 38–55, and J. A. Brinkman, "Foreign Relations of Babylonia from 1600 to 625 B.C.: The Documentary Evidence," *American Journal of Archaeology* 76 (1972): 271–81, 275. M. Powell, "Identification and Interpretation of Long Term Price Fluctuations in Babylonia: More on the History of Money in Mesopotamia," *Altorientalische Forschungen* 17 (1990): 76–99, 79, argues that because gold quality was still noted in the Middle Babylonian period while silver quality was not, silver remained the real standard for money transactions. For the variety of moneys, see M. Müller, "Gold, Silber und Blei als Wertmesser in Mesopotamien während der zweiten Hälfte des 2. Jahrtausends v.u.Z.," in *I. M. Diakonoff A. V.,* J. N. Postgate, ed., 270–78. For the use of a copper standard from 1175 to 1130 B.C.E., see J. A. Brinkman, "Twenty Minas of Copper," in *E. Reiner A. V.,* F. Rochberg-Halton, ed., 33–36.

33. See H. Freydank, "Fernhandel und Warenpreise nach einer mittelassyrischen Urkunde des 12. Jahrhunderts v.u.Z.," in *I. M. Diakonoff A. V.,* J. N. Postgate, ed., 64–75. Compare also the doubtful suggestion that there was a Middle Assyrian tariff, which Freydank derives from the expression "to read in lead at (so many/each)," "Anzeichen für einen mittelassyrischen Preistarif?" *Altorientalische Forschungen* 12 (1985): 162–64.

34. R. R. Stieglitz, "Commodity Prices at Ugarit," *JAOS* 99 (1979): 15–23. Compare M. Heltzer, *Goods, Prices and the Organization of Trade in Ugarit.*

    M. Powell, "Identification and Interpretation of Long Term Price Fluctuations in Babylonia," *Altorientalische Forschungen* 17 (1990): 76–99, 88, 93.

35. For the Middle Assyrian Laws and their focus, see G. R. Driver and J. C. Miles, *The Assyrian Laws,* and C. Saporetti, *Le Leggi medioassire.* On the tax, see J. N. Postgate, *Taxation and Conscription in the Assyrian Empire,* 161.

36. See Dominique Valbette, *"Les Ouvriers de la Tombe." Deir-el-Medinah à l'Epoque ramesside,* 342.

37. P. Vernus, "Production, Pouvoir et Parenté dans l'Égypte pharaonique," in *Production, Pouvoir, et Parenté dans le Monde méditerranéen,* C.-H. Breteau, ed., 103–16, 109, 110, 114.

A. Théoridès, "A propos de Pap. Lansing, 4,8–5,2 et 6,8–7,5," *Revue internationale des droits de l'antiquité* 5 (1958): 65–119, 75, 89.

38. See M. Lichtheim, *Ancient Egyptian Literature*, 2. W. F. Reineke, "Waren die *šwtjw* wirklich Kaufleute?" *Altorientalische Forschungen* 6 (1979): 5–14. See C. J. Eyre, "Work and the Organization of Work in the New Kingdom," in *Labor*, M. Powell, ed., 166–221. Donald Redford, *A Study of the Biblical Story of Joseph*, 197, 199, and, in general, Abd el-Mohsen Bakir, *Slavery in Pharaonic Egypt*.

39. See J. J. Jannsen, *Commodity Prices from the Ramesside Period*, 2, 101, 546–47, and his broad-ranging and stimulating "Prolegomena to the Study of Egypt's Economic History during the New Kingdom," *Studien zur altägyptischen Kultur* 3 (1975): 127–85. T. G. H. James, *Pharaoh's People*, 240–47, discusses how barter worked, based on letters from the period. K. Bauer, "The Low Price of Land in Ancient Egypt," *Journal of the American Research Center in Egypt* 1 (1962): 25–45, 29. E. Castle, "Shipping and Trade in Ramesside Egypt," *JESHO* 35 (1992): 234–77, 256, 262, 273.

40. The vast literature has been summarized by D. Redford, *Akhnaton*.

41. Trigger, *Ancient Egypt*, 206, and B. Kemp, *Ancient Egypt*, 223–29, 252. The Hyksos are closely associated with Amorites, who dominated the politics of Western Asia in the period, as argued by J. Van Seters, *The Hyksos*, 191–95. For the Asian empire, see James M. Weinstein, "The Egyptian Empire in Palestine: A Reassessment," *Bulletin of the American Schools of Oriental Research* 241 (1981): 1–28.

42. See note 12 above for Moran's translation.

43. On the Peoples of the Sea, see A. Strobel, *Der spätbronzezeitliche Seevölkersturm*. M. Liverani, "The Collapse of the Near Eastern Regional System at the End of the Bronze Age: The Case of Syria," in *Centre and Periphery in the Ancient Near Eastern World*, M. Rowlands et al., eds., 66–73, 69.

44. I. M. Diakonoff, "Die hethitische Gesellschaft," *Mitteilungen des Instituts für Orientforschung* 13 (1967): 313–66, but note that he is merely reviewing E. A. Menabde's monograph, which he sees as inadequate. See Menabde, *Khettskoe Obshchestvo. Ekonomika, sobstvennost', semya i nasledovanie*, drawing largely from the Hittite Laws. Similar to Diakonoff's view is A. Archi, "Bureaucratie et Communauté d'hommes libres dans le système économique hittite," in *H. Otten A.V.*, 17–23. H. Klengel, "The Economy of the Hittite Household (E₂)," *Oikumene* 5 (1986): 23–31. K. Riemschneider, "Die hethitischen Landschenkungsurkunden," *Mitteilungen des Instituts für Orientforschung* 6 (1958): 322–81. See A. Archi, "Il 'Feudalismo' ittita," *Studi micenei ed egeoanatolici* 18 (1977): 7–18, 16, versus, for example, A. Goetze, *Kleinasien*, 107.

45. H. Klengel, "Die Rolle der Ältesten (LU₂.MEŠ.ŠU.GI) im Kleinasien der Hethiterzeit," *ZA* 57 (1965): 223–36. A. Archi, "L'Organizzazione amministrativa ittita e il regime delle offerte cultuali," *Oriens Antiquus* 12 (1973): 209–26, 220. Compare Clelia Mora, "Il Ruolo politico-sociale di *pankus* e *tulijas*," in *Studi Orientalistici in Ricordo di Franco Pintore*, O. Carruba et al., eds., 159–84.

46. See H. Otten, "Geschwisterehe in Hatti," *RlA* 3:231a.

47. J. Friedrich, *Die hethitische Gesetze;* the laws were translated by A. Goetze in *ANET*, 188–96.

48. B. Rosenkranz, "Ein hethitischer Wirtschaftstext," *ZA* 57 (1965): 237–48. See S. Košak, *Hittite Inventory Texts*.

49. G. G. Giorgadze, "Two Forms of Non-Slave Labor in Hittite Society," in *Labor*, M. Powell, ed., 251–55.

50. See A. Archi, "Anatolia in the Second Millennium, B.C.," in *Circulation,* Archi, ed., 195–206, 201–02. G. Beckman, "Herding and Herdsmen in Hittite Culture," in *H. Otten A.V.,* 33–44.

CHAPTER 5
ASSYRIAN DOMINATION

1. See, in general, the bibliographic summary of A. Strobel, *Der spätbronzezeitliche Seevölkersturm,* 8, 11.

2. On desiccation, see J. Neumann and S. Parpola, "Climate Change and the Eleventh-Tenth Century Eclipse of Assyria and Babylonia," *JNES* 46 (1987): 161–82.

3. M. Liverani, "Le 'Origini' d'Israele: Progetto irrealizzabile di ricerca ethnogenetica," *Rivista Biblica* 28 (1980): 9–31, correctly emphasizes how little we know from direct contemporary evidence about the origins of Israel and labels finding its origins an impossible scholarly project. See, in general, J. Callaway's chapter "The Settlement in Canaan," in *Ancient Israel,* H. Shanks, ed., 53–84, and I. Finkelstein, *The Archaeology of the Israelite Settlement.*

4. See M. Liverani, "The Ideology of the Assyrian Empire," in *Power and Propaganda,* M. T. Larsen, ed., 297–317, but compare also F. R. Kraus's article "Assyrisch Imperialism," *Jaarbericht Ex Oriente Lux* 15 (1958): 232–39 (to my knowledge never translated from the Dutch), which is a reaction to the invasion of Hungary, a rare instance of modern politics' direct influence on Assyriological research. Note that A. Vagts, *A History of Militarism* (New York: Meridien, 1959), 15, admits that Assyrians "afford the clearest demonstration of past imperialism and militarism"; nonetheless, he begins his study only with the breakdown of European feudalism, arguing that militarism then developed specific traits, including the leisure to develop narcissism. See also P. Machinist, "Assyria and Its Image in the First Isaiah," *JAOS* 103 (1983): 719–37.

5. B. Oded, *Mass Deportation and Deportees in the Neo-Assyrian Empire,* 116–19, lists places from which persons are attested as having been deported, and J. Zabłocka, *Stosunki agrarne w Państvie Sargonidów,* 67–79, lists individual instances of deportation. The main place to which people were deported was Assyria itself (Oded, 28, 62), although the place of exile of half the recorded deportations is unknown.

   Compare J. A. Brinkman on the decimation of the Chaldeans of Bit-Yakin in Babylonia, "Babylonia under the Assyrian Empire, 745–627 B.C.," in *Power and Propaganda* M. T. Larsen, ed., 223–50, 234.

6. The background of the story is that told in 2 Kings 18:13–19:37, retold in Isaiah 36:1–37:38 as well as in 2 Chronicles 32:1–21.

7. Adams, *Heartland,* 152, 192, and note Brinkman, *Prelude to Empire: Babylonian Society and Politics, 747–626,* 1–4 n. 5. Brinkman stresses, 3, that surface survey has covered only one-third of the area between the Tigris and Euphrates.

8. The physical concomitants of settlement are emphasized by J. Callaway in *Ancient Israel,* H. Shanks, ed. But see below.

9. Liverani, "Ideology." Note J. N. Postgate, "The Economic Structure of the Assyrian Empire," in *Power and Propaganda,* M. T. Larsen, ed., 193–221, 200, prefers to divide the empire into a palace sector associated directly with the king, a government sector including the army, and a private sector. The relation between the first two is unclear to me, and elsewhere it constitutes a problem, too, that is, what is the king's and what is the government's.

10. Brinkman, "Babylonia," 226, and compare F. Fales, "West Semitic Names in the Assyrian Empire: Diffusion and Social Relevance," *Studi epigrafici e linguistici* 8 (1991): 99–117, who shows West Semitic, including Aramaic, elements were present in all social contexts, 115, but no contexts had exclusively West Semitic names. And see Brinkman, *Prelude,* 12 n. 46.

11. Oded, *Deportation,* 82. Oded writes, 86, "The Assyrian attitude to a person was based first and foremost on his political affiliation and the territory he lived in, and not on his ethnic-national identity, and . . . territorial unity rather than national purity determined the attitude of the Assyrian kings to conquered population." For the change under Sargon II, see 90–92. Compare J. N. Postgate, "'Princeps Judex' in Assyria," *RA* 74 (1980): 180–82, 181, on the implication in a Neo-Assyrian letter that being an Assyrian was "a precise social status," though not one we can now define. See also his "The Land of Assur and the Yoke of Assur," *World Archaeology* 23 (1992): 247–63, arguing that the distinction between Assyria proper and dominated areas was always clearly maintained.

12. Oded, *Deportations,* 22, 81.

13. Brinkman, "Babylonia," 237–38. And see G. Van Driel, "Land and People in Assyria," *BiOr* 27 (1970): 168–75, 173.

14. Fales, *Censimenti e catasti di Epoca neo-assira,* 117 and n. 6, referring to a modern Lebanese village in which families have an average of 3.7 children. Compare J. N. Postgate, "Grundeigentum und Nutzung von Land in Assyrien im 1. Jt. v.u.Z.," in *Grundeigentum,* B. Brentjes, ed., 89–110, 95. See, in general, R. Harris, "Images of Women in the Gilgamesh Epic," in *W. L. Moran A. V.,* T. Abusch et al., eds., 219–30. Compare Postgate, "On Some Assyrian Ladies," *Iraq* 41 (1979): 89–103, 94. Note that although female scribes do not appear frequently, goddesses are sometimes given that title; see W. von Soden, *Akkadisches Handwörterbuch,* 1395b under *tupšarratu.* Also queen mothers and harem members were involved as actors in the economy; compare T. Kwasman and S. Parpola, *Legal Transactions of the Royal Court of Nineveh Part I,* texts 81–99 and 247–52. On women in cult, see B. Menzel, *Assyrische Tempel,* 295–96.

   Note also the role of the powerful female administrator, the *šakintu* in the queen's household at Kalhu, as sketched by S. Dalley and J. N. Postgate, *Tablets from Fort Shalmaneser,* 9–14. See H. Lewy, "Nitokris/Zakaya," *JNES* 11 (1952) 264–86, 273, for a Neo-Assyrian queen and her power. For scribes, see S. Meier, "Women and Communication in the Ancient Near East," *JAOS* 111 (1991): 540–47, 541–42. See T. Kwasman, *Neo-Assyrian Legal Documents in the Kouyunjik Collection of the British Museum,* number 120, 145–46, among others. Compare also Postgate, "Ladies," 94, 97, including sales by a slave family. Postgate notes, 99, that apparently "normal" marriage contracts do not exist, only texts dealing with odd situations.

15. See J. N. Postgate, *Taxation and Conscription;* Oded, *Deportations,* 92–99, presents a nuanced view of the status and work of deportees, arguing that much depended on circumstances and deportees' skills. Most probably were settled in family units as farmers, a very few were enslaved, others managed to bring slaves and wealth with them. P. Garelli, "Problèmes de Stratification sociale dans l'empire assyrien," in *Gesellschaftsklassen im Alten Zweistromland,* D. O. Edzard, ed., 73–79, 72, stresses that the key divisions in society seem to have been between those who were subject to the state and could be made to work for it and those who were not, 79.

16. W. Manitius, "Das stehende Heer der Assyrerkönige und seine Organisation," *ZA* 24

(1910): 97–149, 185–224, noted, 220–24, that the king's host was expanded with foreign troops, even including former enemies. The major question, which Manitius does not satisfactorily answer, is whether the Neo-Assyrian army really was partly a standing professional mercenary army, 106, 114–17. Manitius reasonably guesses that sometime in the reign of Tiglath-Pilesar III (his IV), 744–727 B.C.E., a separate "royal host" was constituted as a full-time mercenary force. Compare F. Malbran-Labat, *L'Armée et l'Organisation militaire de l'Assyrie*, and R. Henshaw, "The Assyrian Army and Its Soldiers, 9th-7th C. B.C.," *Paleologia* 16 (1969): 1–24, and for change after Sargon, S. Dalley and J. N. Postgate, *Fort Shalmaneser*, 27–47. Compare F. M. Fales, "Grain Reserves, Daily Rations, and the Size of the Assyrian Army: A Quantitative Study," *State Archives of Assyria. Bulletin* 4 (1990): 23–34, confirming the ability to feed twenty-five thousand to thirty thousand men.

Compare Henshaw, "Army," 14, on equality of officers and men. Note that there were certainly some mercenaries in the Assyrian army, Oded, *Deportations*, 50 and n. 60. See F. Malbran-Labat, *L'Armée*, 172, and compare W. Mayer, "Die Finanzierung einer Kampagne," *Ugaritforschung* 11 (1979): 571–95, arguing that Sargon II attacked deeper into Urartu, now eastern Turkey, on his campaign in 714 B.C.E. in order to get booty to pay his troops. Note also that there were problems with desertions from the army, Malbran-Labat, *L'Armée*, 107–09, including the fugitive shepherd who had been deported from Babylon in Fales, *Censimenti*, 123, and the peasants listed as "fled," noted by Van Driel, "Land," 174. As Van Driel notes, "This proves that the right to go elsewhere did not exist in many cases." Postgate argues, *Taxation*, 218–19, that army service was of three types: (1) permanent, professional soldiers, (2) persons serving as part of their duties to the state, and (3) those called up for a single campaign.

17. Fales, *Censimenti*, 125 and n. 24. Van Driel, "Land," 169, notes that these people were tied to the land but could and did own things themselves. Compare similarly J. Zabłocka, "Landarbeiter im Reich der Sargoniden," in *Gesellschaftsklassen* D. O. Edzard, ed., 209–15, 209; individuals could, however, sometimes be sold apart from the land. She asserts, 210, that there was a great labor shortage in the period.

18. Fales, *Censimenti*, 130 31, 6, 135. Compare Postgate, *Taxation*, 36–38, and see his "Some Remarks on Conditions in the Assyrian Countryside," *JESHO* 17 (1974): 225–43, 228–29, against Fales's vaguer idea.

Garelli, "Stratification," 78–79 and n. 30, denies that the term *latifundia* "broad fields," taken from Roman history, is helpful in describing that process because the plots bought tended to be scattered and small, and concentrations of slaves were not used to work them. Compare also Van Driel, "Land," 169, on the scattered plots, and Postgate, "Grundeigentum," 93, 101, as well as Postgate, "Employer, Employee and Employment in the Neo-Assyrian Empire," in *Labor,* M. Powell, ed., 257–70, 260–61.

19. Compare Oded, *Deportations,* 28, and, in general, Fales, *Censimenti.* Note that W. F. Leemans denies that there is any trace of village communal ownership of land in the period, "Trouve-t-on des 'Communautés rurales' dans l'ancienne Mésopotamie?" *Recueils de la société Jean Bodin* 41 (1983): 43–106, 98–99. See J. N. Postgate, "The Economic Structure of the Assyrian Empire," in *Power and Propaganda,* M. T. Larsen, ed., 193–221, 202. And see Postgate, "Structure," 214, and *Neo-Assyrian Royal Grants and Decrees,* 2. Because it took about ten hectares of land to maintain a family of six, purchases bigger than twenty hectares must have been speculative investments, and they are frequently attested, as shown by Postgate, "Grundeigentum," 103.

20. Postgate, *Taxation,* 213, quoting Van Driel, *The Cult of Assur,* 185–91. And compare Postgate, *Taxation,* 202, noting, n. 1, Van Driel's dissent, "Land," 175b.

21. Postgate, *Taxation,* 211, noting that "royal contingents" of workers included shepherds among craftsmen, and temples also employed shepherds, B. Menzel, *Tempel,* 265–66. Brinkman, "Babylonia," 237, notes silence there about sheepherding practices.

    The payment is called an *iškaru,* perhaps "work allotment," Postgate, *Taxation,* 101–02, and compare 207–08. Note that temples had shepherds and bird-catchers; B. Menzel, *Assyrische Tempel,* 265–66. See Postgate, "Employers," 265 and n. 21, and his *The Governor's Palace Archive,* 103–04 and 20–21 on sealings for sheep.

22. Postgate, "Taxation," 211–12, and "Employer," 259, 268, on the "royal contingents" and their apparent quotas, but a large proportion of these may have been paid in silver instead of in finished goods. Compare the Assur temple's handicraft workers in B. Menzel, *Tempel,* 287.

23. Brinkman, *Prelude,* 32. And see J. Muhly, "The Setting," 47, 51, in *The Coming of the Age of Iron* (New Haven: Yale, 1980), J. Muhly and T. Wertime, referring to Snodgrass, 335–74 in the same volume. But contrast C. Zaccagnini, "The Transition from Bronze to Iron in the Near East and the Levant," *JAOS* 110 (1990): 493–502, arguing, 502, that a crisis of supply is too simplistic an explanation.

24. I. Eph'al, *The Ancient Arabs,* 123. But note that the flourishing of the spice trade through the deserts had to wait for the spread of the camel, which may have been domesticated as early as 3000 B.C.E.; see R. Bulliet, *The Camel and the Wheel* (Cambridge: Harvard University Press, 1975), 56, perhaps in South Arabia but only became common after a useful camel saddle had been invented, 87, between 1000 and 500 B.C.E., and only gradually did the camel-borne trade take off between 500 B.C.E. and 300 of our era, 90.

    See Postgate, "Structure," 206–07, versus N. B. Jankowska, "Some Problems of the Economy of the Assyrian Empire," *Ancient Mesopotamia,* I. M. Diakonoff, ed., 253–76. Only trade in slaves and horses is known; Postgate, "Structure," 208. Trade in private hands is not attested, 206, but that may not mean that it did not exist because most sources for information are royal, 195.

    Compare Oded, *Deportations,* 103–04, though not so many Aramaic names occur as would be expected if Oppenheim were right that overland trade was mostly in Aramaic hands, "Overland," as noted by M. Elat, *Kishre kalkalah ben 'artzot ha-Miqra' bi-yeme Bayit Rishon,* 232–33. See S. Kaufman on Elat's efforts to read trade contacts into lists of tribute, *JAOS* 98 (1978): 344–45. Elat, "Der *Tamkāru* im neuassyrischen Reich," *JESHO* 80 (1987): 233–54, found that the people called "merchant" in Neo-Assyrian texts did not have the private interests which people with that title had in earlier periods.

    See also Postgate, *Taxation,* 201, and compare also S. Zawadzki, "The Economic Crisis in Uruk during the Last Years of Assyrian Rule in the Light of the So-called Nabu-ušallim Archives," *Folia Orientalia* 20 (1974): 175–84, 183, documenting price rises for lucrative temple offices in Uruk in southern Babylonia, though the rises were a secondary effect of the fall and not a cause.

25. Postgate, "Structure," 215, 218, on reports of prices. Compare Brinkman, *Prelude,* 34 n. 177. We will consider coinage in the next chapter.

26. Postgate, "Grundeigentum," 103 n. 107; for the homer, see M. Powell, "Masse und Gewichte," *RlA* 7:487–88.

27. Postgate, "Structure," says actual prisoners of war were treated less mildly than deportees, 210. Compare also Oded, *Deportation,* 98–99.

28. Garelli, "Remarques sur l'Administration de l'Empire assyrien," *RA* 68 (1974): 129–40, 135, comparing the Ottoman court of fifteen thousand. Compare Postgate, "Grundeigentum," 97.

29. Brinkman, *Prelude*, 31, 123.

30. Postgate, "Structure," 215–16, and Zabłocka, "Palast und König: Ein Beitrag zu den neuassyrischen Eigentumsverhältnissen," *Altorientalische Forschungen* 1 (1974): 91–113, 98–99. Compare also, for the use of prices in propaganda, J. Hawkins, "Royal Statements of Ideal Prices: Assyrian, Babylonian and Hittite," in *M. J. Mellink A. V.,* J. Canby et al., eds., 93–102. Postgate studied the different kinds of taxes levied in *Taxation*, 40–199.

 P. Garelli, "Le Système fiscal de l'empire assyrien," in *Points de vue sur la fiscalité antique*, H. van Effenterre, ed., 7–18, 8, 11. Note that Garelli asserts that the tax system did not allow for any middle class between administrators and subjects, 18. Contrast Zabłocka, "Zum Problem der neuassyrischen Dorfgemeinde," *Studia Historiae Oeconomicae* 13 (1978): 61–72, 71–72, who says temple cities and their people did have some more bourgeois-seeming rights.

31. B. R. Foster, "The Late Bronze Age Palace Economy—A View from the East," in *The Function of the Minoan Palaces*, R. Hägg and N. Marinatos, eds., 11–16, 14.

32. Trigger, *Ancient Egypt*, 248–49.

33. See Assurbanipal's annals, A. L. Oppenheim, translator, in J. Pritchard, *ANET,* 294–95, about Necho I, who must have died before 700 B.C.E. according to Herodotus, *Histories* 2.152.

34. See the brief sketch of J. Soggin, "Ancient Israel: An Attempt at a Social and Economic Analysis of the Available Data," in *F. C. Fensham A. V.,* W. Classen, ed., 201–08, and the older efforts of N. Gottwald, "Israel, Social and Economic Development of," *Interpreter's Dictionary of the Bible. Supplement,* 465–68, and E. Ginzberg, "Studies in the Economics of the Bible," *Jewish Quarterly Review* 22 (1931): 343–408. R. de Vaux, *Ancient Israel,* is useful as a compendium of biblical references, and J. Pedersen, *Israel,* retains some value. Also helpful is N. Lemche, *Early Israel,* which, however, does not footnote sources and appears to be intended as a general textbook.

35. G. Garbini, *History and Ideology in Ancient Israel,* has emphasized that few biblical accounts are confirmed by sources outside the Bible. Compare also Liverani, "Le 'Origini,'" mentioned above.

 On the extrabiblical sources for the period, see the stimulating papers in Italian from the colloquium published in *Rivista Biblica* 32 (1984): 3–151 and 34 (1986): 1–238, especially F. Israel, "Classificazione tipologica delle Iscrizioni ebraiche antiche," 85–110, and R. Gelio, "Fonti mesopotamiche relative al territorio palestinese," 121–51.

36. The problem of what models one might use to describe the coming into the land has been exercised, but the data, except archaeological, are sparse. Compare G. Mendenhall, "Social Organization in Early Israel," in *G. Wright A. V.,* F. Cross, ed., 132–51, N. Gottwald, *The Tribes of Yahweh*, with N. Lemche, *Early Israel.* J. Sasson's perceptive essay "On Choosing Models for Recreating Israelite Pre-Monarchic History," *Journal for the Study of the Old Testament* 21 (1981): 3–24, argues that our preference for models derives from our particular national experience, with Germans preferring a slow amalgamation and Americans a sudden revolution starting on the frontier. On the very difficult problems involved in the patriarchal stories, set presumably in an earlier period, see the bibliography and discussion of S. Warner, "The Patriarchs and Extra-Biblical Sources," *Journal for the Study of the Old Testament* 2 (1977): 50–61.

On surface survey results, see M. Kokhavi et al., *Judaea, Samaria and the Golan,* with summaries of sites in periods, 85, 147, 190, 238, 295. This survey, which was only of the areas captured by the modern state of Israel during the 1967 war, shows that the number of sites occupied jumped strikingly in all the regions surveyed between Late Bronze and Early Iron, when the Israelites presumably arrived. The Golan area had 2.2 times the number of Iron sites as Late Bronze ones, Ephraim 5.4 times, Benjamin 12.5 times, the wilderness of Judah 22.5 times, and Judah itself 24 times, going from just one occupied site to 24. For the regions surveyed, see the map, 8.

Stager, "The Archaeology of the Family in Ancient Israel," *Bulletin of the American Schools of Oriental Research* 260 (1985): 1–35, 3, on the basis of these data says that in the whole central hill country populated sites increased from 23 to 114; Late Bronze sites had individually been larger than Iron I sites, but total settled area jumped from 69 hectares to 192 hectares (28 to about 78 acres); he estimates that this would take a population increase of 2 percent per year between 1200 and 1150 B.C.E., much larger than could be expected from reproduction only. By contrast, the population of the United States, which enjoys rather better health care than ancient Israelites, is estimated to have increased only 1 percent a year between 1980 and 1989, *New York Times* January 4, 1990, 11. Similar to Stager is Hopkins, *The Highlands of Canaan,* 139, estimating Late Bronze sites at 24 and early Iron sites at 136. More recently, I. Finkelstein, *The Archaeology of the Israelite Settlement,* confirms the outlines of a nomadic group slowly taking marginal land with little armed conflict, 353, 355.

On Joshua 24 as a possible record of an early amalgamation, see the commentaries, though J. Van Seters, "Joshua 24 and the Problem of Tradition in the Old Testament," in *G. Ahlström A. V.,* W. Barrick, J. Spence, eds., 139–58, would date it after Deuteronomy.

Y. Shiloh, "The Population of Iron Age Palestine in Light of a Sample Analysis of Urban Plans, Areas, and Population Densities," *Bulletin of the American Schools of Oriental Research* 239 (1980): 25–35, 33, reducing previous estimates of between 1 and 6 million on the basis of density of houses at Tell Beit Mirsim and reducing the number of persons per house to 8 on the basis of ethnographic observations. The West Bank now has about 1.4 million persons.

37. The direction of the occupation is suggested by M. Kochavi, "The Israelite Settlement in Canaan in the Light of Archaeological Surveys," in *Biblical Archaeology Today,* 54–60, 56, for the territory of Ephraim on the basis of an unpublished M.A. thesis in Hebrew.

See J. Callaway, "Ai (et-Tell): Problem Site for Biblical Archaeologists," in *Archaeology and Biblical Interpretation,* L. Perdue et al., eds., 87–99, and compare L. Marfoe, "The Integrative Transformation: Patterns of Sociopolitical Organization in Southern Syria," *Bulletin of the American Schools of Oriental Research* 234 (1979): 1–42, 8–9, for somewhat similar marginal microenvironments in Lebanon.

See also Hopkins, *Highlands,* 183–85, 266, and Stager, "Family," 6–11, noting that the alleged Philistine monopoly on metals, 1 Samuel 13:19–22, does not mention iron. The move toward iron later may have come, as T. Wertime suggested in Stager, "Family," 11, from the need to conserve charcoal fuel because copper smelting takes twice to four times as much charcoal as iron, and deforestation probably accelerated as Israelites cleared the hills for agriculture, making wood for charcoal scarcer.

Another issue that is not directly related to population but undoubtedly affected it is sanitation. J. Callaway, "A Visit with Ahilud," *Biblical Archaeology Review* 9 (1983):

42–53, 45, notes that people in early Israel relieved themselves "Outside. Anywhere." This was undoubtedly true of almost all of the people of the Ancient Near East as of many in the region today, and it was a way for disease to spread. There is no scholarly discussion about this absolutely essential matter, but compare the cliche "a pisser against the wall," as in 1 Samuel 25:22, usually bowdlerized into "one male."

38. On the tribes the vast literature may be surveyed from R. de Vaux, *Ancient Israel,* but note the uncertainty of the meaning of the tribe and the terms for it, in J. van der Ploeg, "Sociale Groepeeringen in het oude Israël," *Jaarbericht Ex Oriente Lux* 2 (1942): 642–50, 646, and W. Johnstone, "Old Testament Technical Expressions in Property Holding," *Ugaritica* 6 (1969): 308–17, 312.

   Compare Numbers 7 and the commentaries on it, especially B. Levine, "The Descriptive Tabernacle Texts of the Pentateuch," *JAOS* 85 (1965): 307–18. See J. Flanagan, "Chiefs in Israel," *Journal for the Study of the Old Testament* 20 (1981): 47–73.

39. This is the conclusion of J. van der Ploeg, "Les 'Nobles' israélites," *Oudtestamentische Studiën* 9 (1951): 49–64; in "Les Chefs du Peuple d'Israël et leurs Titres," *Revue Biblique* 57 (1950): 40–61, he studies the individual terms, concluding that the large number of terms shows that such people were important, 60.

40. See W. McKane, "The *Gibbōr ḥayil* in the Israelite Community," *Glasgow University Oriental Society Transactions* 17 (1959): 28–37. The term has no Canaanite analogues, 33, and eventually came to connote a rich and influential man who could afford the fifty shekels that King Menahem of the northern kingdom, 745–27 B.C.E., exacted to pay tribute to the Assyrians, 2 Kings 15:20. J. van der Ploeg, "Le Sens de *Gibbōr ḥayil,*" *Revue Biblique* 48 (1941): 120–25, is adamant that the second element never means "property" but always "strength" or "power."

   See the sketch by J. McKenzie, "The Elders in the Old Testament," *Biblica* 40 (1959): 522–40. In the 700s they were viewed as oppressors by prophets, 539, probably because they had bought up land. See also H. Reviv, *The Elders in Ancient Israel: A Study of a Biblical Institution.*

41. See, in general, de Vaux, *Ancient Israel.* I. Cardellini, *Die biblischen "Sklaven"-Gesetze im Lichte des keilschriftlichen Sklavenrechts,* is a detailed study of laws about slaves in the Ancient Near East and Bible. On returners and Ziba, see I. Shifman, "Pravovoe polozhenie rabov v Iudee po dannym bibleiskoi traditsii," *VDI* (1963–3): 54–80, 56, 72.

42. M. Haran, "The Gibeonites, the Nethinim and the Sons of Solomon's Servants," *Vetus Testamentum* 11 (1961): 159–69, emphasizing the non-Israelite origins of these groups, which, however, were eventually merged with the community, 169. Haran's view of "permanent forced labor," 162, should be contrasted with A. Rainey, "Compulsory Labour Gangs in Ancient Israel," *Israel Exploration Journal* 20 (1970): 191–202, and with B. Levine, "The *Netînîm,*" *JBL* 82 (1963): 207–12, arguing that they were free members of a guild. Note that the Gibeonites' tasks of hewing wood and drawing water, Joshua 9:21, focused on two critical areas of labor shortage in early Israel as outlined by D. Hopkins, "The Subsistence Struggles of Early Israel," *Biblical Archaeologist* 50 (1987): 178–91. And see van der Ploeg, "Groepeeringen," 642–46.

43. See H. Schulz, *Leviten im vorstaatlichen Israel und im Mittleren Osten,* dealing with the premonarchical period mainly, for which many students would question whether we have much evidence. For an example of conflict, see Exodus 32.

44. In spite of the tradition's concern for corporate responsibility there is no evidence of agrarian community organization in which peasant groups larger than families owned

and farmed land together. See C. H. J. De Geus, "Agrarian Communities in Biblical Times," *Recueils de la Société Jean Bodin* 41 (1983): 207–37, 232 and 207.

The classic study is by E. Würthwein, *Der ᶜAmm ha'arez im alten Testament*, who argues that the term means all of the Judean citizens, 16, and after the exile it refers to people who had been resettled by the Assyrians and Babylonians in the land, 70, thus mostly untrustworthy foreigners. This also is the conclusion of I. Amusin, "Narod zemli," *VDI* (1955–2): 14–36. J. Soggin, "Der judäischen ᶜAm-Ha-aretz und das Königtum in Juda," *Vetus Testamentum* 13 (1963): 187–95, emphasizes the group's political role in installing kings whom the Deuteronomistic historians viewed as good, and Soggin proposes that the "people of the land" were bearers of Yahwistic tradition, 194; similar is R. de Vaux, "Le Sens de l'Expression 'Peuple du Pays' dans l'ancien testament et le rôle politique du peuple en Israël," *RA* 58 (1964): 167–72. E. Nicholson, "The Meaning of the Expression ᶜam ha-aretz in the Old Testament," *Journal of Semitic Studies* 10 (1965): 59–66, proposes instead that the term is not a technical class designation at all but always refers very generally to people living in the land, 60–61. His formulation seems the most sensible. For the term in rabbinical usage in later antiquity, see A. Oppenheimer, *The ᶜAm Ha-Aretz: A Study in the Social History of the Jewish People in the Hellenistic-Roman Period,* 10–11.

45. See M. Lurje, *Studien zur Geschichte der wirtschaftlichen und sozialen Verhältnisse im Israelitisch-jüdischen Reiche,* 57–59, although he says that the prophets were not very radical and did not propose a real revolution but just a diminution of the oppression of the poor by the rich. This accords with A. Kuschke, "Arm und Reich im Alten Testament," *Zeitschrift für die Alttestamentliche Wissenschaft* 57 (1939): 31–57, 40, saying that prophets did not oppose wealth but just the abuse of it. Lurje's work is in many points stimulating as an attempt at a Marxist analysis published in 1927, before Stalin's definition of what constituted the party line was clear. But Lurje is frequently unreliable even on matters of fact, as, 61, where he says Deuteronomy was the first to prohibit interest, although Exodus 22:25 clearly does so, and presumably earlier.

The idea that Canaanite practices conflicted with Israelite desert equality is still H. Donner's view, "Der soziale Botschaft der Propheten im Licht der Gesellschaftsordnung in Israel," *Oriens Antiquus* 2 (1963): 329–45. Contrast M. Fendler, "Zur Sozial-Kritik des Amos," *Evangelische Theologie* 33 (1973): 32–53, who sees Israel as having a middle class consisting both of oppressors and oppressed, 51. See also Hopkins, "Subsistence," 184.

The prevalence of debt slavery is central to the argument of B. Lang, "The Social Organization of Peasant Poverty in Biblical Israel," *Journal for the Study of the Old Testament* 24 (1982): 47–63, 53–58, noting that our evidence for rent capitalism is slim, especially for peasants' renting of land, 56 n. 25.

See W. Thiel, *Die soziale Entwicklung Israels in vorstaatlicher Zeit,* 151, on 1 Samuel 22:2 showing the disenfranchised flocking to David's side in Saul's reign, though he denies, 161, that there was a real class structure in premonarchic Israel.

It is controversial whether increased differences in wealth can be read in different sizes and qualities of houses in the archaeological record. See Y. Shiloh, "The Four-Room House: Its Situation and Function in the Israelite City," *Israel Exploration Journal* 20 (1970): 180–90, 188, denying that that is clear, and J. K. de Gees, "Die Gesellschaftskritik der Propheten und die Archaeologie," *Zeitschrift des deutschen Palästina-Vereins* 98 (1982): 50–57, 53–55. Shiloh, "The Four-Room House—The

Israelite Type House?" *Eretz-Israel* 11 (1973): 277–85, 280–82, shows that the house plan went out of use with the destruction of the divided kingdoms.

46. Ruth 3:10. See, in general, the quirky survey by I. Mendelsohn, "The Family in the Ancient Near East," *Biblical Archaeologist* 11 (1948): 24–40. See, for example, Genesis 24 and contrast the indications in Proverbs that choice may have been possible, Proverbs 19:14: "House and wealth are inherited from fathers, but a prudent wife is from the Lord" (RSV).

See the controversial suggestions of J. Van Seters, *Abraham in History and Tradition*, and compare Warner, "Patriarchs."

47. On the principle in general, see D. Herlihy, *Medieval Households* (Cambridge: Harvard, 1985), 114. C. Meyers, "The Roots of Restriction: Women in Early Israel," *Biblical Archaeologist* 41 (1978): 91–103, 98, suggests that dowries were rarely given, but the bride-price paid from the groom to the bride's family compensated them for her work. Compare M. Morrison, "The Jacob and Laban Narrative in Light of Near Eastern Sources," *Biblical Archaeologist* 46 (1983): 155–64, 162.

48. Compare Naomi in Ruth with two sons, both of whom died before her, and Isaiah with two sons, still children. Childlessness could in the patriarchal stories be overcome by using slaves as mothers, as in T. Frymer-Kensky, "Patriarchal Family Relationships and Near Eastern Law," *Biblical Archeologist* 44 (1981): 209–14, but the alternative of adoption seems not to have been a live one, as she notes, 211. S. Feigin's suggestions, "Some Cases of Adoption in Israel," *Journal of Biblical Literature* 50 (1931): 186–200, that Jephthah in Judges 11 was adopted and that Ezra 10:44's "putting" of children has to do with it seem doubtful, as does I. Mendelsohn, "A Ugaritic Parallel to the Adoption of Ephraim and Manasseh," *Israel Exploration Journal* 9 (1959): 180–83, noting Genesis 48:16, where Jacob acknowledges Ephraim and Menasseh to allow Joseph a double share of inheritance, 180. Mendelsohn's other cases, 181 n. 3, Ezra 2:61 = Nehemiah 7:63 and 1 Chronicles 2:35–36, seem equally unlikely. Compare also Tosato, *Il Matrimonio israelitico*, 77, suggesting other instances: Exodus 2:10, 2 Samuel 7:14 = 1 Chronicles 17:13, 22:10, and 1 Samuel 18:17.

On evaluation of children, see Leviticus 27:5–6, as noted by C. Meyers, "Procreation, Production, and Protection: Male-Female Balance in Early Israel," *Journal of the American Academy of Religion* 51 (1983): 569–93, 586, and on children in graves, Meyers, "The Roots of Restriction: Women in Early Israel," *Biblical Archaeologist* 41 (1978): 91–103, 95. On the nuclear family, see Stager, "Family," 16, 18.

49. See M. Cogan, "A Technical Term for Exposure," *JNES* 27 (1968): 133–35. On selling children, see Nehemiah 5:5 from the postexilic period. On weaning, see C. Meyers, *Discovering Eve: Ancient Israelite Women in Context*, 151 n. 30, on 1 Samuel 1:21–28, with Samuel presented with a three-year-old bull, and 2 Chronicles 31:16, mentioning male children from three years old and older. See on the rabbinic developments Z. Kaplan, "Bar Mitzvah," *Encyclopaedia Judaica* B, 243a-47a.

50. On "clans," see F. Anderson, "Israelite Kinship Terminology and Social Structure," *Bible Translator* 20 (1969): 29–39, 36, estimating that there may have been about sixty of these "phratries." The *mišpāhāh* was usually composed of more than one *bēt āb* "father's house," which probably included a nuclear family and its unmarried children and probably its married sons and their families, Frymer-Kensky, "Patriarchal," 210. Stager, "Family," 20, sees *bēt āb* as a "lineage" itself including several nuclear families, but, because of high mortality rates, usually including only two generations at one time. Anderson,

"Kinship," 37, on Deuteronomy. The *mišpāḥāh* is also sometimes called an '*elef* "thousand." These words along with the two words for tribe, *šēbeṭ* and *maṭṭeh*, should be investigated more thoroughly.

Hopkins, *Highlands*, 252, notes that only three generations appear as live actors in stories. Note that Hopkins sees the *mišpāḥāh* as a "risk-sharing unit" in Israel before the monarchy, *Highlands*, 256–61. Judges 18:22 may show Micah's large family living in several houses, as Meyers, *Eve*, 133–34, suggests. For grandchildren, compare Proverbs 13:22 and 17:6.

51. See, in general, G. Lerner, *The Creation of Patriarchy*, 176–79. For an example note that in Numbers 27:8–11 widows could not inherit from their husbands as they could elsewhere in the Ancient Near East, although the text notes that daughters may inherit; see E. Davies, "Inheritance Rights and the Hebrew Levirate Marriage. Part I," *Vetus Testamentum* 31 (1981): 138–44, 138–39. Compare J. Otwell, *And Sarah Laughed*, and contrast A. Brenner, *The Israelite Woman*.

52. See R. Westbrook, "Biblical and Cuneiform Law Codes," *Revue Biblique* 91 (1985): 247–64, 262–64. Contrast R. Sonsino, *Motive Clauses in Israelite Law*.

53. On recalling a woman's oath, see Numbers 30:4–16 = English 3–15. Misogynism can be seen in Proverbs 21:9 = 25:24 on the "woman of strifes." On dating Proverbs, see introductions to commentaries by R. B. Y. Scott and W. McKane.

54. This is the argument of Meyers, "Procreation," 574, 585. On causes of death, see Meyers, "Roots," 95, based on studies of bones in graves.

55. Examples of leaders include Deborah in the period of the Judges and Huldah around 621 B.C.E. See Meyers, "Roots," 101–02, 95–99, though it is difficult to accept her idea that archaeological destruction levels may derive from the burning out of places that had had plagues, 96–97. See also her *Eve*, 189.

   The absence of unilinear development goes against the thesis of G. Lerner, *Creation*, which appears to me to be unproved. See, in general, G. I. Emmerson, "Women in Ancient Israel," in *The World of Ancient Israel*, R. E. Clements, ed., 371–94.

56. G. Dalman's seven-volume *Arbeit und Sitte in Palästina* remains a useful if rambling encyclopaedia of work and environment in early twentieth-century Palestine; Dalman collected his information from 1899 till 1914 and returned for some months in 1921 and 1925 (I, i-vi), and he was clearly trying to do what we would now call ethnoarchaeology, for which see *Ethnoarchaeology*, C. Kramer, ed. (New York: Columbia University Press, 1980). For a more modern approach than Dalman's to the same problems of climate and environment, see Hopkins, *Highlands*, 107–20.

   See Deuteronomy 24:14: "Do not oppress a hired man who is poor and needy," which implies that there might be some that were not in such a state. But the only detailed story concerning one seems to be that about Jacob as a shepherd, Genesis 30–31, which is in a foreign context. Compare also Zechariah 11:4–17, probably from after the exile, in which the prophet gets thirty shekels of silver as wages as a hired shepherd.

57. For the references to forced labor, see A. Rainey, "Labour Gangs." See 1 Kings 9:21–22, *mas ᶜōbēd* versus 1 Kings 5:27 = English 5:13, *mas*. R. Kessler, *Staat und Gesellschaft im vorexilischen Juda*, 152, notes that corvée is much better attested than taxes and may have been more important.

58. I. Lurje, *Verhältnisse*, 39, guessing on the basis of 1 Samuel 25:42; Ziba in 2 Samuel 9:10 has fifteen sons and twenty slaves; see Lauterbach, *Der Arbeiter in Recht und Rechtspraxis*

des alten Testaments und des alten Orients, 8. Lauterbach, 4, asserts that the Hebrew vocabulary did not distinguish between the slave and the worker, using ^c*ebed* for both; although it is clear that free persons in addressing their superiors not infrequently referred to themselves as "slaves," I doubt that the word really did not consistently mean "person who could be bought and sold," as opposed to hired laborer, *śākīr.*

Slavery for debt is implied in Exodus 21:7–11 for daughters, as pointed out by Lauterbach, *Arbeiter,* 17. After the exile, Nehemiah 5:5 also stresses the sale of daughters but mentions sons as well. See, in general, G. Chirichigno, *Debt-Slavery in Israel and the Ancient Near East,* 355–56, locating debt-slavery particularly in the monarchic period. See Exodus 21:2–7, updated and made more humane in Deuteronomy 15:12–18.

59. J. Sasson, *Ruth,* 229.

60.` See, in general, R. Westbrook, "Redemption of Land," *Israel Law Review* 6 (1971): 367–75, though I doubt his assumption that the preserved stories had a uniform approach to the problem, especially Ruth. For bibliography, see D. Leggett, *The Levirate and Goel Institutions in the Old Testament.* The discussion by K. Baltzer, "Naboths Weinberg (1 Kön. 21): Der Konflikt zwischen israelitischem und Kanaanäischem Bodenrecht," *Wort und Dienst* NF 8 (1965): 73–88, argues that Ahab in 1 Kings 21 wanted to act like a Canaanite king, as seen in Ugarit four centuries earlier, where the king could confiscate the land of criminals and perhaps had some claim to land he had granted to his subjects. The idea, 81, that Naboth simply could not sell to the king because of an obligation to keep the land in the family contradicts other apparent land sales and is intrinsically unlikely, as J. Dearman, *Property Rights in the Eighth-Century Prophets,* 67, says. Proverbs 31 does not envision that. We are clearly dealing here with a view of the land perhaps current among people who recently took possession of it, but it may have been dying out over the centuries. Compare K. Henrey, "Land Tenure in the Old Testament," *Palestine Exploration Quarterly* 86 (1954): 5–15, for references, but his discussion is very general. Compare also E. W. Davies, "Land: Its Rights and Privileges," in *The World of Ancient Israel,* R. E. Clements, ed., 349–69.

See Hopkins, *Highlands,* 257–58, and C. De Geus, "Communities," 232. The effort by W. Johnstone, "Technical Expressions," to find remains of feudal institutions in the rather untechnical sounding terms for clan, place, and city, is unconvincing.

The renting of fields is not attested in the biblical period, and the first cases of it are in the Mishnah of the 200s C.E., as noted by G. Prenzel, *Über die Pacht im antiken hebräischen Recht,* 5.

For prices of land, see below and note that the most detailed story about such a purchase, Genesis 23, does not clearly reflect Hittite law but might well be a dialogue document attested in the Neo-Assyrian and Neo-Babylonian periods; see G. Tucker, "The Legal Background of Genesis 23," *JBL* 85 (1966): 77–84, 83–84.

S. Kaufman, "A Reconstruction of the Social Welfare Systems of Ancient Israel," in *G. Ahlström A. V.,* W. Barrick and J. Spence, eds., 277–86, has usefully summarized legal approaches to land and personal freedom.

61. See the sensitive study by K. Bardtke, "Die Latifundien in Juda während der zweiten Hälfte des achten Jahrhunderts v.C.," in *Hommages à André Dupont-Sommer,* A. Caquot, M. Philonenko, eds., 235–54, 247–54. On the problems of saying what latifundia were in the Roman world, see K. White, "The Problem of Latifundia in Roman History," *Bulletin—The British School of Archaeology* 14 (1967): 62–79. The Roman use of the term is not widespread and tends not to be from contemporaries of the phenomenon. G. E.

M. de Ste. Croix, *The Class Struggle in the Ancient World* (Ithaca: Cornell University Press, 1981), 242, adds a reference, apparently the earliest, from 30 C.E.

On the roles of the prophets, see R. Wilson, *Prophecy and Society in Ancient Israel* (Philadelphia: Fortress, 1980). The quotations are from the Revised Standard Version.

See J. Dearman, *Property Rights*, 56, 77, 133–35. Contrast I. Hahn, "Representation of Society in the Old Testament and the Asiatic Mode of Production," *Oikumene* 2 (1978): 27–41, who sees the prophets' blaming the importation of Egyptian, not Assyrian, practices as the source for oppression, 35–36, and compare, Henrey, "Land Tenure," 13, who says the narrator in the Joseph story was projecting Canaanite practices into an Egyptian environment.

62. Saul's remark is in 1 Samuel 22:7, and David's acts are mentioned in 2 Samuel 16:1–4, 19:25–30; see Z. Ben-Barak, "Meribaal and the System of Land Grants in Ancient Israel," *Biblica* 62 (1981): 73–91. Note that Baltzer, "Weinberg," 83, reasonably suggested that 1 Samuel 8 referred to Canaanite kings of the region whose practices were known to the Israelite leaders. J. Gray, "Feudalism in Ugarit and Early Israel," *Zeitschrift für die Alttestamentliche Wissenschaft* 64 (1952): 49–55, is an unsatisfactory attempt at reading 1 Samuel 22:7 in light of royal grants at Ugarit earlier. Compare O. Borowski, *Agriculture in Iron Age Israel*, 21–30, surveying land tenure.

63. On the rhythm of the agricultural year, see G. Dalman, *Arbeit und Sitte*, 1, and the chart in Hopkins, "Subsistence," 186, and on general conditions see his *Highlands*, especially 274 on the importance of keeping one's land exploitation options open in a fragile environment like central Israel.

Hopkins, "Subsistence," questions the importance of technological innovation in early Israel's taming of the highlands, noting, 183, that cisterns are not archaeologically attested early, and terracing too may have become important only in the 700s B.C.E. Borowski, *Agriculture*, 163–64, notes that Israelites introduced no new plant species to the Late Bronze repertoire, though their invention of the oil-beam press in Iron II and utilization of the techniques discussed above did contribute to their productivity.

The Babylonian influence on the new year has been noted by J. Vanderkam, "Calendars," *Anchor Bible Dictionary*, 1:810–820, 817.

64. R. Westbrook, "Jubilee Laws," *Israel Law Review* 6 (1971): 209–26, and S. Kaufman, "Social Welfare."

65. Marfoe, "Integrative," 7. Hopkins, *Highlands*, 248. See Proverbs 27:23–27 on herding, especially verse 26: "the lambs will provide your clothing, and the goats the price of a field" and Proverbs 14:4 on oxen. For the use of manure in agriculture, see Hopkins, *Highlands*, 202–07. And for the importance of sheep and goats among the faunal remains at Hesban, see ibid., 246–47. Note that the "fatted calf," mentioned for example in 1 Samuel 28:24, was actually the "stall(-fed) calf," indicating a process of fattening; see Stager, "Family," 15.

66. See M. Morrison, "Jacob and Laban." Compare, in general, G. Dalman, *Arbeit*, 6.

67. 2 Samuel 13:23–24 on Absalom's sheepshearers, but perhaps the prince was seen only as a private landowner, and 2 Chronicles 26:10 on King Uzziah's many herds, again, possibly his own private possessions; compare Lurje, *Verhältnisse*, 26. See also 1 Samuel 21:8 (English :7) on Doeg the Edomite, the chief of Saul's herdsmen, or perhaps runners, for which see the commentaries. On herd size, see 1 Samuel 25:2 (Nabal's with three thousand sheep and one thousand goats) and Job 1:3 (seven thousand sheep, three thousand camels, five hundred yoke of oxen, and five hundred she-asses), as in Hopkins, *Highlands*, 249.

See Hopkins, *Highlands,* 246–47. But compare the odd symbolic story in Zechariah 11:4–17, probably long after the exile, in which a prophet becomes a hired shepherd.

68. On women's work, see R. Kennett, *Ancient Hebrew Social Life and Customs as Indicated in Law, Narrative, and Metaphor,* 47, referring to Proverbs 31:19 and Judges 16:13, the latter in a Philistine context, and 86–87 on potters.

See, too, Lauterbach, *Arbeiter,* 20. On crafts, see Kennett, *Social Life,* 82–89. He suggests that there may have been guilds, after the return from exile, 88, referring to Nehemiah 3:8. Much less detailed is M. Aberbach, *Labor, Crafts and Commerce in Ancient Israel,* only 1–27 deal with the biblical period. On Ezion-Geber, see Y. Aharoni, *Archaeology of the Land of Israel,* 169, 143. On iron, see P. M. McNutt, *The Forging of Israel: Iron, Technology, Symbolism in Ancient Society.*

69. See F. Pintore, "Osservazioni sulle Vie e l'orientamento dei commerci nella Siria-Palestina meridionale dall'inizio del I millennio all'anno 841 A.C.," in *Studi . . . F. Pintore,* O. Carruba et al., eds., 257–83, and J. Dorsey, *The Roads and Highways of Ancient Israel.*

See Ikeda, "Solomon's Trade in Horses and Chariots in Its International Setting," in *Studies in the Period of David and Solomon,* T. Ishida, ed., 215–38, and note with M. Elat, *Kishre,* 181, that only in connection with Solomon do we have direct discussion of trade in the Hebrew Bible. From the aspect of military expenditures, see C. Hauer, "The Economics of National Security in Solomonic Israel," *Journal for the Study of the Old Testament* 18 (1980): 63–73.

70. R. B. Y. Scott, "Solomon and the Beginning of Wisdom in Israel," *Vetus Testamentum Supplement* 3 (1955): 262–69. See Garbini, "L'impero," 16.

71. See C. Wolf, "Merchant," *Interpreter's Dictionary of the Bible* 3:351–52, and compare Elat, *Kishre,* 202–03, on words for *trader;* he says that besides Solomon's the only merchants mentioned in stories about the period were Canaanites. I wonder if the cliche *hālak rākīl,* e.g. Leviticus 19:16, "he bore tales, spread scandal," literally perhaps "he went as a *r.,*" does not have something to do with the merchant, *rōkēl,* and the distrust of people who travel for a living.

For a study of the foreign goods mentioned, see H. Gowen, "Hebrew Trade and Trade Terms in Old Testament Times," *Journal of the Society for Oriental Research* 6 (1922): 9–16.

72. See T. Ikeda's list of chariot and horse prices from elsewhere in the Ancient Near East, "Horses," 226.

De Vaux, *Ancient Israel,* 203–09, on weights and money is helpful, but he does not attempt to list all prices. The prices come from such diverse texts and the texts from such different times that any analysis would be difficult, but the prices are definite evidence for the use of silver as money in Israel in the period.

On silver chunks and bundles, see R. Loewe, "The Earliest Biblical Allusion to Coined Money," *Palestine Exploration Quarterly* (1955)87: 141–50, 141, 146.

73. Gold frequently occurs in the cliche "silver and gold" but appears as a money in some cases: 2 Kings 5:5, 2 Kings 18:14, 2 Kings 23:33, and 2 Chronicles 36:30. Note that Nehemiah 5:10 shows that grain was also lent and functioned as money in the postexilic period. But bronze and brass seem not to function as moneys. Compare K. Singer, *Die Metalle Gold, Silber, Bronze, Kupfer und Eisen im Alten Testament und ihre Symbolik.* On Numbers 7, see B. Levine, "The Descriptive Tabernacle Texts of the Pentateuch," *JAOS* 85 (1965): 307–18.

74. B. Gordon, "Lending at Interest: Some Jewish, Greek, and Christian Approaches, 800 B.C.–A.D.100," *History of Political Economy* 14 (1982): 406–26, surveys Israelite and comparative material from Aristotle, 417. R. Maloney, "Usury and Restrictions on Interest-Taking in the Ancient Near East," *Catholic Biblical Quarterly* 36 (1974): 1–20, emphasizes the isolation of this Israelite prohibition with regard to the rest of the Ancient Near East.

75. Amos 2:6, 8:6. See, in general, M. Fendler, "Sozial-Kritik," for a summary of Amos's complaints. H. Donner, "Botschaft," represents an earlier point of view that saw the prophets as longing for a simpler nomadic time.

76. On the relations of kings to people, see H. Tadmor, "'The People' and the Kingship in Ancient Israel: The Role of Political Institutions in the Biblical Period," *Cahiers d'Histoire Mondu..e* 11 (1968): 46–68, emphasizing the importance of the army commanders in the north as sources for kings and for their support, 63–64. C. Wolf's thesis in "Traces of Primitive Democracy in Ancient Israel," *JNES* 6 (1947): 98–108, assumes a broad definition of what democracy is; it seems true that politics certainly mattered in ancient Israel, in the sense of what opinion leaders thought about the despots' acts. But it does not seem that it exerted any consistent or institutionalized control on kings, as Tadmor shows. See also L. Marfoe's stimulating "The Integrative Transformation: Patterns of Sociopolitical Organization in Southern Syria," *Bulletin of the American Schools of Oriental Research* 234 (1979): 1–42, suggesting that personal loyalty to rulers was a key to the creation of complex states in the region.

 Compare Golka, "Die Königs- und Hofsprüche und der Ursprung der israelitischen Weisheit," *Vetus Testamentum* 36 (1986): 13–36, and my brief note "The Wheel In Proverbs XX 26," *Vetus Testamentum* 39 (1989): 503–07.

77. Note that the administrative structures in Israel may have been imported from Egypt and thus have been sensed as foreign; see J. Bright, "The Organization and Administration of the Israelite Empire," in *G. Wright A.V.*, F. Cross, ed., 193–208, 203–04, and G. Ahlström, *Royal Administration and National Religion in Ancient Palestine*, 27–36. Ahlström has even suggested, "Was David A Jebusite Subject?" *Zeitschrift für die Alttestamentliche Wissenschaft* 92 (1980): 285–87, that David, the first successful king, may have been a Jebusite subject. In contrast note that other scholars see the formation of the monarchy not as a foreign import but just an internal development responding to Philistine pressure and also to trade opportunities; so R. Coote and K. Whitelam, "The Emergence of Israel: Social Transformation and State Formation Following the Decline in Late Bronze Age Trade," in *Social Scientific Criticism of the Hebrew Bible and Its Social World*, N. Gottwald, ed., 107–47, 123, 129.

 The phrase *piety-minded opposition* is M. Hodgson's, *Venture of Islam*, (Chicago: University of Chicago Press, 1974), 1:248–56, describing the analogous group in Islam; it may be equated to M. Smith's "Yahweh-alone Party," *Palestinian Parties and Politics That Shaped the Old Testament*, 29–30. On kingship, see 1 Samuel 8 and Deuteronomy 17:14–20.

78. See C. Hauer, "National Security," 67–70; contrast David's more cost-effective concentration on a small corps of mercenaries supported by ad hoc levies, as shown by C. Hauer, "David's Army," *Concordia Journal* 4 (1978): 68–72.

 See also D. Hopkins, *Highlands*, 22, 275, the latter on the kings' wanting a "regular levy," which conflicted with village needs. Hopkins sees royal pressures to specialize and be regular in payment of taxes as fundamentally altering the early system his book describes. This approach assumes that kings were as efficient as their enemies claimed, and that is not certain. It seems to me that Israel and Judah were more like Bronze Age Ugarit and Alalah in Syria as described by L. Marfoe, "Integrative," 16: "The state . . . was not 'oriental despotism' writ small; nor was it a genuine territorial unit, much less a unified one. It was in effect a network of personal and political ties centered in the palace-temple." His emphasis, 32, on deforestation's happening much earlier in Israel than in the Lebanese Biqa seems, however, only one factor among many to explain why new political arrangements might have been tried. See R. Oden, "Taxation in Biblical Israel," *Journal of Religious Ethics* 12 (1984): 162–81, 172, on the dissolution of the united monarchy as a tax revolt, as also B. Quilici, *L'Evoluzione finanziaria del Popolo Ebraico,* 137–38.

79. R. Oden, "Taxation," 167, and Rainey, "Labour Gangs."
80. As M. Delcor, "Le trésor de la maison de Yahweh des origines à l'Exil," *Vetus Testamentum* 12 (1962): 353–77, 367, seems to assume.
81. See F. Pintore, "I Dodici Intendenti di Salomone," *Rivista degli Studi Orientali* 45 (1970): 177–207, 198–202. Pintore did not see the text as exempting Judah, 205–06, but Judah's burden might have predated the north's supply system and thus have dated back to David.
82. W. Claburn, "The Fiscal Basis for Josiah's Reform," *JBL* 92 (1973): 11–22.
83. See M. Fendler, "Sozial-Kritik." On the prophets' condemnation of cities, see F. Frick, *The City in Ancient Israel,* 220–30. Their critique was not universal; some prophets came from cities, but they condemned individual cities as "a symbol of man's attempt to provide for his own material security" apart from the god of Israel, 230.
84. See Dearman, *Property Rights,* 133–41.
85. Some ostraca have been translated in *ANET* by W. F. Albright, 321. The original edition is by G. Reisner in *Harvard Excavations at Samaria,* G. Reisner et al., eds., 1:227–46, transliterated and summarized by H. Gressmann, *Zeitschrift für die alttestamentliche Wissenschaft* 2 (1925): 147–50. On the meaning of the ostraca, see Dearman, *Property,* 117–23, and 123–26 on the later sealings "for the king."

    On the role of the ostraca, see M. Noth, "Das Krongut der israelitischen Könige und seine Verwaltung," *Zeitschrift des deutschen Palästina-Vereins* 50 (1927): 211–44. For a similar function for the seals inscribed as "royal property," see A. Rainey, "Wine from Royal Vineyards," *Bulletin of the American Schools of Oriental Research* 245 (1982): 57–62. And compare on a collection of sealed clay bits, or bullae, that were probably attached in the early sixth century B.C.E. to documents on papyrus that have themselves decayed N. Avigad, *Hebrew Bullae from the Time of Jeremiah.*
86. M. Silver, *Prophets and Markets.*
87. See W. Dever, "Monumental Architecture in Ancient Israel in the Period of the United Monarchy," in *Studies in the Period of David and Solomon,* T. Ishida, ed., 269–306.

    For an attempt at comparing Israel with contemporary Neo-Assyria, see my "Ancient Israelite and Neo-Assyrian Societies and Economies," in *The Tablet and the Scroll, Near Eastern Studies in Honor of William W. Hallo,* M. Cohen, D. Snell, and D. Weisberg, eds., 223–26.
88. See J. Brown's stimulating "Proverb-Book, Gold Economy, Alphabet," *JBL* 100 (1981): 169–91. Note that J. Muhly, "Phoenicia and the Phoenicians," in *Biblical Archaeology Today,* 177–91, showed that Phoenician expansion into the Mediterranean was not so early as previously thought, dating only to the latter part of the 800s or later, 183, and

Greeks traded in the area earlier, according to pottery remains. This means that the biblical picture of Hiram of Tyre as an international trader in the 900s is anachronistic, 185. In the western Mediterranean the Phoenicians may have been seeking metals, but the evidence for that is scant before 700 B.C.E., 187. See also Y. B. Tsyrkin, "Some Problems of Phoenicia's Social-Political Structure," *VDI* (1991–4): 3–13, and E. Lipiński, "Economie phénicienne; Travaux récents et desiderata," *JESHO* 37 (1994): 322–27. For the achievement in writing of isolating phonological segments, see P. Daniels, "Fundamentals of Grammatology," *JAOS* 110 (1990): 727–31, 730.

 The comparison with Hesiod may work if Amos can be seen as representing Israel's peasants. See M. Andrews, "Hesiod and Amos," *Journal of Religion* 23 (1943): 194–205.

89. See the surveys of J. Pritchard, "New Evidence on the Role of the Sea Peoples in Canaan at the Beginning of the Iron Age," in *The Role of the Phoenicians in the Interaction of Mediterranean Civilizations,* W. Ward, ed., 99–112, and T. Dothan, "The Philistines Reconsidered," in *Biblical Archaeology Today,* 165–76. Dothan argues, 172, that the anthropoid clay coffins are not all Philistine because they are found in Late Bronze levels before the Philistines arrived, but some are.

90. See, in general, K. C. Chang, *The Archaeology of Ancient China.* See J. Needham in *Iron, Wertime and Muhly,* eds., 539, and Cho-yun Ssu, *Ancient China in Transition: An Analysis of Social Mobility, 722–222 B.C.* (Stanford: Stanford University Press, 1965), 107, 179.

91. For the early culture of Thailand, see C. Gorman and P. Charoenwongsa, "Ban Chiang: A Mosaic of Impressions from the First Two Years," *Expedition* 18:4 (1976): 14–26, 26, and D. Bayard, "Excavations at Non Nok Tha, Northeastern Thailand, 1978," *Asian Perspectives* 13 (1980): 104–43.

92. See S. Wolpert, *India,* 37–54; for castes, see L. Dumont, *Homo Hierarchicus* (Chicago: University of Chicago Press, 1970). This is the period of the composition of the Mahabharata (1000 B.C.E.?, Wolpert, 37) and the Ramayana (500 B.C.E.?, 39), and marks the expansion of settled agriculture directed by the Aryans into the north of India, 41. Floor plans at the site of Mohenjo-daro are felt to show a social hierarchy, 42. Against the religious domination of the Brahman class Upanishadic sages rebelled around 700 B.C.E., 44, stressing release from worldly cares as the goal of meditation.

93. On the economy of prehistoric Europe, see J. Sahlins, *Stone-Age Economics* (Chicago, New York: Aldine, Atherton, 1972).

CHAPTER 6
BABYLON AND A PERSIAN WORLD

1. See, in general, L. Cagni, "Le Fonti mesopotamiche dei periodi neo-babilonese, achemenide e seleucide (vi–iii sec. a. C.)," *Rivista Biblica* 34 (1986): 11–53. J. Oelsner, *Materialien zur babylonischen Gesellschaft und Kultur in hellenistischer Zeit,* studies each site and its archives for the Seleucid period. On Persian policy and the Jews, see *The Cambridge History of Judaism* 1, W. D. Davies, L. Finkelstein, eds. On the limited organization before Darius, see H. Sancisi-Weerdenburg, "Meden en Perzen," *Lampas* 12 (1979): 208–22. On the surprisingly small archaeological impact of the Persians, see P. Briant, "Pouvoir central et Polycentrisme culturel dans l'empire achéménide," in *Achaemenid History* 1, H. Sancisi-Weerdenburg, ed., 1–31. On their general policy, see M. Dandamayev, "Achaemenid Babylonia," in *Ancient Mesopotamia,* I. M. Diakonoff, ed., 296–311, and A. Kuhrt, "The Cyrus Cylinder and Achaemenid Imperial Policy,"

Journal for the Study of the Old Testament 25 (1983): 83–97, arguing that Cyrus's toleration was selective; Libyans were deported, and the evidence for toleration comes from Jews, who benefited from his policies, 94.

2. None of the Persian inscriptions come from Mesopotamia, as noted by Cagni, "Le Fonti," 30–31. Compare the Persian spin put on these events by A. Olmstead, *A History of Persia*, 151–61.

3. See Herodotus, *History* 1.199. On the misunderstandings of Herodotus, see W. Baumgartner, "Herodots babylonische und assyrische Nachrichten," *Archiv Orientální* 18 (1950): 69–106, and compare A. Kuhrt, "Non-Royal Women in the Late Babylonian Period: A Survey," in *Women's Earliest Records*, B. Lesko, ed., 215–39, 237. See also O. Ravn, *Herodotus' Description of Babylon* (Copenhagen: Nordisk, 1942).

4. On the passage, see A. Kuhrt, "Women," 237, arguing that one should not assume that Herodotus misunderstood the role of professional cult prostitutes. On his treatment of society and economy, see M. Nenci, "Economie et société chez Hérodote," in *Actes du IX Congrs. Association Guillaume Budé*, 1:133–46; Nenci sees Herodotus as believing that economic development leads to the fall of ethical values, which leads to decadence, 146.

5. Adams, *Heartland*, 177–78. Sites number 134 in the Middle Babylonian, 182 in the Neo-Babylonian, 221 in the Achaemenid, and 415 in the Seleucid-Parthian periods. Probably marginal land was being exploited, 188.

6. See J. A. Brinkman, "Babylonia under the Assyrian Empire, 745–627 B.C.E.," in *Power and Propaganda*, M. T. Larsen, ed. 223–50, 226. Hurrians continued to be present, and they had higher status than in earlier periods; see J. A. Brinkman, "Hurrians in Babylonia in the Late Second Millennium B.C.," in *Studies . . . Nuzi*, M. Morrison and D. Owen, eds., 27–35, 33.

7. On Medes and Persians, see H. Sancisi-Weerdenburg "Meden." On the presence of Persians in the population, see R. Zadok, "On Some Foreign Population Groups in First-Millennium Babylonia," *Tel Aviv* 6 (1979): 164–81, 169–72.

8. On Greeks at the Persian court, see G. Goossens, "Artistes et artisans étrangers en Perse sous les Achéménides," *La Nouvelle Clio* 1 (1949): 32–44, and, most famously, Xenophon's *Anabasis*, the story of a group of mercenaries caught on the wrong side of a Persian dynastic dispute. Compare also the adventures of the Greek physician Ctesias at the Persian court traced by H. Sancisi-Weerdenburg, "Decadence in the Empire or Decadence in the Sources? From Source to Synthesis: Ctesias," in *Achaemenid History* 1, Sancisi-Weerdenburg, ed., 33–45.

9. See J. Oelsner, "Erwägungen zum Gesellschaftsaufbau Babyloniens von der neubabylonischen bis zur achämenidischen Zeit (7–4 Jh. v.u.Z.)," *Altorientalische Forschungen* 4 (1976): 131–49, 134 on "nobles," 138 on "oblates." But M. Dandamayev maintains the *mār banê* meant that one was a member of an assembly and not particularly noble; see "The Neo-Babylonian Popular Assembly," in *Šulmu*, 63–71, 66–67.

10. On women in the Neo-Babylonian and Persian periods, see A. Kuhrt, "Non-Royal Women," and M. Roth, "Age at Marriage and the Household: A Study of Neo-Babylonian and Neo-Assyrian Forms," *Comparative Studies in Society and History* 29 (1987): 715–47, showing that more brides than grooms had living fathers, indicating a likelihood that many were spring-fall marriages since old grooms would be less likely to have living fathers than young brides. She also noted in the Assyrian "Doomsday Book" that girls were absent and must therefore have been married out early, 733, 735–36. See also F. Joannès, "Contrats de marriage d'Epoque récente," *RA* 78 (1984): 71–82.

11. See still, in general, V. Marx, "Die Stellung der Frauen in Babylonien, gemäss den Kontrakten aus der Zeit von Nebukadnezer bis Darius (604–485)," *Beiträge zur Assyriologie* 4 (1902): 1–77, 11–12 on a son's dependence; 61–62 on witnesses. And see now M. Roth, "Marriage and Matrimonial Relations in First Millennium B.C. Mesopotamia," in *Women's Earliest Records,* B. Lesko, ed. 245–55, 248 on dependence and 252 on inheritance. Roth has edited the available marriage contracts in *Babylonian Marriage Agreements, 7th-3rd Centuries B.C.* M. Roth, "The Neo-Babylonian Widow," *JCS* 43–5 (1991): 1–26, shows that widows probably held property only for the remainder of life and could not pass it on freely, 25.

12. W. Lambert, "Ancestors, Authors, and Canonicity," *Journal of Cuneiform Studies* 11 (1957): 1–14, 112. But note that scribes did not always inherit their positions, and some could be rich while others were poor; so M. Dandamayev, "The Social Position of the Neo-Babylonian Scribes," in *Gesellschaft und Kultur im alten Vorderasien,* H. Klengel, ed., 35–39, summarizing his *Vavilonskie Pisty.* For powerful families, see H. M. Kümmel, *Familie, Beruf und Amt im spätbabylonischen Uruk.*

13. Herodotus 1.184–87 on Semiramis and Nitocris. See J. Nougayrol, "Les présages historiques dans l'extispicine babylonienne," *École pratique des hautes études. Annuaire* (1944–45): 5–40, 14 #49. Ku-Bau appears in the Sumerian King List, T. Jacobsen, *The Sumerian King List,* 104–05. For Adad-Guppi, see A. L. Oppenheim in *ANET,* J. Pritchard, ed., 560–62.

14. An important source for information on labor for the Persian government is the two archives from Persepolis, the "Fortification Texts" and the "Treasury Texts," which are in Elamite language; see, in general, G. Cameron, "Persepolis Treasury Tablets Old and New," *JNES* 47 (1958): 161–76, and R. T. Hallock, "A New Look at the Persepolis Treasury Tablets," *JNES* 19 (1960): 90–100. Forced labor was used in a huge royal economy unrivaled elsewhere in the first millennium; see Dandamayev, "Forced Labor in the Palace Economy of Achaemenid Iran," *Altorientalische Forschungen* 2 (1975): 71–78, and A. Uchitel, "Organization of Manpower in Achaemenid Persia according to the Fortification Archive," *ASJ* 11 (1989): 225–38.

    On the highly structured bureaucracy, see W. Hinz, "Achämenidische Hofverwaltung," *ZA* 61 (1971): 260–311, and his interesting suggestion that this bureaucracy was directly borrowed eventually into the Arab world, Sicily, and even Germany; compare on Persian bureaucratic accounting his "Das Rechnungswesen orientalischer Reichfinanzämter im Mittelalter," *Der Islam* 29 (1950): 1–29, 111–41.

15. See the detailed study of M. Dandamayev, *Slavery in Babylonia, 626–331.* And also note V. A. Belyavskij, "Die Sklavenelite des Hauses Egibi," *Jahrbuch für Wirtschaftsgeschichte* (1973/1): 133–58, and Dandamayev, "Social Stratification in Babylonia (7th-4th Centuries B.C.)," *Acta Antiqua* 22 (1974): 433–44. On slaves manipulating land, see M. Dandamayev, "The Economic and Legal Character of the Slave's Peculium in the Neo-Babylonian and Achaemenid Periods," in *Gesellschaftsklassen,* D. O. Edzard, ed., 35–39.

16. Dandamayev, *Slavery,* 277. And see Dandamayev, "Svobodnye nayëmnye rabotniky v pozdnei Vavilonii," 31–50, in *Assiriologia i Yegiptologia,* L. A. Lipin, ed., 44, 46, and "Free Hired Labor during the Sixth through Fourth Centuries B.C.," in *Labor,* M. Powell, ed., 271–79.

17. See B. Porten, *Archives from Elephantine;* a selection of their documents is translated in *ANET,* 222–23, 491–92, 548–49, and the Instructions of Ahiqar, also found at Elephantine, 426–30. For the scroll with the temple petition, see 491–92.

18. On the possible origins and end of the outpost, see Porten, *Elephantine*, 13, 301.

19. See M. Dandamayev, "The Domain-Lands of Achaemenes in Babylonia," *Altorientalische Forschungen* 1 (1974): 123–27. This practice may actually date back to the Neo-Assyrian period, as suggested by A. Kuhrt, "Babylonia from Cyrus to Xerxes" in *Cambridge Ancient History* 4, J. Boardman et al, eds., 112–38, 128. She also questions the usefulness of calling the Achaemenid system feudal, 129. On the possible reform, see J. Oelsner, "Grundbesitz/Grundeigentum im achämenidischen und seleukidischen Babylonien," in *Grundeigentum*, B. Brentjes, ed., 117–34, 121. He notes, 122, that people could at the same time hold fief land and private land. Fief land could be inherited but not sold, 124. On Murašû, see G. Cardascia, *Les Archives de Murašû*, and M. Stolper, *Entrepreneurs and Empire: The Murašû Archive, and Murašû Firm, and Persian Rule in Babylonia.*

20. Stolper, *Entrepreneurs and Empire*, 149–50.

21. See D. Cocquierillat, *Palmeraies et cultures de l'Eanna d'Uruk (559–520).*

22. See M. Dandamayev, "Die Agrarbeziehungen im neubabylonischen Königsreich," in *Grundeigentum*, B. Brentjes, ed., 111–15, 113, and C. Wunsch, "Zur Entwicklung und Nutzung privaten Grossgrundbesitzes in Babylonien während des 6 Jh. v.u.Z., nach dem Archiv des Ṭābiya," in *Šulmu*, 361–78 showing a landholder trying to increase holdings and produce, 371. See also J. Oelsner, "Grundbesitz," 122, to K. Nemet-Nejat, *Late Babylonian Field Plans in the British Museum,* and J. Oelsner, "Gesellschaftsaufbau," 198.

23. See M. San Nicolò, "Materialien zur Viehwirtschaft in den neubabylonischen Tempeln," *OrNS* 18 (1948): 273–93, 19 (1949): 288–306, 20 (1950): 129–50, 23 (1954): 351–82, 25 (1956): 24–38, and G. van Driel, "Neo-Babylonian Sheep and Goats," *Bulletin of Sumerian Agriculture* 7 (1993): 219–58, noting, 224, the existence of private herding contracts.

    Also note the existence of large flocks recorded in the Persepolis texts; see W. Hinz, "Hofverwaltung," 288–90. For a comparison between animal hire contracts in the Roman period Egyptian papyri and the Neo-Babylonian texts, see S. von Bolla-Kotek, *Untersuchungen zur Tiermiete und Viehpacht im Alterum.* On fishing, see M. Dandamayev, "Dannye vavilonskix tekstov vi–v vv. do n.e. o rubolovstve," *Peredneaziatskii Sbornik* 3 (1979): 81–100.

24. We have records of very fancy textiles that were to be cleaned for the use of the cult statues, as shown by D. Weisberg, "Wool and Linen Material in Texts from the Time of Nebuchadnezzar," *Eretz-Israel* 16 (1982): 218–23. See D. Weisberg, *Guild Structure and Political Allegiance in Early Achaemenid Mesopotamia* versus E. Leichty, reviewing the book, *JNES* 29 (1970): 296–98, and J. Renger, *JAOS* 91 (1971): 494–503, and D. Weisberg, *JAOS* 104 (1984): 739–42, 741.

25. On Persian art and its artists, see Goossens, "Artistes."

26. A. L. Oppenheim, "Essay on Overland Trade in the First Millennium B.C.," *JCS* 21 (1967): 236–54.

27. M. Dandamayev, "Die Rolle des *Tamkārum* in Babylonien im 2. und 1. Jahrtausend v.u.Z.," in *Beiträge zur sozialen Struktur des alten Vorderasien*, 1, H. Klengel, ed., 69–78.

28. See H. Lanz, *Die neubabylonischen harrânu-Geschäftsunternehmen,* 97, 138 on profit. B. Hruška in his review, *Archiv Orientální* 46 (1978): 170–73, does not doubt the profit-making goal of these contracts but does doubt that they were very important in the context of a temple-dominated economy. For a participant in such texts, see G. van Driel, "Uit het leven van een Nieuw-Babylonische handelaar," *Phoenix* 38 (1992): 30–45.

Compare on risk taking in one Neo-Babylonian archive L. Shiff, "The Nur-Sin Archive: Private Entrepreneurship in Babylon (603–507 B.C.)," (Ph.D. diss., University of Pennsylvania, 1987), 214–15. This enterprise was incorporated into the House of Egibi, the documents for which are less completely published than Murašû's. See on it A. Ungnad, "Das Haus Egibi," *AfO* 14 (1941–44): 57–64, dating from 690 to 610 B.C.E. M. Lambert, "Le Destin d'Ur et les Routes commerciales," *Rivista degli Studi Orientali* 39 (1964): 89–109, argued that the concern of Nabonidus, the last Babylonian king, for Arabia might have derived from his desire to secure a southern trade route for Ur.

29. Herodotus 5.52–54 on the road and its stations from Sardis to Susa; 8.98 speaks of messengers, as does Xenophon, *Cyropaedaeia,* 8.6.17–18.

30. Herodotus 1.94 locates the development in Lydia, as do modern numismatists; see Nenci, "Économie et société," 142, suggesting that Herodotus's view is that coinage led to degeneration of the Lydians because it encouraged retail sales even of one's own daughter's services as a prostitute. Persians began minting in 517 under Darius; see M. Dandamayev, "Politische und Wirtschaftliche Geschichte," 45.

31. On rights to coin under the Persians, see M. Giacchero, "L'Intuizione dei fenomeni e dei comportamenti economici nelle storie di Erodoto," in *Studi di Storia Antica in memoria di Luca de Regibus,* 91–134, esp. 115 on Herodotus 4.166:2. And compare the still sensible remarks on the continued importance of weighing by F. Hrozný, "Zum Geldwesen der Babylonier," *Beiträge zur Assyriologie* 4 (1902): 546–50.

32. W. Dubberstein, "Comparative Prices in Late Babylonia (625–400 B.C.)," *American Journal of the Semitic Languages* 56 (1939): 27–43, esp. 25, 33, 37, 41, 34, 43, though many more are known now than when Dubberstein wrote; compare D. Wiseman, "A Note on Some Prices in Late Babylonian Astronomical Diaries," in *A Scientific Humanist: A. Sachs A. V.,* E. Leichty et al., eds., 363–73. And see A. L. Slotsky, "Prices in Astronomical Diaries," (Ph.D. diss., Yale University, 1992). And see M. Powell, "Identification and Interpretation of Long Term Price Fluctuations," 94.

33. Dubberstein, "Prices," 43.

34. Dubberstein, "Prices," 42. S. Zawadzki, "Great Families of Sippar during the Chaldean and Early Persian Periods (626–482 B.C.)," *RA* 84 (1990): 17–25, shows that the conquest did not cause personnel changes, but the rise of Darius as Persian king in 521 B.C.E. did, 24.

35. M. Dandamayev, "Achaemenid Babylonia," in *Ancient Mesopotamia,* I. M. Diakonoff, ed., 296–311, 309–10. Nabonidus had also taxed temples, Dandamayev, "Geschichte," 53, and idem, "State and Temple in Babylonia in the First Millennium B.C.," in *State and Temple,* 2, E. Lipiński, ed., 589–96.

36. J. Oelsner, "Die Neu- und Spätbabylonische Zeit," in *Circulation,* Archi, ed., 221–40, 222–23.

37. G. van Driel, "Continuity and Decay in the Late Achaemenid Period: Evidence from Southern Mesopotamia," in *Achaemenid History,* 1, H. Sancisi-Weerdenburg, ed., 159–81, 180.

38. On the so-called Saite renaissance, see Trigger, *Ancient Egypt,* 279–348. On the criticism of kings, see 296–99.

39. Ibid., 302. See also E. Bresciani, "La Satrapia d'Egitto," *Studi classici e orientali* 7 (1958): 132–88, noting, however, that later Persian kings did give votives to Egyptian temples, 166.

40. Trigger, *Ancient Egypt,* 301.

41. Ibid., 304–08, 332.
42. Ibid., 310–11.
43. Ibid., 311–12.
44. Ibid., 312–14. See S. Allam, "Women as Holders of Rights in Ancient Egypt (During the Late Period)," *JESHO* 32 (1990): 1–34, on Demotic texts.
45. Trigger, *Ancient Egypt,* 315.
46. Ibid., 325–28.
47. On Egyptian money in the period, see ibid., 328–29.
48. Ibid., 329.
49. Ibid., 331, 333–34, 336.
50. For conditions during the exile, see M. Coogan, "Life in the Diaspora: Jews at Nippur in the Fifth Century B.C.," *Biblical Archeologist* 37 (1974): 6–12, and compare W. F. Albright, "King Jehoiakin in Exile," *Biblical Archeologist* 5 (1942): 49–55. E. J. Bickerman, "The Generation of Ezra and Nehemiah," *American Academy for Jewish Research* 45 (1978): 1–28, noted, 7, that for unknown reasons names including the divine name Yahweh, the personal name of the God of Israel, become more popular over time between 480 and 470 B.C.E.
51. Ezra 1:2–4. On the Jews in Babylonia, see R. Zadok, *The Jews in Babylonia during the Chaldean and Achaemenian Periods,* noting that few names show up in documents, 1–2. Most Jews were in agriculture; some were shepherds and fishermen in Murašû texts from Nippur, 74. The idea that the Persians economically supported autochthonous religious establishments is reinforced by the contemporaneous Persian documentation; see H. G. M. Williamson, "Ezra and Nehemiah in the Light of the Texts from Persepolis," *Bulletin for Biblical Research* 1 (1991): 41–61, 50–54.

   For the considerable archaeological continuity in the period, see E. Stern, *Material Culture of the Land of the Bible in the Persian Period, 538–332 B.C.* Note that Greek objects appear long before Alexander, 236, and Persians had no archaeological influence. There was devastation at many sites in 332 as Alexander's army moved through, 255.
52. Ezra 4:1–5 and Nehemiah 4:1–20.
53. On the dating of Ezra and Nehemiah, see F. M. Cross, "A Reconstruction of the Judean Restoration," *JBL* 94 (1975): 4–18, arguing that Ezra must have come in 458, Nehemiah in 445, and the Chronicler wrote around 400. Perhaps Ezra was dispatched to shore up southern Syria in the wake of the Egyptian rebellion against the Persians in 459; see A. F. Rainey, "The Satrapy 'Beyond the River,'" *Australian Journal of Biblical Archaeology* 1 (1969): 51–78, 62.
54. Nehemiah 5:1–5. The class of *netînîm,* attested only in Ezra and Nehemiah, apparently were Levites "devoted (to the temple)"; they might not be slaves, as has usually been assumed; see B. Levine, "The Netînîm," *JBL* 82 (1963): 207–12. Both Ezra and Nehemiah may have been sent by the Persians to shore up the Levant against revolt in Egypt, as seen in K. Hoglund, *Achaemenid Imperial Administration in Syria-Palestine and the Missions of Ezra and Nehemiah,* 242–44.
55. On Nehemiah's purposes, see S. Mowinckel, "Die vorderasiatischen Königs- und Fürsteninschriften: Eine stilistische Studie," in *Eucharisterion, H. Gunkel A.V.,* 1, H. Schmidt, ed., 278–322. H. Kippenberg, *Religion und Klassenbildung im antiken Judäa,* sees Nehemiah's reforms as an effort by the Persian government to build solidarity among Jews and support for the Persians, 75.
56. See Nehemiah 13:15–22 on the sabbath, 13:23–29 on intermarriage. What Ezra says in

Ezra 10:11 is, in general, similar to Deuteronomy 7:3, but not in detail; see D. Bossman, "Ezra's Marriage Reform," *Biblical Theology Bulletin* 9 (1979): 32–38. The Persians had demanded a codification of Egyptian law, and Ezra may be connected with a parallel effort in Judah; so K. Koch, "Ezra and the Origins of Judaism," *Journal of Semitic Studies* 19 (1974): 173–97, 183.

57. Ezra 9:1–10:44, and note the opposition in 10:15. It has been pointed out that several of the social reforms attempted in Israel after the exile have parallels in Greece earlier, including the prohibition of usury at Megara around 570–60, the cancellation of debts and release of slaves at Athens in 594, and the reassignment of land at Athens around 538. The prohibition of intermarriage at Athens in 451 B.C.E. was fairly close in time to Nehemiah's similar efforts. See M. Smith, *Palestinian Parties and Politics That Shaped the Old Testament,* 140. M. Smith, 124–25, speculated that Ezra's mission was ended because of the controversial marriage trials.

58. On a possible reference to coinage in Haggai 1:6, see R. Loewe, "The Earliest Biblical Allusion to Coined Money," *Palestine Exploration Quarterly* 87 (1955): 141–50, though wages in a "pierced bundle" might still be uncoined silver fragments, as Loewe admits. Compare also with reference to Persian coins Ezra 2:69, 8:27, Nehemiah 7:70–72, and 1 Chronicles 29:7.

59. On the king's tax, see Nehemiah 5:4, and on the leadership's views of the loss of independence, see Ezra's eloquent prayer, which, for the very first time, recapitulates all of Israelite history, Ezra 9:6–15. Note that it is possible that some Jews were divided into large, male-descent groups, the *beit abōt* "house of the fathers," as argued by J. Weinberg, "Das Bēit 'Abōt im 6.–4. Jh. v.u.Z.," *Vetus Testamentum* 23 (1973): 400–14.

60. Zechariah 9:3, perhaps referring to Alexander's long siege of Tyre. On the impact of Hellenism, see A. Momigliano, *Alien Wisdom,* 74–122.

61. On the relations between Greeks and Phoenicians archaeologically, see J. Elayi, *Pénétration grecque en Phénicie sous l'empire perse,* who finds many more Greek things in Phoenicia than vice versa and thinks the trade goods going to Greece were perishable, most likely food, 159.

62. This roughshod and simplified sketch of Greek cities relies on H. Kloft, *Die Wirtschaft der griechisch-römischen Welt,* 98–152.

63. See M. I. Finley, *Ancient Slavery and Modern Ideology.* See D. MacDowell, *The Law in Classical Athens,* 245–46, on testimony, and N. Brockmeyer, *Antike Sklaverei.*

64. On helots, see M. I. Finley, "Between Freedom and Slavery," *Comparative Studies in Society and History* 6 (1964): 233–49, 240–41.

65. Finley, *Slavery,* 80.

66. On Pericles' law on intermarriage, see Plutarch, *Pericles,* 37, and see W. K. Lacey, *The Family in Classical Greece,* 100–03. But there was contact at Dor on the coast of Israel, an Athenian base, as F. Heichelheim emphasized, "Ezra's Palestine and Periclean Athens," *Zeitschrift für Religions- und Geistesgeschichte* 3 (1951): 251–53.

67. See Polanyi, "Aristotle," and, in general, T. Pekáry, *Der Wirtschaft der griechisch-römischen Antike,* 18–42, and H. Kloft, *Die Wirtschaft,* 110–27. T. Gallant, *Risk and Survival in Ancient Greece,* focuses on the rural economy, which did not regularly use markets, 98.

68. See, in general, J. Heurgon, *Daily Life of the Etruscans,* and M. Pallottino, *Etruscologia,* 233.

69. Compare the similar swift success of the even more youthful Safavid Persian leader Ismail, who inherited in 1500 C.E. at an even younger age than Alexander generations

of loyalty to his family on the part of the Kizilbash "red-hat" soldier families and used their loyalty to conquer a wide swatch of what is now Iran, Iraq, and Turkey. For a sketch, see M. Hodgson, *The Venture of Islam,* 3, 27–33.

70. Political developments are grippingly narrated, ironically enough, by M. Rostovzeff, *Social and Economic History of the Hellenistic World,* 1:1–73.

71. K. Jaspers, *The End and Goal of History,* 51–60. See the symposium edited by S. N. Eisenstadt, *The Origins and Diversity of Axial Age Civilizations,* and the earlier, briefer, and much more insightful *Wisdom, Revelation, and Doubt, Perspectives on the First Millennium B.C., Daedalus* 104 (1975).

72. On Nabonidus, see P.-A. Beaulieu, *The Reign of Nabonidus, 556–539 B.C.*

73. This is the implicit argument about the traditional scribal art's being superseded in A. L. Oppenheim, "The Position of the Intellectual in Mesopotamian Society," *Daedalus* 104 (1975): 37–46.

74. Trigger, *Ancient Egypt,* 347–48. One is tempted to invoke A. Toynbee's very general idea of challenge and response, *A Study of History,* 81–102. Some civilizations managed to face direct challenges and to improve their lots because of their success in facing the challenges, while others did not.

CHAPTER 7
TRENDS AND IMPLICATIONS

1. Note that Postgate, *Early Mesopotamia,* xxii, denies that generalization over so much time will have meaning. I understand his reticence, but I believe that one must make an effort, especially since others, perhaps less well-informed, will feel free to generalize. Contrast the call of C. Cahen for nuanced generalization and comparison within the Islamic world exactly because it is so vast but shares some elements; see "L'Histoire économique et sociale de l'Orient musulman médiéval," *Studia Islamica* 3 (1955): 93–115.

    Compare the correct observation that imperialisms got a bit more efficient in the course of the period we have been considering, M. T. Larsen, "Tradition of Empire in Mesopotamia," in *Power and Propaganda,* M. T. Larsen, ed., 75–103, 103, and P. Novick, *That Noble Dream* (Cambridge: Cambridge University Press, 1988), 465–68, on the deterioration of belief among historians in recent America in progress in history.

2. See the discussion of the origin of the ages idea in W. W. Hallo and W. K. Simpson, *The Ancient Near East: A History,* 6.

3. M. Powell, "Götter, Könige, und 'Kapitalisten' im Mesopotamien des 3. Jahrtausends v.u.Z.," *Oikumene* 2 (1978): 127–44, 140.

4. D. North, *Structure and Change in Economic History,* 164–65. That people were aware of trends toward innovation can be clearly shown. See Thucydides, *The Peloponnesian War* 1.71, R. Warner, trans. (Harmondsworth: Penguin, 1972), 76–77, when the Corinthians observe to the Spartans, "Your whole way of life is out of date when compared with [the Athenians']. And it is just as true in politics as it is in any art or craft: new methods must drive out old ones." But not, it appears, in any systematic or necessarily enduring way.

    See M. I. Finley, "Technical Innovation and Economic Progress in the Ancient World," *Economic History Review* 18 (1965): 29–45, 36, 43; note that K. D. White, *Greek and Roman Technology* (Ithaca: Cornell, 1984), refuses to conclude that there was

much advance, 172–73. K. Hopkins, "Economic Growth and Towns in Classical Antiquity," in *Towns in Societies,* P. Abrams and E. A. Wrigley, eds. (Cambridge: Cambridge
University Press, 1978), 35–77, argues that even barbarian pressure on the Romans led
not to innovation, but only to increased state repression, 77.

5. North argues that it derives from increased rights over innovations, *Structure,* 164.

6. I. Hahn, "From Antiquity to the Third World," *Oikumene* 5 (1986): 371–88, 381, 387.
Compare C. Cahen, "L'Histoire," on the neglect in modern studies of rural life because
Islam is seen as a civilization of cities, 96 n. 1 and 105.

7. For full documentation of generalizations and trends in this chapter, the reader should
turn to the relevant chapters above; here I shall note only conclusions that have been
arrived at by other scholars, not usually the phenomena on which the conclusions are
based, which have been discussed earlier.

8. This contrasts with the assertions of G. Lerner, *The Creation of Patriarchy,* but I believe
it is quite clear in the record. Lerner wishes to argue that things have gotten progressively
worse over time, culminating in Israelite society, the norms of which were taken over by
the West. It is definitely part of her argument to see Israel as a nadir, and I do not see that
the evidence supports that view.

9. See I. M. Diakonoff, "Slaves, Helots and Serfs in Early Antiquity," *Acta Antiqua* 22
(1974): 45–78. Compare M. I. Finley on the great variety of terms for the unfree in various Greek societies, "The Servile Statuses of Ancient Greece," *Revue internationale des
droits de l'Antiquité* 7 (1960): 164–89.

10. I prefer I. M. Finley's strictures against invoking the term *feudalism* in ancient studies,
"The Mycenaean Tablets and Economic History," *Economic History Review* 10 (1957):
141 and n. 2.

11. The continuity in field names is documented in G. Pettinato, *Untersuchungen zur
neusumerischen Landwirtschaft,* 2:25, finding forty-one names of fields in both periods at
Lagaš.

12. Compare T. Jacobsen, *Salinity and Irrigation Agriculture in Antiquity,* and M. Powell,
"Salt, Seed, and Yields in Sumerian Agriculture: A Critique of the Theory of Progressive Salinization," *ZA* 75 (1985): 7–38.

    On seed ratios, see Powell, "Salt, Seed, and Yields," 34, 36. For low numbers in
Egypt, Palestine, Rome, and modern Iraq, compare K. Butz, "Landwirtschaft," *RlA*
6:470–86, 483. For Europe, see F. Braudel, *The Mediterranean and the Mediterranean
World in the Age of Philip II* (New York: Harper and Row, 1972 [French 1949, 1966]),
1:425–26.

13. Hammurapi paragraphs 250–52, closely related to Exodus 21:28–32, though these pas-
sages may not reflect a real problem as a way to get at a real principle, that of responsibility for the behavior of animals under one's nominal control. See J. J. Finkelstein, *The
Ox That Gored,* 21.

14. See J. Jacobs, *Cities and the Wealth of Nations* (New York: Vintage, 1985).

15. On the camel, see W. Heimpel, "Kamel," *RlA* 5:330–32.

16. As I noted in *Ledgers and Prices,* 201–03; dates and wool have similar prices from Ur
III through Neo-Babylonian, but sesame oil, copper, and barley vary. M. Powell, "Identification and Interpretation of Long Term Price Fluctuation in Babylonia: More on the
History of Money in Mesopotamia," *Altorientalische Forschungen* 17 (1990): 76–99,
finds that barley appears to fall in silver price in the Ur III and Old Babylonian periods,
then to rise again, reaching very high levels again in the Neo-Babylonian period.

17. So M. Rostovzeff, *Social and Economic History of the Hellenistic World*, 1:165–69.

18. Compare J. Cooper, *The Curse of Agade*, 61, lines 242–44. J. Renger, "Zur Rolle von Preisen und Lönen im Wirtschaftssystem des alten Mesopotamien an der Wende vom 3. zum 2. Jahrtausend v. Chr.,—Grundsätzliche Fragen und Überlegungen," *Altorientalische Forschungen* 16 (1989): 234–52, 252, sees the passage as showing that high silver equivalents were results of the general catastrophe.

19. See B. Foster, "*Agoranomos* and *Muhtasib*," *JESHO* 13 (1970): 128–44. Nonetheless, some would see the Old Babylonian Eshnunna Code as a guide for market supervisors given that it lacks a prologue and epilogue and begins with a tariff of prices.

20. For a preliminary study of the "police" in the Ur III period, see D. F. Katz, "A Computerized Study of the AGA-Uš of the Ur III Period," (Master's thesis, University of Minnesota, 1979), and for the Old Babylonian period, V. Jacobson, "Pravovoe i imushchestvennoe polozhenie voina *rēdûm* vremeni I vavilonskoi dinastii," *VDI* (1963–2): 129–40.

21. Compare M. Rostovzeff, *Social and Economic History*, with the more modern popular treatment, A. K. Bowman, *Egypt after the Pharaohs* (Berkeley: University of California Press, 1986).

22. J. Renger, "Das Privateigentum an der Feldflur in der altbabylonischen Zeit," in *Das Grundeigentum in Mesopotamien*, B. Brentjes, ed., 49–67, 50–51, and H. Klengel, "Einige Bemerkungen zur sozialökonomischen Entwicklung in der altbabylonischen Zeit," *Acta Antiqua* 22 (1974): 249–57, 249–50.

23. See E. Le Roy Ladurie and M. Baulant, "Grape Harvests from the Fifteenth through the Nineteenth Centuries," in *Climate and History*, R. I. Rotberg and T. K. Rabb, eds. (Princeton: Princeton University Press, 1981), 259–69.

24. This is the argument of F. Braudel, "History and the Social Sciences: The *longue durée*," in *On History* (Chicago: University of Chicago Press, 1980 [French: 1958]), 25–54. On change in pre-Revolutionary French agriculture, see J. Goldsmith, "The Agrarian History of Preindustrial France: Where Do We Go from Here?" *Journal of European Economic History* 13 (1984): 175–99.

25. M. Rowton's series of articles on nomads approaches such a study of long duration, but the level of generalization he attains is higher than what I envision. His works include "Autonomy and Nomadism in Western Asia," *OrNS* 42 (1973): 247–58, "Urban Autonomy in a Nomadic Environment," *JNES* 32 (1973): 201–15, "Enclosed Nomadism," *JESHO* 17 (1974): 1–30, "Dimorphic Structure and Typology," *Oriens Antiquus* 15 (1976): 17–31, and "Dimorphic Structure and the Tribal Elite," *Anthropos* 30 (1976): 219–57, and twelve more. What we need is a study of several defined archives that deal with similar phenomena.

26. P. Kennedy, *The Rise and Fall of the Great Powers* (New York: Random House, 1987). On ancient decline, see N. Yoffee and G. Cowgill, *The Collapse of Ancient States and Civilizations*.

27. Note the analogy of the decline of Syrian Christian institutions in the High Muslim Caliphate. Syrian youths may not have abandoned their religion, but they saw service to the Muslim state as more rewarding than service to their church; see Hodgson, *The Venture of Islam*, 1:236, 298, and note that their piety may still have influenced the dominant Muslim piety, 305–08.

28. L. T. Doty, "Nikarchos and Kephalon," in *A Scientific Humanist; A. Sachs A. V.*, E. Leichty, M. Ellis, eds., 95–118.

29. See A. L. Oppenheim, "The Position of the Intellectual in Mesopotamian Society," *Daedalus* 104 (1975): 37–46. And see Trigger, *Ancient Egypt,* 348; and on decline see 346–48; on new attitudes toward kings in the late period, see 295–99. See also, in general, N. Yoffee and Cowgill, *The Collapse of Ancient States,* but the emphasis there is certainly on states and not on cultures. Also, as J. A. Brinkman pointed out in his paper "Continuity and Discontinuity in Babylonian Civilization," American Oriental Society Annual Meeting, March 21, 1994, Madison, Wisconsin, periods of weakness exceeded periods of strength anyway, and we may suggest contemporaries would not notice weakness as particularly unusual.

30. On modern illiteracy, see A. Lestage, *Literacy and Illiteracy* (Paris: UNESCO, 1982), and on its historical dimensions, C. Cipollo, *Literacy and Development in the West* (Baltimore: Penguin, 1969).

31. This is the point made by A. L. Oppenheim, "Trade in the Ancient Near East," *Vth Congress of Economic History,* 1–37, and seconded by J. Oelsner, "Die Neu- und Spätbabylonische Zeit," in *Circulation,* Archi, ed., 221–40, 239.

32. As seen by Gerald Gunderson, "Economic Behavior in the Ancient World," in *Explorations in the New Economic History; Essays . . . Douglass C. North,* R. Ransom et al., eds. (New York: Academic, 1982), 235–56, 256.

EPILOGUE

1. The lives of the Uruk families were sketched by G. Goossens, "Au déclin de la civilisation babylonienne: Uruk sous les Seleucides," *Académie royale de Belgique: Bulletin de la Classe des lettres et des sciences morales et politiques* (1941): 223–44, and L. T. Doty, "Cuneiform Archives from Hellenistic Uruk" (Ph.D. diss., Yale University, 1977). There is administrative continuity from Nabonidus to the successors of Alexander as shown by continuity in sealed letter-orders, as pointed out by A. Kuhrt, "Survey of Written Sources Available for the History of Babylonia under the Late Achaemenids," in *Achaemenid History,* 1, H. Sancisi-Weerdenburg, ed., 147–57, 156. Compare also her "Berossus' *Babyloniaka* and Seleucid Rule in Babylonia," in *Hellenism in the East,* A. Kuhrt and S. Sherwin-White, eds., 32–56, emphasizing that Alexander's conquest was for Babylonians just a change in foreign rulers that did not affect local conditions, 49–50. See, in general, still M. Rostovzeff, *The Social and Economic History of the Hellenistic World.*

   On changes in record keeping, see especially Doty, "Uruk," 323–33; slave sales stopped after year 37 of the Seleucid era (= 274 B.C.E.), and sales of arable land after 38. M. Stolper, "Registration and Taxation of Slave Sales in Achaemenid Babylonia," *ZA* 79 (1989): 30–101, shows that Persians also had taxed at least slave sales, but the Greeks apparently had insisted that they be recorded in a nontraditional way.

2. On Berossos, see A. Kuhrt, "Berossus' *Babyloniaka.*"

3. See the sketch of the phenomenon of the limits of Hellenization by A. Momigliano, *Alien Wisdom.* And particularly compare L. T. Doty, "Nikarchos and Kephalon," in *A Scientific Humanist; A. Sachs A.V.,* E. Leichty, M. Ellis, eds., 95–118, for two families, one with many Greek names and one without, who are both attested in cuneiform texts. On the small Greek influence as seen in personal names, see G. Sarkisian, "Greek Personal Names in Uruk and the *Graeco-Babyloniaca* Problem," *Acta Antiqua* 22 (1974): 495–503.

   In Syria and in Palestine the impact of Hellenism appears archaeologically to have been very limited; see F. Millar, "The Problem of Hellenistic Syria," in *Hellenism in the East*, A. Kuhrt, S. Sherwin-White, eds., 110–13, noting that the first use of "Hellenism" is in 2 Maccabees 4:13—usually dated around 100 B.C.E.—where it is definitely a bad thing, 110.

4. On the Graeco-X traditions, see, in general, F. W. Peters, *The Harvest of Hellenism*.

5. See, in general, A. K. Bowman, *Egypt after the Pharaohs, 332 B.C.–A.D. 642*, and K. Schippmann, *Grundzüge der parthischen Geschichte*.

6. See, in general, J. Neusner, *A History of the Jews in Babylonia*, vol. 1, *The Parthian Period*, and A. Ben-David, *Talmudische Oekonomie*.

7. See I. Lapidus, *A History of Islamic Societies* (Cambridge: Cambridge University, 1988), 120–21, and R. Bulliet, *Conversion to Islam in the Medieval Period* (Cambridge: Harvard University Press, 1979).

8. On Muslim attitudes toward the past, see F. Rosenthal, *A History of Muslim Historiography* (Leiden: Brill, 1968); the history of pre-Islamic peoples was valued, but it was not seen as a separate discipline, 30–53, and the historical value of what was passed down varied a good deal.

9. The last cuneiform tablet was published by A. Sachs, "The Latest Datable Cuneiform Tablets," in *Kramer A. V.*, B. Eichler, ed., 379–98. On the history of the Coptic language, see briefly T. Lambdin, *Introduction to Sahidic Coptic* (Macon, Ga.: Mercer University, 1983), vii–ix, and on its death as a spoken language, A. F. Shore, "Christian and Coptic Egypt," in *The Legacy of Egypt*, J. R. Harris, ed., 390–433 (Oxford: Clarendon, 1971), noting, 417, that by the thirteenth century most literary communication between Copts was in Arabic. On the end of Demotic writing, see, in brief, J. Johnson, *Thus wrote 'Onchsheshonqy: An Introductory Grammar of Demotic* (Chicago: Oriental Institute, 1986), 1.

APPENDIX
THEORIES OF ANCIENT ECONOMIES AND SOCIETIES

1. See the sketch of the history of thought about society and trade by A. Archi, *Circulation*, 9–15, and compare, too, W. Röllig, "Gesellschaft," *RlA* 3:233–36, complaining that he could find no one willing to write comprehensively about society for the reference work. Note that C. Cahen many years ago observed that in Islamic studies the concepts of economic history and social history were not clearly distinguished, "L'Histoire économique et sociale de l'Orient musulman médiéval," *Studia Islamica* 3 (1955): 93–115, 97 n. 1. This is still true for the Ancient Near East.

2. Compare Will A. Boelcke, *Wirtschafts- und Sozialgeschichte: Einführung, Bibliographie, Methoden, Problemfelder* (Darmstadt: Wissenschaftliche Buchgesellschaft, 1987), 15, on the practical necessity of plurality of methods, and, 111, on the lack of help from modern economic theory on earlier situations. See also the essays in A. J. Field, *The Future of Economic History* (Boston: Kluwer-Nijhoff, 1987). E. J. Hobsbawm, "From Social History to the History of Society," *Daedalus* 100 (1971): 20–45, notes that social history can never be isolated, as economic history sometimes can, from other aspects of the past, 24. Though he calls for new techniques of study, and especially for more self-conscious theorizing, he does admit that good work can be produced without theory, 35–36, noting "horses can be recognized and ridden by those who can't define them."

3. B. Gordon, *Economic Analysis before Adam Smith: Hesiod to Lessius*, has a chapter, 70–110, on biblical and patristic sources.

4. E. Wilson, *To the Finland Station* (Garden City, N.Y.: Doubleday, 1940 [1953 reprint]), 139–228, offers a critical appraisal of the relationship of the two men.

5. See especially M. I. Finley, *Ancient Slavery and Modern Ideology*. I. M. Diakonoff, "Slaves, Helots."

6. Compare M. Rostovzeff's emphasis on the importance of the Greek bourgeoisie, which he defines as "a class of men who had achieved by their efforts or inherited from their parents a certain degree of prosperity, and lived not on the income derived from their manual labour but from the investment of their accumulated capital in some branch of economic activity," *The Social and Economic History of the Hellenistic World*, 1116. Others would be less sanguine about our ability to identify such a class. In particular the papers in *Gesellschaftsklassen*, D. O. Edzard, ed., do not manage to identify classes.

7. See J. Fogel, "The Debates over the Asiatic Mode of Production in Soviet Russia, China, and Japan," *American Historical Review* 93 (1988): 56–79, 57–58, for the scattered references in Marx and Engels. One problem with the Asiatic Mode is that Marx and Engels did not give it an extended treatment because in fact they were not interested in it and the stagnation it supposedly represented for essentially racist and Eurocentric reasons.

8. Fogel, "Debates," 74, has sources that argued that the mode is inconsistent with some basic Marxist ideas in that it implies the primacy of geography over productive forces, stagnation over progress, and the uniqueness of the Western experience over the usual claim for its universality, 74. The mode debate heats up when "a Marxist orthodoxy is just taking form, is breaking down, or does not exist at all," 79. The latter is the case in our own day.

9. K. Wittfogel, *Oriental Despotism*. R. McC. Adams, "Die Rolle des Bewässergungsbodenbaus bei der Entwicklung von Institutionen in der altmesopotamischen Gesellschaft," in *Produktivkräfte und Gesellschaftsformationen in vorkapitalistischer Zeit*, J. Hermann, I. Sellnow, eds. (Berlin: Akademie, 1982), 119–40, 129–30, 135 on Sassanians.

10. "Modo di produzione asiatico e Vicino Oriente antico: Appunti per una discussione," *Dialoghi di Archeologia* 3 (1981): 3–65.

11. Ibid., 19–20 and 39–65 on the transfer of villages. One student has suggested that the Asiatic Mode is best seen in the Joseph story in the Bible, Genesis 41, in which the state stores food and then acquires peasants' land; see I. Hahn, "Representation of Society in the Old Testament and the Asiatic Mode of Production," *Oikumene* 2 (1978): 27–41.

12. See E. Wallerstein, *The Modern World-System* (New York: Academic, 1974), and, in general, the studies in *Centre and Periphery in the Ancient World*, M. Rowlands et al., eds., though none of them is completely uncritical about the analogy to the modern situation. Compare also G. Algaze, *The Uruk World System*, 7–8, who criticizes Wallerstein for failing to see that ancient empires were not homeostatic but unstable and dynamic.

13. "Main Features of the Economy in the Monarchies of Ancient Western Asia," *Troisième conférence internationale d'Histoire économique*, 13–32, 14, 22, 33–40; note 37: "No historical theory can be applied without ultimately apologetic purposes," meaning that we are trying to defend or explain our own situations. I. M. Diakonoff, "Three Ways of Development of the Ancient Oriental Society," in *Stato Economia Lavoro nel Vicino Oriente antico*, A. Zanardo, ed., 1–8. Compare Oppenheim's helpful but atheoretical "Trade in the Ancient Near East," in *Vth International Congress of Economic History*, 1–37.

14. M. Weber, *The Agrarian Sociology of Ancient Civilizations*, 46, 406, 385. See also John R. Love, *Antiquity and Capitalism: Max Weber and the Sociological Foundations of Roman*

Civilization (London: Routledge, 1990), dealing only with Weber's Roman studies. For a critique of Weber's sloppy use of biblical texts but also a rather unfair attack on the use of theory in general, see J. Holstein, "Max Weber and Biblical Scholarship," *Hebrew Union College Annual* 46 (1975): 159–79. See the characterization of Weber by R. Frank, in Weber, *Agrarian Sociology*, 24–25.

15. A. Schneider, *Die Anfänge der Kulturwirtschaft: Die sumerische Tempelstadt.*

16. A. Falkenstein, "Le Cité-temple sumérien," *Cahiers d'Histoire Mondiale* 1 (1953–4): 784–814. See also F. R. Kraus, "Le rôle des temples depuis la troisième dynastie d'Ur jusqu'à la première dynastie de Babylone," *Cahiers d'Histoire Mondiale* 1 (1953–54): 518–54. R. Harris, "On the Process of Secularization under Hammurapi," *JCS* 15 (1961): 117–20. On the centrality of the temple and the rise of a middle class, see most clearly Falkenstein, "Temple City."

17. I. J. Gelb, "On the Alleged Temple and State Economies in Ancient Mesopotamia," *Studi in onore di Edouardo Volterra*, 137–54. R. Cameron, *A Concise Economic History of the World from Paleolithic Times to the Present* (Oxford: Oxford University Press, 1989), 30, for example, still asserts that temples owned all land. This is not particularly the fault of Cameron and others who synthesize, but rather those who know better but do not share knowledge in accessible ways. B. Foster, "A New Look at the Sumerian Temple State," *JESHO* 24 (1981): 225–441. H. J. Nissen, "Die 'Tempelstadt': Regierungsform der frühdynastischen Zeit in Babylonien?" in *Gesellschaft und Kultur im alten Vorderasien*, H. Klengel, ed., 195–200, 198–99.

18. "Marketless Trading in Hammurabi's Time," in *Trade and Market in the Early Empires*, K. Polanyi et al., eds., 12–26. This reciprocity had been earlier studied in illuminating ways by Marcel Mauss, *The Gift: Form and Reason for Exchange in Archaic Societies* (1923–24; reprint, London: Routledge, 1990).

19. Polanyi, "Marketless Trading," 16, on Herodotus, *History* 1.152b-153a.

20. "Aristotle Discovers the Economy," in *Trade and Market in the Early Empires*, Polanyi, ed., 64–94. And see K. Polanyi, "Marketless Trading," 20.

21. K. Veenhof, *Aspects of the Old Assyrian Trade and Its Terminology*, 348–400. W. Röllig, "Der altmesopotamische Markt," *Welt des Orients* 8 (1976): 286–95, and compare C. Zaccagnini, "Markt," *RlA* 7:421–26. See S. Cook, "The Obsolete 'Anti-Market' Mentality: A Critique of the Substantive Approach to Economic Anthropology," *American Anthropologist* 68 (1966): 323–45. G. Dalton, "Karl Polanyi's Analysis of Long-Distance Trade and His Wider Paradigm," in *Ancient Civilization and Trade*, J. Sabloff and C. Lamberg-Karlovsky, eds., 63–132, 104. Compare also Robin Law, "Posthumous Questions for Karl Polanyi: Price Inflation in Pre-Colonial Dahomey," *Journal of African History* 33 (1992): 387–420, studying a case of apparently government-administered trade in Dahomey in West Africa that Polanyi had looked at and concluding that the governments involved did try to regulate prices, but in fact prices varied, 389, 418, creating a century of inflation, which stabilized from 1750 to 1850, though wage rates were stable, 419, meaning that porters and other workers were being exploited. Basic in the critique of Polanyi's ill-informed views on Dahomey is W. Peukert, *Die atlantische Sklavenhandel von Dahomey, 1740–1797*, 2–29, 229–41. Reference courtesy of John Thornton.

22. Compare J. Renger, "Patterns of Non-Institutional Trade," in *Circulation*, Archi, 31–123. And compare, too, Renger, "Formen des Zugangs zu den lebensnotwendigen Gütern: Die Austauschverhältnisse in der altbabylonischen Zeit," *Altorientalische*

Forschungen 20 (1993): 87–119, 98–99. D. Snell, "Marketless Trading in Our Time," *JESHO* 39 (1991): 129–41.

23. M. W. Frederiksen, reviewing M. I. Finley's *The Ancient Economy* (1973), which deals only with Greece and Rome and is heavily influenced by Polanyi, observes, "In the final reckoning, we may submit that the status-based model is not wholly false, but it is not a substitute for economic history," *Journal of Roman Studies* 65 (1975): 164–71. Compare T. Figueira, "Karl Polanyi and Ancient Greek Trade: The Port of Trade," *Ancient World* 10 (1984): 15–30. And even ostensible supporters of Polanyi admit that the market does play a role, if a small one, in early societies; see M. Sahlins, *Stone Age Economics* (Chicago, New York: Aldine, Atherton, 1972), 297. See too D. North, "Markets and Other Allocation Systems in History: The Challenge of Karl Polanyi," *Journal of European Economic History* 6 (1977): 703–16, 715, 711.

24. Timothy Earle, "Prehistoric Economics and the Evolution of Social Complexity: A Commentary," in *Prehistoric Production and Exchange: The Aegean and Eastern Mediterranean*, A. B. Knapp and T. Stech, eds., 106–11.

25. "Aspects of Ceremonial Exchange in the Near East during the Late Second Millennium B.C.," in *Centre and Periphery*, M. Rowlands, ed., 57–65.

26. Preface to M. Weber, *The Protestant Ethic and the Spirit of Capitalism* (New York: Scribner's, 1958), 1b–1c.

27. Adams, "Anthropological Reflections on Ancient Trade," *Current Anthropology* 15 (1974): 239–58, 240, and he asserts that one must question authors' denial that gain is a goal outside the West, 248. Donald McCloskey, "Bourgeois Virtue," *The American Scholar* 63 (1994): 177–91.

28. "Götter, Könige, und 'Kapitalisten' im Mesopotamien des 3. Jahrtausands v.u.Z.," *Oikumene* 2 (1978): 127–44, 139: "Eine eigenartige Mischung von Polanyis Wiederverteilungswirtschaft und den kapitalistischen Prinzipien," 140, 143. Though Powell may be right in some periods, P. R. S. Moorey, "The Archaeological Evidence for Metallurgy and Related Techniques in Mesopotamia, c. 5500–2100 B.C.," *Iraq* 44 (1982): 13–38, 31, denies that metalwork technology was really important in economic development in the late fourth and early third millennia.

29. "The Polanyi Paradigm and a Dynamic Analysis of Archaic States," in *Theory and Explanation in Archaeology*, C. Renfrew et al., eds., 197–229, 198, 226.

30. "Land Tenure and Inheritance in the Ancient Near East: The Interaction between 'Palace' and 'Family' Sectors," in *Land Tenure and Social Transformation in the Middle East*, T. Khalidi, ed., 33–44, 35, 39.

31. *Economic Structures of the Ancient Near East*, 51. For transaction costs he draws on D. North, "Markets and Other Allocation Systems in History: The Challenge of Karl Polanyi," *Journal of European Economic History* 6 (1977): 703–16. See John F. Robertson, "On Profit-Seeking Market Orientations and Mentality in the Ancient Near East," *JAOS* 113 (1993): 437–43, noting that Silver lumps together the diverse cultures of the area. Compare Silver's earlier *Prophets and Markets,* seeing prophetic reform as a bad thing because it sought to restrain markets in the interests of justice, 250!

North argues, "Challenge," 713, "In effect reciprocity societies can be considered as a least-cost trading solution where no system of enforcing the terms of exchange between trading units exists."

32. "Les Limites de l'information textuelle," in *L'Archéologie,* M.-T. Barrelet, ed., 225–32, 225–26: "Il y a des renseignements, souvent essentiels pour la solution de nos prob-

lèmes, qui ne figurent pas dans les textes non parce qu'ils n'étaient point *perçus* par les scribes mais tout au contraire parce qu'ils étaient *trop connus* des scribes."

33. D. R. Bender, "A Refinement of the Concept of Household: Families, Co-residence, and Domestic Functions," *American Anthropologist* 69 (1967): 493–504, argues for a distinction between family groups and co-residence groups. In the Ancient Near East when we speak of households we mean coresidence groups; members may or may not be related to each other. I. J. Gelb, "Household and Family in Early Mesopotamia," in *State and Temple Economy,* E. Lipiṅsnki, 1–97, and compare, admittedly without much data, M. Powell, "Economy of the Extended Family According to Sumerian Sources," *Oikumene* 5 (1986): 9–13. D. Herlihy, *Medieval Households* (Cambridge: Harvard University Press, 1985), sketches the variety in European households of his period, and compare in general the studies in *Households: Comparative and Historical Studies of the Domestic Group,* R. M. Netting, R. Wilk, E. Arnould, eds. (Berkeley: University of California, 1984).

34. Silver, *Structures,* passim.

35. See J. Strayer and R. Coulborn, "The Idea of Feudalism," in *Feudalism in History,* R. Coulborn, ed., 3–11, 5, defining feudalism as the predominance of the personal in politics: "Political authority is treated as a private possession. . . . there is relatively little separation of functions; the military leader is usually an administrator and the administrator is usually a judge."

36. Liverani, "Land Tenure," 35.

37. Called in Arabic *iqṭāᶜ*, literally, "cutting up" of the land. On the term and institution, see B. Spuler, "The Disintegration of the Caliphate in the East," in *The Cambridge History of Islam,* vol. IA, P. M. Holt et al., eds. (1970; reprint, Cambridge: Cambridge University Press, 1977), 143–74, 153–54, and, in more detail, C. Cahen, "L'Evolution de l'*iqṭāᶜ* du ixᵉ au xiiiᵉ siècles," *Annales: Economies Sociétés Civilisations* 8 (1953): 25–52.

38. J. Renger, in personal communication, March 15, 1989, and compare "autarkic village communities" discussed by J. Gledhill, "The Transformation of Asiatic Formations; The Case of Late Prehispanic Mesoamerica," in *Marxist Perspectives in Archaeology,* M. Spriggs, ed., 135–48.

39. See E. Stone, "Economic Crisis and Social Upheaval in Old Babylonian Nippur," in *Mountains and Lowlands,* L. Levine and T. Cuyler Young, Jr., eds., 267–89, and see C. Zaccagnini, "Modo di produzione," 39–65.

   On Rome, see K. D. White, "Latifundia," *Bulletin—The Institute of Classical Studies* 14 (1967): 62–79.

40. Compare, defending Diakonoff's descriptive efforts against Oppenheim, I. J. Gelb, "Comparative Method in the Study of the Society and Economy of the Ancient Near East," *Rocznik Orientalistyczny* 2 (1980): 29–36.

BIBLIOGRAPHY

Aberbach, M. *Labor, Crafts, and Commerce in Ancient Israel,* Jerusalem: Magnes, 1984.

Adams, Robert McC. "Anthropological Reflections on Ancient Trade." *Current Anthropology* 15 (1974): 239–58.

———. *The Evolution of Urban Society.* Chicago: University of Chicago Press, 1966.

———. *Heartland of Cities.* Chicago: University of Chicago Press, 1981.

———. "Historic Patterns of Mesopotamian Irrigation Agriculture." In *Irrigation's Impact on Society,* edited by T. Downing and McGuire Gibson, 1–6. Tucson: University of Arizona Press, 1979.

———. *The Land behind Baghdad.* Chicago: University of Chicago Press, 1965.

———. "The Mesopotamian Social Landscape: A View from the Frontier." In *Reconstructing Complex Societies,* edited by C. Moore, 1–20. Cambridge: Bulletin of the American Schools of Oriental Research, 1974.

———. "Die Rolle des Bewässerungsbodenbaus bei der Entwicklung von Institutionen in der altmesopotamischen Gesellschaft." In *Produktivkräfte und Gesellschaftsformationen in vorkapitalistischer Zeit,* edited by J. Hermann and I. Sellnow, 119–40. Berlin: Akademie, 1982.

———. "Strategies of Maximization, Stability and Resilience in Mesopotamian Society, Settlement, and Agriculture." *Proceedings of the American Philosophical Society* 122 (1978): 329–35.

Adams, Robert McC., and Hans Nissen. *The Uruk Countryside.* Chicago: University of Chicago Press, 1972.

Aharoni, Yohanan. *Archaeology of the Holy Land.* Philadelphia: Westminster, 1978.

Ahlström, Gösta. *Royal Administration and National Religion in Ancient Palestine.* Leiden: Brill, 1982.

———. "Was David a Jebusite Subject?" *Zeitschrift für die alttestamentliche Wissenschaft* 92 (1980): 285–87.

AHR Forum: The Old History and the New. American Historical Review 94 (1989): 654–98.

Albright, William F. "King Jehoiakin in Exile." *Biblical Archeologist* 5 (1942): 49–55.

Algaze, Guillermo. "The Uruk Expansion: Cross-Cultural Exchange in Early Mesopotamian Civilization." *Current Anthropology* 30 (1989): 571–608.

———. *The Uruk World System.* Chicago: University of Chicago Press, 1993.

Allam, S. "Women as Holders of Rights in Ancient Egypt (During the Late Period)." *JESHO* 32 (1990): 1–34.

Amusin, I. D. "'Narod zemli' (The People of the Land)." *VDI* (1955–2): 14–36.

Anbar, Moshe. *Les Tribus amurrites de Mari.* Freiburg, Schweiz: Universität; Göttingen: Vandenhoek, Ruprecht, 1991.

Anderson, F. "Israelite Kinship Terminology and Social Structure." *Bible Translator* 20 (1969): 29–39.

Andrews, M. E. "Hesiod and Amos." *Journal of Religion* 23 (1943): 194–205.

Appleby, Joyce, L. Hunt, and M. Jacob. *Telling the Truth About History.* New York: Norton, 1994.

Archi, Alfonso. "Allevamento e distribuzione del bestiame ad Ebla." *Studi Eblaiti* 7 (1984): 45–81.

————. "Anatolia in the Second Millennium, B.C." In *Circulation of Goods in Non-Palatial Context in the Ancient Near East,* edited by Alfonso Archi, 195–206. Rome: Ateneo, 1984.

————. "Bureaucratie et Communauté d'hommes libres dans le système économique hittite." In *Heinrich Otten A.V.,* 17–23. Wiesbaden: Harrassowitz, 1973.

————. "Ebla: La formazione di uno Stato del III millenio a.C." *La Parola del Passato* 46 (1991): 195–219.

————. "Il 'Feudalismo' ittita." *Studi micenei ed egeo- anatolici* 18 (1977): 7–18.

————. "L'Organizzazione amministrativa ittita e il regime delle offerte cultuali." *Oriens Antiquus* 12 (1973): 209–26.

————. "Prices, Workers' Wages and Maintenance at Ebla." *Altorientalische Forschungen* 15 (1988): 24–29.

————. "Les Rapports politiques et économiques entre Ebla et Mari." *M.A.R.I.* 4 (1985): 63–83.

————. "Trade and Administrative Practice." *Altorientalische Forschungen* 20 (1993): 43–58.

————. "Wovon Lebte man in Ebla?" *AfO Beiheft* 19 (1982): 175–88.

————, editor. *Circulation of Goods in Non-Palatial Context in the Ancient Near East.* Rome: Ateneo, 1984.

Ariès, Philippe. *Centuries of Childhood. A Social History of Family Life.* New York: Knopf, 1962.

Asher-Greve, Julia M. *Frauen in altsumerischer Zeit.* Malibu: Undena, 1985.

Aspects du Contact suméro-akkadien = Genava 8 (1960).

Astour, Michael. "The Merchant Class of Ugarit." In *Gesellschaftsklassen im alten Zweistromland,* edited by Dietz Otto Edzard, 11–26. Munich: Bayerische Akademie, 1972.

————. Review of Gernot Wilhelm, *The Hurrians. JNES* 53 (1994): 225–30.

Åström, P., editor. *International Colloquium on Absolute Chronology: High, Middle or Low?* Gothenburg: Åström, 1987.

Avigad, Nigel. *Hebrew Bullae from the Time of Jeremiah.* Jerusalem: Israel Exploration Society, 1986.

Baer, Klaus. "The Low Price of Land in Ancient Eypt." *Journal of the American Research Center in Egypt* 1 (1962): 25–43.

————. *Rank and Title in the Old Kingdom.* Chicago: Univeristy of Chicago Press, 1960.

Baffi Guardata, Francesca, and Rita Dolce. *Archeologia della Mesopotamia: L'Età cassita e medio-assira.* Rome: Bretschneider, 1990.

Bakir, Abd el-Mohsen. *Slavery in Pharaonic Egypt.* Cairo: Institut français, 1952.

Balkan, Kemal. *Kassitenstudien I. Die Sprache der Kassiten.* New Haven: American Oriental Society, 1954.

————. *Studies in Babylonian Feudalism of the Kassite Period.* Malibu: Undena, 1986.

Baltzer, Klaus. "Naboths Weinberg (1 Kön. 21): Der Konflikt zwischen israelitischem und kanaanäischem Bodenrecht." *Wort und Dienst* NF 8 (1965): 73–88.

Barber, Elizabeth W. *Women's Work.* New York: Norton, 1994.

Bardtke, Hans. "Die Latifundien in Juda während der zweiten Hälfte des achten Jahrhunderts v.C.; zum Verständnis von Jes 5, 8–10." In *Hommages à André Dupont-Sommer,* edited by André Caquot and M. Philonenko, 235–54. Paris: Adrien-Maisonneuve, 1971.

Batto, Bernard. "Land Tenure and Women at Mari." *JESHO* 23 (1980): 210–32.

————. *Studies on Women at Mari.* Baltimore: Johns Hopkins University Press, 1974.

Baumgartner, Walther. "Herodots babylonische und assyrische Nachrichten." *Archiv Orientální* 18 (1950): 69–106.

Bayard, D. "Excavations at Non Nok Tha, Northeastern Thailand, 1968." *Asian Perspectives* 13 (1970): 104–43.

Beaulieu, Paul-Alain. *The Reign of Nabonidus, 556–539 B.C.* New Haven: Yale University Press, 1989.

Beckman, Gary. "Herding and Herdsmen in Hittite Culture." In *Heinrich Otten A.V.,* 33–44. Wiesbaden: Harrassowitz, 1988.

Belyavskij, V. "Die Sklavenelite des Hauses Egibi." *Jahrbuch für Wirtschaftsgeschichte* (1973–1): 133–58.

Ben-Barak, Z. "Meribaal and the System of Land Grants in Ancient Israel." *Biblica* 62 (1981): 73–91.

Ben-David, Abba. *Talmudische Oekonomie.* Hildesheim: Olms, 1974.

Bender, Donald R. "A Refinement of the Concept of Household: Families, Co-residence, and Domestic Functions." *American Anthropologist* 69 (1967): 493–504.

Berlev, Oleg D. *Obshchestvennye otnosheniya v Yegipte epoxi srednego tsarstva.* Moskow: Nauka, 1978.

Bertholet, Alfred. "Landbau und Altes Testament." *Schweizerisches Archiv für Volkskunde* 20 (1916): 29–37.

Bickerman, Elias. "The Generation of Ezra and Nehemiah." *American Academy for Jewish Research* 45 (1978): 1–28.

Biga, Maria. "Donne alla corte di Ebla." *La Parola del Passato* 46 (1991): 285–303.

———. "Frauen in der Wirtschaft von Ebla." In *Wirtschaft und Gesellschaft von Ebla,* edited by Hartmut Waetzoldt and Harald Hauptmann, 159–71. Heidelberg: Orient, 1988.

Biggs, Robert. "Semitic Names in the Fara Period." *OrNS* 36 (1967): 55–66.

Bloch, Marc. *Feudal Society.* Chicago: University of Chicago Press, 1961.

Boelcke, Willi A. *Wirtschafts- und Sozialgeschichte: Einführung, Bibliographie, Methoden, Problemfelder.* Darmstadt: Wissenschaftliche Buchgesellschaft, 1987.

Bogoslovsky, E. S. "Drevneyegiptskaya ekonomika na puti k vozniknoveniyu deneg." *VDI* (1982–1): 3–12.

Bohanan, Paul, and Philip Curtin. *Africa and Africans.* Garden City: Natural History, 1971.

Bolla-Kotek, S. Von. *Untersuchungen zur Tiermiete und Viehpacht im Altertum.* Munich: Beck, 1969.

Borowski, Oded. *Agriculture in Iron Age Israel.* Winona Lake, Ind.: Eisenbrauns, 1987.

Bossman, David M. "Ezra's Marriage Reform." *Biblical Theology Bulletin* 9 (1979): 32–38.

Boswell, John. *The Kindness of Strangers: The Abandonment of Children in Western Europe from Late Antiquity to the Renaissance.* New York: Pantheon, 1988.

Bottéro, Jean. "Désordre économique et annulation des dettes en Mésopotamie à l'époque paléo-babylonienne." *JESHO* 4 (1961): 113–64.

———. "Habiru." *RIA* 4:14–27.

Bowman, Alan K. *Egypt after the Pharaohs.* Berkeley: University of California Press, 1986.

Braidwood, Robert. "Prehistoric Investigations in Southwestern Asia." *Proceedings of the American Philosophical Society* 116 (1972): 310–20.

Braudel, Fernand. "History and the Social Sciences: The *longue durée.*" In F. Braudel, *On History,* Sarah Matthews, trans., 25–54. Chicago: University of Chicago Press, 1980.

———. *On History,* Sarah Matthews, trans., 25–54. Chicago: University of Chicago Press, 1980.

————. *The Mediterranean and the Mediterranean World in the Age of Philip II.* New York: Harper and Row, 1972.

Brenner, Adele. *The Israelite Woman.* Sheffield: JSOT Press, 1985.

Brentjes, Burchard, editor. *Das Grundeigentum in Mesopotamien.* = *Jahrbuch für Wirtschaftsgeschichte—Sonderband.* Berlin: Akademie, 1988.

————. "Klimaschwankungen und Siedlungsgeshichte Vorder-und Zentralasiens." *AfO* 40–41 (1993/4): 74–87.

Bresciani, Edda. "La Satrapia d'Egitto." *Studi classici e orientali* 7 (1958): 132–88.

Briant, Pierre. "Pouvoir central et Polycentrisme culturel dans l'empire achéménide." In *Achaemenid History* 1, edited by Helen Sancisi-Weerdenburg, 1–31. Leiden: Nederlands Instituut, 1987.

Bright, John. "The Organization and Administration of the Israelite Empire." In *Magnalia Dei . . . G. Ernest Wright,* edited by Frank M. Cross, 193–208. Garden City: Doubleday, 1976.

Brinkman, John A. "Babylonia under the Assyrian Empire, 745–627 B.C." In *Power and Propaganda,* edited by M. Trolle Larsen, 223–50. Copenhagen: Akademisk, 1979.

————. "Continuity and Discontinuity in Babylonian Civilization." Paper March 21, 1994, at the Annual Meeting of the American Oriental Society, Madison, Wisconsin.

————. "Forced Labor in the Middle Babylonian Period." *JCS* 32 (1980): 17–22.

————. "Foreign Relations of Babylonia from 1600 to 625 B.C.: The Documentary Evidence." *American Journal of Archaeology* 76 (1972): 271–81.

————. "Hurrians in Babylonia in the Late Second Millennium B.C.: An Unexploited Minority Resource for Socioeconomic and Philological Analysis." In *Studies in the Civilization and Culture of Nuzi and the Hurrians* 1, edited by Martha Morrison and David Owen, 27–35. Winona Lake, Ind.: Eisenbrauns, 1981.

————. "Kassiten." *RlA* 5:464b-473b.

————. "Kudurru." *RlA* 6:267–74.

————. *Materials for Kassite History* 1. Chicago: Oriental Institute, 1976.

————. *Prelude to Empire: Babylonian Society and Politics, 747–626.* Philadelphia: Babylonian Fund, 1984.

————. "Settlement Surveys and Documentary Evidence: Regional Variation and Secular Trend in Mesopotamian Demography." *JNES* 43 (1984): 169–80.

————. "Sex, Age, and Physical Condition Designations for Servile Laborers in the Middle Babylonian Period: A Preliminary Survey." In *Zikir Šumim, Assyriological Studies Presented to F. R. Kraus,* edited by Govert Van Driel et al., 1–8. Leiden: Brill, 1982.

————. "Twenty Minas of Copper." In *Language, Literature, and History: Philological and Historical Studies Presented to Erica Reiner,* edited by Francesca Rochberg-Halton, 33–36. New Haven: American Oriental Society, 1987.

Brockmeyer, N. *Antike Sklaverei.* Darmstadt: Wissenschaftliche Buchgesellschaft, 1979.

Brombert, Victor. Review of Edward Said, *Orientalism. American Scholar* 48 (1979): 532–42.

Brown, J. "Proverb-Book, Gold-Economy, Alphabet." *JBL* 100 (1981): 169–91.

Brüschweiler, Françoise. "La Ville dans les Textes littéraires sumériens." In *La Ville dans le Proche-Orient ancien,* 191–98. Louvain: Peeters, 1993.

Buccellati, Giorgio. "ᶜApiru and Munnabtūtu—The Stateless of the First Cosmopolitan Age." *JNES* 32 (1977): 145–47.

————. *Amorites of the Ur III Period.* Naples: Istituto Orientale, 1966.

———. "A Note on the *muškēnum* as a 'Homesteader.'" *Maarav* 7 (1991): 91–100.

———. "The Origin of Writing and the Beginning of History." In *The Shape of the Past: Studies in Honor of Franklin D. Murphy,* edited by Giorgio Buccellati and C. Sperioni, 3–13. Los Angeles: University of California Press, 1981.

———. "Popolo del paese." *Bibbia e Oriente* 3 (1959): 77.

———. "Salt at the Dawn of History: The Case of the Beveled-Rim Bowls." In *Resurrecting the Past: Adnan Bounni A.V.,* edited by Paolo Matthiae et al., 17–32. Leiden: Nederlands Instituut, 1990.

Budge, W.A. *The Rise and Progress of Assyriology.* London: Hopkinson, 1925.

Bulliet, Richard. *Conversion to Islam in the Medieval Period.* Cambridge: Harvard University Press, 1979.

———. *The Camel and the Wheel.* Cambridge: Harvard University Press, 1975.

Butz, Karl. "Konzentrationen wirtschaftlicher Macht im Königreich Larsa: Der Nanna-Nungal-Tempelkomplex in Ur." *WZKM* 65/66 (1973/4): 1–58.

———. "Landwirtschaft." *RlA* 6:470–86.

Butz, Karl, and P. Schröder. "Zu Getreideerträgen in Mesopotamien und dem Mittelmeergebiet." *Baghdader Mitteilungen* 16 (1985): 165–209.

Butzer, Karl. *Early Hydraulic Civilization in Egypt.* Chicago: University of Chicago Press, 1976.

———. "The Late Prehistoric Environmental History of the Near East." In *The Environmental History of the Near and Middle East since the Last Ice Age,* edited by W. Brice, 5–12. London: Academic, 1978.

Cagni, Luigi. "Le Fonti mesopotamiche dei periodi neo-babilonese, achemenide e seleucide (vi–iii sec. a.C.)." *Rivista Biblica* 34 (1986): 11–53.

Cahen, Claude. "L'Evolution de l'iqtāᶜ du ixᵉ au xiiiᵉ siècles." *Annales: Economies Sociétés Civilisations* 8 (1953): 25–52.

———. "L'Histoire économique et sociale de l'Orient musulman médiéval." *Studia Islamica* 3 (1955): 93–115.

Callaway, Joseph A. "Ai (et-Tell): A Problem Site for Biblical Archaeologists." In *Archaeology and Biblcial Interpretation,* edited by Leo G. Perdue, Lawrence E. Toombs, and Gary Lance Johnson, 87–99. Atlanta: John Knox, 1987.

———. "The Settlement in Canaan." In *Ancient Israel,* edited by Hershel Shanks, 53–84. Englewood Cliffs, N.J., Washington, D.C.: Prentice-Hall and Biblical Archaeology Society, 1988.

———. "A Visit with Ahilud." *Biblical Archaeology Review* 9 (1983): 42–53.

Cameron, George. "Darius Carved History on Ageless Rock." *National Geographic* 98 (1958): 825–44.

———. "Persepolis Treasury Tablets Old and New." *JNES* 47 (1958): 161–76.

Cameron, R. *A Concise Economic History of the World from Paleolithic Times to the Present.* Oxford: Oxford University Press, 1989.

Campbell, Edward. "The Shechem Area Survey." *Bulletin of the American Schools of Oriental Research* 190 (1968): 19–41.

Cardascia, Guillaume. *Les Archives de Murašû.* Paris: Imprimerie nationale, 1951.

———. "Le Statut de la femme dans les droits cunéiformes." *Recueils de la Société Jean Bodin* 11 (1957): 79–94.

———. "Les Valeurs morales dans le droit assyrien." *Acta Antiqua* 22 (1974): 363–71.

Cardellini, Innocenzo. *Die biblischen "Sklaven"-Gesetze im Lichte des keilschriftlichen "Sklavenrechts."* Bonn: Hanstein, 1981.

Carerro, O. *History of the Near Eastern Historiography and its Problems, 1852–1985.* Part 1. Neukirchen: Neukirchen-Vluyn, 1989.

Caspers, E. C. L. During. "Harappan Trade in the Arabian Gulf in the Third Millennium B.C." *Mesopotamia* 7 (1972): 167–91.

Cassin, Elena. "Pouvoirs de la femme et structures familiales." *RA* 63 (1969): 121–48.

———. "Techniche della guerra e strutture sociali in Mesopotamia nella seconda metà del II millennio." *Rivista storica italiana* 77 (1965): 445–55.

Castle, E. "Shipping and Trade in Ramesside Egypt." *JESHO* 35 (1992): 239–77.

Castleden, Rodney. *Minoans.* London and New York: Routledge, 1994.

Chadwick, John. "Minoan Scripts." In *Oxford Classical Dictionary,* edited by N. G. L. Hammond and H. H. Scullard, 692. Oxford: Clarendon, 1970.

Chang, K. C. *The Archaeology of Ancient China.* New Haven: Yale University Press, 1963.

Charpin, Dominique. "L'*Andurārum* à Mari." *M.A.R.I.* 6 (1990): 253–70.

———. *Archive familiale et propriété privée en Babylonie ancienne: Etudes des documents de "Tell Sifr."* Geneva: Droz, 1980.

———. *Le Clergé d'Ur au siècle d'Hammurabi.* Geneva-Paris: Droz, 1986.

———. "Les Décrets royaux à l'Epoque paléo-babylonienne." *AfO* 34 (1987): 36–44.

———. "Marchand du palais et marchand du temple à la fin de la Ire Dynastie de Babylone." *Journal Asiatique* 270 (1982): 25–65.

———. "Le Rôle économique du Palais en Babylonie sous Hammurapi et ses successeurs." In *Le Système palatial en Orient, en Grèce, et à Rome,* edited by Edmond Lévy, 111–26. Strasbourg: University of Strasbourg; Leiden: Brill, 1987.

———. "Le Sumérien, langue morte parlée." *N.A.B.U.* (1994–1): 7 #6.

Chirichigno, Gregory C. *Debt-Slavery in Israel and the Ancient Near East.* Sheffield: Journal for the Study of the Old Testament, 1993.

Cipollo, Carlo M. *Literacy and Development in the West.* Baltimore: Penguin, 1969.

Civil, Miguel. "Les Limites de l'information textuelle." In *L'Archéologie de l'Iraq du début de l'époque néolithique à 333 avant notre ère,* edited by Marie-Thérèse Barrelet, 225–32. Paris: Centre National du Recherche Scientifique, 1980.

———. "On Mesopotamian Jails and Their Lady Warden." In *The Tablet and the Scroll: Near Eastern Studies in Honor of William W. Hallo,* edited by Mark Cohen, Daniel Snell, and David Weisberg, 72–78. Bethesda, Md.: CDL, 1993.

———. "Ur III Bureaucracy: Quantitative Aspects." In *The Organization of Power,* edited by McGuire Gibson and Robert Biggs, 213–53. Chicago: Oriental Institute, 1987.

Claburn, W. "The Fiscal Basis of Josiah's Reform." *JBL* 92 (1973): 11–22.

Cocquierillat, Denise. *Palmeraies et cultures de l'Eanna d'Uruk (559–520).* Berlin: Gebr. Mann, 1968.

Cogan, Morton. "A Technical Term for Exposure." *JNES* 27 (1968): 133–35.

Coogan, Michael. "Life in the Diaspora: Jews at Nippur in the Fifth Century B.C." *Biblical Archeologist* 37 (1974): 6–12.

Cook, S. "The Obsolete 'Anti-Market' Mentality: A Critique of the Substantive Approach to Economic Anthropology." *American Anthropologist* 68 (1966): 323–45.

Cooper, Jerrold S. *The Curse of Agade.* Baltimore: Johns Hopkins University Press, 1983.

———. *Sumerian and Akkadian Royal Inscriptions.* Volume 1. New Haven: American Oriental Society, 1987.

Cottrell, L., editor. *The Concise Encyclopedia of Archaeology.* New York: Hawthorn, 1960.

Coote, Robert, and Keith Whitelam. "The Emergence of Israel: Social Transformation and

State Formation following the Decline in Late Bronze Age Trade." In *Social Scientific Criticism of the Hebrew Bible and Its Social World,* edited by Norman Gottwald, 107–47. Decatur: Scholars, 1986.

Crawford, H. E. W. "Mesopotamia's Invisible Exports in the Third Millennium B.C." *World Archaeology* 5 (1973): 232–41.

Cross, Frank M. "A Reconstruction of the Judean Restoration." *JBL* 94 (1975): 4–18.

Cuno, Kenneth M. "The Origins of Private Ownership of Land in Egypt: A Reappraisal." In *The Modern Middle East: A Reader,* edited by Albert Hourani, 195–228. Berkeley and Los Angeles: University of California Press, 1993.

Curtin, Philip. "Prices and Market Mechanisms of the Senegambia." *Ghana Social Science Journal* 2 (1973): 19–41.

Dalley, Stephanie. "Old Babylonian Dowries." *Iraq* 42 (1980): 53–74.

———. "Old Babylonian Trade in Textiles at Tell el Rimah." *Iraq* 39 (1977): 155–59.

Dalley, Stephanie, and J. Nicholas Postgate, eds. *The Tablets from Fort Shalmaneser.* London: British School of Archaeology in Iraq, 1984.

Dalman, Gustav. *Arbeit und Sitte in Palästina.* 7 volumes. 1928–42. Reprint. Hildesheim: Olms, 1964.

Dalton, George. "Karl Polanyi's Analysis of Long-Distance Trade and His Wider Paradigm." In *Ancient Civilization and Trade,* edited by J. Sabloff and C. Lamberg-Karlovsky, 63–132. Albuquerque: University of New Mexico Press, 1975.

Dandamayev, Muhammad. "Achaemenid Babylonia." In *Ancient Mesopotamia,* edited by Igor M. Diakonoff, 296–311. Moscow: Nauka, 1969.

———. "Die Agrarbeziehungen im neubabylonischen Königsreich." In *Das Grundeigentum in Mesopotamien,* edited by Burchard Brentjes, 111–15. Berlin: Akademie, 1985.

———. "Dannye Vavilonskikh tekstov vi–v vv. do n.e. o rubolovstve." *Peredneaziatskii Sbornik* 3 (1979): 81–100.

———. "The Domain-Lands of Achaemenes in Babylonia." *Altorientalische Forschungen* 1 (1974): 123–27.

———. "The Economic and Legal Character of the Slave's Peculium in the Neo-Babylonian and Achaemenid Periods." In *Gesellschaftsklassen im alten Zweistromland,* edited by Dietz Otto Edzard, 35–39. Munich: Bayerische Akademie, 1972.

———. "Forced Labor in the Palace Economy of Achaemenid Iran." *Altorientalische Forschungen* 2 (1975): 71–78.

———. "Free Hired Labor during the Sixth through Fourth Centuries B.C." In *Labor in the Ancient Near East,* edited by Marvin A. Powell, 271–79. New Haven: American Oriental Society, 1987.

———. "The Neo-Babylonian Popular Assembly." In *Šulmu,* 63–71. Prague: Charles University, 1988.

———. "Neo-Babylonian Society and Economy." In *Cambridge Ancient History,* 3:2, edited by J. Boardman et al., 252–75. Cambridge: Cambridge University Press, 1991.

———. "Politische und wirtschaftliche Geschichte." In *Beiträge zur Achämenidengeschichte,* edited by G. Walser, 15–58. Wiesbaden: Steiner, 1972.

———. "Die Rolle des *Tamkārum* in Babylonien im 2. und 1. Jahrtausend v.u.Z." In *Beiträge zur sozialen Struktur des alten Vorderasien,* 1, edited by Horst Klengel, 69–78. Berlin: Akademie, 1971.

———. *Slavery in Babylonia, 626–331.* Translated by Victoria Powell. Dekalb, Ill.: Northern Illinois University, 1984.

———. "The Social Position of the Neo-Babylonian Scribes." In *Gesellschaft und Kultur im alten Vorderasien,* edited by Horst Klengel, 35–39. Berlin: Akademie, 1982.

———. "Social Stratification in Babylonia (7th-4th Centuries B.C.)." *Acta Antiqua* 22 (1974): 433–44.

———. "State and Temple in Babylonia in the First Millennium B.C." In *State and Temple Economy in the Ancient Near East,* 2, edited by Edward Lipiński, 589–96. Louvain: Departement Oriëntalistiek, 1979.

———. "Svobodnye naëmnye rabotniki v pozdnei Vavilonii." In *Assiriologia i Yegiptologia,* edited by L. A. Lipin, 31–50. Leningrad: Leningrad University, 1964.

———. *Vavilonskie Pisty.* Moscow: Nauka, 1983.

Daniels, Peter. "Fundamentals of Grammatology." *JAOS* 110 (1990): 727–31.

———. "'Shewing of Hard Sentences and Dissolving Doubts': The First Decipherment." *JAOS* 108 (1988): 419–36.

Davidović, Vesna. "Guruš in the Administrative Texts from Ebla." In *Wirtschaft und Gesellschaft von Ebla,* edited by Hartmut Waetzoldt and Harald Hauptmann, 199–204. Heidelberg: Orient, 1988.

———. "The Women's Ration System in Ebla." *Oriens Antiquus* 26 (1987): 299–307.

Davies, Eryl W. "Inheritance Rights and the Hebrew Levirate Marriage. Part I." *Vetus Testamentum* 31 (1981): 138–44.

———. "Land: Its Rights and Privileges." In *The World of Ancient Israel,* edited by Ronald E. Clements, 349–69. Cambridge: Cambridge University Press, 1984.

Davies, W. D., and Louis Finkelstein, eds. *The Cambridge History of Judaism,* 1. Cambridge: Cambridge University Press, 1984.

Dearman, John A. *Property Rights in the Eighth-Century Prophets.* Atlanta: Scholars, 1988.

Delcor, Matthias. "Le trésor de la maison de Yahweh des origines à l'Exil." *Vetus Testamentum* 12 (1962): 353–77.

Del Monte, G.F. "Razioni e classi d'età in Nippur medio-babilonese." In *Stato Economia Lavoro nel Vicino Oriente antico,* edited by A. Zanardi, 17–30. Milan: Angeli, 1988.

Desroches, M. J. "Aspects of the Structure of Dilbat during the Old Babylonian Period." Ph.D. dissertation, University of California at Los Angeles, 1978.

De Vaux, Roland. *Ancient Israel: Its Life and Institutions.* New York: McGraw-Hill, 1961.

———. "Le Sens de l'Expression 'Peuple du Pays' dans l'ancien testament et le rôle politique du peuple en Israël." *RA* 58 (1964): 167–72.

Dever, William G. "Funerary Practices in EB IV (MB I) Palestine: A Study in Cultural Discontinuity." In *Marvin Pope A.V.,* edited by John Marks and Robert Good, 9–19. Guilford, Conn.: Four Quarters, 1987.

———. "Monumental Architecture in Ancient Israel in the Period of the United Monarchy." In *Studies in the Period of David and Solomon,* edited by T. Ishida, 269–306, Winona Lake, Ind.: Eisenbrauns, 1982.

Diakonoff, Igor M. "Extended Families in Old Babylonian Ur." *ZA* 75 (1985): 47–65.

———. "Die hethitische Gesellschaft." *Mitteilungen des Instituts für Orientforschung* 13 (1967): 313–66.

———. "Kuplia-prodazha zemli v drevneishem Shumere i vopros o shumerskoi obshchine." *VDI* (1955–4): 10–40.

———. *Lyudi goroda Ura.* Moskow: Nauka, 1990.

———. "Main Features of the Economy in the Monarchies of Ancient Western Asia." In *Troisième conférence internationale d'Histoire économique,* 13–32. Paris: École pratique, 1969.

———. *Obshchestvennyi i gosudarstvennyi Stroi drevnego dvurech'ya. Šumer.* Moscow: Vostochnaya Literatura, 1959.

———. "On the Structure of Old Babylonian Society." In *Beiträge zur sozialen Struktur des alten Vorderasien* 1, edited by Horst Klengel, 15–31. Berlin: Akademie, 1971.

———. *Razvitie zemel'nyx otnoshenii v Assirii.* Leningrad: Universitet Zhdanova, 1949.

———. "Sale of Land in Pre-Sargonic Sumer." In *Papers Presented by the Soviet Delegation to the XXIIId International Congress of Orientalists.* 5–32. Moscow: 1954.

———. "Slaves, Helots and Serfs in Early Antiquity." *Acta Antiqua* 22 (1974): 45–78.

———. "Slave Labour versus Non-Slave Labour: The Problem of Definition." In *Labor in the Ancient Near East,* edited by Marvin A. Powell, 1–3. New Haven: American Oriental Society, 1987.

———. "Socio-Economic Classes in Babylonia and the Babylonian Concept of Social Stratification." In *Gesellschaftsklassen im alten Zweistromland,* edited by Dietz Otto Edzard, 41–52. Munich: Bayerische Academie, 1972.

———. "The Structure of Near Eastern Society before the Middle of the 2nd Millennium." *Oikumene* 3 (1982): 7–100.

———. "Three Ways of Development of the Ancient Oriental Society." In *Stato Economia Lavoro nel Vicino Oriente antico,* edited by A. Zanardo, 1–8. Milan: Angeli, 1988.

Dietrich, Manfred, and Oswald Loretz. "Die soziale Struktur von Alalah und Ugarit." *Welt des Orients* 3 (1964–5): 188–205, 5 (1969–70): 57–93.

Donbaz, Veysal. "Four Old Assyrian Tablets from the City of Assur." *JCS* 26 (1974): 81–87.

Donner, Herbert. "Die soziale Botschaft der Propheten im Licht der Gesellschaftsordnung in Israel." *Oriens Antiquus* 2 (1963): 329–45.

Dorian, Nancy. *Language Death.* Philadelphia: University of Pennsylvania Press, 1981.

Dorsey, J. *The Roads and Highways of Ancient Israel.* Baltimore: Johns Hopkins University Press, 1991.

Dosch, Gudrun. "Non-Slave Labor in Nuzi." In *Labor in the Ancient Near East,* edited by Marvin A. Powell, 223–35. New Haven: American Oriental Society, 1987.

Dossin, Georges. "La Route de l'Étain en Mésopotamie au temps de Zimri-Lim." *RA* 64 (1970): 97–106.

Dothan, Trudy. "The Philistines Reconsidered." In *Biblical Archaeology Today,* 165–76. Jerusalem: Israel Exploration Society, 1985.

Doty, L. Timothy. "Cuneiform Archives from Hellenistic Uruk." Ph.D. dissertation, Yale University, 1977.

———. "Nikarchos and Kephalon." In *A Scientific Humanist: Studies in Memory of Abraham Sachs,* edited by Earle Leichty and Maria deJ. Ellis, 95–118. Philadelphia: Babylonian Fund, 1988.

Driel, Govert van. "Continuity and Decay in the Late Achaemenid Period: Evidence from Southern Mesopotamia." In *Achaemenid History,* 1, edited by Helen Sancisi-Weerdenburg, 159–81. Leiden: Nederlands Instituut, 1987.

———. "Land and People in Assyria." *BiOr* 27 (1970): 168–75.

———. "Neo-Babylonian Sheep and Goats." *Bulletin of Sumerian Agriculture* 7 (1993): 219–58.

———. "Uit het leven van een Nieuw-Bablonische handelaar." *Phoenix* 38 (1992): 30–45.

Driver, Geoffrey R., and J. C. Miles, editors. *The Assyrian Laws.* Oxford: Clarendon, 1935.

Dubberstein, Walter. "Comparative Prices in Late Babylonia (625–400 B.C.)." *American Journal of Semitic Languages* 56 (1939): 27–43.

Dumont, Louis. *Homo Hierarchicus.* Chicago: University of Chicago Press, 1970.

Dunham, Sally. "Beads for Babies." *ZA* 83 (1993): 236–57.

Durand, Jean-Marie. "Les Dames du Palais de Mari à l'epoque du Royaume de Haute-Mésopotamie." *M.A.R.I.* 4 (1985): 385–436.

Durand, Jean-Marie, and Dominique Charpin. "Remarques sur l élévage intensif dans l'Iraq ancien." In *L'Archéologie de l'Iraq,* edited by Marie-Thérèse Barrelet, 131–56. Paris: Centre National de Recherche Scientifique, 1980.

Earle, T. "Prehistoric Economics and the Evolution of Social Complexity: A Commentary." In *Prehistoric Production and Exchange: The Aegean and Eastern Mediterranean,* edited by A. Bernard Knapp and T. Stech, 106–11. Los Angeles: Institute of Archaeology, 1985.

Ebeling, Erich. "Erbe, Erbrecht, Enterbung." *RlA* 2:458b-460b.

———. "Familie." *RlA* 3:15b.

———, editor. *Reallexikon der Assyriologie.* Berlin: de Gruyter, 1937– .

Edzard, Dietz Otto. "Die Beziehungen Babyloniens und Ägyptens in der mittelbabylonischen Zeit und das Gold." *JESHO* 3 (1960): 38–55.

———. "Indusschrift aus der Sicht des Assyriologen." *ZA* 80 (1990): 124–34.

———. "Mebaragesi." *RlA* 7:614.

———. "Soziale Reformen im Zweistromland bis 1600 v.Chr.: Realität oder literarischen Topos?" *Acta Antiqua* 22 (1974): 145–56.

———. "Sumerer und Semiten in der frühen Geschichte Mesopotamiens." In *Aspects du contact = Genava* 8 (1960): 241–48.

———. *Die Zweite Zwischenzeit Babyloniens.* Wiesbaden: Harrasowitz, 1957.

———, editor. *Gesellschaftsklassen im alten Zweistromland und in den angrenzenden Gebieten.* Munich: Bayerische Akademie, 1972.

———, editor. *Sumerische Rechtsurkunden des III. Jahrtausends.* Munich: Bayerische Akademie, 1968.

Eichler, Barry. *Indenture at Nuzi.* New Haven: Yale University Press, 1973.

Eilers, Wilhelm. "Akkad. *kaspum,* 'Silber, Geld' und Sinnverwandtes." *Welt des Orients* 2 (1957): 322–37, 4 (1959): 465–569.

Eisenstadt, Shmuel N., editor. *The Origins and Diversity of Axial Age Civilizations.* Albany: State University of New York Press, 1986.

Elat, Moshe. *Qishre kalkalah ben 'artzot ha-Miqra' bi-yeme Bayit rishon* (Economic Relations in the Lands of the Bible c. 1000–539 B.C.). Jerusalem: Bialik, 1977.

———. "Der *Tamkārum* im neuassyrischen Reich." *JESHO* 30 (1987): 233–54.

Elayi, J. *Pénétration grecque en Phénicie sous l'empire perse.* Nancy: Universitaires, 1988.

Ellis, Maria deJ. *Agriculture and the State in Ancient Mesopotamia.* Philadelphia: Babylonian Fund, 1976.

———. "*ṣimdatu* in the Old Babylonian Sources." *JCS* 24 (1972): 74–82.

———. "Taxation in Ancient Mesopotamia: The History of the Term *miksu.*" *JCS* 26 (1974): 211–50.

Ellison, R. "Diet in Mesopotamia: The Evidence of the Barley Ration Texts (c. 3000–1400 B.C.)." *Iraq* 43 (1981): 35–45.

Emmerson, Grace I. "Women in Ancient Israel." In *The World of Ancient Israel,* edited by Ronald E. Clements, 371–94. Cambridge: Cambridge University Press, 1984.

Engels, D. "The Use of Demography in Ancient History." *Classical Quarterly* 34 (1984): 386–93.

Englund, Robert K. "Hard Work—Where Will It Get You? Labor Management in Ur III Mesopotamia." *JNES* 50 (1991): 255–80.

——. *Organisation und Verwaltung der Ur III-Fischerei.* Berlin: Reimer, 1990.

Eph'al, Israel. *The Ancient Arabs: Nomads on the Borders of the Fertile Crescent, 9th-5th Centuries B.C.* Jerusalem: Magnes, 1984.

Erdmann, Elisabeth. "Römischer 'Imperialismus'—Schlagwort oder Begriff?" *Geschichte in Wissenschaft und Unterricht* 28 (1977/8): 461–77.

Evans, D. "The Incidence of Labour-Service in the Old Babylonian Period." *JAOS* 83 (1963): 20–26.

Eyre, Christopher J. "Work and the Organization of Work in the New Kingdom." In *Labor in the Ancient Near East,* edited by Marvin A. Powell, 166–221. New Haven: American Oriental Society, 1987.

Fales, Frederick M. *Censimenti e catasti di Epoca neo-assira.* Roma: Centro per le antichità, 1973.

——. "Grain Reserves, Daily Rations, and the Size of the Assyrian Army: A Quantitative Study." *State Archives of Assyria. Bulletin* 4 (1990): 23–34.

——. "West Semitic Names in the Assyrian Empire: Diffusion and Social Relevance." *Studi epigrafici e linguistici* 8 (1991): 99–117.

Falkenstein, Adam. "Le Cité-temple sumérien." *Cahiers d'Histoire Mondiale* 1 (1953–4): 784–814, revised and translated as *The Sumerian Temple City,* Maria deJ. Ellis, trans. Malibu: Undena, 1974.

——. "Gilgameš." *RlA* 3: 357–63.

——, editor. *Die Neusumerischen Gerichtsurkunden,* 1. Munich: Bayerische Akademie, 1956.

Farber, Howard. "An Examination of Long Term Fluctuations in Prices and Wages for North Babylonia during the Old Babylonian Period." M.A. thesis, Northern Illinois University, 1974.

——. "A Price and Wage Study for Northern Babylonia during the Old Babylonian Period." *JESHO* 21 (1978): 1–51.

Fariz, Muhammad el-. "Salinité et histoire de l'Irak pré-Islamique." *JESHO* 33 (1990): 105–13.

Feigin, Samuel. "Some Cases of Adoption in Israel." *JBL* 50 (1931): 186–200.

Fendler, M. "Zur Sozial-Kritik des Amos." *Evangelische Theologie* 33 (1973): 32–53.

Fensham, F. Charles. "Widow, Orphan, and the Poor in Ancient Near Eastern Legal and Wisdom Literature." *JNES* 21 (1962): 129–39.

Field, A.J., editor. *The Future of Economic History.* Boston: Kluwer-Nijhoff, 1987.

Figueira, T. "Karl Polanyi and Ancient Greek Trade: The Port of Trade." *Ancient World* 10 (1984): 15–30.

Finkbeiner, U., and Wolfgang Röllig, eds. *Ǧamdat Nasr: Period or Regional Style?* Wiesbaden: Reichert, 1986.

Finkel, Ira. "An Issue of Weights from the Reign of Amar-Sin." *ZA* 77 (1987): 192–93.

Finkelstein, Israel. *The Archaeology of the Israelite Settlement.* Jerusalem: Israel Exploration Society, 1988.

Finkelstein, Jacob J. "Mesopotamia." *JNES* 21 (1962): 73–92.

——. "An Old Babylonian Herding Contract and Genesis 31:38f." *JAOS* 88 (1968): 30–36.

————. *The Ox That Gored. Transactions of the American Philosophical Society* 71:2 (1981).

————. "Subartu and Subarians in Old Babylonian Sources." *JCS* 9 (1955): 1–7.

————. "Ammisaduqa's Edict and the Babylonian 'Law Codes.'" *JCS* 15 (1961): 91–104.

Finley, Moses I. "The Alienability of Land in Ancient Greece; A Point of View." *Eirene* 7 (1968): 28–32.

————. *Ancient Slavery and Modern Ideology.* Harmondsworth: Penguin, 1983.

————. "Between Freedom and Slavery." *Comparative Studies in Society and History* 6 (1964): 233–49.

————. "The Mycenaean Tablets and Economic History." *Economic History Review* 10 (1957): 128–41.

————. "The Servile Statuses of Ancient Greece." *Revue internationale des droits de l'Antiquité* 7 (1960): 164–89.

————. "Technical Innovation and Economic Progress in the Ancient World." *Economic History Review* 18 (1965): 29–45.

Firmage, Edwin. "Zoology." In *Anchor Bible Dictionary,* 6, edited by David N. Freedman, 1109–67. New York: Doubleday, 1992.

Flanagan, James. "Chiefs in Israel." *Journal for the Study of the Old Testament* 20 (1981): 47–73.

Flannery, Kent V. "Origins and Ecological Effects of Early Domestication in Iran and the Near East." In *Prehistoric Agriculture,* edited by S. Streuver, 50–79. Garden City: American Museum of Natural History, 1971.

Fogel, Joshua A. "The Debates over the Asiatic Mode of Production in Soviet Russia, China, and Japan." *American Historical Review* 93 (1988): 56–79.

Foster, Benjamin R. *Administration and Use of Institutional Land in Sargonic Sumer.* Copenhagen: Akademisk, 1982.

————. "*Agoranomos* and *Muhtasib.*" *JESHO* 13 (1970): 128–44.

————. "Agriculture and Accountability in Ancient Mesopotamia." In *The Origins of Cities in Dry-Farming Syria in the Third Millennium B.C.,* edited by Harvey Weiss, 109–28. Guilford, Conn.: Four Quarters, 1986.

————. "Commercial Activity in Sargonic Mesopotamia." *Iraq* 39 (1979): 31–43.

————. "Ethnicity and Onomastics in Sargonic Mesopotamia." *OrNS* 51 (1982): 297–354.

————. "The Late Bronze Age Palace Economy: A View from the East." In *The Function of the Minoan Palaces,* edited by R. Hägg and N. Marinatos, 11–16. Stockholm: Åström, 1987.

————. "A New Look at the Sumerian Temple State." *JESHO* 24 (1981): 225–441.

————. "Notes on Women in Sargonic Society." In *La Femme dans le Proche-Orient antique,* edited by Jean-Marie Durand, 53–61. Paris: Recherche sur les Civilisations, 1987.

————. *Umma in the Sargonic Period.* Hamden: Archon, 1982.

Fox-Talbot, W.H. et al. "Comparative Translations by W.H. Fox-Talbot . . . of the Inscription of Tiglath Pileser I." *Journal of the Royal Asiatic Society* 18 (1861): 150–212.

Foxvog, Daniel, "A Third Arua Summary from Ur III Lagash." RA 80 (1986): 19–29.

Frankfort, Henri. *The Art and Architecture of the Ancient Orient.* Harmondsworth: Penguin, 1954.

————. *Kingship and the Gods.* Chicago: University of Chicago Press, 1948.

Frederiksen, M.W. Review of M.I. Finley, *The Ancient Economy. Journal of Roman Studies* 65 (1975): 164–71.

Freydank, Helmut. "Anzeichen für einen mittelassyrischen Preistarif?" *Altorientalische Forschungen* 12 (1985): 162–64.

———. "Fernhandel und Warenpreise nach einer mittelassyrischen Urkunde des 12. Jahrhunderts v. u. Z." In *Societies and Languages of the Ancient Near East: Studies in Honor of I. M. Diakonoff,* edited by J. Nicholas Postgate, 64–75. Warminster: Aris & Phillips, 1982.

———. "Untersuchungen zur sozialen Struktur in mittelassyrischer Zeit." *Altorientalische Forschungen* 4 (1976): 111–30.

Frick, Frank. *The City in Ancient Israel.* Missoula: Scholars, 1977.

Friedrich, Johannes. *Extinct Languages.* New York: Philosophical, 1957.

———. *Die hethitische Gesetze.* Leiden: Brill, 1971.

Fritz, Volkmar. *Einführung in die biblische Archäologie.* Darmstadt: Wissenschaftliche Buchgesellschaft, 1985.

Frymer-Kensky, Tiqva. "Patriarchal Family Relationships and Near Eastern Law." *Biblical Archeologist* 44 (1981): 209–14.

Gadd, Cyril J. "The Spirit of Living Sacrifices in Tombs." *Iraq* 22 (1960): 51–59.

Garbini, Giovanni. "L'Impero di David." *Annali della Scuola Normale Superiore di Pisa, Classe di Lettere e Filosofia,* Serie III, 13/1 (1983): 1–20.

———. *History and Ideology in Ancient Israel.* New York: Crossroad, 1988.

Garelli, Paul. *Les Assyriens en Cappadoce.* Paris: Institut français, 1963.

———. "Marchands et *Tamkārū* assyriens en Cappadoce." *Iraq* 39 (1977): 99–107.

———. "Le Problème de la 'Féodalité' assyrienne du xvᵉ au xiiᵉ siècle av. J.-C." *Semitica* 17 (1967): 5–21.

———. "Problèmes de stratification sociale dans l'Empire assyrien." In *Gesellschaftsklassen im alten Zweistromland,* edited by Dietz Otto Edzard, 73–79. Munich: Bayerische Akademie, 1972.

———. "Remarques sur l'Administration de l'Empire assyrien." *RA* 68 (1974): 129–40.

———. "Le Système fiscal de l'empire assyrien." In *Points de vue sur la fiscalité antique,* edited by H. van Effenterre, 7–18. Paris: Sorbonne, 1979.

———, editor. *Le Palais et la Royauté.* Paris: Geuthner, 1974.

Garelli, Paul, and Dominique Charpin. "Rôle des prisonniers et des déportés à l'époque médio-assyrienne." In *Gesellschaft und Kultur im alten Vorderasien,* edited by Horst Klengel, 69–75. Berlin: Akademie, 1982.

Gates, Marie-Henriette. *Alalakh Levels VI and V: A Chronological Reassessment.* Malibu: Undena, 1981.

Gees, J. K. de. "Die Gesellschaftskritik der Propheten und die Archaeologie." *Zeitschrift des deutschen Palästina-Vereins* 98 (1982): 50–57.

Gelb, Ignace J. "The Ancient Mesopotamian Ration System." *JNES* 24 (1965): 230–43.

———. "The Arua Institution." *RA* 66 (1972): 1–32.

———. "Comparative Method in the Study of the Society and Economy of the Ancient Near East." *Rocznik Orientalistyczny* 2 (1980): 29–36.

———. "Definition and Discussion of Slavery and Freedom." *Ugaritforschungen* 11 (1979): 283–97.

———. "Ebla and Lagash: Environmental Contrast." In *The Origins of Cities in Dry-Farming Syria in the Third Millennium B.C.,* edited by Harvey Weiss, 157–67. Guilford, Conn.: Four Quarters, 1986.

———. "The Growth of a Herd of Cattle in Ten Years." *JCS* 21 (1967): 64–69.

———. *Hurrians and Subarians.* Chicago: University of Chicago Press, 1944.

———. "Household and Family in Early Mesopotamia." In *State and Temple Economy in the*

Ancient Near East, 1, edited by Edward Lipiński, 1–97. Louvain: Departement Oriëntal-istiek, 1979.

———. "On the Alleged Temple and State Economies in Ancient Mesopotamia." In *Studi in onore di Edouardo Volterra,* 137–54. Rome, 1969.

———. "An Old Babylonian List of Amorites." *JAOS* 88 (1968): 39–46.

———. "Prisoners of War in Early Mesopotamia." *JNES* 32 (1973): 70–98.

———. "Quantitative Estimates of Slavery and Serfdom." In *Cuneiform Studies in Honor of Samuel Noah Kramer,* edited by Barry Eichler, 195–208. Kevelaer: Butzon & Bercker; Neukirchen-Vluyn: Neukirchener, 1976.

———. "Social Stratification in the Old Akkadian Period." In *25th International Congress of Orientalists,* 1, 225–26. Moskow: Nauka, 1960.

———. "Terms for Slaves in Ancient Mesopotamia." In *Societies and Languages of the Ancient Near East: Studies in Honor of I. M. Diakonoff,* edited by J. Nicholas Postgate, 81–98. Warminster: Aris & Phillips, 1982.

Gelb, Ignace J., Pyotr Steinkeller, and Robert Whiting, eds. *Earliest Land Tenure Systems in the Near East: The Ancient Kudurrus.* Chicago: University of Chicago Press, 1991.

Gelb, Ignace J., Benno Landsberger, A. Leo Oppenheim, and Erica Reiner, eds. *The Assyrian Dictionary.* Chicago, Glückstadt: Oriental Institute and J.J. Augustin, 1956–.

Gelio, R. "Fonti mesopotamiche relative al territorio palestinese (1000–500 a. C.)." *Rivista Biblica* 32 (1984): 121–51.

Geus, C. de. "Agrarian Communities in Biblical Times: 12th to 10th Centuries B.C.E." *Recueils de la Société Jean Bodin* 41 (1983): 207–37.

Giacchero, M. "L'Intuizione dei fenomeni e dei comportamenti economici nelle storie di Erodoto." In *Studi di Storia Antica in memoria di Luca de Regibus,* 91–134. Genoa: Istituto di Storia antica, 1969.

Gibson, McGuire. *The City and Area of Kish.* Miami: Field Research, 1972.

———. "Violation of Fallow and Engineered Disaster in Mesopotamian Civilization." In *Irrigation's Impact on Society,* edited by T. Downing and McGuire Gibson, 7–19. Tucson: University of Arizona Press, 1974.

Gibson, McGuire, and Robert Biggs, editors. *Seals and Sealings in the Ancient Near East.* Malibu: Undena, 1977.

Ginzberg, E. "Studies in the Economics of the Bible." *Jewish Quarterly Review* 22 (1931): 343–408.

Giorgadze, G. G. "Two Forms of Non-Slave Labor in Hittite Society." In *Labor in the Ancient Near East,* edited by Marvin A. Powell, 251–55. New Haven: American Oriental Society, 1987.

Gledhill, J., "The Transformation of Asiatic Formations: The Case of Late Prehispanic Mesoamerica." In *Marxist Perspectives in Archaeology,* edited by M. Spriggs, 135–48. Cambridge: Cambridge University Press, 1984.

Gledhill, J., and Mogens Trolle Larsen. "The Polanyi Paradigm and a Dynamic Analysis of Archaic States." In *Theory and Explanation in Archaeology,* edited by Colin Renfrew et al., 197–229. New York: Academic, 1982.

Goetze, Albrecht. *Kleinasien.* Munich: Beck, 1957.

———. *The Laws of Eshnunna.* New Haven: American Schools of Oriental Research, 1956.

———. "Umma Texts Concerning Reed Mats." *JCS* 2 (1948): 165–202.

Goldsmith, James. "The Agrarian History of Preindustrial France. Where Do We Go from Here?" *Journal of European Economic History* 13 (1984): 175–99.

Golka, Friedemann. "Die Königs- und Hofsprüche und der Ursprung der israelitischen Weisheit." *Vetus Testamentum* 36 (1986): 13–36.

Gomi, Tohru. "On the Critical Economic Situation at Ur Early in the Reign of Ibbi-Sin." *JCS* 36 (1984): 211–42.

———. "On Dairy Productivity at Ur in the Late Ur III Period." *JESHO* 23 (1979): 1–42.

Goossens, Geoffrey. "Artistes et artisans étrangers en Perse sous les Achéménides." *La Nouvelle Clio* 1 (1949): 32–44.

———. "Au déclin de la civilisation babylonienne: Uruk sous les Seleucides." *Académie royale de Belgique: Bulletin de la Classe des lettres et des sciences morales et politiques* (1941): 223–44.

Gordon, Barry. *Economic Analysis before Adam Smith: Hesiod to Lessius.* New York: Harper & Row, Barnes & Noble, 1975.

———. "Lending at Interest: Some Jewish, Greek, and Christian Approaches, 800 B.C.–A.D. 100." *History of Political Economy* 14 (1982): 406–26.

Gordon, Edmund. *Sumerian Proverbs.* Philadelphia: University Museum, 1959.

Gorelick, Leonard, and A. John Gwinnett. "The Ancient Near Eastern Cylinder Seal as Social Emblem and Status Symbol." *JNES* 49 (1990): 45–56.

Gottwald, Norman. "Israel, Social and Economic Development of." In *Interpreter's Dictionary of the Bible,* Supplement, edited by Keith Crim, 465–68. Nashville: Abingdon, 1976.

———. "Social Class as an Analytic and Hermeneutical Category in Biblical Studies." *JBL* 112 (1993): 3–22.

———. *The Tribes of Yahweh: A Sociology of the Religion of Liberated Israel, 1250–1050 B.C.E.* New York: Orbis, 1979.

Gowen, Herbert. "Hebrew Trade and Trade Terms in Old Testament Times." *Journal of the Society for Oriental Research* 6 (1922): 1–16.

Gray, John. "Feudalism in Ugarit and Early Israel." *Zeitschrift für die alttestamentliche Wissenschaft* 64 (1952): 49–55.

Green, Margaret W. "Animal Husbandry at Uruk in the Archaic Period." *JNES* 39 (1980): 1–36.

Green, Margaret W., and Hans Nissen. *Zeichenliste der archäischen Texte aus Uruk.* Berlin: Gebr. Mann, 1987.

Greenberg, Moshe. *Hab/piru.* New Haven: American Oriental Society, 1956.

Greengus, Samuel. "Old Babylonian Marriage Ceremonies and Rites." *JCS* 20 (1966): 55–72.

Gressmann, H. "Die Ausgrabungen in Samaria." *Zeitschrift für die alttestamentliche Wissenschaft* 2 (1925): 147–50.

Grosz, Katarzyna. "Dowry and Brideprice at Nuzi." In *Studies on the Civilization and Culture of Nuzi and the Hurrians in Honor of Ernest R. Lacheman,* vol. 1, edited by Martha Morrison and David Owen, 161–82. Winona Lake, Ind.: Eisenbrauns, 1981.

Gunderson, Gerald. "Economic Behavior in the Ancient World." In *Explorations in the New Economic History; Essays . . . Douglass C. North,* edited by Roger Ransom et al., 235–56. New York: Academic, 1982.

Gurney, Oliver R. *The Hittites.* Harmondsworth: Pelican, 1954.

Hahn, I. "From Antiquity to the Third World." *Oikumene* 5 (1986): 371–88.

———. "Representation of Society in the Old Testament and the Asiatic Mode of Production." *Oikumene* 2 (1978): 27–41.

Hallock, R. "A New Look at the Persepolis Treasury Tablets." *JNES* 19 (1960): 90–100.

Hallo, William W. "The Coronation of Ur-Nammu." *JCS* 20 (1966): 133–41.

————. "Gutium." *RlA* 3:708–20.

————. Review of W. Leemans, *Foreign Trade, JCS* 17 (1963): 60.

————. "A Sumerian Amphictyony." *JCS* 14 (1960): 88–114.

Hallo, William W., and Briggs Buchanan. "A Persian Gulf Seal on an Old Babylonian Mercantile Agreement." In *Studies in Honor of Benno Landsberger*, 199–203. Chicago: University of Chicago Press, 1965.

Hallo, William W., and William Kelly Simpson. *The Ancient Near East: A History*. New York: Harcourt, Brace, Jovanovich, 1971.

Hallo, William W., and J. J. A. Van Dijk. *The Exaltation of Inanna*. New Haven: Yale University Press, 1968.

Haran, Menahem. "The Gibeonites, the Nethinim and the Sons of Solomon's Servants." *Vetus Testamentum* 11 (1961): 159–69.

Harlan, Jack. "A Wild Wheat Harvest in Turkey." *Archaeology* 20 (1967): 197–201.

Harris, Rivkah. *Ancient Sippar*. Istanbul: Nederlands Instituut, 1975.

————. "Biographical Notes on the Naditu Women of Sippar." *JCS* 16 (1962): 1–12.

————. "On Foreigners in Old Babylonian Sippar." *RA* 70 (1976): 145–52.

————. "Images of Women in the Gilgamesh Epic." In *Lingering over Words: W. L. Moran A. V.*, edited by Tzvi Abusch, John Huehnergard, and Pyotr Steinkeller, 219–30. Atlanta: Scholars, 1990.

————. "The *naditu* Laws of the Code of Hammurapi in Praxis." *OrNS* 30 (1961): 163–69.

————. "The *Naditu* Woman." In *Studies Presented to A. Leo Oppenheim*, edited by Robert Biggs and John A. Brinkman, 106–35. Chicago: Oriental Institute, 1964.

————. "Notes on the Slave Names of Old Babylonian Sippar." *JCS* 29 (1977): 45–51.

————. "The Organization and Administration of the Cloister in Ancient Babylonia." *JESHO* 6 (1963): 121–57.

————. "On the Process of Secularization under Hammurapi." *JCS* 15 (1961): 117–20.

Hauer, Chris, Jr. "David's Army." *Concordia Journal* 4 (1978): 68–72.

————. "The Economics of National Security in Solomonic Israel." *Journal for the Study of the Old Testament* 18 (1980): 63–73.

Hawkins, J. D. "Royal Statements of Ideal Prices: Assyrian, Babylonian, and Hittite." In *Ancient Anatolia . . . M. J. Mellink A.V.*, edited by Jean Canby et al., 93–102. Madison: University of Wisconsin Press, 1986.

Hawkins, J. D., editor. *Trade in the Ancient Near East* = *Iraq* 39 (1977).

Heichelheim, F. "Ezra's Palestine and Periclean Athens." *Zeitschrift für Religions- und Geistesgeschichte* 3 (1951): 251–53.

Heimpel, Wolfgang. "Kamel." *RlA* 5:330–32.

————. "Sumerische und akkadische Personennamen in Sumer und Akkad." *AfO* 25 (1974/77): 171–74.

Helck, Wolfgang. *Wirtschaftsgeschichte des alten Ägypten im 3. und 2. Jahrtausend vor Chr.* Leiden: Brill, 1975.

Heltzer, Michael. *Goods, Prices and the Organization of Trade in Ugarit*. Wiesbaden: Reichert, 1975.

————. "Labour in Ugarit." In *Labor in the Ancient Near East*, edited by Marvin A. Powell, 237–50. New Haven: American Oriental Society, 1987.

————. "The Metal Trade of Ugarit and the Problem of Transportation of Commercial Goods." *Iraq* 39 (1977): 203–11.

———. "Private Property in Ugarit." In *Circulation of Goods in Non-Palatial Context in the Ancient Near East,* edited by Alfonso Archi, 161–93. Rome: Ateneo, 1984.

———. "Raby, rabovladenie, i rol' rabstva v Ugarite xiv-xii veka." *VDI* (1968–3): 85–95.

———. *The Rural Community in Ancient Ugarit.* Wiesbaden: Reichert, 1976.

———. *The Suteans.* Naples: Istituto universitario orientale, 1981.

———. "Tamkar i ego rol' v Perednei Azii, xiv-xiii vv. do n.e." *VDI* (1964–2): 3–16.

Henrey, K. H. "Land Tenure in the Old Testament." *Palestine Exploration Quarterly* 86 (1954): 5–15.

Henshaw, Richard. "The Assyrian Army and Its Soldiers, 9th-7th C. B.C." *Paleologia* 16 (1969): 1–24.

Herlihy David. *Medieval Households.* Cambridge: Harvard University Press, 1985.

Herodotus. *The History.* Translated by David Grene. Chicago: University of Chicago Press, 1987.

Herrmann, Georgina. "Lapis Lazuli: The Early Phases of Its Trade." *Iraq* 39 (1968): 21–37.

Hertzler, Joyce O. *The Social Thought of the Ancient Civilizations.* New York: McGraw-Hill, 1936.

Heurgon, J. *Daily Life of the Etruscans.* New York: Macmillan, 1964.

Hinz, Walther. "Achämenidische Hofverwaltung." *ZA* 61 (1971): 260–311.

———. "Das Rechnungswesen oreintalischer Reichfinanzämter im Mittelalter. *Der Islam* 29 (1950): 1–29, 111–41.

Hobsbawm, Eric J. "From Social History to the History of Society." *Daedalus* 104 (1971): 20–45.

Hodgson, Marshall. "Hemispheric Interregional History as an Approach to World History." *Cahiers d'Histoire Mondiale* 1 (1953–4): 715–23.

———. *The Venture of Islam,* 1. Chicago: University of Chicago Press, 1974.

Hoglund, K. *Achaemenid Imperial Administration in Syria-Palestine and the Missions of Ezra and Nehemiah.* Atlanta: Scholars, 1992.

Hole, Frank. "Environmental Instabilities and Urban Origins." In *Chiefdoms and Early States in the Near East,* edited by Gil Stein and Mitchell Rothman, 121–51. Madison: Prehistory, 1994.

Holstein, J. "Max Weber and Biblical Scholarship." *Hebrew Union College Annual* 46 (1975): 159–79.

Hood, M. "Minoan Civilization." In *Oxford Classical Dictionary,* edited by N. G. L. Hammond, H. H. Scullard, 690–92. Oxford: Clarendon, 1970.

Hooker, J. T. "Minoan and Mycenean Administration: A Comparison of the Knossos and Pylos Archives." In *The Function of the Minoan Palaces,* edited by R. Hägg, N. Marinatos, 312–15. Stockholm: Åström, 1987.

Hopkins, David. *The Highlands of Canaan: Agricultural Life in the Early Iron Age.* Sheffield: Almond, 1985.

———. "The Subsistence Struggles of Early Israel." *Biblical Archaeologist* 50 (1987): 178–91.

Hopkins, K. "Economic Growth and Towns in Classical Antiquity." In *Towns in Societies,* edited by P. Abrams and E.A. Wrigley, 35–77. Cambridge: Cambridge University Press, 1978.

Hourani, Albert. Review of Edward Said, *Orientalism. New York Review of Books* 26 (March 8, 1979): 27–30.

Hrozný, Friedrich. "Zum Geldwesen der Babylonier." *Beiträge zur Assyriologie* 4 (1902): 546–50.

Hruška, Blahoslav. "Zur Verwaltung der Handwerker in der frühdynastischen Zeit." In *Gesellschaft und Kultur im alten Vorderasien,* edited by Horst Klengel, 99–115. Berlin: Akademie, 1982.

———. Review of H. Lanz, *harrânu-Geschäftsunternehmen. Archiv Orientální* 46 (1978): 170–73.

Hsu, Cho-yun. *Ancient China in Transition: An analysis of Social Mobility, 722–222 B.C.* Stanford: Stanford University Press, 1965.

Hunt, Robert C. "The Role of Bureaucracy in the Provisioning of Cities: A Framework for Analysis of the Ancient Near East." In *The Organization of Power,* edited by McGuire Gibson, Robert Biggs, 161–92. Chicago: Oriental Institute, 1987.

Ikeda, Yutaka. "Solomon's Trade in Horses and Chariots in Its International Setting." In *Studies in the Period of David and Solomon,* edited by Tomoo Ishida, 215–38. Winona Lake, Ind.: Eisenbrauns, 1982.

Israel, Felice. "Classificazione tipologica delle iscrizioni ebraiche antiche." *Rivista Biblica* 32 (1984): 85–110.

Jacobs, Jane. *Cities and the Wealth of Nations.* New York: Vintage, 1985.

Jacobsen, Thorkild. "The Assumed Conflict between Sumerians and Semites in Early Mesopotamian History." *JAOS* 59 (1939): 485–95.

———. "Early Political Development in Mesopotamia." *ZA* 52 (1957): 91–170.

———. *The Harps That Once . . .* New Haven: Yale University Press, 1987.

———. "The Reign of Ibbi-Sin." *JCS* 7 (1953): 36–47.

———. "On the Textile Industry at Ur under Ibbi-Sîn." In *Studia Orientalia Ioanni Pedersen dedicata,* 172–87. Copenhagen: E. Munksgaard, 1953. Reprinted in *Toward the Image of Tammuz,* edited by William Moran, 218–29. Cambridge: Harvard University Press, 1970.

———. *Salinity and Irrigation Agriculture in Antiquity.* Malibu: Undena, 1982.

———, editor. *The Sumerian King List.* Chicago: University of Chicago Press, 1939.

Jacobson, V. A. "Pravovoe i imushchestvennoe polozhenie voina *rēdûm* vremeni I vavilonskoi dinastii." *VDI* (1963–2): 129–40.

———. "Some Problems Connected with the Rise of Landed Property (Old Babylonian Period)." In *Beiträge zur sozialen Struktur des alten Vorderasien* 1, edited by Horst Klengel, 33–37. Berlin: Akademie, 1971.

James, T.G.H. *Pharaoh's People.* Chicago: University of Chicago Press, 1984.

Jankowska, N.B. "Some Problems of the Economy of the Assyrian Empire." In *Ancient Mesopotamia,* edited by I.M. Diakonoff, 253–76. Moscow: Nauka, 1969.

Jannsen, Jacob J. *Commodity Prices from the Ramesside Period.* Leiden: Brill, 1975.

———. "Prolegomena to the Study of Egypt's Economic History during the New Kingdom." *Studien zur altägyptischen Kultur* 3 (1975): 127–85.

Jaritz, Karl. "Quellen zur Geschichte der Kaššû-Dynastie." *Mitteilungen des Instituts für Orientforschung* 6 (1958): 187–265.

———. "Die Kulturreste der Kassiten." *Anthropos* 55 (1960): 17–64.

Jaspers, Karl. *The End and Goal of History.* New Haven: Yale University Press, 1953.

Joannès, François. "Contrats de marriage d'Epoque récente." *RA* 78 (1984): 71–82.

———. "La Culture matérielle à Mari (iv); les Méthodes de Pesée." *RA* 83 (1989): 113–52.

Johnson, Janet. *Thus Wrote 'Onchsheshonqy: An Introductory Grammar of Demotic.* Chicago: Oriental Institute, 1986.

Johnstone, W. "Old Testament Technical Expressions in Property Holding: Contributions from Ugarit." *Ugaritica* 6 (1969): 308–17.

Jones, Tom B. *The Sumerian Problem*. New York: John Wiley, 1969.

Jones, Tom B., and John W. Snyder. *Sumerian Economic Texts from the Third Ur Dynasty*. Minneapolis: University of Minnesota Press, 1961.

Jordan, Gregory. "Usury, Slavery, and Land-Tenure: The Nuzi *tidennūtu* Transaction." *ZA* 80 (1990): 76–92.

Kamp, Kathryn, and Norman Yoffee. "Ethnicity in Ancient Western Asia during the Early Second Millennium B.C.: Archaeological Assessments of Ethnoarchaeological Perspectives." *Bulletin of the American Schools of Oriental Research* 237 (1980): 85–104.

Kanawati, Naguib. "Polygamy in the Old Kingdom of Egypt?" *Studien zur altägyptischen Kultur* 4 (1976): 149–60.

Kaplan, Zvi. "Bar Mitzvah." *Encyclopaedia Judaica* B, 243–47. Jerusalem: Keter, 1971.

Katz, Debra F. "A Computerized Study of the AGA-UŠ of the Ur III Period." M.A. thesis, University of Minnesota, 1979.

Kaufman, Stephen. "A Reconstruction of the Social Welfare Systems of Ancient Israel." In *In the Shelter of Elyon: Essays on Ancient Palestinian Life and Literature in Honor of Gösta Ahlström*, edited by W. Barrick and J. Spence, 277–86. Sheffield: Journal for the Study of the Old Testament, 1984.

———. Review of M. Elat, *Kishre Kalkalah*. JAOS 98 (1978): 344–45.

Kemp, Barry. *Ancient Egypt*. London: Routledge, 1991.

Kennedy, Paul. *The Rise and Fall of the Great Powers*. New York: Random House, 1987.

Kennett, Robert H. *Ancient Hebrew Social Life and Custom as Indicated in Law, Narrative, and Metaphor*. London: British Academy, 1933.

Kessler, Rainer. *Staat und Gesellschaft im vorexilischen Juda*. Leiden: Brill, 1992.

Kienast, Burkhart. "Ist das Neusumerische eine lebende Sprache?" *AfO Beiheft* 19 (1982): 105–11.

Kientz, J.-M., and Maurice Lambert. "L'Élévage du gros Bétail à Lagash au temps de Lugalanda et d'Urukagina." *Rivista degli Studi orientali* 38 (1963): 93–117, 198–218.

Kilmer, Anne D. "The Mesopotamian Concept of Overpopulation and Its Solution as Reflected in the Mythology." *OrNS* 41 (1972): 160–77.

King, Leonard. *Babylonian Boundary-Stones and Memorial Tablets in the British Museum*. London: The British Museum, 1912.

Kinnier Wilson, J. V. *Indo-Sumerian: A New Approach to the Problem of the Indus Script*. Oxford: Clarendon, 1974.

———. *The Nimrud Wine Lists*. London: British School of Archaeology in Iraq, 1972.

Kippenberg, H. *Religion und Klassenbildung im antiken Judäa*. Göttingen: Vandenhoeck & Ruprecht, 1978.

Klein, Jacob. "Šeleppūtum, a Hitherto Unknown Ur III Princess." *ZA* 80 (1990): 20–39.

Klengel, Horst. "The Economy of the Hittite Household (É)." *Oikumene* 5 (1986): 23–31.

———. "Einige Bemerkungen zur sozialökonomischen Entwicklung in der altbabylonischen Zeit." *Acta Antiqua* 22 (1974): 249–57.

———. *König Hammurapi und der Alltag Babylons*. Darmstadt: Wissenschaftliche Buchgesellschaft, 1992.

———. "Non-Slave Labour in the Old Babylonian Period: The Basic Outlines." In *Labor in the Ancient Near East*, edited by Marvin A. Powell, 159–66. New Haven: American Oriental Society, 1987.

———. "Die Rolle der Ältesten (LU$_2$.MEŠ.ŠU.GI) im Kleinasien der Hethiterzeit." *ZA* 57 (1965): 223–36.

————. "Zur Sklaverei in Alalah." *Acta Antiqua* 11 (1963): 1–15.

————. "Zu den *šibūtum* in altbabylonischer Zeit." *OrNS* 29 (1960): 357–75.

————, editor. *Kulturgeschichte des alten Vorderasien.* Berlin: Akademie, 1989.

Kloft, H. *Die Wirtschaft der griechisch-römischen Welt.* Darmstadt: Wissenschaftliche Buchgesellschaft, 1992.

Knapp, A. Bernard. *The History and Culture of Ancient Western Asia and Egypt.* Chicago: Dorsey, 1988.

Koch, K. "Ezra and the Origins of Judaism." *Journal of Semitic Studies* 19 (1974): 173–97.

Kochavi, Moshe. "The Israelite Settlement in Canaan in the Light of Archaeological Surveys." In *Biblical Archaeology Today,* 54–60. Jerusalem: Israel Exploration Society, 1985.

————, et al., eds. *Judaea, Samaria and the Golan: Archaeological Survey 1967–1968.* Jerusalem: Carta, 1972 (in Hebrew).

Kohl, Philip L., and R. Wright. "Stateless Cities: The Differentiation of Societies in the Near Eastern Neolithic." *Dialectical Anthropology* 2:4 (1977): 271–83.

Kohlmeyer, Kay. "'Wovon man nicht sprechen kann.' Grenzen der Interpretation von bei Oberflächenbegehungen gewonnenen archäologischen Informationen." *Mitteilungen der Deutschen Orientgesellschaft* 113 (1981): 53–79.

Kolchin, Peter. *Unfree Labor.* Cambridge and London: Harvard University Press, 1987.

Komoróczy, Géza. "Lobpreis auf das Gefängnis in Sumer." *Acta Antiqua* 23 (1975): 153–74.

Koschaker, Paul. "Zur staatlischen Wirtschaftsverwaltung in altbabylonischer Zeit, insbesondere nach Urkunden aus Larsa." *ZA* 47 (1942): 135–80.

Koshurnikov, S. G. "A Family Archive from Old Babylonian Dilbat." *VDI* (1984–2): 123–33.

Košak, S. *Hittite Inventory Texts.* Heidelberg: Winter, 1982.

Kovacs, Maureen Gallery. *The Epic of Gilgamesh.* Stanford: Stanford University Press, 1989.

(Kovacs), Maureen Gallery. Review of R. Harris, *Ancient Sippar. JAOS* 99 (1979): 73–80.

Kozyreva, N. V. *Drevnyaya Larsa.* Moscow: Nauka, 1988.

————. "Nekotorye dannye o chastnom skotovodcheskom khozyaystve v starovavilonskom gorode Larsa." *Peredneaziatskii Sbornik* 3 (1979): 135–41.

————. Nekotorye produkty tovoro-denezhnyx otnoshenii v starovavilonskoi Mesopotamii." *VDI* (1984–2): 3–14.

————. "Sel'skaya okruga v gosudarstve Larsa." *VDI* (1975–2): 3–17.

————. "Serebro kak odno iz sredstv vyplaty naloga i ekvivalent trudovoi povinnosti v starovavilonskoi Mesopotamii." *VDI* (1986–1): 76–81.

Kraeling, Emil G. *The Old Testament since the Reformation.* New York: Schocken, 1955.

Kraus, Fritz R. "Assyrisch Imperialism." *Jaarbericht Ex Oriente Lux* 15 (1958): 232–39.

————. "Zum altbabylonischen Erbrecht." *Archiv Orientální* 17 (1949): 406–13.

————. *Königliche Verfügungen in altbabylonischer Zeit.* Leiden: Brill, 1984.

————. "Der 'Palast,' Produzent und Unternehmer im Königsreiche Babylon nach Hammurabi (ca. 1750–1600 v. Chr)." In *State and Temple Economies in the Ancient Near East,* edited by Edward Lipiński, 423–34. Louvain: Departement Oriëntalistiek, 1979.

————. Review of M. Ellis, *Agriculture and the State.* BiOr 34 (1977): 147–53.

————. "Le rôle des temples depuis la troisième dynastie d'Ur jusqu'à la première dynastie de Babylone." *Cahiers d'Histoire Mondiale* 1 (1953–54): 518–45. Translated as *The Role of Temples from the Third Dynasty of Ur to the First Dynasty of Babylon,* Benjamin Foster, trans. Malibu: Undena, 1990.

———. *Staatliche Viehhaltung im altbabylonischen Lande Larsa.* Amsterdam: Ned. Akademie, 1966.

———. *Vom mesopotamischen Menschen der altbabylonischen Zeit und seiner Welt.* Amsterdam: North Holland, 1973.

———. "Ein zentrales Problem des altmesopotamischen Rechtes: Was Ist der Kodex-Hammurabi?" In *Aspects du Contact suméro-akkadien = Genava* 8 (1960): 283–96.

Kramer, Carol, editor. *Ethnoarchaeology.* New York Columbia University Press, 1980.

Kramer, Samuel N. *Lamentation over the Destruction of Ur.* Chicago: University of Chicago Press, 1940.

———. "The Ur-Nammu Law Code: Who Was Its Author?" *OrNS* 52 (1983): 453–56.

Krecher, Joachim. "/ur/ 'Mann', /eme/ 'Frau' und die sumerische Herkunft des Wortes urdu (-ud) 'Sklave.'" *Welt des Orients* 18 (1987): 7–19.

Kuhrt, Amélie. "Babylonia from Cyrus to Xerxes." In *Cambridge Ancient History* 4, edited by J. Boardman, 112–38. Cambridge: Cambridge University Press, 1988.

———. "The Cyrus Cylinder and Achaemenid Imperial Policy." *Journal for the Study of the Old Testament* 25 (1983): 83–97.

———. "Non-Royal Women in the Late Babylonian Period: A Survey." In *Women's Earliest Records,* edited by Barbara Lesko, 215–39. Atlanta: Scholars, 1989.

———. "Berossus' *Babyloniaka* and Seleucid Rule in Babylonia." In *Hellenism in the East,* edited by Amélie Kuhrt and Susan Sherwin-White, 32–56. Berkeley and Los Angeles: University of California Press, 1987.

———. "Survey of Written Sources Available for the History of Babylonia under the Late Achaemenids." In *Achaemenid History* 1, edited by Helen Sancisi-Weerdenburg, 147–57. Leiden: Nederlands Instituut, 1987.

Kümmel, H. *Familie, Beruf und Amt im spätbabylonischen Uruk.* Berlin: Mann, 1979.

Kupper, Jean-Robert. "Mari." In *La Ville dans le Proche-Orient ancien,* 113–21. Louvain: Peeters, 1983.

——— *Les Nomades en Mésopotamie au temps des rois de Mari.* Paris, 1957.

Kuschke, Arnulf. "Arm und Reich im Alten Testament mit besonderer Berücksichtigung der nachexilischen Zeit." *Zeitschrift für die alttestamentliche Wissenschaft* 57 (1939): 31–57.

Kuyper, J. de. "Grundeigentum in Mari." *Das Grundeigentum in Mesopotamien,* edited by Burchard Brentjes, 69–78. Berlin: Akademie, 1988.

Kwasman, Theodore. *Neo-Assyrian Legal Documents in the Kouyunjik Collection of the British Museum.* Rome: Pontificial Biblical Institute, 1988.

Kwasman, Theodore, and Simo Parpola. *Legal Transactions of the Royal Court of Nineveh, Part I.* Helsinki: Helsinki University Press, 1991.

Lacey, W.K. *The Family in Classical Greece.* Ithaca: Cornell University Press, 1984.

Lafont, Bertrand. "Les Filles du Roi de Mari." In *La Femme dans le Proche-Orient antique,* edited by Jean-Marie Durand, 113–23. Paris: Centre National de Recherche Scientifique, 1987.

Lambdin, Thomas. *Introduction to Sahidic Coptic.* Macon, Ga.: Mercer University Press, 1983.

Lamberg-Karlovsky, C. C. "Patterns of Interaction in the Third Millennium: From Mesopotamia to the Indus Valley." *VDI* (1990–1): 3–21 (in Russian).

Lambert, Maurice. "Le Destin d'Ur et les Routes commerciales." *Rivista degli Studi Orientali* 39 (1964): 89–109.

———. "Recherches sur la vie ouvrière: Les Ateliers de tissage de Lagash au temps de Luga-landa et d'Urukagina." *Archiv Orientální* 29 (1961): 422–43.

———. "Ur-Emush, 'Grand marchand' de Lagash." *Oriens Antiquus* 20 (1981): 175–85.

———. "L'Usage de l'Argent-Métal à Lagash au temps de la 3e Dynastie d'Ur." *RA* 57 (1963): 79–92, 193–299.

Lambert, Wilfred. "Ancestors, Authors, and Canonicity." *JCS* 11 (1957): 1–14, 112.

Landsberger, Benno. "Remarks on the Archive of the Soldier Ubarum." *JCS* 9 (1955): 121–31.

Lang, Bernhard. "The Social Organization of Peasant Poverty in Biblical Israel." *Journal for the Study of the Old Testament* 24 (1982): 47–63.

Lanz, H. *Die neubabylonischen harrânu-Geschäftsunternehmen.* Berlin: Schweitzer, 1976.

Lapidus, Ira. *A History of Islamic Societies.* Cambridge: Cambridge University Press, 1988.

Larsen, C., and G. Evans. "The Holocene Geological History of the Tigris-Euphrates-Karun Delta." In *The Environmental History of the Near and Middle East since the Last Ice Age,* edited by W. Brice, 226–34. London: Academic, 1978.

Larsen, Mogens Trolle. "Early Assur and International Trade." *Sumer* 35 (1979): 349–7 (*sic*).

———. *Old Assyrian Caravan Procedures.* Leiden: Nederlands Instituut, 1967.

———. *The Old Assyrian City-State and Its Colonies.* Copenhagen: Akademisk, 1976.

———. "The Tradition of Empire in Mesopotamia." In *Power and Propaganda,* edited by Mogens Trolle Larsen, 75–103. Copenhagen: Akademisk, 1979.

Lauterbach, W. *Der Arbeiter in Recht und Rechtspraxis des alten Testaments und des alten Orients.* Heidelberg: Pilger, 1936.

Law, R. "Posthumous Questions for Karl Polanyi: Price Inflation in Pre-Colonial Dahomey." *Journal of African History* 33 (1992): 387–420.

Lebrun, A., and F. Vallat. "L'Origine de l'Ecriture à Suse." *Délégation archéologique française en Iran, Cahiers* 8 (1975): 11–59.

Leemans, Wilhelmus F. "The Importance of Trade: Some Introductory Remarks." *Iraq* 39 (1977): 1–10.

———. "The Family in the Economic Life of the Old Babylonian Period." *Oikumene* 5 (1986): 15–22.

———. *Foreign Trade in the Old Babylonian Period.* Leiden: Brill, 1960.

———. "Handel." *RlA* 4:76–90.

———. *The Old Babylonian Merchant, His Business and Social Position.* Leiden: Brill, 1950.

———. "The Rate of Interest in Old Babylonian Times." *Revue internationale des Droits de l'Antiquité* 1 (1950): 7–34.

———. "The Trade Relations of Babylonia and the Question of Relations with Egypt in the Old Babylonian Period." *JESHO* 3 (1960): 21–37.

———. "Trouve-t-on des 'Communautés rurales' dans l'ancienne Mésopotamie?" *Recueils de la Société Jean Bodin* 41 (1983): 43–106.

Leggett, D. *The Levirate and Goel Institutions in the Old Testament.* Cherry Hill, N.J.: Mack, 1974.

Leichty, Earle. Review of D. Weisberg, *Guild Structure. JNES* 29 (1970): 296–98.

Lemche, Nels. *Ancient Israel: A New History of Israelite Society.* Sheffield: Journal for the Study of the Old Testament, 1988.

———. *Early Israel: Anthropological and Historical Studies on the Israelite Society before the Monarchy.* Leiden: Brill, 1985.

Lerner, Gerda. *The Creation of Patriarchy.* New York: Oxford University Press, 1986.

Le Roy Ladurie, Emmanuel and M. Baulant. "Grape Harvests from the Fifteenth Through the Nineteenth Centuries." In *Climate and History,* edited by R.I. Rotberg and T.K. Rabb, 259–69. Princeton: Princeton University Press, 1981.

Lestage, A. *Literacy and Illiteracy.* Paris: U. N. E. S. C. O., 1982.

Levine, Baruch. "The Descriptive Tabernacle Texts of the Pentateuch." *JAOS* 85 (1965): 307–18.

———. "The Netînîm." *JBL* 82 (1963): 207–12.

Lewis, T. "The Ancestral Estate . . . in 2 Samuel 14:16." *JBL* 110 (1991): 597–612.

Lewy, Hildegard. "Nitokris-Naqî'a." *JNES* 11 (1952): 264–86.

Lichtheim, Muriel. *Ancient Egyptian Literature.* 3 volumes. Berkeley and Los Angeles: University of California Press, 1975–80.

Liddell, Henry G. and Robert Scott. *A Greek-English Lexicon.* Oxford: Clarendon, 1968.

Lieberman, Stephen. "Of Clay Pebbles, Hollow Clay Balls, and Writing: A Sumerian View." *American Journal of Archaeology* 84 (1980): 340–58.

Limet, Henri. "La Condition de L'Enfant en Mésopotamie autour de l'an 2000 av. J.-C." In *L'Enfant dans les civilisations orientales,* edited by Aristide Théodoridès, Paul Naster, and Julien Ries, 5–17. Louvain: Peeters, 1980.

———. "Les Métaux à l'Epoque d'Agadé." *JESHO* 15 (1972): 3–34.

———. "Le Rôle du palais dans l'économie néo-sumérienne." In *State and Temple Economy in the Ancient Near East,* vol. 1, edited by Edward Lipiński, 235–48. Louvain: Departement Oriëntalistiek, 1979.

———. "Les Schémas du Commerce néo-sumérien." *Iraq* 39 (1977): 51–58.

———. "Ur et sa région à l'époque de la 3e dynastie." *Altorientalische Forschungen* 20 (1993): 115–22.

Lipiński, Edward. "Economie phénicienne: Travaux récents et desiderata." *JESHO* 37 (1994): 322–37.

———, editor. *State and Temple Economy in the Ancient Near East,* 2 vols. Louvain: Departement Oriëntalistiek, 1979.

Liverani, Mario. *Antico Oriente: Storia, Società, Economia.* Roma: Laterza, 1988.

———. "The Collapse of the Near Eastern Regional System at the End of the Bronze Age: The Case of Syria." In *Centre and Periphery in the Ancient Near Eastern World,* edited by Michael Rowlands, Mogens Trolle Larsen, and Kristian Kristiansen, 66–73. Cambridge: Cambridge University Press, 1987.

———. "Communautés de village et palais royal dans la Syrie du IIe millénaire." *JESHO* 18 (1975): 146–64.

———. "Communautés rurales dans la Syrie du IIe millénaire A.C." *Recueils de la Société Jean Bodin* 41 (1983): 147–85.

———. "Dono, Tributo, Commercio: Ideologia dello Scambio nella tarda età di Bronzo." *Istituto Italiano di Numismatica: Annali* (1979): 9–28.

———. "La Dotazione dei Mercanti di Ugarit." *Ugaritforschungen* 11 (1979): 495–503.

———. "Economia delle fattorie palatine ugaritiche." *Dialoghi di Archeologia* 1 (1979): 57–72.

———. "Elementi 'irrazionali' nel commercio amariano." *Oriens Antiquus* 11 (1972): 297–317. Translated in *Three Amarna Essays,* Matthew L. Jaffe, trans. Malibu: Undena, 1979.

———. "L'Estradizione dei refugiati in AT 2." *Rivista degli Studi Orientali* 39 (1964): 111–15.

———. "Il Fuoruscitismo in Siria nella tarda età del Bronzo." *Rivista Storica Italiana* 77 (1965): 315–36.

————. "The Ideology of the Assyrian Empire." In *Power and Propaganda,* edited by M.T. Larsen, 297–317. Copenhagen: Academisk, 1979.

————. "Land Tenure and Inheritance in the Ancient Near East: The Interaction between 'Palace' and 'Family' Sectors." In *Land Tenure and Social Transformation in the Middle East,* edited by Tarif Khalidi, 33–44. Beirut: American University, 1984.

————. "Le 'Origini' d'Israele: Progetto irrealizzabile di ricerca etnogenetica." *Rivista Biblica* 28 (1980): 9–31.

————. "Problemi e indirizze degli studi storici sul vicino oriente antico." *Cultura e scuola* 220 (1966): 72–79.

————. "Il Rendimento dei Cereali durante la III Dinastia di Ur: Contributo ad un approcio realistico." *Origini* 15 (1990): 359–68.

Loding, Darlene. "A Craft Archive from Ur." Ph.D. dissertation, University of Pennsylvania, 1974.

Loewe, Raphael. "The Earliest Biblical Allusion to Coined Money." *Palestine Exploration Quarterly* 87 (1955): 141–50

Loretz, Oswald. *Habiru-Hebräer.* Berlin: de Gruyter, 1984.

Love, John R. *Antiquity and Capitalism: Max Weber and the Sociological Foundations of Roman Civilization.* London: Routledge, 1990.

Lurje, M. *Studien zur Geschichte der wirtschaftlichen und sozialen Verhältnisse im Israelitisch-Jüdischen Reiche, von der Einwanderung in Kanaan bis zum bab. Exil. = Beiheft der Zeitschrift für die alttestamentliche Wissenschaft* 45. Giessen: Töpelmann, 1927.

Lutzman, Heiner. *Die neusumerischen Schulddurkunden.* Münster: Ph.D. dissertation, Erlangen, 1976.

MacDowell, Dwight. *The Law in Classical Athens.* Ithaca: Cornell University Press, 1971.

Machinist, Peter. "Assyria and Its Image in the First Isaiah." *JAOS* 103 (1983): 719–37.

Maekawa, K. "Cereal Cultivation in the Ur III Period." *Bulletin of Sumerian Agriculture* 1 (1984): 73–96.

————. "Collective Labor Service in Girsu-Lagash: The Pre-Sargonic and Ur III Periods." In *Labor in the Ancient Near East,* edited by Marvin A. Powell, 49–71. New Haven: American Oriental Society, 1987.

————. "The Development of the E_2-MI_2 in Lagash during Early Dynastic III." *Mesopotamia* 8–9 (1973–74): 77–144.

————. "The $Erin_2$ People in Lagash of Ur III Times." *RA* 70 (1976): 9–44.

————. "Female Weavers and Their Children in Lagash—Pre-Sargonic and Ur III." *ASJ* 2 (1980): 81–125.

————. "The Management of Fatted Sheep (udu-niga) in Ur III Girsu/Lagash." *ASJ* 6 (1983): 81–111.

————. "Rations, Wages and Economic Trends in the Ur III Period." *Altorientalische Forschungen* 16 (1989): 42–50.

Mahadevan, I. "Terminal Ideograms in the Indus Script." In *Harappan Civilization,* edited by G. Possehl, 311–17. Warminster: Aris and Phillips, 1982.

Maisels, Charles K. *The Emergence of Civilization from Hunting and Gathering to Agriculture, Cities, and the State in the Near East.* London, New York: Routledge, 1990.

Majidzadeh, Y. "Lapis Lazuli and the Great Khorasan Road." *Paléorient* 8 (1983): 59–69.

Makkay, J. "The Origins of the 'Temple Economy' as Seen in the Light of Prehistoric Evidence." *Iraq* 45 (1983): 1–6.

Malbran-Labat, Françoise. *L'Armée et l'Organisation militaire de l'Assyrie.* Geneva and Paris: Droz, 1982.

Mallowan, Max. "Noah's Flood Reconsidered." *Iraq* 26 (1964): 62–82.

Malone, Dumas. *Jefferson, the Virginian.* New York: Little, Brown, 1948.

Maloney, R. "Usury and Restrictions on Interest-Taking in the Ancient Near East." *Catholic Biblical Quarterly* 36 (1974): 1–20.

Manassini, P. "Note sugli Apporti patrimoniali in occasione del Matrimonio nella Siria de II. Millennio." In *Il Trasferimento dei Beni del Matrimonio privato del Vicino Oriente Antico,* edited by Claudio Saporetti, 65–75. – *Geo-Archaeologica* (1984–2).

Manitius, W. "Das stehende Heer der Assyrerkönige und seine Organisation." *ZA* 24 (1910): 97–149, 185–224.

Marazzi, M. "Tarife und Gewichte in einem althethitischen Königserlass." *OrNS* 63 (1994): 88–92.

Marfoe, Lee. "Cedar Forest to Silver Mountain: Social Change and the Development of Long-Distance Trade in Early Near Eastern Societies." In *Centre and Periphery in the Ancient World,* edited by Michael Rowlands, Mogens Trolle Larsen, and Kristian Kristiansen, 25–35. Cambridge: Cambridge University Press, 1987.

———. "The Integrative Transformation: Patterns of Sociopolitical Organization in Southern Syria." *Bulletin of the American Schools of Oriental Research* 234 (1979): 1–42.

Margueron, Jean. "L'Apparition du Palais au Proche-Orient." In *Le Système palatial en Orient, en Grèce et à Rome,* edited by Edmond Lévy, 8–38. Strasbourg: Université de Strasbourg, 1987.

Martin, Harriet. *Fara: A Reconstruction of the Ancient Mesopotamian City of Shuruppak.* Birmingham: C. Martin, 1988.

Marx, Victor. "Die Stellung der Frauen in Babylonien, gemäss den Kontrakten aus der Zeit von Nebukadnezer bis Darius (604–485)." *Beiträge zur Assyriologie* 4 (1902): 1–77.

Matthews, Victor. *Pastoral Nomadism in the Mari Kingdom.* Cambridge: American Schools of Oriental Research, 1978.

Mauss, M. *The Gift: Form and Reason for Exchange in Archaic Societies.* 1923–24. Reprint. London: Routledge, 1990.

Mayer, Walter. "Die Finanzierung einer Kampagne." *Ugaritforschung* 11 (1979): 571–95.

———. *Nuzi-Studien I. Die Archive des Palastes und die Prosopographie der Berufe.* Neukirchen-Vluyn: Neukirchener, 1978.

McClellan, Thomas. "Irrigation and Hydraulic Systems in Syria." *Syrian Archaeology Bulletin* 2 (1990): 12–13.

———. "Towns to Fortresses: The Transformation of Urban Life in Judah from the 8th to 7th Century B.C." In *Society of Biblical Literature Seminar Papers,* edited by Paul Achtemeier, 277–85. Chico, Cal.: Scholars, 1978.

McCloskey, Donald. "Bourgeois Virtue." *The American Scholar* 63 (1994): 177–91.

McKane, William. "*The Gibbōr hayil* in the Israelite Community." *Glasgow University Oriental Society Transactions* 17 (1959): 28–37.

———. *Proverbs. A New Approach.* Philadelphia: Westminister, 1975.

McKenzie, John. "The Elders in the Old Testament." *Biblica* 40 (1959): 522–40.

McNutt, Paula M. *The Forging of Israel: Iron Technology, Symbolism and Tradition in Ancient Society.* Sheffield: Almond, 1990.

Meier, Samuel A. "Women and Communication in the Ancient Near East." *JAOS* 111 (1991): 540–47.

Menabde, E.A. *Khettskoe Obschestvo, Ekonomika, sobstvennost', semya i nasledovanie.* Tbilisi: Metsniereba, 1965.

Mendelsohn, Isaac. "On Slavery in Alalah." *Israel Exploration Journal* 5 (1955): 65–72.

———. "The Family in the Ancient Near East." *Biblical Archaeologist* 11 (1948): 24–40.

———. *Slavery in the Ancient Near East.* New York: Oxford, 1949.

———. "A Ugaritic Parallel to the Adoption of Ephraim and Manasseh." *Israel Exploration Journal* 9 (1959): 180–83.

Mendelsohn, Kurt. *The Riddle of the Pyramids.* New York: Praeger, 1974.

Mendenhall, George. "Social Organization in Early Israel." In *Magnalia Dei . . . G. Wright A. V.,* edited by Frank M. Cross, 132–51. Garden City: Doubleday, 1976.

Menzel, B. *Assyrische Tempel.* Rome: Biblical Institute, 1981.

Meyers, Carol. *Discovering Eve: Ancient Israelite Women in Context.* New York: Oxford, 1988.

———. "Procreation, Production, and Protection: Male-Female Balance in Early Israel." *Journal of the American Academy of Religion* 51 (1983): 569–93.

———. "The Roots of Restriction: Women in Early Israel." *Biblical Archaeologist* 41 (1978): 91–103.

Michalowski, Pyotr. *Lamentation over the Destruction of Sumer and Ur.* Winona Lake, Ind.: Eisenbrauns, 1989.

———. "Mental Maps and Ideology: Reflections on Subartu." In *The Origins of Cities in Dry-Farming Syria and Mesopotamia in the Third Millennium B.C.,* edited by Harvey Weiss, 129–56. Guilford, Conn.: Four Quarters, 1988.

———. "The Neo-Sumerian Silver Ring Texts." *Syro-Mesopotamian Studies* 2 (1978): 1–16.

Milano, Lucio. "Alimentazione e regimi alimentari nella Siria preclassica." *Dialoghi di Archeologia* 3 (1981): 85–121.

———. "Barley for Rations and Barley for Sowing." *ASJ* 9 (1987): 177–202.

———. "Food Rations at Ebla: A Preliminary Account of the Ration Lists Coming from the Ebla Palace Archive L. 2712." *M.A.R.I.* 5 (1987): 519–50.

———. "Le Razioni alimentari nel vicino oriente antico: per un'articolazione storica del sistema." In *Il pane del re: Accumulo e distribuzione dei cereali nell'oriente antico,* edited by Rita Dolce and Carlo Zaccagnini, 65–100. Bologna, 1989.

Millar, F. "The Problem of Hellenistic Syria." In *Hellenism in the East,* edited by Amélie Kuhrt and Susan Sherwin-White, 110–13. Berkeley and Los Angeles: University of California Press, 1987.

Millard, A.R. "The Bevelled-Rim Bowls: Their Purpose and Significance." *Iraq* 50 (1988): 49–57.

Momigliano, Arnauldo. *Alien Wisdom.* Cambridge: Cambridge University Press, 1975.

Moore, John. "The Evolution of Exploitation." *Critique of Anthropology* 8 (1977): 33–58.

Moorey, P. R. S. "The Archaeological Evidence for Metallurgy and Related Techniques in Mesopotamia, c. 5500–2100 B.C." *Iraq* 44 (1982): 13–38.

———. "On Tracking Cultural Transfers in Prehistory: The Case of Egypt and Lower Mesopotamia in the Fourth Millennium B.C." In *Centre and Periphery in the Ancient World,* edited by Michael Rowlands, Mogens Trolle Larsen, and Kristian Kristiansen, 36–46. Cambridge: Cambridge University Press, 1987.

Mora, Clelia. "Il Ruolo politico-sociale di *pankus* e *tulijas.*" In *Studi Orientalistici in Ricordo di Franco Pintore,* edited by O. Carruba et al., 159–84. Pavia: GJES, 1983.

Moran, William L., editor. *The Amarna Letters.* Baltimore: Johns Hopkins University Press, 1992.

Morrison, Martha. "Evidence for Herdsmen and Animal Husbandry in the Nuzi Documents." In *Studies on the Civilization and Culture of Nuzi and the Hurrians in Honor of*

Ernest R. Lacheman, vol. 1, edited by Martha Morrison and David Owen, 257–96. Winona Lake, Ind.: Eisenbrauns, 1981.

———. "The Jacob and Laban Narrative in Light of Near Eastern Sources." *Biblical Archaeologist* 46 (1983): 155–64.

Mowinckel, Sigmund. "Die vorderasiatischen Königs- und Fürsteninschriften: Eine stilistische Studie." In *Eucharisterion, H. Gunkel A.V.,* 1, edited by H. Schmidt, 278–322. Göttingen: Vandenhoeck & Ruprecht, 1923.

Mueller, D. "Some Remarks on Wage Rates in the Middle Kingdom." *JNES* 34 (1975): 249–63.

Müller, Manfred. "Gold, Silber und Blei als Wertmesser in Mesopotamien während der zweiten Hälfte des 2. Jahrtausends v.u.Z." In *Societies and Languages of the Ancient Near East: Studies in Honor of I. M. Diakonoff,* edited by J. Nicholas Postgate, 270–78. Warminster: Aris & Phillips, 1982.

———. "Ein neuer Beleg zur staatlichen Viehhaltung in altsumerischer Zeit." *Festschrift Lubor Matouš,* 2, edited by Blahoslav Hruška and Géza Komoróczy, 151–66. Budapest: Eötvös Loránd Tudományegyetem, 1978.

Muhly, James. "Phoenicia and the Phoenicians." In *Biblical Archaeology Today,* 177–91. Jerusalem: Israel Exploration Society, 1985.

Muhly, James, and T. Wertime. *The Coming of the Age of Iron.* New Haven: Yale University Press, 1980.

Muntingh, A. L. M. "The Social and Legal Status of a Free Ugaritic Female." *JNES* 26 (1967): 102–12.

Murzoev, M. I. "O rabstve v kassitskoi Vavilonii." *VDI* (1988–4): 109–31.

Nashef, Khaled. *Rekonstruktion der Reiserouten zur Zeit der altassyrischen Handelsniederlassungen.* Wiesbaden: Reichert, 1987.

Nemet-Nejat, Karen. *Late Babylonian Field Plans in the British Museum.* Rome: Pontifical Biblical Institute, 1982.

Nenci, M. "Economie et société chez Hérodote." In *Actes du IX Congrs. Association Guillaume Budé,* 1:133–46. Paris: Les Belles Lettres, 1975.

Netting, R.M., R. Wilk, and E. Armould, editors. *Households: Comparative and Historical Studies of the Domestic Group.* Berkeley: University of California Press, 1984.

Neumann, Hans. "Einige Erwägungen zu Recht und Gesellschaft in frühstaatlicher Zeit." In *Šulmu,* edited by Petr Vavrošek, 211–24. Prague: Charles University, 1988.

———. "Zu den Geschäften des Kaufmanns Ur-Dumuzida aus Umma." *Altorientalische Forschungen* 20 (1993): 69–86.

———. "Handel und Händler in der Zeit der III. Dynastie von Ur." *Altorientalische Forschungen* 6 (1979): 15–67.

———. *Handwerk in Mesopotamien.* Berlin: Akademie, 1987.

———. "Zum Problem des privaten Bodeneigentums in Mesopotamien." In *Das Grundeigentum in Mesopotamien,* edited by Burchard Brentjes, 29–49. Berlin: Akademie, 1988.

———. "Zur privaten Geschäftstätigkeit in Nippur in der Ur III-Zeit." In *Nippur at the Centennial,* edited by Maria deJ. Ellis, 161–76. Philadelphia: University Museum, 1992.

Neumann, J., and Simo Parpola. "Climate Change and the Eleventh-Tenth Century Eclipse of Assyria and Babylonia." *JNES* 46 (1987): 161–82.

Neusner, Jacob. *A History of the Jews in Babylonia.* Volume 1, *The Parthian Period.* Leiden: Brill, 1965.

Nicholson, Ernest. "The Meaning of the Expression ᶜam ha-āretz in the Old Testament." *Journal of Semitic Studies* 10 (1965): 59–66.

Nissen, Hans. "Die 'Tempelstadt': Regierungsform der frühdynastischen Zeit in Babylonien?" In *Gesellschaft und Kultur im alten Vorderasien,* edited by Horst Klengel, 195–200. Berlin: Akademie, 1982.

———. "Zur Frage der Arbeitsorganisation in Babylonien während der Späturuk-Zeit." *Acta Antiqua* 22 (1974): 5–14.

Nissen, Hans, Peter Damerow, and Robert Englund. *Archaic Bookkeeping.* Chicago: Chicago University Press, 1993.

North, Douglass. "Markets and Other Allocation Systems in History: The Challenge of Karl Polanyi." *Journal of European Economic History* 6 (1977): 703–16.

———. *Structure and Change in Economic History.* New York: Norton, 1981.

Noth, Martin. "Das Krongut der israelitischen Könige und seine Verwaltung." *Zeitschrift des deutschen Palästina-Vereins* 50 (1927): 211–44.

Nougayrol, Jean. "Les présages historiques dans l'extispicine babylonienne." *Ecole pratique des hautes études. Annuaire.* (1944–45): 5–40.

Novick, Peter. *That Noble Dream: The "Objectivity" Question and the American Historical Profession.* Cambridge: Cambridge University Press, 1988.

Oates, Joan. "Mesopotamian Social Organisation: Archaeological and Philological Evidence." In *The Evolution of Social Systems,* edited by J. Friedman and M. J. Rowlands, 457–85. Pittsburgh: University of Pittsburgh Press, 1978.

———. "Urban Trends in Prehistoric Mesopotamia." In *La Ville dans le Proche-Orient ancien,* 81–92. Louvain: Peeters, 1983.

———, et al. "Seafaring Merchants of Ur?" *Antiquity* 5 (1977): 221–34.

Oded, B. *Mass Deportations and Deportees in the Neo-Assyrian Empire.* Wiesbaden: Reichert, 1979.

Oden, Robert. "Taxation in Biblical Israel." *Journal of Religious Ethics* 12 (1984): 162–81.

Oelsner, Joachim. "Erwägungen zum Gesellschaftsaufbau Babyloniens von der neubabylonischen bis zur achämenidischen Zeit (7–4 Jh. v.u.Z.)." *Altorientalische Forschungen* 4 (1976): 131–49.

———. "Grundbesitz/Grundeigentum im achämenidischen und seleukidischen Babylonien." In *Das Grundeigentum in Mesopotamien,* edited by Burchard Brentjes, 117–34. Berlin: Akademie, 1988.

———. "Landvergabe im kassitischen Babylonien." In *Societies and Languages of the Ancient Near East: Studies in Honor of I. M. Diakonoff,* edited by J. Nicholas Postgate, 279–84. Warminster: Aris & Phillips, 1982.

———. *Materialien zur babylonischen Gesellschaft und Kultur in hellenistischer Zeit.* Budapest: Kultura, 1986.

———."Neue Daten zur sozialen und wirtschaftlichen Situation Nippurs in altbabylonischer Zeit." *Acta Antiqua* 22 (1974): 259–65.

———. "Die Neu- und Spätbabylonische Zeit." In *Circulation of Goods in Non-Palatial Context in the Ancient Near East,* edited by Alfonso Archi, 221–40. Rome: Ateneo, 1984.

———. "Zur Organisation des gesellschaftlichen Lebens im kassitischen und nachkassitischen Babylonien: Verwaltungsstruktur und Gemeinschaften." *AfO Beiheft* 19 (1982): 403–10.

Olmstead, Alfred. *A History of Persia.* Chicago: University of Chicago Press, 1948.

Oppenheim, A. Leo. *Ancient Mesopotamia.* Chicago: University of Chicago Press, 1964.

————. *Catalogue of the Cuneiform Tablets of the Wilberforce Eames Babylonian Collection.* New Haven: American Oriental Society, 1948.

————. "Essay on Overland Trade in the First Millennium B.C." *JCS* 21 (1967): 236–54.

————. "A New Look at the Structure of Mesopotamian Society." *JESHO* 10 (1967): 1–16.

————. "The Position of the Intellectual in Mesopotamian Society." *Daedalus* 104 (1975): 37–46.

————. "The Seafaring Merchants of Ur." *JAOS* 74 (1954): 6–17.

————. "Trade in the Ancient Near East." In *Vth International Congress of Economic History,* 1–37. Moscow: Nauka, 1970.

Oppenheimer, A. *The ʿAm Ha-Aretz: A Study in the Social History of the Jewish People in the Hellenistic-Roman Period.* Leiden: Brill, 1977.

Otten, Heinrich. "Geschwisterehe in Hatti." *RlA* 3:231a.

Otto, Eberhard. "Sozialgeschichte Israels: Probleme und Perspektive. Ein Diskussionspapier." *Biblische Notizen* 15 (1981): 87–92.

Otwell, John. *And Sarah Laughed.* Philadelphia: Westminister, 1977.

Otzen, Benedikt. "Israel under the Assyrians." In *Power and Propaganda,* edited by Mogens Trolle Larsen, 251–61. Copenhagen: Akademisk, 1979.

Owen, David I. *Neo-Sumerian Archival Texts Primarily from Nippur.* Winona Lake, Ind. Eisenbrauns, 1982.

————. "Widow's Rights in Ur III Sumer." *ZA* 70 (1981): 170–84.

Pallis, S. *The Antiquity of Iraq.* Copenhagen: Munksgaard, 1956.

————. *Early Exploration in Mesopotamia.* Copenhagen: Munksgaard, 1954.

Pallottino, J. *Etruscologia.* Milan: Hoepli, 1984.

Parrot, André. *Archéologie mésopotamienne: Les Étapes.* Paris: Albin Michel, 1946, and *Techniques et Problèmes.* 1953.

Peat, Jerome A. "*Hanšu* Land and the *rab hanši.*" *Iraq* 45 (1983): 124–27.

Pedersen, Johannes. *Israel, Its Life and Culture.* 2 vols. London: Cumberdge; Copenhagen: Branner, 1926, 1940.

Peebles, Christopher, and Susan Kus. "Some Archaeological Correlates of Ranked Societies." *American Antiquity* 42 (1977): 421–48.

Peiser, Felix. *Skizze der babylonischen Gesellschaft, Mitteilungen der Vorderasiatischen Gesellschaft* (1896:3): 1–31.

Pekáry, T. *Die Wirtschaft der griechisch-römischen Antike.* Wiesbaden: Steiner, 1976.

Perkins, Ann L. *The Comparative Archeology of Early Mesopotamia.* Chicago: Oriental Institute, 1949.

Peters, F. *The Harvest of Hellenism.* New York: Simon & Schuster, 1970.

Petschow, Herbert. "Die [Paragraphen] 45 und 46 des Codex Hammurapi. Ein Beitrag zum altbabylonischen Bodenpachtrecht und zum Problem: Was ist der Codex Hammurapi?" *ZA* 74 (1984): 181–212.

Pettinato, Giovanni. "Il Commercio con l'Estero della Mesopotamia meridionale nel 3 millenio av. Cr. alla luce delle fonti letterarie e lessicali sumeriche." *Mesopotamia* 7 (1972): 43–166.

————. *Untersuchungen zur neusumerischen Landwirtschaft,* 2. Napoli: Istituto orientale di Napoli, 1967.

Peukert, W. *Die atlantische Sklavenhandel von Dahomey, 1740–1797.* Wiesbaden: F. Steiner, 1978.

Pinnock, F. "About the Trade of Early Syrian Ebla." *M.A.R.I.* 4 (1985): 85–92.

————. "The Lapis Lazuli Trade in the Third Millennium B.C. and the Evidence from the Royal Palace G of Ebla." In *Insight Through Images . . . Edith Porada A.V.,* edited by Marilyn Kelly-Buccellati, 221–28. Malibu: Undena, 1986.

Pintore, Franco. "I Dodici Intendenti di Salomone." *Rivista degli Studi Orientali* 45 (1970): 177–207.

————. "Osservazioni sulle Vie e l'orientamento dei commerci nella Siria-Palestina meridionale dall'inizio del I millennio all'anno 841 A.C." In *F. Pintore A.V.,* edited by O. Carruba et al., 257–83. Pavia: GJES, 1983.

————. *Il Matrimonio interdinastico nel vicino oriente durante i secoli ix-xii a.C.* Rome: Centro per le antichità, 1978.

Ploeg, Jean van der. "Les Chefs du Peuple d'Israël et leurs Titres." *Revue Biblique* 57 (1950): 40–61.

————. "Les 'Nobles' israélites." *Oudtestamentische Studiën* 9 (1951): 49–64.

————. "Le sens de *gibbōr hail.*" *Revue Biblique* 48 (1941): 120–25.

————. "Sociale en economische vraagstukken uit de geschiedenis van Israël tijd der Koningen." *Jaarbericht Ex Oriente Lux* 7 (1940): 390–99.

————. "Sociale Groepeeringen in het oude Israël." *Jaarbericht Ex Oriente Lux* 2 (1942): 642–50.

Plutarch. *Pericles.* In *Lives,* translated by Bernadotte Perrin. London, New York: Heinemann, Putnam, 1916.

Polanyi, Karl. "Aristotle Discovers the Economy." In *Trade and Market in the Early Empires,* edited by Karl Polanyi, Conrad M. Arensberg, and Harry W. Pearson, 64–94. Chicago: Regnery, 1957.

————. *The Livelihood of Man.* Edited by Harry W. Pearson. New York: Academic, 1977.

————. "Marketless Trading in Hammurabi's Time." In *Trade and Market in the Early Empires,* edited by Karl Polanyi, Conrad M. Arensberg, and Harry W. Pearson, 12–26. Chicago: Regnery, 1957.

Pomponio, Francesco. "The Reichskalendar of Ur III in the Umma Texts." *ZA* 79 (1989): 10–13.

Porten, Bezalel. *Archives from Elephantine.* Berkeley: University of California Press, 1968.

Postgate, J. Nicholas. *Early Mesopotamia: Society and Economy at the Dawn of History.* London: Routledge, 1992.

————. "The Economic Structure of the Assyrian Empire." In *Power and Propaganda,* edited by Mogens Trolle Larsen, 193–221. Copenhagen: Akademisk, 1979.

————. "Employer, Employee and Employment in the Neo-Assyrian Empire." In *Labor in the Ancient Near East,* edited by Marvin A. Powell, 257–70. New Haven: American Oriental Society, 1987.

————. *Fifty Neo-Assyrian Legal Documents.* Warminster: Aris & Phillips, 1976.

————. *The Governor's Palace Archive.* London: British School of Archaeology in Iraq, 1973.

————. "Grundeigentum und Nutzung von Land in Assyrien im 1. Jt. v. u. Z." In *Das Grundeigentum in Mesopotamien,* edited by Burchard Brentjes, 89–110. Berlin: Akademie, 1988.

————. "The Land of Assur and the Yoke of Assur." *World Archaeology* 23 (1992): 247–63.

————. "Land Tenure in the Middle Assyrian Period: A Reconstruction." *Bulletin of the School of Oriental and African Studies* 34 (1971): 496–519.

————. *Neo-Assyrian Royal Grants and Decrees.* Rome: Pontifical Biblical Institute, 1969.

————. "Nomads and Sedentaries in the Middle Assyrian Sources." In *Nomads and Seden-*

tary Peoples, edited by Jorge Silva Castillo, 47–56. Mexico City: Collegio de México, 1981.

―――. "Palm-Trees, Reeds and Rushes in Iraq Ancient and Modern." In *L'Archéologie de l'Iraq*, edited by Marie-Thérèse Barrelet, 99–109. Paris: Centre National de Recherche Scientifique, 1980.

―――. "'Princeps Iudex' in Assyria." *RA* 74 (1980): 180–82

―――. "The Role of the Temple in the Mesopotamian Secular Community." In *Man, Settlement, and Urbanism*, edited by Peter Ucko et al., 811–25. Cambridge: Schenkman, 1972.

―――. "On Some Assyrian Ladies." *Iraq* 41 (1979): 89–103.

―――. "Some Remarks on Conditions in the Assyrian Countryside." *JESHO* 17 (1974): 225–43.

―――. *Taxation and Conscription in the Assyrian Empire*. Rome: Pontificial Biblical Institute, 1974.

Postage, J. Nicholas, and S. Payne. "Some Old Babylonian Shepherds and Their Flocks." *Journal of Semitic Studies* 20 (1975): 1–21.

Potts, D. "On Salt and Salt Gathering in Ancient Mesopotamia." *JESHO* 27 (1984): 225–71.

―――. "Salt of the Earth: The Role of a Non-Pastoral Resource in a Pastoral Economy." *Oriens Antiquus* 22 (1983): 205–15.

Powell, Marvin A. "A Contribution to the History of Money in Mesopotamia prior to the Invention of Coinage." In *Festschrift Lubor Matouš*, 2, edited by Blahoslav Hruška and Géza Komoróczy, 211–43. Budapest: Eötvös Loránd Tudományegyetem, 1978.

―――. "Economy of the Extended Family According to Sumerian Sources." *Oikumene* 5 (1986): 9–13.

―――. "Götter, Könige, und 'Kapitalisten' im Mesopotamien des 3. Jahrtausands v.u.Z." *Oikumene* 2 (1978): 127–44.

―――. "Identification and Interpretation of Long Term Price Fluctuations in Babylonia: More on the History of Money in Mesopotamia." *Altorientalische Forschungen* 17 (1990): 76–99.

―――. "Masse und Gewichte." *RlA* 7· 487–88

―――. "Salt, Seed, and Yields in Sumerian Agriculture: A Critique of the Theory of Progressive Salinization." *ZA* 75 (1985): 7–38.

―――. "Sumerian Area Measures and the Alleged Decimal Substratum." *ZA* 62 (1972): 165–221.

―――, editor. *Labor in the Ancient Near East*. New Haven: American Oriental Society, 1987.

Premnath, D. "The Process of Latifundialization Mirrored in the Oracles Pertaining to 8th Century B.C.E. in the Books of Amos, Hosea, Isaiah, and Micah." Ph.D. dissertation, Graduate Theological Union, 1984.

Prenzel, G. *Über die Pacht im antiken hebräischen Recht*. Stuttgart: Kohlhammer, 1971.

Pritchard, James. "New Evidence on the Role of the Sea Peoples in Canaan at the Beginning of the Iron Age." In *The Role of the Phoenicians in the Interaction of Mediterranean Civilizations*, edited by W. Ward, 99–112. Beirut: American University, 1968.

―――, editor. *Ancient Near Eastern Texts Relating to the Old Testament*. Princeton: Princeton University Press, 1969.

Quilici, B. *L'Evoluzione finanziaria del Popolo Ebraico*. Bologna: Cappelli, 1927.

Rainey, Anson. "Compulsory Labour Gangs in Ancient Israel." *Israel Exploration Journal* 20 (1970): 191–202.

————. "The Satrapy 'Beyond the River.'" *Australian Journal of Biblical Archaeology* 1 (1969): 51–78.

————. "Wine from Royal Vineyards." *Bulletin of the American Schools of Oriental Research* 245 (1982): 57–62.

Rao, S. R. *Lothal and the Indus Civilization.* London: Asia, 1973.

Ravn, O. *Herodotus' Description of Babylon.* Copenhagen: Nordisk, 1942.

Reade, Julian E. "Kassites and Assyrians in Iran." *Iran* 16 (1978): 137–43.

Redford, Donald. *Akhnaton.* Princeton: Princeton University Press, 1984.

Redford, Donald, and J. Weinstein. "Hyksos." In *Anchor Bible Dictionary,* vol. 3, edited by David N. Freedman, 341–48. New York: Doubleday, 1992.

————. *A Study of the Biblical Story of Joseph.* Leiden: Brill, 1970.

Reineke, Walter F. "Waren die *šwtjw* wirklich Kaufleute?" *Altorientalische Forschungen* 6 (1979): 5–14.

Reisner, George. "Israelite Inscriptions." In *Harvard Excavations at Samaria,* vol. 1, edited by George Reisner et al., 227–46. Cambridge: Harvard University Press, 1924.

Renger, Johannes. "Zur Bewirtschaftung von Dattelpalmgärten während der altbabylonischen Zeit." In *Zikir Šumim, Assyriological Studies Presented to F. R. Kraus,* edited by Govert van Driel et al., 290–97. Leiden: Brill, 1982.

————. "Flucht als soziales Problem in der altbabylonischen Gesellschaft." In *Gesellschaftsklassen im alten Zweistromland,* edited by Dietz Otto Edzard, 166–82. Munich: Bayerische Akademie, 1972.

————. "Formen des Zugangs zu den lebensnotwendigen Gütern: Die Austauschverhältnisse in der altbabylonischen Zeit." *Altorientalische Forschungen* 20 (1993): 87–119.

————. "Interaction of Temple, Palace and 'Private Enterprise' in the Old Babylonian Economy." In *State and Temple Economy in the Ancient Near East,* edited by Edward Lipiński, 249–56. Louvain: Departement Oriëntalistiek, 1979.

————. "*mārat ilim*: Exogamie bei den semitischen Nomaden des 2. Jahrtausends." *AfO* 24 (1973): 103–07.

————. "Patterns of Non-Institutional Trade and Non-Commercial Exchange in Ancient Mesopotamia at the Beginning of the Second Millennium B.C." In *Circulation of Goods in Non-Palatial Context in the Ancient Near East,* edited by Alfonso Archi, 131–23. Rome: Ateneo, 1984.

————. "Das Privateigentum an der Feldflur in der altbabylonischen Zeit." In *Das Grundeigentum in Mesopotamien,* edited by Burchard Brentjes, 49–67. Berlin: Akademie, 1988.

————. "Zur Rolle von Preisen und Löhnen im Wirtschaftssystem des alten Mesopotamien an der Wende vom. 3 zum 2. Jahrtausend v. Chr., —Grundsätzliche Fragen und Überlegungen." *Altorientalische Forschungen* 16 (1989): 234–52.

————. "Überlegungen zur räumlichen Ausdehnung des Staates von Ebla an Hand der agrarischen und viehwirtschaftlichen Gegebenheiten." In *Ebla 1975–1985,* edited by Luigi Cagni, 293–311. Naples: Istituto orientale, 1987.

————. Review of D. Weisberg, *Guild Structure. JAOS* 91 (1971): 494–503.

————. "Who Are All Those People?" *OrNS* 42 (1973): 259–73.

Reviv, Haim. *The Elders in Ancient Israel: A Study of a Biblical Institution.* Jerusalem: Magnes, 1989.

————. "Some Comments on the *Maryannu*." *Israel Exploration Journal* 22 (1972): 218–28.

Riemschneider, Klaus. "Die hethitischen Landschenkungsurkunden." *Mitteilungen des Instituts für Orientforschung* 6 (1958): 322–81.

Rivista Biblica 32 (1984): 3–151 and 34 (1986): 1–238. (Conference on the Hebrew World in Light of Extra-Biblical Sources.)

Roaf, Michael. *Cultural Atlas of Mesopotamia and the Ancient Near East.* New York, Oxford: Facts on File, 1990.

Robertson, John. "The Internal Political and Economic Structure of Old Babylonian Nippur: The Guennakkum and His 'House.'" *JCS* 36 (1984): 145–90.

———. "On Profit-Seeking, Market Orientations, and Mentality in the Ancient Near East." *JAOS* 113 (1993): 437–43.

———. "The Temple Economy of Old Babylonian Nippur: The Evidence for Centralized Management." In *Nippur at the Centennial,* edited by Maria deJ. Ellis, 177–88. Philadelphia: University Museum, 1992.

Röllig, Wolfgang. "Der altmesopotamische Markt." *Welt des Orients* 8 (1976): 286–95.

———. "Gesellschaft." *RlA* 3:233–36.

———. "Politische Heiraten im Alten Orient." *Saeculum* 25 (1975): 11–23.

Rosenkranz, B. "Ein hethitischer Wirtschaftstext." *ZA* 57 (1965): 237–48.

Rosenthal, Franz. *A History of Muslim Historiography.* Leiden: Brill, 1968.

Rostovzeff, Michael. *The Social and Economic History of the Hellenistic World,* 3 vols. Oxford: Clarendon, 1941.

Roth, Ann M. *Egyptian Phyles in the Old Kingdom.* Chicago: Oriental Institute, 1991.

Roth, Martha. "Age at Marriage and the Household: A Study of Neo-Babylonian and Neo-Assyrian Forms." *Comparative Studies in Society and History* 29 (1987): 715–47.

———. *Babylonian Marriage Agreements, 7th–3rd Centuries B.C.* Neukirchen-Vluyn: Butzon & Bercker Kevelaer, Neukirchener, 1989.

———. "Marriage and Matrimonial Relations in First Millennium B.C. Mesopotamia." In *Women's Earliest Records,* edited by Barbara Lesko, 245–55. Atlanta: Scholars, 1989.

———. "The Neo-Babylonian Widow." *JCS* 43–45 (1991–93): 1–26.

Rowlands, Michael, Mogens Trolle Larsen, and Kristian Kristiansen, eds. *Centre and Periphery in the Ancient World.* Cambridge: Cambridge University Press, 1987.

Rowley, Harold Henry. *The Old Testament and Modern Study.* Oxford: Clarendon, 1952.

Rowton, Michael B. "Ancient Western Asia." In *Cambridge Ancient History* 1:1, edited by I. E. S. Edwards, Cyril J. Gadd, and N. G. L. Hammond, 193–217, 231–33. Cambridge: Cambridge University Press, 1970.

———. "Autonomy and Nomadism in Western Asia." *OrNS* 42 (1973): 247–58.

———. "Dimorphic Structure and the Tribal Elite." *Anthropos* 30 (1976): 219–57.

———. "Dimorphic Structure and Typology." *Oriens Antiquus* 15 (1976): 17–31.

———. "Enclosed Nomadism." *JESHO* 17 (1974): 1–30.

———. "Urban Autonomy in a Nomadic Environment." *JNES* 32 (1973): 201–15.

———. "The Woodlands of Ancient Western Asia." *JNES* 26 (1967): 261–77.

Sachs, Abraham. "The Latest Datable Cuneiform Tablets." In *Kramer Anniversary Volume: Cuneiform Studies in Honor of Samuel Noah Kramer,* edited by Barry Eichler, 379–98. Kevelaer: Butzon & Bercker; Neukirchen-Vluyn: Neukirchener, 1976.

Safar, Fuad, et al. *Eridu.* Baghdad: Ministry of Culture and Information, 1981.

Sahlins, Marshall D. *Stone-Age Economics.* Chicago, New York: Aldine, Atherton, 1972.

Said, Edward. *Orientalism.* New York: Pantheon, 1978.

Ste. Croix, G. E. M. de. *The Class Struggle in the Ancient World.* Ithaca: Cornell University Press, 1981

―――. "Greek and Roman Accounting." In *Studies in the History of Accounting,* edited by A. C. Littleton, B. S. Yamey, 14–74. New York: Sweet & Maxwell, 1956.

Sancisi-Weerdenburg, Helen. "Decadence in the Empire or Decadence in the Sources? From Source to Synthesis: Ctesias." In *Achaemenid History,* 1, edited by Helen Sancisi-Weerdenburg, 33–45. Leiden: Nederlands Instituut, 1987.

―――. "Meden en Perzen." *Lampas* 12 (1979): 208–22.

San Nicolò, Mario. "Materialien zur Viehwirtschaft in den neubabylonischen Tempeln." *OrNS* 18 (1948): 273–93, 19 (1949): 288–306, 20 (1950): 129–50, 23 (1954): 351–82, 25 (1956): 24–38.

Saporetti, Claudio. "La Figura del *Tamkāru* nell'Assira del xiii secolo." *Studi micenei ed egeo-anatolici* 18 (1977): 93–101.

―――, editor. *Le Leggi medioassire.* Malibu: Undena, 1979.

Sarkisian, G. K. "Greek Personal Names in Uruk and the *Graeco-Babyloniaca* Problem." *Acta Antiqua* 22 (1974): 495–503.

Sass, Benjamin. *The Genesis of the Alphabet and its Development in the Second Millennium B.C.* Wiesbaden: Harrassowitz, 1988.

Sasson, Jack M. "Biographical Notices on Some Royal Ladies from Mari." *JCS* 25 (1973): 59–78.

―――. "Canaanite Maritime Involvement in the Second Millennium B.C." *JAOS* 86 (1966): 126–38.

―――. "On Choosing Models for Recreating Israelite Pre-Monarchic History." *Journal for the Study of the Old Testament* 21 (1981): 3–24.

―――. "Hurrians and Hurrian Names in the Mari Texts." *Ugaritforschung* 6 (1974): 353–400.

―――. *Ruth.* Baltimore, London: Johns Hopkins University Press, 1979.

―――. "A Sketch of North Syrian Economic Relations in the Middle Bronze Age." *JESHO* 9 (1966): 161–81.

―――. "Thoughts of Zimri-Lim." *Biblical Archaeologist* 47 (1984): 110–20.

Scandone Matthiae, Gabriella. "Les Relations entre Ebla et l'Egypte au IIIème et au IIème Millénaire av. J.-Chr." In *Wirtschaft und Gesellschaft von Ebla,* edited by Hartmut Waetzoldt and Harald Hauptmann, 67–73. Heidelberg: Orient, 1988.

Schippmann, Klaus. *Grundzüge der parthischen Geschichte.* Darmstadt: Wissenschaftliche Buchgesellschaft, 1980.

Schmandt-Besserat, Denise. *Before Writing.* Volume I. *From Counting to Cuneiform.* Austin: University of Texas Press, 1992.

―――. "From Token to Tablets: A Re-evaluation of the So-called 'Numerical Tablets.'" *Visible Language* 15 (1981): 321–44.

Schneider, Anna. *Die Anfänge der Kulturwirtschaft: Die sumerische Tempelstadt.* Essen: Baedeker, 1920.

Schneider, Nicholas. "Der dub-sar als Verwaltungsbeamter im Reiche von Sumer und Akkad zur Zeit der III Dynastie von Ur." *OrNS* 15 (1946): 64–88.

Schulz, H. *Leviten im vorstaatlichen Israel und im Mittleren Osten.* Munich: Kaiser, 1987.

Scott, Robert B. Y. *Proverbs and Ecclesiastes.* Garden City, N.Y.: Doubleday, 1965.

―――. "Solomon and the Beginnings of Wisdom in Israel." *Vetus Testamentum Supplement* 3 (1955): 262–69.

Shahar, Shulamit. *Childhood in the Middle Ages.* London, New York: Routledge, 1990.

Sharashenidze, Dj. *Formy ekspluatatsii rabochei sily v gosudarstvennom khozyaystve Shumera II pol. III tys. do n. e.* Tbilisi: Metsniereba, 1986.

———. "Die 'Träger' in der Zeit der III Dynastie von Ur." In *Gesellschaft und Kultur im alten Vorderasien,* edited by Horst Klengel, 229–33. Berlin: Akademie, 1982.

Shiff, Laurence. "The Nur-Sin Archive: Private Entrepreneurship in Babylon (603–507 B.C.)." Ph.D. dissertation, University of Pennsylvania, 1987.

Shifman, I. S. "Pravovoe polozhenie rabov v Iudee po dannym bibleiskoi traditsii" (The Legal Position of Slaves in Judah according to the Data of the Biblical Tradition). *VDI* (1963–3): 54–80.

———. *Ugaritskoe Obshchestvo, xiv–xii vv. do n. e.* Moskow: Nauka, 1982.

Shiloh, Yigael. "The Four-Room House—The Israelite Type House?" *Eretz-Israel* 11 (1973): 277–85 (in Hebrew).

———. "The Four-Room House. Its Situation and Function in the Israelite City." *Israel Exploration Journal* 20 (1970): 180–90.

———. "The Population of Iron Age Palestine in Light of a Sample Analysis of Urban Plans, Areas, and Population Densities." *Bulletin of the American Schools of Oriental Research* 239 (1980): 25–35.

Shore, A. F. "Christian and Coptic Egypt." In *The Legacy of Egypt,* edited by J. R. Harris, 390–433. Oxford: Clarendon, 1971.

Sigrist, Marcel. *Drehem.* Bethesda, Md.: CDL, 1992.

———. "Erin$_2$ Un-il$_2$." *RA* 73 (1979): 101–20, 74 (1980): 11–28.

———. "Le Trésor de Drehem." *OrNS* 48 (1979): 26–53.

Silva Castillo, Jorge. "Tribus pastorales et Industrie textile à Mari." In *Nomads and Sedentary Peoples,* edited by Jorge Silva Castillo, 109–22. Mexico City: Colegio de México, 1981.

Silver, Morris. *Economic Structures of the Ancient Near East.* New York: Barnes & Noble, 1985.

———. *Prophets and Markets.* New York: Barnes & Noble, 1983.

Simpson, William Kelly. "Polygamy in Egypt in the Middle Kingdom?" *Journal of Egyptian Archaeology* 60 (1974): 100–05.

Singer, Karl. *Die Metalle Gold, Silber, Bronze, Kupfer und Eisen im Alten Testament und ihre Symbolik.* Würzburg: Echter, 1980.

Sjöberg, Åke. "Zu Einige Verwantschaftsbezeichnungen im Sumerischen." *Heidelberger Studien zum alten Orient: Adam Falkenstein A. V.,* 201–31. Wiesbaden: Harrassowitz, 1967.

Slotsky, A.L. "Prices in Astronomical Diaries." Ph.D. dissertation. Yale University, 1992.

Smith, Morton. *Palestinian Parties and Politics that Shaped the Old Testament.* New York: Columbia, 1971.

Snell, Daniel. "The Activities of Some Merchants of Umma." *Iraq* 39 (1977): 45–50.

———. "The Allocation of Resources in the Umma Silver Balanced Account System." *JESHO* 31 (1988): 1–13.

———. "Ancient Israelite and Neo-Assyrian Societies and Economies." In *The Tablet and the Scroll, Near Eastern Studies in Honor of William W. Hallo,* edited by Mark Cohen, Daniel Snell, and David Weisberg, 223–26. Bethesda, Md.: CDL, 1993.

———. "The Aramaeans." In *From Ebla to Damascus,* edited by Harvey Weiss, 326–29. Washington, D.C.: Smithsonian Institution Traveling Exhibitions, 1985.

———. "The Lager Texts." *ASJ* 11 (1989): 155–224.

———. *Ledgers and Prices.* New Haven: Yale University Press, 1982.

———. "The Mari Livers and the Omen Tradition." *Journal of the Ancient Near Eastern Society* 6 (1974): 117–23.

———. "Marketless Trading in Our Time." *JESHO* 39 (1991): 129–41.

———. "The Rams of Lagash." *ASJ* 8 (1986): 133–217.

———. "The Wheel in Proverbs XX 26." *Vetus Testamentum* 39 (1989): 503–7.

Soggin, J. Alberto. "Ancient Israel: An Attempt at a Social and Economic Analysis of the Available Data." In *F. Charles Fensham A.V.*, edited by W. Claasen, 201–08. Sheffield: Journal for the Study of the Old Testament, 1988.

———. "Der judäische ᶜAm-Ḥaʾares und das Königtum in Juda." *Vetus Testamentum* 13 (1963): 187–95.

Sollberger, Edmond. *Ur Excavation Texts* 8, *Royal Inscriptions* 2. London: The British Museum, 1965.

Sonsino, R. *Motive Clauses in Israelite Law.* Chico, Calif.: Scholars, 1980.

Sorokin, P. "What Is a Social Class?" In *Class, Status and Power,* edited by R. Bendix and S. Lipset, 87–92. 1947. Reprint. Glencoe, Ill.: Free Press, 1953.

Spalinger, Anthony. "A Redistributive Pattern at Assiut." *JAOS* 105 (1985): 7–20.

Spuler, B. "The Disintegration of the Caliphate in the East." In *The Cambridge History of Islam,* edited by P.M. Holt et al., volume IA, 143–74. Cambridge: Cambridge University Press, 1977.

Stager, Lawrence. "The Archaeology of the Family in Ancient Israel." *Bulletin of the American Schools of Oriental Research* 260 (1985): 1–35.

Stein, Gil. "Economy, Ritual, and Power in 'Ubaid Mesopotamia.'" In *Chiefdoms and Early States in the Near East,* edited by Gil Stein and Mitchell Rothman, 35–46. Madison: Prehistory, 1994.

Steinkeller, Pyotr. "The Administrative and Economic Organization of the Ur III State: The Core and the Periphery." In *The Organization of Power,* edited by McGuire Gibson and Robert Biggs, 19–42. Chicago: Oriental Institute, 1987.

———. "The Foresters of Umma." In *Labor in the Ancient Near East,* edited by Marvin A. Powell, 73–115. New Haven: American Oriental Society, 1987.

———. "Grundeigentum in Babylonien von Uruk IV bis zur früdynastischen Periode II." In *Das Grundeigentum in Mesopotamien,* edited by Burchard Brentjes, 11–27. Berlin: Akademie, 1988.

———. "The Reforms of Uru-KA-gina and an Early Sumerian Term for 'Prison.'" *Aula Orientalis* 9 (1991): 227–33.

———. "The Rent of Fields in Early Mesopotamia and the Development of the Concept of 'Interest" in Sumerian." *JESHO* 24 (1981): 113–45.

———. *Sale Documents of the Ur-III-Period.* Stuttgart: F. Steiner, 1989.

Steinmetzer, Franz X. *Die babylonische Kudurru (Grenzsteine) als Urkundenform.* Paderborn: Schöningh, 1922.

Stern, Ephraim. *Material Culture of the Land of the Bible in the Persian Period, 538–332 B.C.* Warminster: Aris & Phillips; Jerusalem: Israel Exploration Society, 1982; Hebrew: 1973.

Stieglitz, Robert R. "Commodity Prices at Ugarit." *JAOS* 99 (1979): 15–23.

Stolper, Matthew. *Entrepreneurs and Empire. The Murašû Archive, the Murašû Firm, and Persian Rule in Babylonia.* Leiden: Nederlands Instituut, 1985.

———. "Registration and Taxation of Slave Sales in Achaemenid Babylonia." *ZA* 79 (1989): 30–101.

Stone, Elizabeth. "Economic Crisis and Social Upheaval in Old Babylonian Nippur." In *Mountains and Lowlands,* edited by Louis Levine and T. Cuyler Young, Jr., 267–89. Malibu: Undena, 1977.

————. *Nippur Neighborhoods.* Chicago: Oriental Institute, 1987.

————. "The Social Role of the *Nadītu* Women in Old Babylonian Nippur." *JESHO* 25 (1982): 50–70.

————. "The Spatial Organization of Mesopotamian Cities." In *Velles Paraules, Ancient Near Eastern Studies in Honor of Miguel Civil,* edited by Pyotr Michalowski et al. = *Aula Orientalis* 9 (1991): 235–42.

————. "Texts, Architecture and Ethnographic Analogy: Patterns of Residence in Old Babylonian Nippur." *Iraq* 43 (1981): 19–33.

Stone, Elizabeth, and David I. Owen. *Adoption in Old Babylonian Nippur.* Winona Lake: Eisenbrauns, 1991.

Strayer, J., and R. Coulborn. "The Idea of Feudalism." In *Feudalism in History,* edited by R. Coulborn, 3–11. Hamden, Conn.: Archon, 1965.

Strobel, August. *Der spätbronzezeitliche Seevölkersturm.* Berlin: De Gruyter, 1976.

Struve, V. V. "Naëmnyi trud i sel'skaya obshchina v iuzhnom Mezhdurech'e kontsa III tysacheletia do n.e." *VDI* (1948-2): 13–33.

Sweet, Ronald. "On Prices, Moneys, and Money Uses in the Old Babylonian Period." Ph.D. dissertation, University of Chicago, 1957.

Tadmor, Haim. "'The People' and the Kingship in Ancient Israel: The Role of Political Institutions in the Biblical Period." *Cahiers d'Histoire Mondiale* 11 (1968): 46–68.

Tawney, Richard Henry. Preface to M. Weber, *The Protestant Ethic and the Spirit of Capitalism.* New York: Scribner's, 1958.

Théoridès, A. "A propos de Pap. Lansing, 4, 8–5,2 et 6,8–7,5," *Revue internationale des droits de l'antiquité* 5 (1958): 65–119.

Thiel, Winfried. *Die soziale Entwicklung Israels in vorstaatlicher Zeit.* Neukirchen-Vluyn: Neukirchener, 1980.

Thomsen, Marie-Louise. *The Sumerian Language.* Copenhagen: Akademisk, 1984.

Thucydides. *The Peloponnesian War.* Translated by R. Warner. Harmondsworth: Penguin, 1972.

Tiumenev, A. I. *Gosudarstvennoe Khozyaystvo drevnego Shumera.* Moscow, Leningrad: Nauk, 1956.

Tosato, Angelo. *Il Matrimonio israelitico.* Rome: Pontifical Biblical Institute, 1982.

Toynbee, Arnold. *A Study of History.* Abridged by D.C. Somerwell. New York: Dell, 1965.

Trigger, B. G., B. J. Kemp, D. O'Connor, and A. B. Lloyd. *Ancient Egypt: A Social History.* Cambridge: Cambridge University Press, 1983.

Tsyrkin, Y. B. "Some Problems of Phoenicia's Social-Political Structure." *VDI* (1991–4): 3–13 (in Russian).

Tucker, G. "The Legal Background of Genesis 23." *JBL* 85 (1966): 77–84.

Uchitel, A. "Organization of Manpower in Achaemenid Persia according to the Fortification Archive." *ASJ* 11 (1989): 225–38.

————. "Women at Work." *Historia* 33 (1984): 257–82.

Ungnad, Arthur. "Das Haus Egibi." *AfO* 14 (1941–44): 57–64.

Vagts, A. *A History of Militarism.* New York: Meridien, 1959.

Valbette, Dominique. *"Les Ouvriers de la Tombe": Deir-el-Medinah à l'Epoque ramesside.* Cairo: Institut français, 1985.

Van de Mieroop, Marc. *Crafts in the Early Isin Period.* Louvain: Departement Oriëntalistiek, 1987.

————. "Old Babylonian Ur: Portrait of an Ancient Mesopotamian City." *Journal of the Ancient Near Eastern Society* 21 (1992): 119–30.

————. "The Reign of Rim-Sin." *RA* 87 (1993): 47–69.

————. "Sheep and Goat Herding according to the Old Babylonian Texts from Ur." *Bulletin of Sumerian Agriculture* 7 (1993): 161–82.

————. *Society and Enterprise in Old Babylonian Ur.* Berlin: Raimer, 1992.

————. "Turām-ilī: An Ur III Merchant." *JCS* 38 (1986): 1–80.

————. "Women in the Economy of Sumer." In *Women's Earliest Records,* edited by Barbara Lesko, 53–66. Atlanta: Scholars, 1987.

Van Seters, John. *Abraham in History and Tradition.* New Haven: Yale University Press, 1975.

————. "Joshua 24 and the Problem of Tradition in the Old Testament." In *In the Shelter of Elyon . . . Gösta Ahlström A.V.,* edited by W. Barrick and J. Spence, 139–58. Sheffield: Journal for the Study of the Old Testament, 1984.

————. *The Hyksos.* New Haven: Yale University Press, 1966.

Veenhof, Klaas. *Aspects of the Old Assyrian Trade and Its Terminology.* Leiden: Brill, 1972.

————. "Some Social Effects of Old Assyrian Trade." *Iraq* 39 (1977): 109–18.

Vernus, Pascal. "Production, Pouvoir et Parenté dans l'Egypte pharaonique." In *Production, Pouvoir, et Parenté dans le Monde méditerranéen,* edited by C.-H. Breteau, 103–16. Paris: Geuthner, 1981.

Walters, Stanley. *Water for Larsa.* New Haven: Yale University Press, 1970.

Waetzoldt, Hartmut. "Compensation of Craft Workers and Officials in the Ur III Period." In *Labor in the Ancient Near East,* edited by Marvin A. Powell, 117–41. New Haven: American Oriental Society, 1987.

————. *Untersuchungen zur neusumerischen Textilindustrie.* Rome: Centro per le antichità, 1972.

Wallerstein, Emmanuel. *The Modern World-System.* New York: Academic, 1974.

Warner, S. "The Patriarchs and Extra-Biblical Sources." *Journal for the Study of the Old Testament* 2 (1977): 50–61.

Weber, Max. *The Agrarian Sociology of Ancient Civilizations.* 1909. Reprint. London: Verso, 1988.

Weiler, Ingomar. "Zum Shicksal der Witwe und Waisen bei den Völkern der alten Welt: Materialien für eine vergleichende Geschichtswissenschaft." *Saeculum* 31 (1980): 157–93.

Weinberg, J. "Das Bēit 'Abōt im 6.–4. Jh. v.u.Z." *Vetus Testamentum* 23 (1973): 400–14.

Weinstein, James M. "The Egyptian Empire in Palestine: A Reassessment." *Bulletin of the American Schools of Oriental Research* 241 (1981): 1–28.

Weisberg, David. *Guild Structure and Political Allegiance in Early Achaemenid Mesopotamia.* New Haven: Yale University Press, 1969.

————. "Wool and Linen Material in Texts from the Time of Nebuchadnezzar." *Eretz-Israel* 16 = *Harry Orlinsky A.V.* (1982): 218–23.

————. Review of H. Kümmel, *Familie. JAOS* 104 (1984): 739–43.

Weiss, Harvey. "The Origins of Tell Leilan and the Conquest of Space in Third Millennium Mesopotamia." In *The Origins of Cities in Dry-Farming Syria and Mesopotamia in the Third Millennium B.C.,* edited by Harvey Weiss, 71–108. Guilford, Conn.: Four Quarters, 1986.

Weiss, Harvey, et al., "The Genesis and Collapse of Third Millennium North Mesopotamian Civilization." *Science* 261 (1993): 995–1004.

Weitemeyer, Mogens. *Some Aspects of the Hiring of Workers in the Sippar Region at the Time of Hammurabi.* Copenhagen: Munksgaard, 1962.

Westbrook, Raymond. "Biblical and Cuneiform Law Codes." *Revue Biblique* 92 (1985): 247–64.

———. "Cuneiform Law Codes and the Origins of Legislation." *ZA* 79 (1989): 201–22.

———. "Jubilee Laws." *Israel Law Review* 6 (1971): 209–26.

———. *Old Babylonian Marriage Law*. Horn: Berger, 1988.

———. "Redemption of Land." *Israel Law Review* 6 (1971): 367–75.

———. *Studies in Biblical and Cuneiform Law*. Paris: Gabalda, 1988.

Westenholz, Aage. "The Sargonic Period." In *Circulation of Goods in Non-Palatial Context in the Ancient Near East,* edited by Alfonso Archi, 17–30. Rome: Ateneo, 1984.

White, K. *Greek and Roman Technology*. Ithaca: Cornell University Press, 1984.

———. "The Problem of Latifundia in Roman History." *Bulletin—The Institute of Classical Studies* 14 (1967): 62–79.

Whiting, Robert. "Some Observations on the Drehem Calendar." *ZA* 69 (1979): 6–33.

Wilcke, Claus. "*CT* 45, 119: Ein Fall legaler Bigamie mit *nadītum* und *šugītum*." *ZA* 74 (1984): 170–80.

———. "E-saĝ-da-na Nibru^ki: An Early Administrative Center of the Ur III Empire." In *Nippur at the Centennial,* edited by Maria deJ. Ellis, 311–24. Philadelphia: University Museum, 1992.

———. Familiengründung im alten Babylonien." In *Geschlectsreife und Legitimation zur Zeugung,* edited by E. Müller, 213–317. Freiburg and Munich: Alber, 1985.

———. "Zur Geschichte der Ammuriter in der Ur-III-Zeit." *Welt des Orients* 5 (1969): 1–31.

Wilhelm, Gernot. *Grundzüge der Geschichte und Kultur der Hurriter*. Darmstadt: Wissenschaftliche Buchgesellschaft, 1982 = *The Hurrians*. Warminster: Aris & Phillips, 1989.

———. "Zur Rolle des Grossgrundbesitzes in der hurritischen Gesellschaft." *Revue hittite et asianique* 36 (1978): 205–13.

Williamson, H.G.M. "Ezra and Nehemiah in Light of the Texts from Persepolis." *Bulletin for Biblical Research* 1 (1991): 41–61.

Wilson, Edmund. *To the Finland Station*. Garden City, N.Y.: Doubleday, 1940.

Wilson, Robert. *Prophecy and Society in Ancient Israel*. Philadelphia: Fortress, 1980.

Wiseman, David. "A Note on Some Prices in Late Babylonian Astronomical Diaries." In *A Scientific Humanist: A. Sachs A.V.,* edited by Earle Leichty and Maria deJ. Ellis, 363–73. Philadelphia: Kramer Fund, 1988.

Wisdom, Revelation, and Doubt: Perspectives on the First Millennium B.C. Daedalus 104 (1975).

Witall, W. "Son of Man—A Pre-Davidic Social Class?" *Catholic Biblical Quarterly* 37 (1975): 331–40.

Wittfogel, Karl. *Oriental Despotism*. New Haven: Yale University Press, 1957.

Wolf, C. "Traces of Primitive Democracy in Ancient Israel." *JNES* 6 (1947): 98–108.

———. "Merchant." In *Interpreter's Dictionary of the Bible,* edited by George Buttrick et al., 3: 351–52. Nashville: Abingdon, 1962.

Woolley, Leonard. *Excavations at Ur*. New York: Crowell, 1965.

Wolpert, Stanley. *A New History of India*. Oxford: Oxford University Press, 1989.

Wunsch, C. "Zur Entwicklung und Nutzung privaten Grossgrundbesitzes in Babylonien während des 6. Jh. v.u.Z., nach dem Archiv des Ṭābiya." In *Šulmu,* 361–78. Prague: Charles University, 1988.

Würthwein, Ernst. *Der ᶜamm ha'arez im alten Testament*. Stuttgart: Kohlhammer, 1936.

Xenophon. *Anabasis*. Translated by Carleton L. Brownson. Cambraidge and London: Harvard University Press and Heinemann, 1968.

————. *Cyropaedaeia.* Translated by Walter Miller. London and New York: Heinemann and Macmillan, 1914–1925.

Yankovskaya, N. B. "Optovaya torgovlya drevnei perednei Azii do vozniknoveniya imperii." *VDI* (1985–3): 3–8.

Yoffee, Norman, and George L. Cowgill, eds. *The Collapse of Ancient States and Civilizations.* Tucson: University of Arizona Press, 1988.

————. *The Economic Role of the Crown in the Old Babylonian Period.* Malibu: Undena, 1977.

————. *Explaining Trade in Ancient Western Asia.* Malibu, Calif.: Undena, 1981.

————. "'Chuzhezemtsy'" v Mesopotamii." *VDI* (1989–2): 95–100.

Young, T. Cuyler, Jr. "Population Densities and Early Mesopotamian Origins." In *Man, Settlement and Urbanism,* edited by Peter Ucko et al., 827–42. London: Duckworth, 1972.

Zabłocka, Julia. "Landarbeiter im Reich der Sargoniden." In *Gesellschaftsklassen im alten Zweistromland,* edited by Dietz Otto Edzard, 209–15. Munich: Bayerische Akademie, 1972.

————. "Palast und König: Ein Beitrag zu den neuassyrischen Eigentumsverhältnissen." *Altorientalische Forschungen* 1 (1974): 91–113.

————. *Stosunki agrarne w Państwie Sargonidów* (Agrarverhältnisse im Reich der Sargoniden). Poznan: Uniwersytet im. Adama Mickiewicza, 1971.

————. "Zum Problem der neuassyrischen Dorfgemeinde." *Studia Historiae Oeconomicae* 13 (1978): 61–72.

Zaccagnini, Carlo. "Aspects of Ceremonial Exchange in the Near East during the Late Second Millennium B.C." In *Centre and Periphery in the Ancient World,* edited by Michael Rowlands, 57–65. Cambridge: Cambridge University Press, 1987.

————. "On Gift Exchange in the Old Babylonian Period." In *Franco Pintore A. V.,* edited by O. Carruba et al., 189–253. Pavia: GJES, 1983.

————. "Ideological and Procedural Paradigms in Ancient Near Eastern Long Distance Exchanges: The Case of Enmerkar and the Lord of Aratta." *Altorientalische Forschungen* 20 (1993): 34–42.

————. "Markt." *RlA* 7:421–26.

————. "The Merchant at Nuzi." *Iraq* 39 (1977): 171–89.

————. "Modo di produzione asiatico e Vicino Oriente antico: Appunti per una discussione." *Dialoghi di Archeologia* 3 (1981): 3–65. (Translated reportedly with many typographical errors in *Production and Consumption in the Ancient Near East* [Budapest: Eötvös Loránd, 1989], unavailable to me.)

————. "The Price of Fields at Nuzi." *JESHO* 22 (1979): 1–32.

————. *The Rural Landscape of the Land of Arraphe.* Rome: Università di Roma, 1979.

————. *Lo Scambio dei Doni nel Vicino Oriente durante i Secoli xv–xiii.* Rome: Centro per le antichità, 1973.

————. "Transfers of Movable Property in Nuzi Private Transactions." In *Circulation of Goods in Non-Palatial Context in the Ancient Near East,* edited by Alfonso Archi, 130–50. Rome: Ateneo, 1984.

————. "The Transition from Bronze to Iron in the Near East and the Levant." *JAOS* 110 (1990): 493–502.

————. "The Yield of the Fields at Nuzi." *Oriens Antiquus* 14 (1975): 181–225.

Zadok, Ran. *The Jews in Babylonia during the Chaldean and Achaemenian Periods.* Haifa: University of Haifa Press, 1979.

―――. "On Some Foreign Population Groups in First-Millennium Babylonia." *Tel Aviv* 6 (1979): 164–81.

Zawadzki, Stefan. "The Economic Crisis in Uruk during the Last Years of Assyrian Rule in the Light of the So-called Nabu-ušallim archives." *Folia Orientalia* 20 (1979): 175–84.

―――. "Great Families of Sippar during the Chaldean and Early Persian Periods (626–482 B.C.)." *RA* 84 (1990): 17–25.

Zeder, Melinda K. *Feeding Cities*. Washington, D.C.: Smithsonian Institution Press, 1991.

―――. "Of Kings and Shepherds: Specialized Animal Economy in Ur III Mesopotamia." In *Chiefdoms and Early States in the Near East,* edited by Gil Stein and Mitchell Rothman, 175–91. Madison: Prehistory, 1994.

Zettler, Richard. "The Genealogy of the House of Ur-Me-me: A Second Look." *AfO* 31 (1984): 1–14.

―――. *The Ur III Temple of Inanna at Nippur*. Berlin: D. Reimer, 1992.

INDEX

BIBLICAL REFERENCES